# The World We Imagine

# THE WORLD
# WE IMAGINE

## SELECTED ESSAYS BY

*Mark Schorer*

*Farrar, Straus and Giroux*

NEW YORK

"Technique as Discovery" was delivered before the Utah Writers' Conference in 1947 and was first published in *Hudson Review*, I, 1 (Spring 1948).

"Fiction and the 'Analogical Matrix'" was originally presented in longer form before the English Institute, Columbia University, and the School of Letters, then at Kenyon College, in 1948. It was first published in *Kenyon Review*, XI, 4 (Autumn 1949).

"Moll Flanders" was written as the introduction to the Modern Library edition of *Moll Flanders* (Copyright © 1950 by Random House, Inc. Reprinted by permission), and was first published in *Thought: Fordham University Quarterly*, XXV, 97 (June 1950), as "A Study in Defoe."

"Emma" was first published as "The Humiliation of Emma Woodhouse" in *The Literary Review*, II, 14 (Summer 1959).

"Jane Eyre" is from the book *Jane Eyre* by Charlotte Brontë, Riverside Edition, with an introduction by Mark Schorer. Published by Houghton Mifflin Company, Boston, Massachusetts. Reprinted by permission.

"The Good Soldier: A Tale of Passion" appeared in its first version in *The Princeton University Library Chronicle*, IX, 3 (April 1948), as "The Good Novelist in *The Good Soldier*," and then, under the same title but in a slightly different form, in *Horizon*, XX, 116 (August 1949). Then, in the present form and called "An Interpretation," it served as the introduction to the reprint of Ford's novel when it was published by Alfred A. Knopf, Inc., in 1951 and in Vintage Books in 1957. Reprinted with permission.

Under the title "Women in Love and Death," the essay on *Women in Love* first appeared in *Hudson Review*, VI, 1 (Spring 1953), and as "Donne, Amore e Morte," in *Inventario*, V, 5–6 (Autumn 1953).

"Lady Chatterley's Lover" was published in *Evergreen Review*, I, 1 (1957), and then served as the introduction to the Grove Press unexpurgated edition of Lawrence's novel, 1959.

"Poste Restante: Lawrence as Traveler" was written as the introduction to Harry T. Moore's *Poste Restante: A Lawrence Travel Calendar* (University of California Press, 1956).

"Elmer Gantry: The Method of Half-Truths" was presented to the English Institute, Columbia University as "Sinclair Lewis and the Method of Half-Truths" in 1955 and was first published in *Society and Self in the Novel*, English Institute Essays 1955, edited by Mark Schorer and published by Columbia University Press, 1956.

"Sinclair Lewis and His Critics" was written as the introduction to the Twentieth Century Views volume, *Sinclair Lewis* (Spectrum Books, Prentice-Hall, Inc., 1962).

"Two Houses, Two Ways: The Florentine Villas of Lewis and Lawrence" first appeared in *New World Writing*, 4 (New American Library of World Literature, 1953).

"The Burdens of Biography" was the Hopwood Lecture at the University of Michigan in 1962 and, after having been delivered as an Alfred Harcourt Lecture at Columbia University, was published in *The Michigan Quarterly Review*, I, 4 (Autumn 1962), and then in *To the Young Writer*, Hopwood Lectures, Second Series, edited by A. L. Bader as an Ann Arbor Paperback Original for the University of Michigan Press. Copyright © 1965 by the University of Michigan. Reprinted with permission.

"Hamlin Garland" was written as the afterword to *Main-Travelled Roads* in the Signet Classic reprint (New American Library of World Literature, Inc., 1962). Reprinted with permission.

"Conrad Aiken, 1" was written as the Preface to *The Collected Short Stories of Conrad Aiken* (Copyright © 1960 by Conrad Aiken. Reprinted by permission of William Heinemann Ltd.). "Conrad Aiken, 2," in a slightly different form, appeared in *The New York Times Book Review* for October 12, 1952, as a review of Aiken's *Ushant: An Essay*.

"Katherine Anne Porter" was written as the afterword to *Pale Horse, Pale Rider* in the Signet Classic reprint (New English Library, 1962). Reprinted with permission.

"Carson McCullers and Truman Capote," under the title "McCullers and Capote: Basic Patterns," was written for the volume edited by Nona Balakian and Charles Simmons called *The Creative Present* (Copyright © 1963 by Nona Balakian and Charles Simmons. Doubleday and Co., Inc.). Reprinted with permission.

"Some Relationships: Gertrude Stein, Sherwood Anderson, F. Scott Fitzgerald, and Ernest Hemingway" in its earliest form served as the introduction to the selections from the last three of those writers in *Major Writers of America*, II, general editorship of Perry Miller (Copyright © 1962 by Harcourt, Brace and World, Inc.). It was then much expanded to serve as the basis for a series of lectures delivered in many

Italian universities under the Fulbright Act. The present version reduces the second but takes account of certain publications like *A Moveable Feast* that were not available in the spring of 1964, when the Italian lectures were delivered.

"The World We Imagine: Notes on the Creative Act and Its Function" began as notes for a lecture delivered in a series called "The Silent Revolution," organized by Dr. Frank X. Barron for the University of California Extension Division in San Francisco in 1962. Later this material was so arranged as to provide the introduction to *Techniques of Fiction Writing: Measure and Madness* by Leon Surmelian, published by Doubleday and Co., Inc., in 1968. The text published here lies somewhere between those two earlier versions.

FOR

*ROBERT GUTWILLIG*

AND

*PETER KEMENY*

# Contents

# PART ONE

❁

# Technique as Discovery

MODERN CRITICISM, through its exacting scrutiny of literary texts, has demonstrated with finality that in art beauty and truth are indivisible and one. The Keatsian overtones of these terms are mitigated and an old dilemma solved if for beauty we substitute form, and for truth, content. We may, without risk of loss, narrow them even more, and speak of technique and subject matter. Modern criticism has shown us that to speak of content as such is not to speak of art at all, but of experience; and that it is only when we speak of the *achieved* content, the form, the work of art as a work of art, that we speak as critics. The difference between content, or experience, and achieved content, or art, is technique.

When we speak of technique, then, we speak of nearly everything. For technique is the means by which the writer's experience, which is his subject matter, compels him to attend to it; technique is the only means he has of discovering, exploring, developing his subject, of conveying its meaning, and, finally, of evaluating it. And it follows that certain techniques are sharper tools than others, and will discover more; that the writer capable of the most exacting technical scrutiny of his subject matter will produce works with the most satisfying content, works with thickness and resonance, works which reverberate, works with maximum meaning.

We are no longer able to regard as seriously intended criticism of poetry which does not assume these generalizations; but the case for fiction has not yet been established. The novel is still read as though its content has some value in itself, as though the subject matter of fiction has greater or lesser value in itself, and as though technique were not a primary but a supplementary element, capable perhaps of not unattractive embellishments upon the surface of the subject, but hardly of its essence. Or technique is thought of in blunter terms than those that one associates with poetry, as such relatively obvious matters as the arrangement of events to create plot; or, within plot, of suspense and climax; or as the means of revealing character motivation, relationship, and development; or as the use of point of view, but point of view as some nearly arbitrary device for the heightening of dramatic interest through the narrowing or broadening of perspective upon the material, rather than as a means toward the positive definition of theme. As for the resources of language, these, somehow, we almost never think of as a part of the technique of fiction—language as used to create a certain texture and tone which in themselves state and define themes and meanings; or language, the counters of our ordinary speech, as forced, through conscious manipulation, into all those larger meanings that our ordinary speech almost never intends. Technique in fiction, all this is a way of saying, we somehow continue to regard as merely a means to organizing material which is "given" rather than as the means of exploring and defining the values in an area of experience which, for the first time *then,* are being given.

Is fiction still regarded in this odd, divided way because it is really less tractable before the critical suppositions which now seem inevitable to poetry? Let us look at some examples: two well-known novels of the past, both by writers who may be described as "primitive," although their relative innocence of technique is of a different sort—Defoe's *Moll Flanders* and Emily Brontë's *Wuthering Heights;* and three well-known novels of this century—*Tono Bungay,* by a writer who claimed to eschew technique; *Sons and Lovers,* by a novelist whose ideal of subject matter ("the poetry of the immediate present") led him in effect to eschew technique; and *A Portrait of the Artist as a Young Man,* by a novelist whose practice made claims for the supremacy of technique beyond those made by anyone in the past or by anyone else in this century.

Technique in fiction is, of course, all those obvious forms of it which are usually taken to be the whole of it, and many others; but for present purposes, let it be thought of in two respects particularly: the uses to which language, as language, is put to express the quality of the experience in question; and the uses of point of view not only as a mode of dramatic delimitation, but more particularly, of thematic definition. Technique is really what T. S. Eliot means by "convention": any selection, structure, or distortion, any form or rhythm imposed upon the world of action; by means of which, it should be added, our apprehension of the world of action is enriched or renewed. In this sense, everything is technique which is not the lump of experience itself, and one cannot properly say that a writer has no technique, or that he eschews technique, for, being a writer, he cannot do so. We can speak of good and bad technique, of adequate and inadequate, of technique which serves the novel's purpose, or disserves.

2

In the prefatory remarks to *Moll Flanders,* Defoe tells us that he is not writing fiction at all, but editing the journals of a woman of notorious character, and rather to instruct us in the necessities and the joys of virtue than to please us. We do not, of course, take these professions seriously, since nothing in the conduct of the narrative indicates that virtue is either more necessary or more enjoyable than vice. On the contrary, we discover that Moll turns virtuous only after a life of vice has enabled her to do so with security; yet it is precisely for this reason that Defoe's profession of didactic purpose has interest. For the actual morality which the novel enforces is the morality of any commercial culture, the belief that virtue pays—in worldly goods. It is a morality somewhat less than skin deep, having no relation to motives arising from a sense of good and evil, least of all, of evil-*in*-good, but exclusively from the presence or absence of food, drink, linen, damask, silver, and timepieces. It is the morality of measurement, and without in the least intending it, *Moll Flanders* is our classic revelation of the mercantile mind: the morality of measurement, which Defoe has completely neglected to measure. He fails not only to evaluate this material in his announced way, but to evaluate it at all. His announced purpose is, we admit, a pious humbug, and he meant us to read the book as a series of scandalous events; and thanks to his inexhaustible pleasure in excess and exaggeration, this element in the book continues to amuse us. Long before the book has been finished, however, this element has also become an absurdity; but not half the absurdity as that which Defoe did not intend at all—the notion that Moll could live a rich and full life of crime, and yet, repenting, emerge spotless in the end. The point is, of course, that she has no moral being, nor has the book any moral life. Everything is external. Everything can be weighed, measured, handled, paid for in gold, or expiated by a prison term. To this, the whole texture of the novel testifies—the bolts of goods, the inventories, the itemized accounts, the landlady's bills, the lists, the ledgers —all this, which taken together comprises what we call Defoe's method of circumstantial realism.

He did not come upon that method by any deliberation; it represents precisely his own world of value, the importance of external circumstance to Defoe. The point of view of Moll is indistinguishable from the point of view of her creator. We discover the meaning of the novel (at unnecessary length, without economy, without emphasis, with almost none of the distortions or the advantages of art) in spite of Defoe, not because of him. Thus the book is not the true chronicle of a disreputable female, but the true allegory of an impoverished soul, the author's; not an anatomy of the criminal class, but of the middle class. And we read it as an unintended comic revelation of self and of a social mode. Because he had no adequate resources of technique to separate himself from his material, thereby to discover and to define the meanings of his material, his contribution is not so much to fiction as to the history of fiction, and to social history.

The situation in *Wuthering Heights* is at once somewhat the

same and yet very different. Here, too, the whole novel turns
upon itself, but this time to its estimable advantage; here, too,
is a revelation of what is perhaps the author's secret world of
value, but this time, through what may be an accident of technique, the revelation is meaningfully accomplished. Emily
Brontë may merely have stumbled upon the perspectives which
define the form and the theme of her book. Whether she knew
from the outset, or even at the end, what she was doing, we
may doubt; but what she did and did superbly we can see.

We can assume, without at all becoming involved in the author's life but merely from the tone of somnambulistic excess
which is generated by the writing itself, that this world of monstrous passion, of dark and gigantic emotional and nervous
energy, is for the author, or was in the first place, a world of
ideal value; and that the book sets out to persuade us of the
moral magnificence of such unmoral passion. We are, I think,
expected, in the first place, to take at their own valuation these
demonic beings, Heathcliff and Cathy: as special creatures, set
apart from the cloddish world about them by their heightened
capacity for feeling, set apart, even, from the ordinary objects
of human passion as, in their transcendent, sexless relationship,
they identify themselves with an uncompromising landscape
and cosmic force. Yet this is absurd, as much of the detail that
surrounds it ("Other dogs lurked in other recesses") is absurd.
The novelist Emily Brontë had to discover these absurdities to
the girl Emily; her technique had to evaluate them for what
they were, so that we are persuaded that it is not Emily who is
mistaken in her estimate of her characters, but they who are
mistaken in their estimate of themselves. The theme of the
moral magnificence of unmoral passion is an impossible theme
to sustain, and what interests us is that it was device—and, this
time, mere mechanical device—which taught Emily Brontë—
the needs of her temperament to the contrary, all personal longing and reverie to the contrary, perhaps—that this was indeed
not at all what her material must mean as art. Technique objectifies.

To lay before us the full character of this passion, to show us how it first comes into being and then comes to dominate the world about it and the life that follows upon it, Emily Brontë gives her material a broad scope in time, lets it, in fact, cut across three generations. And to manage material which is so extensive, she must find a means of narration, points of view, which can encompass that material, and, in her somewhat crude concept of motive, justify its telling. So she chooses a foppish traveler who stumbles into this world of passionate violence, a traveler representing the thin and conventional emotional life of the far world of fashion, who wishes to hear the tale; and for her teller she chooses, almost inevitably, the old family retainer who knows everything, a character as conventional as the other, but this one representing not the conventions of fashion, but the conventions of the humblest moralism.

What has happened is, first, that she has chosen as her narrative perspective those very elements, conventional emotion and conventional morality, which her hero and heroine are meant to transcend with such spectacular magnificence; and second, that she has permitted this perspective to operate throughout a long period of time. And these two elements compel the novelist to see what her unmoral passions come to. Moral magnificence? Not at all; rather, a devastating spectacle of human waste; ashes. For the time of the novel is carried on long enough to show Heathcliff at last an emptied man, burned out by his fever ragings, exhausted and will-less, his passion meaningless at last. And it goes even a little further, to Lockwood, the fop, in the graveyard, sententiously contemplating headstones. Thus in the end the triumph is all on the side of the cloddish world, which survives.

Perhaps not all on that side. For, like Densher at the end of *The Wings of the Dove*, we say, and surely Hareton and the second Cathy say, "We shall never be again as we were!" But there is more point in observing that a certain body of materials, a girl's romantic daydreams, have, through the most conventional devices of fiction, been pushed beyond their inception in fancy to their meanings, their conception as a written book—that they, that is, are not at all as they were.

## 3

Technique alone objectifies the materials of art; hence technique alone evaluates those materials. This is the axiom which demonstrates itself so devastatingly whenever a writer declares under the urgent sense of the importance of his materials— whether these are autobiography, or social ideas, or personal passions—whenever such a writer declares that he cannot linger with technical refinements. That art will not tolerate such a writer H. G. Wells handsomely proves. His enormous literary energy included no respect for the techniques of his medium, and his medium takes its revenge upon his bumptiousness.

> I have never taken any very great pains about writing. I am outside the hierarchy of conscious and deliberate writers altogether. I am the absolute antithesis of Mr. James Joyce. . . . Long ago, living in close conversational proximity to Henry James, Joseph Conrad, and Mr. Ford Madox Hueffer, I escaped from under their immense artistic preoccupations by calling myself a journalist.

Precisely. And he escaped—he disappeared—from literature into the annals of an era.

Yet what confidence! "Literature," Wells said,

> is not jewelry, it has quite other aims than perfection, and the more one thinks of "how it is done" the less one gets it done. These critical indulgences lead along a fatal path, away from every natural interest towards a preposterous emptiness of technical effort, a monstrous egotism of artistry, of which the later work of Henry James is the monumental warning. "It," the subject, the thing or the thought, has long since disappeared in these amazing works; nothing remains but the way it has been manipulated.

Seldom has a literary theorist been so totally wrong; for what we learn as James grows for us and Wells disappears is that without what he calls "manipulation," there *is* no "it," no "subject" in art. There is again only social history.

The virtue of the modern novelist—from James and Conrad down—is not only that he pays so much attention to his medium, but that, when he pays most, he discovers through it a new subject matter, and a greater one. Under the "immense artistic preoccupations" of James and Conrad and Joyce, the form of the novel changed, and with the technical change, analogous changes took place in substance, in point of view, in the whole conception of fiction. And the final lesson of the modern novel is that technique is not the secondary thing that it seemed to Wells, some external machination, a mechanical affair, but a deep and primary operation; not only that technique *contains* intellectual and moral implications, but that it *discovers* them. For a writer like Wells, who wished to give us the intellectual and the moral history of his times, the lesson is a hard one; it tells us that the order of intellect and the order of morality do not exist at all, in art, except as they are organized in the order of art.

Wells's ambitions were very large. "Before we have done, we will have all life within the scope of the novel." But that is where life already is, within the scope of the novel; where it needs to be brought is into novels. In Wells we have all the important topics in life, but no good novels. He was not asking too much of art, or asking that it include more than it happily can; he was not asking anything of it—as art, which is all that it can give, and that is everything.

A novel like *Tono Bungay*, generally thought to be Wells's best, is therefore instructive. "I want to tell—*myself*," says George, the hero, "and my impressions of the thing as a whole" —the thing as a whole being the collapse of traditional British institutions in the twentieth century. George "tells himself" in terms of three stages in his life which have rough equivalents in modern British social history, and this is, to be sure, a plan, a framework; but it is the framework of Wells's abstract thinking, not of his craftsmanship, and the primary demand which one makes of such a book as this—that means be discovered

whereby the dimensions of the hero contain the experiences
he recounts—is never met. The novelist flounders through a
series of literary imitations—from an early Dickensian episode,
through a kind of Shavian interlude, through a Conradian episode, to a Jules Verne vision at the end. The significant failure
is in that end, and in the way that it defeats not only the entire
social analysis of the bulk of the novel, but Wells's own ends
as a thinker. For at last George finds a purpose in science. "I
decided that in power and knowledge lay the salvation of my
life; the secret that would fill my need; that to these things I
would give myself."

But science, power, and knowledge are summed up at last in
a destroyer. As far as one can tell Wells intends no irony, although he may here have come upon the essence of the major
irony in modern history. The novel ends in a kind of meditative
rhapsody which denies every value that the book had been aim-
ing toward. For of all the kinds of social waste which Wells has
been describing, this is the most inclusive, the final waste. Thus
he gives us in the end not a novel, but a hypothesis; not an
individual destiny, but a theory of the future; and not his
theory of the future, but a nihilistic vision quite opposite from
everything that he meant to represent. With a minimum of
attention to the virtues of technique, Wells might still not
have written a great novel; but he would at any rate have
established a point of view and a tone that would have told
us what he meant.

To say what one means in art is never easy, and the more
intimately one is implicated in one's material, the more difficult
it is. If, besides, one commits fiction to a therapeutic function
which is to be operative not on the audience but on the author,
declaring, as D. H. Lawrence did, that "one sheds one's sicknesses in books—repeats and presents again one's emotions, to
be master of them," the difficulty is vast. It is an acceptable
theory only with the qualification that technique, which objectifies, is under no other circumstances so imperative. For
merely to repeat one's emotions, merely to look into one's heart
and write, is also merely to repeat the round of emotional

bondage. If our books are to be exercises in self-analysis, then technique must—and alone can—take the place of the absent analyst.

Lawrence, in the introductory note to his *Collected Poems*, made a distinction between his "real" poems and what he seemed to think of as his "composed" poems, between the poems which expressed his demon directly and created their own form "willy-nilly," and the poems which, through the hocus-pocus of technique, he spuriously put together and could, if necessary, revise. His belief in a "poetry of . . . the immediate present," poetry in which nothing is fixed, static, or final, where all is shimmeriness and impermanence and vitalistic essence, arose from this notion of technique as a frustration of the demon, one's genius. And from this notion, an unsympathetic critic like D. S. Savage can construct a case which shows Lawrence driven "concurrently to the dissolution of personality and the dissolution of art." The argument suggests that Lawrence's early, crucial novel, *Sons and Lovers*, is another example of meanings confused by an impatience with technical resources.

The novel has two themes: the crippling effects of a mother's love on the emotional development of her son; and the "split" between kinds of love, physical and spiritual, which the son develops, the kinds represented by two young women, Clara and Miriam. The two themes should, of course, work together, the second being, actually, the result of the first: this "split" is the "crippling." So one would expect to see the novel developed, and so Lawrence, in his famous letter to Edward Garnett, where he says that Paul is left at the end "with the drift towards death," apparently thought he had developed it. Yet in the last few sentences of the novel, Paul rejects his desire for extinction and turns toward "the faintly humming, glowing town," to life—as nothing in his previous history persuades us that he could unfalteringly do.

The discrepancy suggests that the book may reveal certain confusions between intention and performance.

One of these is the contradiction between Lawrence's explicit characterizations of the mother and father and his tonal evaluations of them. It is a problem not only of style (of the contradiction between expressed moral epithets and the more general texture of the prose which applies to them) but of point of view. Morel and Lawrence are never separated, which is a way of saying that Lawrence maintains for himself in this book the confused attitude of his character. The mother is a "proud, *honorable* soul," but the father has a "small, *mean* head." This is the sustained contrast; the epithets are characteristic of the whole, and they represent half of Lawrence's feelings. But what is the other half? Which of these characters is given his real sympathy—the hard, self-righteous, aggressive, demanding mother who comes through to us, or the simple, direct, gentle, downright, fumbling, ruined father? There are two attitudes here. Lawrence (and Morel) loves his mother, but he also hates her for compelling his love; and he hates his father with the true Freudian jealousy, but he also loves him for what he is in himself, and he sympathizes more deeply with him because his wholeness has been destroyed by the mother's domination, just as his, Lawrence-Morel's, has been.

This is a psychological tension which disrupts the form of the novel and obscures its meaning, because neither the contradiction in style nor the confusion in point of view is made to right itself. Lawrence is merely repeating his emotions, and he avoids an austerer technical scrutiny of his material because it would compel him to master them. He would not let the artist be stronger than the man.

The result is that, at the same time that the book condemns the mother, it justifies her; at the same time that it shows Paul's failure, it offers rationalizations which place the failure elsewhere. The handling of the girl, Miriam, if viewed closely, is pathetic in what it signifies for Lawrence, both as man and artist. For Miriam is made the mother's scapegoat, and in a different way from the way that she was in life. The central section of the novel is shot through with alternate statements as to the source of the difficulty: Paul is unable to love Miriam wholly, and Miriam can love only his spirit. These contradictions appear sometimes within single paragraphs, and the point of view is never adequately objectified and sustained to tell us which is true. The material is never seen as material; the writer is caught in it exactly as firmly as he was caught in his experience of it. "That's how women are with me," said Paul. "They want me like mad, but they don't want to belong to me." So he might have said, and believed it; but at the end of the novel, Lawrence is still saying that, and himself believing it.

For the full history of this technical failure, one must read *Sons and Lovers* carefully and then learn the history of the manuscript from the book called *D. H. Lawrence: A Personal Record*, by one E. T., who was Miriam in life. The basic situation is clear enough. The first theme—the crippling effects of the mother's love—is developed right through to the end; and then suddenly, in the last few sentences, turns on itself, and Paul gives himself to life, not death. But all the way through, the insidious rationalizations of the second theme have crept in to destroy the artistic coherence of the work. A "split" would occur in Paul; but as the split is treated, it is superimposed upon rather than developed in support of the first theme. It is a rationalization made from it. If Miriam is made to insist on spiritual love, the meaning and the power of theme one are reduced; yet Paul's weakness is disguised. Lawrence could not separate the investigating analyst, who must be objective, from Lawrence, the subject of the book; and the sickness was not healed, the emotion not mastered, the novel not perfected. All this, and the character of a whole career, would have been altered if Lawrence had allowed his technique to discover the full meaning of his subject.

*A Portrait of the Artist as a Young Man*, like *Tono Bungay* and *Sons and Lovers*, is autobiographical, but unlike these it analyzes its material rigorously, and it defines the value and the quality of its experience not by appended comment or moral epithet, but by the texture of the style. The theme of *A Portrait*, a young artist's alienation from his environment, is explored and evaluated through three different styles and methods as Stephen Dedalus moves from childhood through boyhood into maturity. The opening pages are written in something like the Ulyssesean stream of consciousness, as the environment impinges directly on the consciousness of the infant and the child, a strange, opening world which the mind does not yet subject to questioning, selection, or judgment. But this style changes very soon, as the boy begins to explore his surroundings; and as his sensuous experience of the world is enlarged, it takes on heavier and heavier rhythms and a fuller and fuller body of sensuous detail, until it reaches a crescendo of romantic opulence in the emotional climaxes which mark Stephen's rejection of domestic and religious values. Then gradually the style subsides into the austere intellectuality of the final sections, as he defines to himself the outlines of the artistic task which is to usurp his maturity.

A highly self-conscious use of style and method defines the quality of experience in each of these sections, and, it is worth pointing out in connection with the third and concluding section, the style and method evaluate the experience. What has happened to Stephen is, of course, a progressive alienation from the life around him as he progressed in his initiation into it, and by the end of the novel, the alienation is complete. The final portion of the novel, fascinating as it may be for the developing esthetic creed of Stephen-Joyce, is peculiarly bare. The life experience was not bare, as we know from *Stephen Hero*; but Joyce is forcing technique to comment. In essence, Stephen's alienation is a denial of the human environment; it is a loss; and the austere discourse of the final section, abstract and almost wholly without sensuous detail or strong rhythm, tells us of that loss. It is a loss so great that the texture of the notation-like prose here suggests that the end is really all an illusion, that when Stephen tells us and himself that he is going forth to forge in the smithy of his soul the uncreated conscience of his race, we are to infer from the very quality of the icy, abstract void he now inhabits, the implausibility of his aim. For *Ulysses* does not create the conscience of the race; it creates our consciousness.

In the very last two or three paragraphs of the novel, the style changes once more, reverts from the bare, notative kind to the romantic prose of Stephen's adolescence. "Away! Away! The spell of arms and voices: the white arms of roads, their promise of close embraces and the black arms of tall ships that stand against the moon, their tale of distant nations. They are held out to say: We are alone—come." Might one not say that the austere ambition is founded on adolescent longing? That the excessive intellectual severity of one style is the counterpart of the excessive lyric relaxation of the other? And that the final passage of *A Portrait* punctuates the illusory nature of the whole ambition?

For *Ulysses* does not create a conscience. Stephen, in *Ulysses,* is a little older, and gripped now by guilt, but he is still the cold young man divorced from the human no less than the institutional environment. The environment of urban life finds a separate embodiment in the character of Bloom, and Bloom is as lost as Stephen, though touchingly groping for moorings. Each of the two is weakened by his inability to reach out, or to do more than reach out to the other. Here, then, is the theme again, more fully stated, as it were in counterpoint.

But if Stephen is not much older, Joyce is. He is older as an artist not only because he can create and lavish his godlike pity on a Leopold Bloom, but also because he knows now what both Stephen and Bloom mean, and *how much,* through the most brilliant technical operation ever made in fiction, they can be made to mean. Thus *Ulysses,* through the imaginative force which its techniques direct, is like a pattern of concentric circles, with the immediate human situation at its center, this passing on and out to the whole dilemma of modern life, this passing on and out beyond that to a vision of the cosmos, and this to the mythical limits of our experience. If we read *Ulysses* with more satisfaction than any other novel of this century, it is because its author held an attitude toward technique and the technical scrutiny of subject matter which enabled him to order, within a single work and with superb coherence, the greatest amount of our experience.

4

In the United States during the last twenty-five years, we have had many big novels but few good ones. A writer like James T. Farrell apparently assumes that by endless redundancy in the description of the surface of American life, he will somehow write a book with the scope of *Ulysses*. Thomas Wolfe apparently assumed that by the mere disgorging of the raw material of his experience he would give us at last our epic. But except in a physical sense, these men have hardly written novels at all.

The books of Thomas Wolfe were really journals, and the primary role of his editor in transforming these journals into the semblance of novels is well known. For the crucial act of the artist, the unique act which is composition, a sympathetic blue pencil and scissors were substituted. The result has excited many people, especially the young, and the ostensibly critical have observed the prodigal talent with the wish that it might have been controlled. Talent there was, if one means by talent inexhaustible verbal energy, excessive response to personal experience, and a great capacity for auditory imitativeness, yet all of this has nothing to do with the novelistic quality of the written result; for until the talent is controlled, the material organized, the content achieved, there is simply the man and his life. It remains to be demonstrated that Wolfe's conversations were any less interesting as novels than his books, which is to say that his books are without great interest as novels. Our response to the books is determined not so much by their qualities as novels as by our response to him and his qualities as a temperament.

This is another way of saying that Thomas Wolfe never really knew what he was writing *about*. *Of Time and the River* is merely a euphemism for "Of a Man and His Ego." It is possible that had his conception of himself and of art included an adequate respect for technique and the capacity to pursue it, Wolfe would have written a great novel on his true subject— the dilemma of romantic genius; it was his true subject, but it remains his undiscovered subject, it is the subject which *we* must dig out for him, because he himself had neither the lamp nor the pick to find it in and mine it out of the labyrinths of his experience. Like Emily Brontë, Wolfe needed a point of view beyond his own which would separate his material and its effect.

With Farrell, the situation is opposite. He knows quite well what his subject is and what he wishes to tell us about it, but he hardly needs the novel to do so. It is significant that in sheer clumsiness of style no living writer exceeds him, for his prose is asked to perform no service beyond communication of the most rudimentary kind of fact. For his ambitions the style of the newspaper and the lens of the documentary camera would be quite adequate, yet consider the diminution which Leopold Bloom, for example, would suffer, if he were to be viewed from these technical perspectives. Under the eye of this technique, the material does not yield up enough; indeed, it shrinks.

More and more writers in this century have felt that naturalism as a method imposes on them strictures which prevent them from exploring through all the resources of technique the full amplifications of their subjects, and that thus it seriously limits the possible breadth of esthetic meaning and response. James Farrell is almost unique in the complacency with which he submits to the blunt techniques of naturalism; and his fiction is correspondingly repetitive and flat.

That naturalism had a sociological and disciplinary value in the nineteenth century is obvious; it enabled the novel to grasp materials and make analyses which had eluded it in the past, and to grasp them boldly; but even then it did not tell us enough of what, in Virginia Woolf's phrase, is "really real," nor did it provide the means to the maximum of reality coherently contained. Even the Flaubertian ideal of objectivity seems, today, an unnecessarily limited view of objectivity, for as almost every good writer of this century shows us, it is quite as possible to be objective about subjective states as it is to be objective about the circumstantial surfaces of life. Dublin, in *Ulysses*, is a moral setting: not only a city portrayed in the naturalistic fashion of Dickens's London, but also a map of the modern psyche with its oblique and baffled purposes. The second level of reality in no way invalidates the first, and a writer like Joyce shows us that, if the artist truly respects his medium, he can be objective about both at once. What we need in fiction is a devoted fidelity to every technique which will help us to discover and to evaluate our subject matter, and more than that, to discover the amplifications of meaning of which our subject matter is capable.

Most modern novelists have felt this demand upon them. André Gide allowed one of his artist-heroes to make an observation which considerably resembles an observation we have quoted from Wells.

> My novel hasn't got a subject . . . Let's say, if you prefer it, it hasn't got *one* subject . . . "A slice of life," the naturalist school said. The great defect of that school is that it always cuts its slice in the same direction; in time, lengthwise. Why not in breadth? Or in depth? As for me I should like not to cut at all. Please understand; I should like to put everything into my novel.

Wells, with his equally large blob of potential material, did not know how to cut it to the novel's taste; Gide cut, of course —in every possible direction. Gide and others. And those "cuts" are all the new techniques which modern fiction has given us. None, perhaps, is more important than that inheritance from French symbolism which Huxley, in the glittering wake of Gide, called "the musicalization of fiction." Conrad anticipated both when he wrote that the novel "must strenuously aspire to the plasticity of sculpture, to the colour of painting, and to the magic suggestiveness of music—which is the art of arts," and when he said of that early but wonderful piece of symbolist fiction, *Heart of Darkness,* "It was like another art altogether. That sombre theme had to be given a sinister resonance, a tonality of its own, a continued vibration that, I hoped, would hang in the air and dwell on the ear after the last note had been struck."

The analogy with music, except as a metaphor, is inexact,

and except as it points to techniques which fiction can employ as fiction, not very useful to the sense of craftsmanship. It has had an approximate exactness in only one work, Joyce's final effort, an effort unique in literary history, *Finnegans Wake*, and here, of course, those readers willing to make the effort Joyce demands, discovering what appears to be an inexhaustible wealth and a scope beyond measure, are most forcibly reminded of the primary importance of technique to subject, and of their indivisibility.

The techniques of naturalism inevitably curtail subject and often leave it in its original area, that of undefined social experience. Those of our writers who, stemming from this tradition, yet, at their best, achieve a novelistic definition of social experience—writers like the occasional Sherwood Anderson, William Carlos Williams, the very early Erskine Caldwell, Nathanael West, and Ira Wolfert in *Tucker's People*—have done so by pressing naturalism far beyond itself, into positively Gothic distortions. The structural machinations of Dos Passos and the lyrical interruptions of Steinbeck are the maneuvers of men committed to a method of whose limitations they despair. They are our symbolists *manqué*, who end as allegorists.

Our most accomplished novels leave no such impressions of desperate and intentional struggle, yet their precise technique and their determination to make their prose work in the service of their subjects have been the measure of their accomplishment. Hemingway's *The Sun Also Rises* and Wescott's *The Pilgrim Hawk* are consummate works of art not because they may be measured by some external, neoclassic notion of form, but because their forms are so exactly equivalent with their subjects, and because the evaluation of their subjects exists in their styles.

Hemingway said that his contribution to younger writers lay in a certain necessary purification of the language; but the claim has doubtful value. The contribution of his prose was to his subject, and the terseness of style for which his early work is justly celebrated is no more valuable, as an end in itself, than the baroque involutedness of Faulkner's prose, or the cold elegance of Wescott's. Hemingway's early subject, the exhaustion of value, was perfectly investigated and invested by his bare style, and in story after story, no meaning at all is to be inferred from the fiction except as the style itself suggests that there is no meaning in life. This style, more than that, was the perfect technical substitute for the conventional commentator; it expresses and it measures that peculiar morality of the stiff lip which Hemingway borrowed from athletes. It is an instructive lesson, furthermore, to observe how the style breaks down when Hemingway moves into the less congenial subject matter of social affirmation: how the style breaks down, the effect of verbal economy as mute suffering is lost, the personality of the writer, no longer protected by the objectification of an adequate technique, begins its offensive intrusion, and the entire structural integrity slackens. Inversely, in the stories and the early novels, the technique was the perfect embodiment of the subject and it gave that subject its astonishing largeness of effect and of meaning.

One should correct Buffon and say that style is the subject. In Wescott's *Pilgrim Hawk*—a novel which bewildered its many friendly critics by the apparent absence of subject—the subject, the story, is again in the style itself. This novel, which is a triumph of the sustained point of view, is only bewildering if we try to make a story out of the narrator's observations upon others; but if we read his observations as oblique and unrecognized observations upon himself the story emerges with perfect coherence, and it reverberates with meaning, is as suited to continuing reflection as the greatest lyrics.

The rewards of such respect for the medium as the early Hemingway and the occasional Wescott have shown may be observed in every good writer we have. The involutions of Faulkner's style are the perfect equivalent of his involved structures, and the two together are the perfect representation of the moral labyrinths through which he plunges and gropes, and of the ruined world which his novels repeatedly invoke and in which these labyrinths exist. The cultivated sensuosity of Katherine Anne Porter's style—as of Eudora Welty's and

Carson McCullers's—has charm in itself, of course, but no more than with these others does it have esthetic value in itself; its values lie in the subtle means by which sensuous details become symbols, and in the way the symbols provide a network which is the story, and which at the same time provides the writer and us with a refined moral insight by means of which to test it. When we put such writers against a writer like William Saroyan, whose respect is reserved for his own temperament, we are appalled by the stylistic irresponsibility we find in him, and by the almost total absence of theme, or defined subject matter, and the abundance of unwarranted feeling. Such a writer inevitably becomes a sentimentalist because he has no means by which to measure his emotion. Technique, at last, is measure.

These writers, from Defoe to Porter, are of unequal and very different talent, and technique and talent are, of course, after a point, two different things. What Joyce gives us in one direction, Lawrence, for all his imperfections as a technician, gives us in another, even though it is not always the direction of art. In some of his stories and poems, where the demands of technique are less sustained and the subject matter is not autobiographical, Lawrence, who was less concerned with "perfection of the work" than of "the life," and in a quite different way from Joyce, comes to the same esthetic fulfillment. Emily Brontë, with what was perhaps her intuitive grasp of the need to establish a tension between her subject matter and her perspective upon it, achieves a similar fulfillment; and, curiously, in the same way and certainly by intuition alone, Hemingway's early work makes a moving splendor from nothingness.

And yet, whatever one must allow to talent and forgive in technique, one risks no generalization in saying that modern fiction at its best has been peculiarly conscious of itself and of its tools. The technique of modern fiction, at once greedy and fastidious, achieves as its subject matter not some singleness, some topic or thesis, but the whole of the modern consciousness. It discovers the complexity of the modern spirit, the difficulty of personal morality, and the fact of evil—all the untract-

able elements under the surface which a technique of the
surface alone cannot approach. It shows us—in Conrad's words,
from *Victory*—that we all live in an "age in which we are
camped like bewildered travellers in a garish, unrestful hotel,"
and while it puts its hard light on our environment, it penetrates, with its sharp weapons, the depths of our bewilderment.
These are not two things, but only an adequate technique can
show them as one. In a realist like Farrell, we have the environment only, which we know from the newspapers; in a
subjectivist like Wolfe, we have the bewilderment only, which
we record in our own diaries and letters. But the true novelist
gives them to us together, and thereby increases the effect of
each, and reveals each in its full significance.

Elizabeth Bowen, writing of Lawrence, said of modern fiction, "We want the naturalistic surface, but with a kind of internal burning. In Lawrence every bush burns." But the bush
burns brighter in some places than in others, and it burns
brightest when a passionate private vision finds its objectification in exacting technical search. If the vision finds no such
objectification, as in Wolfe and Saroyan, there is a burning
without a bush. In our committed realists, who deny the resources of art for the sake of life, whose technique forgives
both innocence and slovenliness, there is a bush but it does not
burn. There, at first glance, the bush is only a bush; and then,
when we look again, we see that, really, the thing is dead.

# Fiction and the "Analogical Matrix"

IF THE NOVEL, as R. P. Blackmur proposed, is now to enjoy the kind of attention from criticism that for the past twenty years has been the privilege of poetry, criticism must begin with the simplest assertion: fiction is a literary art. It must begin with the base of language, with the word, with figurative structures, with rhetoric as skeleton and style as body of meaning. A beginning as simple as this must overcome reading habits of long standing; for the novel, written in prose, bears an apparently closer resemblance to discursive forms than it does to poetry, thus easily opening itself to first questions about philosophy or politics, and, traditionally a middle-class vehicle with a reflective social function, it bears an apparently more immediate relation to life than it does to art, thus easily opening itself to first questions about conduct. Yet a novel, like a poem, is not life, it is an image of life; and the critical problem is first of all to analyze the structure of the image. Thus criticism must approach the vast and endlessly ornamented house of fiction with a willingness to do a little at a time and none of it finally, in order to suggest experiences of meaning and of feeling that may be involved in novels, and responsibilities for their style which novelists themselves may forget.

To choose, more or less at random and without premeditated end, one novel by each of only three novelists, and to examine in each only one element in the language, the dominant metaphorical quality—this, positively, is to work piecemeal, and merely to suggest. I emphasize not *metaphor* but *quality*, intending not only the explicit but the buried and the dead metaphors, and some related traits of diction generally, that whole habit of value association suggested in Scott Buchanan's phrase, the "analogical matrix." The novels are *Persuasion, Wuthering Heights,* and *Middlemarch.*

## 2

*Persuasion* is a novel of courtship and marriage with a patina of sentimental scruple and moral punctilio and a stylistic base derived from commerce and property, the counting house and the inherited estate. The first is the expression of the characters, the second is the perception of the author. And whether we should decide that a persistent reliance on commerce and property for concepts of value is the habit of Jane Austen's mind, the very grain of her imagination, or that it is a special novelistic intention, is for the moment irrelevant. It is probable that the essence of her comedy resides, in either case, in the discrepancy between social sentiment and social fact, and the social fact is to be discovered not so much in the professions of her characters as in the texture of her style.

We are told at once that the mother of the three Elliot girls felt in dying that in them she left "an awful *legacy* . . . an awful *charge* rather"; that Sir Walter Elliot is devoted to his eldest daughter, Elizabeth (who opens "every ball *of credit*" and is waiting to be "properly *solicited* by baronet-blood"), but feels that his two younger daughters, Mary and Anne, are "of very inferior *value*"—indeed, "Anne's word had no *weight.*" Anne is befriended by Lady Russell, who "had a *value* for rank and consequence," and even though it was Lady Russell no less than Sir Walter who discouraged Anne's marriage, seven years before, to the property-less Captain Wentworth, Anne "*rated* Lady Russell's influence highly." "Consequence," we are told, "has its *tax,*" and for seven years Anne has been paying it. The problem of the novel is to relieve her of the necessity of paying it and at the same time to increase her value.

We are in a world of substance, a peculiarly material world. Here, indeed, changes are usually named "*material* alterings"— for example, in "style of living" and "degree of consequence."

Perhaps the word is used most tellingly in the phrases "a face not materially *disfigured*" and "a material difference in the *discredit* of it"; for *figure* and *credit* suggest the two large areas of metaphorical interest—arithmetic and business.

Time is *divided*, troubles *multiply*, weeks are *calculated*, and even a woman's prettiness is *reckoned*. Thus, one's independence is *purchased*; one is *rendered* happy or unhappy; one is on *terms*, friendly or unfriendly, with others. Young Mr. Elliot has "nothing to *gain* by being on *terms* with Sir Walter," but Lady Russell is convinced that he hopes "to *gain* Anne" even though Anne cannot "know herself to be so *highly rated*." We are asked to "take all the charms and perfections of Edward's wife upon *credit*," and "to judge of the general *credit due*." Captain Wentworth thought that he had *earned* "every blessing." "I have *valued* myself on honourable toils and just *rewards*." So Mary is in the habit of *claiming* Anne's energies, and Anne does not feel herself "*entitled* to reward." Young ladies have a "*stock* of accomplishments." "Here were *funds* of enjoyment!" Anne does not wish "for the possibility of *exchange*." Experience is thought of as *venture, reversal, prospect, fortune,* and *allowance*. Anne "*ventured* to recommend a larger *allowance* of prose in" Captain Benwick's "daily study." The death of a wife leaves a man with "*prospects* . . . blighted," and Anne contemplates "the *prospect* of *spending*" two months at Uppercross. In this metaphorical context, even the landscape takes on a special shimmer: "all the *precious* rooms and furniture, groves, and *prospects*." An "arrangement" is *prudent* or *imprudent,* and feelings must be *arranged* as prudently as accounts: no one's "feelings could *interest* her, till she had a little better *arranged* her own." One *pays* addresses, of course, but one is also *repaid* for the "trouble of exertion." "It had *cost* her something to encounter Lady Russell's surprise." A town has *worth,* a song is not *worth* staying for, and Anne "had the full *worth* of" tenderness in "Captain Wentworth's affection." Captain Wentworth's account of Captain Benwick ("whom he had always *valued highly*") "*stamped him* well in the esteem of every listener." "Ten minutes were enough to *certify* that" Mr.

Elliot was a sensible man. Stamped, certified; and at last Anne's character is "*fixed* on his mind as perfection itself," which is to say that, like a currency, it has been stabilized.

Moral qualities are persistently put in economic figures: Mary "had no *resources* for solitude" and she had *inherited* "a considerable *share* of the Elliot self-importance." Love, likewise: if Elizabeth is hoping to be *solicited* by baronet-blood, Anne has had to reject the "declarations and proposals" of an improvident sailor. "Alliance" is a peculiarly appropriate word for such prudential arrangements as these, and at the end of the novel, when "the engagement" is "*renewed*," one sees bonded documents. Anne need no longer suffer those fits of dejection in which she contemplates others' "*prosperous* love," for hers at last has prospered, too.

In this context certain colorless words, words of the lightest intention, take on a special weight. The words *account* and *interest* are used hundreds of times in their homeliest sense, yet when we begin to observe that every narration is an *account*, and at least once "an *account* . . . of the *negotiation*," we are reminded that they have more special meanings. When Anne's blighted romance is called "this little history of sorrowful *interest*," we hardly forget that a lack of money was the blight. Is "a man of principle" by any chance a man of substance?

The significance of this metaphorical substructure is clearest, perhaps, not when Jane Austen substitutes material for moral or sentimental values, but when she juxtaposes them. "He had . . . been nothing better than a thick-headed, *unfeeling, unprofitable* Dick Musgrove, who had never done anything to entitle himself to more than the abbreviation of his name, living or dead." More simply, these three from a single paragraph: "a *fund* of good *sense*," "*leisure* to *bestow*," "something that is *entertaining* and *profitable*." "I must endeavour," says Captain Wentworth, in another such juxtaposition near the end of the novel, "I must endeavour to subdue my *mind* to my *fortune*."

*Persuasion* is a novel in which sensibility—and I am not now raising the question whether it is the sensibility of the author

or of her characters or of her characters except for her heroes—
a novel in which sensibility is subdued to property.

The novel explicitly asks, what is "the value of an Anne
Elliot" and where is the man who will "understand" it? Anne
herself feels that her value has sunk:

> A few months hence, and the room now so deserted, occupied
> by her silent, pensive self, might be filled again with all that was
> happy and gay, all that was *glowing and bright* in *prosperous
> love*, all that was most unlike Anne Elliot.

> . . . Anne felt her spirits not likely to be benefited by an increas-
> ing acquaintance among his brother-officers. "These would have
> been all my friends," was her thought; and she had to struggle
> against a great tendency to lowness.

"A great *tendency to lowness.*" The phrase clarifies her situation, for Anne's is finally the problem of a stock that has a
debased value, and when she thinks of doing good in such a
further phrase as "good of a lower standard," we can hardly
escape the recognition that this is a novel about marriage as a
market, and about the female as marketable, and that the
novel makes the observation that to sentimental scruple and
moral fastidiousness, as they are revealed to us in the drama,
much property is not necessary but *some* is essential—and this
is shown us primarily in the style. The basis of the comedy
lies in the difference between the two orders of value which
the metaphors, like the characters, are all the while busily
equating. At the end, in the last sentence, a prosperous sailor's
wife, Anne has been relieved of "the tax of consequence," but
now "she must *pay the tax* of quick alarm for belonging to that
profession which is, if possible, more distinguished in its domestic virtues than in its national importance."

### 3

The style of Jane Austen is so entirely without flamboyance
or gesture, the cited illustrations are so commonplace, so perfectly within the order of English idiom, that, unless we remind

ourselves that our own habits of speech are even more intimately involved in the life of cash than Jane Austen's, no case at all may appear. Yet the inevitability of individual imaginative habit, the impressive fact that every mind selects its own creative gamut from the whole range of possible language, and in thus selecting determines its insights and their scope, in short, its character and the character of its creations, is at once apparent when we open some other novel. Emily Brontë is very different from Jane Austen, yet both were unmarried provincial women, living in the same half of the same century, speaking the same language, both daughters of clergymen, and one might reasonably expect to encounter, even in *Wuthering Heights,* some of those perfectly normal rhetorical figures with which *Persuasion* abounds. There are, I think, none of the same kind. Emily Brontë does not "divide the time" but, on the first page, "the desolation"; "time," when she mentions it, "stagnates," and "prudence" is "diabolical." If there are any figures of the same kind, they are so few, and in their own metaphorical context, function so differently, that the total quality owes nothing to them. Where Wentworth speaks of the "crown" of "all my other success," Lockwood speaks of the "copestone on my rage and humiliation." Both *crown* and *copestone on* mean climax, but "crown" is drawn from rank and money, "copestone" from earth and building. If Nelly Dean's phrase, "the crown of all my wishes," suggests a kingdom at all, it is a heavenly kingdom, quite different from "all my other successes." The difference signifies. *Wuthering Heights* has its own sphere of significant experience, and its metaphors, like its epithets and verbs, tell us different things. They tell us, too, of a special problem.

*Wuthering Heights,* as I understand it, means to be a work of edification: Emily Brontë begins by wishing to instruct her narrator, the dandy, Lockwood, in the nature of a grand passion; she ends by instructing herself in the vanity of human wishes. She means to dramatize with something like approval —the phrase that follows is from *Middlemarch*—"the sense of a stupendous self and an insignificant world." What her metaphors signify is the impermanence of self and the permanence of something larger.

To exalt the power of human feeling, Emily Brontë roots her analogies in the fierce life of animals and in the relentless life of the elements—fire, wind, water. "Wuthering," we are told, is "a significant provincial adjective, descriptive of the atmospheric tumult to which its station is exposed in stormy weather," and, immediately after, that "one may guess the power of the north wind blowing over the edge, by the excessive slant of a few stunted firs at the end of the house; and by a range of gaunt thorns all stretching their limbs one way, as if craving alms of the sun." The application of this landscape to the characters is made explicit in the second half of the novel, when Heathcliff says, "Now, my bonny lad, you are *mine!* And we'll see if one tree won't grow as crooked as another, with the same wind to twist it!" This analogy provides at least half of the metaphorical base of the novel.

Human conditions are like the activities of the landscape, where rains *flood,* blasts *wail,* and the snow and wind *whirl wildly* and *blow* out lights. A serving woman *heaves* "like a sea after a high wind"; a preacher "*poured* forth his zeal in a *shower*"; Mrs. Dean *rushes* to welcome Lockwood, "exclaiming *tumultuously*"; spirits are "at high-water mark"; Linton's soul is as different from Heathcliff's "as a moonbeam from lightning, or frost from fire"; abuse is *lavished* in a *torrent,* or *pours forth* in a *deluge*; illnesses are "*weathered . . .* through"; "sensations" are felt in a *gush*; "your veins are *full* of *ice water*; but mine are *boiling*"; hair *flies,* bodies *toss* or *tremble* like reeds, tears *stream* or *rain down* among ashes; discord and distress arise in a *tumult*; Catherine Linton "was *struck* during a *tempest* of passion with a kind of fit" and "*flew off* in the *height* of it."

Faces, too, are like landscapes: "a *cloud* of meditation" hangs over Nelly Dean's "*ruddy* countenance"; Catherine had "a suddenly *clouded* brow; her humor was a mere *vane* for constantly varying caprices"; "the surface of" the boy Heathcliff's "face and hands was dismally *beclouded*" with dirt; later, his face "*brightened* for a moment; then it was *overcast* afresh." "His forehead . . . *shaded* over with a heavy *cloud*"; and "the *clouded* windows of hell," his eyes, "*flashed*." Hareton, likewise, grows "black as a *thundercloud*"; or "*darkens* with a frown." The older Catherine experienced whole "*seasons* of gloom," and the younger Catherine's "heart was *clouded* . . . in double *darkness*." Her "face was just like the *landscape—shadows* and *sunshine* flitting over it in rapid succession; but the *shadows* rested longer, and the *sunshine* was more transient." Sometimes "her eyes are *radiant* with *cloudless* pleasure," and at the end, Hareton shakes off "the *clouds* of ignorance and degradation," and his "*brightening* mind *brightened* his features."

Quite as important as the imagery of wind and cloud and water is the imagery of fire. In every interior, the fire on the hearth is the center of pictorial interest, and the characters sit "*burning* their eyes out before the fire." Eyes *burn* with anguish but do not *melt*; they always *flash* and *sparkle*. Fury *kindles*, temper *kindles*, a "*spark* of spirit" *kindles*. Catherine has a *fiery* disposition, but so do objects and states: words *brand*, shame is *burning*, merriment *expires* quickly, fevers *consume* life; hot coffee and basins *smoke*, they do not steam; and Isabella shrieks "as if witches were running *red-hot* needles into her." Sometimes fire is identified with other elements, as when a servant urges "*flakes* of *flame* up the chimney," or when Isabella complains that the fire causes the wound on her neck, first stopped by the icy cold, to stream and smart.

Metaphors of earth—earth takes more solid and durable forms than the other elements—are interestingly few. Twice Heathcliff is likened to "an arid wilderness of *furze* and *whinstone*"; there is a reference to his "*flinty* gratification"; and once he speaks scornfully of "the *soil* of" Linton's "shallow cares." Earth and vegetation sometimes result in a happy juxtaposition of the vast or the violent and the little or the homely, as when Heathcliff says of Linton that "he might as well plant *an oak in a flowerpot*," or when he threatens to "crush his ribs in like *a rotten hazelnut*," which is like his saying that Catherine's

passion could be as readily encompassed by Linton as "*the sea
could be . . . contained in that horse-trough.*"

Most of the animals are wild. Hareton's "whiskers en-
croached *bearishly* over his cheeks," and Heathcliff denies the
paternity of "that bear." Hareton had been "cast out like an
unfledged *dunnock*," and Heathcliff is a "fierce, pitiless, *wolfish*
man." He is also "a *bird* of bad omen" and "an evil *beast*"
prowling between a "stray *sheep* . . . and the fold, waiting his
time to spring and destroy." He has a "*ferocious* gaze" and a
*savage* utterance; he *growls* and *howls* "like a beast," and is
many times named "a brute," "a beast," "a brute beast." He
struggles like a *bear*, he has *sharp cannibal teeth* which *gleam*
"through the dark," and "*basilisk* eyes . . . *quenched* by sleep-
lessness." He *gnashes* his teeth and *foams* like a *mad dog*. He is
"like a *bull*" to Linton's "*lamb*," and only at the very end, the
exhausted end, "he breathed as fast as a *cat*."

For the domestic and the gentler animals are generally used
for purposes of harsh satire or vilification. Edgar, "the soft
thing," "possessed the power to depart, as much as a *cat*
possesses the power to leave a *mouse* half killed, or a *bird*
half eaten." He is "not a *lamb*" but "a sucking *leveret*," and his
sister is a "pitiful, slavish, mean-minded *brach*," she is among
those *worms*, who, "the more they writhe, the more" Heathcliff
yearns "to crush out their entrails." Hindley dies in a stupor,
"snorting like a *horse*"; "flaying and scalping" would not have
roused him, and when the doctor arrives, "the *beast* has
changed to *carrion*." Hareton is "an infernal *calf*," and young
Linton is a "*puling chicken*" and a "*whelp*." Like a dying dog,
he "slowly *trailed* himself off, and lay down," or, like a cold
one, he "*shrank* closer to the fire." He "had *shrunk* into a corner
of the settle, as quiet as a *mouse*"; he is called "a little perishing
*monkey*"; and he "achieved his exit exactly as a *spaniel* might."
He is also "an abject *reptile*" and "a *cockatrice*." Hareton, who
is capable on occasion of gathering "*venom* with reflection," is
once called a "*magpie*," and once said to be "obstinate as a
*mule*"—one of the few kindly animal references in the novel.
To be sure, Isabella describes herself as though she were a

deer: "I *bounded, leaped* and *flew* down the steep road; then
. . . *shot* direct across the moor, *rolling* over banks, and *wading*
through marshes." And Catherine, on the whole, is not abused.
She is a "cunning little *fox*" and she runs "like a *mouse*," but
chiefly she is "soft and mild as a *dove*."

Emily Brontë's metaphors color all her diction. As her epithets are charged with passion—"jealous guardianship," "vexatious phlegm," "importunate branch"—so her verbs are verbs of
violent movement and conflict, both contributing to a rhetorical texture where everything is at a pitch from which it can
only subside. The verbs *demand* exhaustion, just as the metaphors *demand* rest. And there is an antithetical chorus in this
rhetoric, a contrapuntal warning, which, usually but not only in
the voice of Nelly Dean, says, "Hush! Hush!" all through the
novel, at the beginning of paragraph after paragraph. At the
end, everything *is* hushed. And the moths *fluttering* over
Heathcliff's grave and "the soft wind *breathing* through the
grass" that grows on it have at last more power than he, for all
his passion. These soft and fragile things paradoxically endure.

The passions of animals, if we may speak of them as passions, have meaning in that they are presumably necessary to
survival; Heathcliff's passion destroys others, himself, and at
last, itself. The tumult of the elements alternates with periods
of peace, and the seasons are not only autumn and winter. The
*fact* of alternation enables nature to endure. The singleness of
Heathcliff's tempestuous and wintry emotional life dooms it.
Thus there is a curious and ironic contrast between the condition and the destiny of Heathcliff, and the full facts of those
areas of metaphor. When, at the end of the novel, Nelly remarks that "the same moon shone through the window; and
the same autumn landscape lay outside" as eighteen years before, she is speaking with metaphorical accuracy; but Heathcliff is *not* the same. He has not indeed come into a "sober,
disenchanted maturity"—that will be the privilege of Hareton
and the second Cathy; but he has completely changed in the
fashion that Joseph described much earlier—"so as by fire."
". . . there is a strange change approaching: I'm in its shadow

at present," he declares when he has found that nothing is worth the feeling of it. At last, after all the windy tumult and the tempests, he says, "I have to remind myself to *breathe.* . . ."

If his life, exhausted at the end, has not been, as he once said of it, "a moral teething," and the novel, therefore, no tragedy, the story of his life has been a moral teething for the author. Lockwood is instructed in the nature of a grand passion, but he and Emily Brontë together are instructed in its final fruits: even roaring fires end in a bed of ashes. Her metaphors instruct her, and her verbs. That besides these rhetorical means (which in their functioning make tolerable the almost impossibly inflated style), she should have found structural means as well which give her whole narrative the remote quality of a twice-told tale, the property of an old wife (and so make its melodrama endurable), should reinforce the point. At the end, the voice that drones on is the perdurable voice of the country, Nelly Dean's. No more than Heathcliff did Emily Brontë quite intend that homespun finality. Like the older Catherine, Emily Brontë could have said of her book, "I've dreamed in my life dreams that have stayed with me ever after, and changed my ideas: they've gone through and through me, like wine through water, and altered the color of my mind." Her rhetoric altered the form of her intention. It is her education; it shapes her insight.

## 4

*Middlemarch* is a novel written on a much grander scale than either of these others, with many points of narrative interest, a much more complex structural pattern, and an important difference in its metaphorical language. Jane Austen's metaphors are generally of the "buried" kind, submerged, woven deep in the ordinary, idiomatic fabric of the language; Emily Brontë's are generally epithetical. George Eliot's tend always to be, or to become, explicit symbols of psychological or moral conditions, and they actually function in such a way as to give symbolical value to much action, as Dorothea's pleasure in planning buildings ("a kind of work which she delighted in") and Casaubon's desire to construct a "Key to all Mythologies." Their significance lies, then, not so much in the choice of area (as, "commerce," or "natural elements" and "animals") as in the choice of function, and one tests them not by their field, their content, but by their conceptual portent. I should like to suggest a set of metaphorical qualities in *Middlemarch* which actually represents a series apparent in the thinking that underlies the dramatic structure. First of all, there are metaphors of unification; then, of antithesis; next, there are metaphors which conceive things as progressive, and then, metaphors of shaping and making, of structure and creative purpose; finally, there are metaphors of what I should call a "muted" apocalypse.

George Eliot's metaphors of unification pivot on her most characteristic verbs—these are of conciliation and reconciliation, of unification, of course, and of inclusion, of mingling, of associating, of merging and mixing, of embracing and comprehending, of connecting, allying, binding together and making room for. The elements to be brought together are as various as the universe—they may be merely "mingled pleasures" or "associated facts which . . . show a mysterious electricity if you touched them," or the relation of urban and rural areas, which "made fresh threads of connection"; again, they may be attitudes—"criticism" and "awe" *mixing*, or qualities *uniting*, as presumably, "the glories of doctor and saint" in dreary Casaubon, of men themselves making more *energetic alliances* "with impartial nature"; or they may be those yearnings of one individual for another which find completion in love, the institution of marriage, and the literal embrace; or, most important, they may be "lofty conceptions" which embrace multitudinousness—for example, the daily life of Tipton parish and Dorothea Brooks's own "rule of conduct." If only we knew more and felt more, these metaphors insist; for there *is*, we are told, "a knowledge which . . . traces out the suppressed transitions which unite all contrasts." This is religious yearning, and it finds occasional pseudo-religious fulfillment, as after Lydgate's successful cogitations on morphology: he finds himself "in that agreeable after-glow of excitement when thought lapses from examination of a specific object into a suffusive sense of its connections with all the rest of our existence," and one can "float with the repose of unexhausted strength."

The metaphors of unification imply the metaphors of antithesis; the first represent yearnings, the second a recognition of fact. Thus we have metaphors of reality vs. appearance, as: "the large vistas and wide fresh air which she had dreamed of finding in her husband's mind were replaced by anterooms and winding passages which seemed to lead no-whither"; or of chaos vs. order (humorously dramatized by Mr. Brooke's "documents," which need arranging but get mixed up in pigeonholes), as Mary Garth's "red fire," which "seemed like a solemn existence calmly independent of the petty passions, the imbecile desires, the straining after worthless uncertainties, which were daily moving her contempt"; or of shapelessness vs. shape, as "a kind Providence furnishes the limpest personality with a little gum or starch in the form of tradition." There are other kinds, of outer vs. inner, for example: "so much subtler is a human mind than the outside tissues which make a sort of blazonry or clock-face for it." It is this, the outer-inner antithesis, which underscores one of George Eliot's favorite words —"inward" or "inwardly," a usage which is frequently annoying because it is tautological, applied to states which can *only* be inward under the circumstances of the fiction, but, for that reason, all the more symptomatic. There are metaphorical antitheses of fact to wish, imbalance to balance, restlessness to repose, and many other opposites. Most important, and perhaps most frequent, are the figures which oppose freedom to various forms of restraint—burdens, ties, bonds, and so on: "he replies by calling himself Pegasus, and every form of prescribed work 'harness,' " to which the answer is, "I shall let him be *tried* by the *test* of freedom." Another example of the restraint-freedom opposition illustrates the way that reported action, when conjoined with these metaphors, pushes both on to explicit symbolism: near the end, Dorothea observes on the road outside her window "a man with a bundle on his back and a woman carrying her baby," and, still nearer the end, when Lydgate has "accepted his narrowed lot," that is, the values of his child-bride, he thinks, "He had chosen this fragile creature, and had taken the burden of her life upon his arms. He must walk as he could, carrying that burden pitifully."

The oppositions in these metaphors of antithesis are the classic oppositions between Things as They Are and Things as They Should Be, between the daily realities of a community like Middlemarch and the "higher" realities of that "New Jerusalem" toward which Dorothea and others are "on the road."

Everyone and everything in this novel is moving on a "way." Life is a *progress*, and it is variously and inevitably described as road, stream, channel, avenue, way, journey, voyage, ride (either on horse or by carriage), vista, chain, line, course, path, and process. To these terms one should add the terms of *growth*, usually biological growth, which carry much the same value. There must be at least a thousand and possibly there are more metaphorical variations on the general idea of life as progress, and this progress is illimitable. At the end of the novel we are told, in words somewhat suggestive of a more orthodox religious spirit than George Eliot, that "Every limit is a beginning as well as an ending."

Everything strains forward. Consciousness is a stream. "In Dorothea's mind there was a current into which all thought and feeling were apt sooner or later to flow—the reaching forward of the whole consciousness toward the fullest truth, the least partial good." "Character, too," we are told, "is a process," and it is a process which we recognize by achievement—"the niceties of inward balance, by which man swims and makes his point or else is carried headlong." Like Leopold Bloom, George Eliot's characters think of their existence as "the stream of life in which the stream of life we trace," but with a difference: the personal life finally flows into the "gulf of death," but the general stream flows on, through vistas of endlessly unfolding good, and that good consists of individual achievements of "the fullest truth, the least partial good," of Lydgate's individually *made points.* This is a progressive, in no sense a cyclical view of human history.

These metaphors of progress, like the restraint-freedom antithesis, involve George Eliot in her many complementary metaphors of hindrance to progress. The individual purpose is sometimes confused by "a social life which seemed nothing but a labyrinth of petty courses, a walled-in maze"; sometimes by the inadequacy of the purpose itself, as Casaubon, who "was lost among small closets and winding stairs"; experience and circumstance over and over become "yokes," which slow the progress, for there are those always "who carry a weight of trials"; one may *toil* "under the fetters of a promise" or move, like Lydgate, more haltingly than one had hoped under the *burden* of a responsibility.

These hindrances are, generally speaking, social, not moral. One submits to them in the interests of the whole procession, and when one does not submit—as Dorothea, refusing to devote herself to Casaubon's scholarship after his death—it is because one has discovered that they are not in the interests of the whole procession. The particular interests of the procession are indicated by the extended metaphors drawn from nearly every known field of physical and medical science. It is by the "serene light of science" that we glimpse "a presentiment of endless processes filling the vast spaces planked out of" our "sight by that wordy ignorance which," in the past, we "had supposed to be knowledge." It is by the same light that we are able to recognize our social obligations, according to the Religion of Humanity.

Thus, quite smoothly, we come to that fourth group of prevailing metaphors, those having to do with purpose. They are of shaping, of forming, of making, of framing; they pivot on notions of pattern or rule, measure or structure. They are all words used in metaphors which, explicitly or by implication, reveal the individual directing his destiny by conscious, creative purpose toward the end of absolute human order. Opposed to them are the many metaphors of derogation of the unorganized, notably the human mind, which, at worst, like Mr.

Brooke's, availing nothing perceptible in the body politic, is a *mass*.

At the end of this grand vista are the metaphors of what I have called the "muted" apocalypse. The frequency with which George Eliot uses the words *up*, *high*, and *higher* in metaphorical contexts is equaled only, perhaps, by her use of the word *light*, until one feels a special significance in "giving *up*" and in all the faces that *beam*, all the ideas that *flash* across the mind, and all the things that are all the time being "taken" in *that light* or *this light*. Fire plays a perhaps predictably important metaphorical role, and, together with light, or alternating with it, usually accompanies or is implied by those frequent metaphors in which things are *gloriously* transformed, transfused, or transfigured. Treating this complex of figures as I do, as a kind of apocalyptic drama which of course does not exist in the novel as such, but surely does in the imagination of George Eliot, we are, now, at the moment before climax, all those metaphors involving ideas of veneration and adoration, or worshipful awe; these, in my factitious series, are immediately followed by the climax itself, which is contained in endless use of the word "revelation" and figurative developments from it. Perception, in this novel, is indeed thought of as revelation, and minds and souls are always "opening" to the influx. Things are many times "manifested" or "made manifest," as if life were a perpetual epiphany. If perception is not a "revelation," it is a "divination," and for the ordinary verb, "to recognize," George Eliot usually prefers to use "to divine." It is here that we come upon her unquestionably favorite word, and the center of her most persistent metaphors. For the word "sight" or "feeling" she almost always substitutes the more portentous word "vision." Visions are of every possible kind, from *dim* to *bright* to *blinding*, from *testing* to *guiding*. The observation of any simple physical detail may be a vision; every insight is of course a vision, usually an *inward* vision.

The experience now subsides. If perception is revelation, then it is, secondarily, nourishment, and the recurrence of metaphors in which perception is conceived as spiritual food and drink, and of all the metaphors of *fullness, filling,* and *ful-fillment,* is perhaps predictable. It is likewise energizing, in various figurative ways, and in moments of climactic under-standing, significantly, a charge of electricity flows through the human organism.

Illumination, revelation, fulfillment. One step remains in this pattern of a classic religious experience; that is expectation. Metaphors of expectation are everywhere; I will represent them in their most frequent form, a phrase so rubbed by usage that it hardly seems metaphorical at all. It is "to look forward," and it appears on nearly every page of *Middlemarch,* a com-monplace there too, yet more than that: it is the clue to the whole system of metaphor I have sketched out; it is the clue to a novel, the clue to a mind.

I have separated into a series a metaphorical habit which of course always appears in conflux, and it is only because these metaphors do constantly associate themselves in the novel that one may justifiably hit upon them as representing George Eliot's selectivity. One of many such elaborate confluences is as follows:

> . . . Mr. Casaubon's talk about his great book was *full* of *new vistas;* and this sense of *revelation,* this *surprise of a nearer intro-duction* to Stoics and Alexandrians, as people who had ideas not totally unlike her own, kept in abeyance for the time her usual eagerness for a *binding theory* which could bring her own life and doctrine into *strict connection* with that amazing past, and give the remotest *sources* of knowledge some *bearing* on her actions . . . she was *looking forward* to *higher initiation* in ideas, as she was *looking forward* to marriage, and *blending* her *dim* conceptions of both. . . . All her eagerness for acquirement lay within that *full current of sympathetic* motive in which her ideas and impulses were habitually *swept along.* She did not want to deck herself with knowledge—to wear it loose from the *nerves and blood that fed her action*; and if she had written a book she must have done it as St. Theresa did, under the *command of an authority that constrained her conscience.* But something she yearned for by which her *life might be filled* with action at once rational and ardent: and since the time was gone by *for guiding*

*visions* and spiritual directors, since prayer *heightened* yearning, but not instruction, *what lamp* was there but knowledge?

Here are nearly all of them: metaphors of unification, of antithesis (restraint-freedom), of progress, of the apocalypse: height, light, revelation, vision, nourishment, and, of course, the forward look. The passage is not in the least exceptional. In my analytical sketch of such persistent confluences, I separated the elements into a series to demonstrate how completely, step by step, they embody a pseudo-religious philosophy, how absolutely expressive is metaphor, even in fiction, and how systematic it can become. This is a novel of religious yearning without religious object. The unification it desires is the unification of human knowledge in the service of social ends; the antitheses that trouble it (and I observe in this otherwise classic series no antitheses either of Permanence and Change, or of Sin and Grace) are the antitheses between man as he is and man as he could be in this world; the hindrances to life as progress are man's social not his moral flaws; the purposive dedication of individuals will overcome those flaws; we see the fulfillment of all truly intellectual passions, for the greater glory of Man.

Our first observation on the function of metaphor in this novel should, then, be of its *absolutely* expressive character. The second is perhaps less evident, and we may call it the interpretive function of metaphor, the extent to which metaphor comments on subject. The subject of this novel may be Middlemarch, a community, but, as even the title metaphorically suggests, the theme is the nature of progress in what is probably meant to be the typical British community in the nineteenth century. (Observe, too, these names: Brooke, a running course, and Lydgate, his progress blocked by his wife, twice-blocked by his name.) Or we can select subjects within the subject, as the clerical subject interpreted by the pseudo-religious theme: the true "religious" dedication of a Dorothea Brooke, and the characters around her falling into various "religious" postures: Casaubon as the false prophet, Bulstrode as the parody-

prophet, Lydgate as the nearly true prophet—a "scientific Phoe-
nix," he is called—somehow deflected from his prophecy; and
Ladislaw as the true prophet. Indeed, given the metaphorical
texture, one cannot escape the nearly systematic Christ analogy
which George Eliot weaves around Ladislaw, omitting from
her figure only the supremely important element of Christ's
sacrifice, and the reason for which He made it. This is to be
expected in a novel which is about progress without guilt.
Here, even the heroic characters cannot be said to have inner
struggles, for all their "inward visions." Here there is much
illumination and nearly no self-doubt; much science, and never
a sin. One recognizes from the metaphorical structure that this
novel represents a decay of the full religious experience into
that part of it which aspires alone: Christian optimism divorced from the basic human tragedy.

The metaphorical complex provides a third, and a more interesting function: a structural function. *Middlemarch* is concerned with nearly every important activity in community life
—political, clerical, agricultural, industrial, professional, domestic, of course, even scholarly. It involves many different characters and groups of characters. The relations between some of
these characters and even between some of these groups are
often extremely tenuous, often merely accidental. The dramatic
structure, in short, is not very taut, yet one feels, on finishing
the book, that this is a superbly constructed work, that, indeed,
as foolish Mr. Brooke observes, "We're all one family, you know
—it's all one cupboard." What makes it so is thematic rather
than dramatic unity.

The measure of Middlemarch is Dorothea's *sublimity*, the
interpretive height from which she judges. From her sublimity,
everything shades off, all the way down to garrulous Mrs. Cad-
wallader and villainous Mr. Bulstrode. The metaphors of unification which George Eliot enjoyed to use, those images of
intermingling and embracing, are important in a double sense:
they express Dorothea's ethical sentiments, and, actually, they
and the others bind the material together. They tell us *how to
take* each Middlemarcher, *in what light*. They do this chiefly

through the creation of symbolic echoes of the major situations in the minor ones, echoes often ironic, sometimes parodic.

Thus, in the imagery of vision, Dorothea's remark, made so early as in Chapter III, has a special ring: "I am rather short-sighted." In the imagery of human progress, Mr. Garth's question about Bulstrode, the pious fraud,—"whether he shall settle somewhere else, as a lasting thing"—has such symbolic value. Mr. Garth's own attitude toward agriculture is a thematic parody of the exaltation of Dorothea, Lydgate, and Ladislaw: "the peculiar tone of fervid veneration, of religious regard in which he wrapped it, as a consecrated symbol is wrapped in its gold-fringed linen." In the imagery of structure, a special meaning seems to attach to the word "dwell," when it refers to characters experiencing some state of mind. Lydgate's morphological research is another such symbolic extension of the metaphors of structure. Dorothea's avenue of limes outside her window, leading toward the sunset, becomes, finally, a representation in the landscape of the idea of progress. The political newspapers, notably unenlightened, are called *The Pioneer* and *The Trumpet,* and these are surely parodies, one of the progress metaphors, the other of the apocalyptic. Even that humble rural tavern, the *Weights and Scales,* reminds us of more exalted concern, in this novel, with justice and with metaphors of balance. And so that wretched farm called Freeman's End, which has nearly destroyed its tenant and his family, is an eloquent little drama of the freedom-restraint metaphors.

"We all of us," says George Eliot, "grave or light, get our thoughts entangled in metaphors, and act fatally on the strength of them." If the writing of a novel is a deed, as Conrad liked to think, she spoke truer than she knew.

## 5

Four tentative proposals seem relevant:

1. Metaphorical language gives any style its special quality, and one may even suggest—only a little humorously—that this quality derives in part from the content of the metaphors, that

quantity shapes quality. Certainly the particular "dryness" of Jane Austen's style is generated in part by the content of her images of the counting house, and certainly the inflatedness of Emily Brontë's is generated in large part by the prominence of wind and of atmospheric tumult in her metaphors. I cannot, unfortunately, suggest that George Eliot's pleasure in "light" has any notable effect on the quality of her style, but we can say that the content of her conceptions as her metaphors express it predicts a style serious always, solemn probably, and heavy perhaps.

2. Metaphorical language expresses, defines, and evaluates theme, and thereby demonstrates the limits and the special poise within those limits of a given imagination. We have seen three novels in which metaphors in effect answered questions that the novels themselves neglected to ask.

3. Metaphorical language, because it constantly strains toward symbolism, can be in novels as in poems the basis of structure, and it can even be counterposed to dramatic structure. We have observed the structural function in *Middlemarch*. In *Wuthering Heights* we may observe the more complicated contrapuntal function of metaphor in structure. Gerard Manly Hopkins, writing of Greek tragedy, spoke of "two strains of thought running together and like counterpointed," the paraphrasable "overthought," and the "underthought"

> conveyed chiefly in the choice of metaphors etc. used, and often only half realized by the poet himself, not necessarily having any connection with the subject in hand but usually having a connection and suggested by some circumstance of the scene or of the story.

The metaphors of *Wuthering Heights* comprise such an "underthought," for although they are equated in the work, the work itself yet somehow develops a stronger and stronger contrast between the obligations of the human and the non-human creation.

4. Finally, metaphorical language reveals to us the character of any imaginative work in that, more tellingly perhaps than

any other elements, it shows us what conceptions the imagination behind that work is able to entertain, how fully and how happily. I mean to say that style *is* conception, and that, for this reason, rhetoric must be considered as existing within— importantly within, and, sometimes, fatally within—what we call poetic. It is really style, and style primarily, that first conceives, then expresses, and finally tests these themes, these subjects, even these "kinds"—Jane Austen's manners, Emily Brontë's passions, George Eliot's morals. "Symbolization," said Susanne Langer (and I could not comfortably close these observations without mentioning her excellent name), "Symbolization is both an end and an instrument." "The right word," said George Eliot, "is always a power, and communicates its definiteness to our action." And "The eye," said William Blake, "sees more than the heart knows."

# PART TWO

# Moll Flanders

IN THE preface of his book, *The Living Novel,* V. S. Pritchett proposes that the novel that lives beyond its time somehow embodies as "new material" the intrinsic values and conflicts that are the peculiar condition of its time. Thus the living novelist is always "on the tip of the wave," not reflecting his age but, for the first time, really discovering the age to itself. Yet "new material" is hardly ever a new "subject." "New material is added only by new seeing, not by new sights. *Moll Flanders* is a book of new material because it is old material—the conventional rogue's tale—seen in a new way." However we may wish to qualify this statement, its essential point must stand; for *Moll Flanders* is the first work of fiction to bring us at a thrust into the very heart of the middle class, even as the middle class was coming into dominant existence. "Seeing" the middle class and "seeing" with its eyes, perhaps without quite knowing, was Defoe's "new way." *Moll Flanders* is all the more entertaining and perhaps all the more telling in that here a middle-class intelligence has been located—has been *seen*—in a criminal life.

To say that we are in the heart of the middle class is to say at the same time that we are in the heart of Daniel Defoe. His life is a nearly incredible account of bourgeois activity in the late seventeenth and early eighteenth century, fantastically crowded and always precarious, edging now up toward aristocracy and secret vice, now trembling on the ledge from

NOTE. This essay, using much more various evidence, attempts to document the point more briefly made about *Moll Flanders* in "Technique as Discovery." I have deleted some material here that merely repeats what is already there.

which it would plunge down into the world of open vice and crime. At the very end, an aged man of seventy, Defoe was forced for reasons still obscure to us to flee his home and live out his last months in hiding. Secret flight was an old and familiar pattern for him, often exciting, often even exhilarating, but the final hiding, which ended with his death in "a lethargy," as his age called it, is pathetic, and if he troubled then to look back over his packed and various years, he might well have found them a spectacle of waste. He seems to us to have been a man so deeply involved in the multiple, immediate activities of daily life that he was never able to pause to observe how remarkable, on various occasions and in a thousand fleeting moments, he actually was, and, in later history, would appear to have been.

He was born merely Daniel Foe in 1660, and remained D. Foe for forty years, when, by an alteration not hard to make, he became the more aristocratic Daniel Defoe. Of aristocracy there was nothing in his blood, nothing in his nature. His father was a dissenting tallow-chandler, and Daniel Defoe received the plain but solid education of a typical Dissenters' academy. The tradition of religious dissent, implicated in the ambitions of the rising lower orders, encouraged a kind of depraved Puritanism that expressed itself in a moralistic piety and a utilitarian morality; and these strains were always to be evident in at least the superficial character of Daniel Defoe. He married prosperously, considerably improving his economic situation through the match; yet had, as a young man in 1685, enough of indiscretion and imprudence to join Monmouth's rebellion, an unsuccessful Protestant attempt to forestall the succession of James II. At about the same time he had entered the world of trade as a merchant in hosiery (a term that indicates approximately those items we associate today with "haberdashery"), but, never content with merely one activity, he engaged at the same time in the merchandising of various other goods including at least wine and tobacco. His enterprises became more ambitious and more involved, and in 1692, with an already tarnished name, he declared himself bankrupt, indebted to the amount of 17,000 pounds. Between the years 1688 and 1694, he was the subject of at least eight lawsuits for fraud in dealings ranging from ships to civet cats, and he was never again to live quite outside the shadow of the debtors' prison.

In the midst of all this, he had in an amateur way already evinced an interest in authorship by composing at least two sets of clumsy verses of a satirical bias, and when he was faced with the necessity of beginning his economic life again at the age of thirty-three, he turned to journalism. Yet even as he moved into the political activities that contemporary journalism inevitably involved (he was at first a tool of the Whig ministry of William III), he began a new mercantile operation, a tile and brick factory at Tilbury, that survived successfully until his next great disaster.

Once launched on his literary career, his pace was reckless, relentless. His published works number over four hundred titles. What drove him? It is the great question in Defoe's life, and there has never been an answer. His first important book, the *Essay on Projects* of 1698, shows us a mind not, certainly, noble, but vastly curious, wide ranging, and genuinely concerned with the public good. It is a mind possessed even of a certain humdrum visionary quality, as in that proposal for the education of women that sprang from his sympathetic recognition of their hideously depressed condition:

> I have often thought of it as one of the most barbarous customs in the world, considering us as a civilized and a Christian country, that we deny the advantages of learning to women. We reproach the sex every day with folly and impertinence, while I am confident, had they the advantages of education equal to us, they would be guilty of less than ourselves.

It is a mind that offers everywhere the unpretentious kernels from which two hundred years of "progress" were to spring; it is the mind of the middle class, with all its humble folly and its often foolish good. Thus it is also a rather self-righteously pious mind, a moralizing rather than a meditative mind, a mind that, even as it is ever alert to the main chance, is imbued with a somewhat uncritical but not unattractive tolerance. This last we see in Defoe's only interesting poem, the *True-Born Eng-lishman* of 1701, which, as a satirical attack on the enemies of the Dutch King William, is at the same time a plea for sympathy between varying national strains. And yet, for all this, one cannot feel that Defoe's motive was ever really altruistic or even disinterested.

His poem brought him money and the friendly eye of the king, and when the king died in 1701, Defoe was already so deeply implicated in the political intrigue of his time that he had no inclination to extricate himself. Until now, he had with most Dissenters been a defender of the Whig position, and it was the Tory attempt to legislate against the device of "occasional conformity," whereby a Dissenter could make himself eligible for public office, that impelled Defoe to write his most brilliant but personally most disastrous satire. For *The Shortest Way with Dissenters* he stood three days in the pillory and thereafter was allowed to languish in Newgate until, his life again and the brickworks too in ruins, he was inconspicuously rescued by a Tory politician, Robert Harley, soon to be the new queen's minister and whose tool Defoe thereafter became. Defoe's newspaper, *The Review*, influential as it may be in the history of journalism, was founded for no better reason than Harley's cause. Long before *The Review* died in 1713, Defoe had come to be regarded as one of the most valuable men that a faction could employ, and one of the most reprehensible. Of him, Swift (who likewise served Harley) wrote in 1708, "One of these authors (the fellow that was pilloried, I have forgot his name) is indeed so grave, sententious, dogmatical a rogue, that there is no enduring him," and Addison, in 1713, "a false, shuffling, prevaricating rascal—unqualified to give his testimony in a Court of Justice."

By 1713, to be sure, Harley had fallen, Defoe had transferred his services to the Whig minister, Godolphin, and, upon his decline, returned them to the once more ascendant Harley. These are twists and turns of conscience that call up no wonder in us over the fact that, in 1712, in a moment of oblique self-scrutiny, Defoe could have written, "I have seen the bottom of all parties." He had seen, besides, the bottom of his own narrow soul. For Harley he had founded a secret intelligence service, himself the agent, and when he went over to Godolphin, he spied with equal ingeniousness for him. A spy is perhaps the nearest political equivalent to the kind of reporter, in the literary world, that Defoe revealed himself to be in his famous short narrative, *A True Relation of the Apparition of One Mrs. Veal*, which he published in 1706. The prying gift of observation, the sense of fact, the feel for mystery, the delight in sensation and danger—all these would seem to relate these diverse occupations in the single man. The constant risk of exposure and jail (Defoe was jailed again in 1713), the willingness to drop one project (*The Review* died in the same year) and get on to a new one (the *Mercator*, an organ of apology for the current policy of free trade), and, finally, the love of masquerade, to which we will presently come—all these seem, too, to be qualities as necessary to the political as to the journalistic spy. The two, in Defoe, at any rate, were one.

Robert Harley, Earl of Oxford, fell finally (and fell into a Tower cell) in 1714. Queen Anne died in the same week. Defoe, once more, fell temporarily. His immediate major effort at rehabilitation was an enormous work of domestic piety called *The Family Instructor*, a moralistic handbook, written in dialogues, to the conduct of marital and parental affairs in the Christian home. This monument to vulgarized righteousness was a stopgap in a bad moment; it was also, conceivably, a hasty payment to conscience. Defoe was as much at home here as anywhere, and it is borne in on us that his easiest gift was the ability to slide into almost any role and believe it real. Observe the next step: although George I seemed at first to feel no kindliness toward even the gifted hangers-on, like Defoe, of even moderate Tories, like Harley, Defoe was nevertheless in the secret employ of the new party by 1718. And now the two occupations of political and literary espionage come together in fact, for he was employed by the new Whigs to write like a Tory for a Tory periodical, that "the sting of that mis-

chievous paper should be entirely taken out." Nor did he emas-
culate only one Tory journal, but several at once, and, further,
by the time that, in the most notable example, he was working
in this artful fashion on Mist's *Weekly Journal*, he wrote at the
same time for a Whig paper, *The Whitehall Evening Post*. The
deviousness is almost dazzling, and it brought Defoe's relation
with Mist to a momentary end.

> What strange adventures could untwist
> Such true-born knaves as Foe and Mist? . . .
> As rats do run from falling houses,
> So Dan another cause espouses;
> Leaves poor Nat sinking in the mire,
> Writes *Whitehall Evening Post* for hire.

The labyrinthine character of political journalism in the eighteenth century is perhaps nowhere more clearly displayed than
in the fact that, after this break, Mist sought out Defoe again
and rehired him on his own terms.

Defoe was nearly sixty years old, and we should expect to
find him now an exhausted literary hack; but it is precisely
now that the miracle occurs. In 1719 he published the first of
the several works by which his literary fame was to be established. *Robinson Crusoe* is a work of fiction based on fact—
the case of Alexander Selkirk. *Moll Flanders*, which followed
three years later (almost unbelievably, together with *Due
Preparations for the Plague, A Journal of the Plague Year,
Colonel Jack,* and another four-hundred-page book of homi-
letic dialogues, *Religious Courtship*), was a work of fiction that
pretended to be fact. The literary energy that brought these
works into being is not to be explained, but the literary evolution is clear enough. They are, indeed, a kind of culmination of
all Defoe's history and quality. In *Moll Flanders*, Defoe the
bankrupt tradesman and Puritan moralist, Defoe the journalist
and popular historian, above all, perhaps, Defoe the pilloried
prisoner and Defoe the spy, come together. His imagination is
the composite gift of all these characters.

## 2

Everything about *Moll Flanders*—its kind and Defoe's extension of that kind, its literary method, its paradoxical morality—everything about it has a naïvely direct relation to his own world of experience and interests. The kind is the biography of a rogue, a conventional if low form of literary expression since Elizabethan times. Rogue biographies were usually the lives of real criminals fictionally foreshortened and sensationalized. Their ostensible purpose was to expose the operations of criminals and thereby to warn; their actual purpose was rather to thrill an undiscriminating audience with melodrama. The convention offered Defoe solid elements to which he would almost at once have responded. The world of crime he had experienced and observed with sufficient directness and even fascination to recognize as a subject matter that he was in a superb position to handle, and it is no accident that Moll's paralyzing fear of Newgate is her most forcibly urged emotion. At the same time, the journalist in Defoe would have responded to a subject that lent itself to exposure, and the Puritan, to the elements that allowed the expression of a ready impulse to admonish and exhort. Add to these the convention of the "secret history," which would be as attractive to the intriguing familiar of party ministers as it would be to the journalistic spy, and the several elements that the rogue biography offered to the special talents of Daniel Defoe should be evident.

The method that Defoe developed to animate the *genre* is perfectly calculated to his talents. The Puritan and the journalist together, the first out of genuine suspicions of the idle and the second out of his conviction that nothing is more persuasive than fact, lead Defoe to deny that he is writing fiction at all. On the contrary, he tells us, he is merely editing the diary of a real and notorious character who must, for reputation's sake, present herself under a pseudonym. Thus at once Defoe saves his conscience and puts himself into his favorite position, the assumed role. He is not telling us about Moll Flanders, he *is* Moll Flanders. The device comes easy to one whose own life had consisted of a series of conflicting roles, and he had had long practice not only in life but in his previous writings. He had written in the past as though he were a Turk, a Scotch soldier, a visionary Scotchman, a Quaker, a lonely but enterprising castaway. Why not now as a sexually abandoned thief? Once the role was assumed, it was easy, too, for the journalist to support the role, or, at any rate, for a journalist with Defoe's special feeling for the telling physical facts in any situation. Out of this gift grows his special kind of verisimilitude, that kind of realism best described as "circumstantial." It is a method that depends not on sensibility but on fact, not on description but on proof, as if a man, wishing to tell us of an excellent dinner, did not bother to say how his food tasted, but merely listed the courses that made up the meal, or, more likely, produced a canceled check to prove that he had paid a good deal for it. On such evidence, we would hardly doubt that he had eaten it. Thus the centrality in Defoe's method (and the resulting texture) of the bolts of goods, the inventories, the itemized amounts, the landlady's bills, the lists, the ledgers.

Defoe's tone is hardly less important to this method than his persuasive details. How matter-of-fact all this is, for such an extraordinary life! Five marriages, a score of recorded lovers, and, if we can count, a score of children, twelve dead and eight alive when Moll's child-bearing ceased at last. *We* exclaim (we may even protest), but Defoe does not. In this story, the birth of a child or the acquisition of a new lover seems hardly as important as the hiring of a coach or the packing of a trunk. Defoe's prevailingly matter-of-fact tone levels all incidents out on a straight narrative plane, and we are lulled into supposing that any account of a life that is so guilelessly without emphasis is necessarily true. Defoe's deepest guile, indeed, always lay in his appearance of being without guile. A narrator with an air of uncomprehending innocence or a narrator so innocent that he comprehends precisely the wrong things in a situation, had been among Defoe's great propagandistic devices throughout his career as a journalist, and over and over again, this device had been the basis of his satire. In *Moll Flanders,* the heroine, like Defoe's earlier narrators, is peculiarly innocent; the meaning of her experience seems to run off her moral skin like quicksilver; nothing touches her; at the end, a woman of seventy, she is almost exactly as bland as she was in the opening scenes, a small girl who wished to be a lady. And this quality again, this very imperceptiveness, lends itself to Defoe's purposes of persuasion. Isn't this, we ask ourselves, exactly what a woman like Moll would be, so wonderfully imperceptive that this is really a book about a remarkable self-deception?

But then the other question comes, and with it, the question whether this is a method adequate to the production of a novel. Whose deception is it—Moll's or Defoe's? And this question takes us into the third consideration, the paradoxical morality of the book. *Moll Flanders* comes to us professing that its purpose is to warn us not only against a life of crime but against the cost of crime. We cannot for very many pages take that profession seriously, for it is apparent all too soon that nothing in the conduct of the narrative indicates that virtue is either more necessary or more enjoyable than vice. At the end we discover that Moll turns virtuous only after a life of vice has enabled her to do so with security. The actualities of the book, then, enforce the moral assumption of any commercial culture, the belief that virtue and worldly goods form an equation.

Security and morality are almost identical in *Moll Flanders,* and we today are hardly in a position to scorn Defoe's observation that it is easier to be pious with a bank account than without one. Like *Robinson Crusoe,* this is a desperate story of survival, a story that tries to demonstrate the possibility of success through unremitting native wit. Security, clearly, is the end of life:

> This was evidently my case, for I was now a loose, unguided creature, and had no help, no assistance, no guide for my conduct; I knew what I aimed at and what I wanted, but knew nothing how to pursue the end by direct means. I wanted to be placed in a settled state of living, and had I happened to meet with a

sober, good husband, I should have been as faithful and true a wife to him as virtue itself could have formed. If I had been otherwise, the vice came in always at the door of necessity, not at the door of inclination; and I understood too well, by the want of it, what the value of a settled life was, to do anything to forfeit the felicity of it.

But if security is the end of life, ingenuity, clever personal enterprise, is its most admirable quality, and, certainly, the only way to security:

I have observed that the account of his life would have made a much more pleasing history than this of mine; and, indeed, nothing in it was more strange than this part, viz. that he had carried on that desperate trade full five-and-twenty years and had never been taken, the success he had met with had been so very uncommon, and such that sometimes he had lived handsomely, and retired in one place for a year or two at a time, keeping himself and a manservant to wait on him, and had often sat in the coffeehouses and heard the very people whom he had robbed give accounts of their being robbed, and of the places and circumstances, so that he could easily remember that it was the same.

Strip *Moll Flanders* of its bland loquacity, its comic excess, its excitement, and we have the revelation of a savage life, a life that is motivated solely by economic need, and a life that is measured at last by those creature comforts that, if we gain them, allow us one final breath in which to praise the Lord. Yet this essence is not the book as we have it, as Defoe wrote it, any more than the acquisitive impulse is the whole of middle-class value. For there is also the secondary interest of the book, which is to reveal to us the condition of women, the small choice (there was only her needle; to be sure, there *was* her needle had she preferred it; but who would ask that she should have?)—the small choice that Moll could have made between disreputable and reputable employment. The infant Moll, born in Newgate, becomes a public charge; education is an impossibility; independent work is likewise an impossibility; and as young men are by nature wolves, so the world at large is wolfish. Women, like men, are forced into the realm of trade; they offer such goods as they have for such prices as they can command.

This secondary interest suggests the softer side of Daniel Defoe, his will to create a less savage world than the world he knew. The paradox of the middle class has always been its hope to create, through its values of mere measurement, values that did not have to measure in its way. And the social pathos of *our* lives is largely to be traced to our illusion that we have done so. This is also the final pathos of Moll Flanders's life, whether Defoe was aware of it or not.

Sympathy exceeds awareness, and throughout *Moll Flanders* (this is probably the main reason that we continue to read it) we are charged by the author's sympathy. It shows as much in the gusto with which he enters Moll's life and participates in her adventures as it does in his tolerance of her errors and her deceits and self-deceits. It shows, furthermore, in a few moments of this vastly episodic narrative when genuinely novelistic values emerge, when, that is, the individual character somehow shines through the social automaton. One such moment occurs when Moll is reunited with her Lancashire husband:

> As soon as he was gone, and I had shut the door, I threw off my hood, and bursting out into tears, "My dear," says I, "do you not know me?" He turned pale, and stood speechless, like one thunderstruck, and, not able to conquer the surprise, said no more but this, "Let me sit down"; and sitting down by a table, he laid his elbow upon the table, and leaning his head on his hand, fixed his eyes on the ground as one stupid. I cried so vehemently, on the other hand, that it was a good while ere I could speak any more; but after I had given some vent to my passion by tears, I repeated the same words, "My dear, do you not know me?" At which he answered, Yes, and said no more a good while.

Such genuinely moving scenes must be observed, of course, against the long stretches of the book where the relentless narrative sense points up the totally deficient sense of plot, where the carelessness of time and causality destroys the illusion of actuality after all the pains to achieve it, where the monotonously summarizing method gives even the fine feeling for separate incident a pallor. These deficiencies all remind us that this is not, after all, the first English novel.

Yet it is very nearly the first English novel. It is the whole groundwork. Given twenty more years of literary convention and just a slightly different set of interests, Defoe would have freed himself from the tyranny of fact and the morality of circumstance and sprung into the liberties of formal fiction, where another morality must prevail. His prose has been called "the prose of democracy," and this has been the characteristic prose of the novel as we know it in English. The prose of democracy is a prose without rhetorical refinement even when it employs rhetorical display; it emerges in sentences as sinewy and emphatically plain as this: "In short, they robbed together, lay together, were taken together, and at last were hanged together." It is also a prose capable of fine, colloquial surprise:

> I made him one present, and it was all I had of value, and that was one of the gold watches, of which I mentioned above, that I had two in my chest, and this I happened to have with me, and I gave it him at his third visit. I told him I had nothing of any value to bestow but that, and I desired he would now and then kiss it for my sake. I did not indeed tell him that I had stole it from a gentlewoman's side, at a meeting-house in London. That's by the way.

Such prose projects us into the future of the novel: Jane Austen, George Eliot, Mark Twain, D. H. Lawrence, Ernest Hemingway.

Yet not entirely. "That's by the way," says Moll; and then comes the voice of Defoe, saying, too, "Yes, that's by the way." He does not, finally, *judge* his material, as a novelist must. He makes us sort out his multiple materials for him and pass our judgment. Our judgment must therefore fall on him, not on his creature, Moll. In her bland, self-deluded way, she asks us not to be harsh; and that again is the voice of Defoe, taking a breath at the end to beg posterity to be kind. As it has been.

# *Emma*

JANE AUSTEN's *Emma*, 1816, stands at the head of her achievements, and, even though she herself spoke of Emma as "a heroine whom no one but myself will much like," discriminating readers have thought the novel her greatest. Her powers here are at their fullest, her control at its most certain. As with most of her novels, it has a double theme, but in no other has the structure been raised so skillfully upon it. The novel might have been called *Pride and Perception,* or *Perception and Self-Deception,* for the comedy is concerned with a heroine who must be educated out of a condition of self-deception brought on by the shutters of pride, into a condition of perception when that pride had been humbled through the exposure of the errors of judgment into which it has led her. No novel shows more clearly Jane Austen's power to take, through the range of her characters, the moral measurement of the society with which she was concerned.

Morality in the novel lies not in spread but in scale, in the discrimination of values on scale and the proportion that is held between values within scale. In *Emma,* the word scale has a special meaning, for its subject is a fixed social scale in need of measurement by moral scale. As the social scale is represented by the scene as a whole, by all the characters, so the chief characters establish, in addition, the moral scale. The story is the progress of the heroine on this second scale toward her position on the first. *Emma* gives us the picture of an externally balanced society which the novel itself readjusts, or puts in perspective, through the internal balance that is the root of moral, not social, judgment.

Can we permit the notion that Jane Austen is capable of making a moral judgment on that social world which she herself accepts and from which her novels emerge? I have argued elsewhere that our surest way of knowing the values out of which a novel comes lies in an examination of style, more particularly, of metaphor. Jane Austen's style is, of course, remarkably non-metaphorical, if we are thinking of explicit metaphor, the stated analogy, but it is no less remarkable in the persistency with which the buried, or dead metaphors in her prose imply one consistent set of values. These are the values of commerce and property, of the counting house and the inherited estate. I will divide this set of values rather arbitrarily into five categories. First of all, of *scale* itself, all that metaphor of high and low, sink and rise, advance and decline, superior and inferior, rank and fortune, power and command; as "held below the level," "raise her expectations too high," "materially cast down," "the intimacy between her and Emma must sink." Second, of *money*: credit, value, interest, rate, reserve, secure, change and exchange, alloy, resources, gain, want, collect (for "assume"), reckon, render, account, claim, profit, loss, accrue, tax, due, pay, lose, spend, waste, fluctuate, dispense, "precious deposit," appropriate, commission, safety. Third, of *business and property*: inherit, certify, procure, solicit, entitle, business, venture, scheme, arrangement, insure, cut off, trust, charge, stock. Fourth, of *number and measure*: add, divide, multiply, calculate, how much and how little, more and less. And fifth, of *matter*: incumbrance, weight, substance, material, as material change, or material alteration, comfort.

These terms are constantly appearing, both singly and in clusters. One or two illustrations must suffice:

> She listened, and found it well *worth* listening to. That very *dear* part of Emma, her fancy, *received* an amusing *supply* . . . it became henceforth her *prime object of interest*; and during the ten days of their stay at Hartfield it was not to be expected—she did not herself expect—that anything beyond occasional fortuitous assistance could be *afforded by her* to the lovers. They *might advance* rapidly if they would, however; they *must advance* some-

how or other, whether they would or no. She hardly wished to have more leisure for them. They are people, who *the more you do* for them, *the less they will do* for themselves. Mr. and Mrs. John Knightley . . . were exciting, of course, rather *more than the usual interest*. Till this year, every long vacation since their marriage had been *divided* between Hartfield and Donwell Abbey.

This language, as a functioning element in the novel, begins to call attention to itself when we discover it in clusters where moral and material values are either juxtaposed or equated: "no *material* injury *accrued* either to body or mind"; "glad to have *purchased* the mortification of having loved"; "except in a moral light, as a penance, a lesson, a source of *profitable humiliation* to her own mind, she would have been thankful to be *assured* of never seeing him again . . . his welfare twenty miles off would *administer* most satisfaction."

It would seem that we are in a world of peculiarly *material* value, a world of almost instinctive material interests in its basic, intuitive response to experience. The style has created a texture, the "special feel" of that world. At the same time, on the surface of the action, this is usually a world of refined sensibility, of concern with moral propriety, and in Emma's case, presumably at least, of intelligent clarity of evaluation. A large portion of Jane Austen's comedy arises from the discrepancy that we see here, from the tension between these two kinds of value, these different *scales*, material and moral, which the characters, like the metaphors, are all the time juxtaposing and equating. But when we say that, we have moved from considerations of language alone, into the function of the language in the whole.

How do we transfer ourselves from one to the other? Notice, first of all, that in some very impressive details, the implicit stylistic values erupt every now and then into explicit evaluations in the action, explicit evaluations that are, of course, ironical illuminations of the characters in their special situations. "You were very popular before you came, because you were Mr. Weston's son; but lay out half a guinea at Ford's, and your popularity will stand upon your own virtues."

"No—I cannot call them gifts; but they are things that I have valued very much."

She held the parcel towards her, and Emma read the words *Most Precious treasures* on the top.

Emma's charity: "Emma was very compassionate; and the distress of the poor were as sure of relief from her personal attention and kindness, her counsel and her patience, as from her purse."

Emma's judgment of Mr. Martin:

". . . He will be a completely gross, vulgar farmer, totally inattentive to appearances, and thinking of nothing but profit and loss."

"Will he, indeed? That will be very bad."

"How much his business engrosses him already, is very plain from the circumstances of his forgetting to inquire for the book you recommended. He was a great deal too full of the market to think of anything else—which is just as it should be, for a thriving man. What has he to do with books? And I have no doubt that he *will* thrive, and be a very rich man in time; and his being illiterate and coarse need not disturb *us*."

Most impressive, because most central to the theme of the book, this passage:

Emma perceived that her taste was not the only taste on which Mr. Weston depended, and felt that to be the favourite and intimate of a man who had so many intimates and confidantes, was not *the very first distinction in the scale of vanity*. She liked his open manners, but a little less of open-heartedness would have made him a higher character.

We may summarize this much as follows:

1. The language itself defines for us, and defines most clearly, that area of available experience and value from which this novel takes its rise, and on which the novel itself must

place the seal of its value. The texture of the style itself announces, therefore, the subject, and warns us, suggesting that
we not be deceived by the fine sentiments and the moral scru-
ples of the surface; that this is a material world where property
and rank are major and probably as important as "character."
More specifically, that this is not simply a novel of courtship
and marriage, but a novel about the economic and social significance of courtship and marriage. (The basic situation in
all the novels arises from the economics of marriage.) There
is other evidence that Jane Austen knew marriage, in her world,
to be a market; in her *Letters,* she wrote, "Single women have a
dreadful propensity for being poor—which is one very strong
argument in favor of matrimony."

2. The implicit textural values created by language become
explicit thematic statements in important key phrases such as
"the scale of vanity" and "their intimacy must sink." In such
phrases we detect the novel's themes (what it has to say about
its subject) and its tone, too (how Jane Austen feels about it).
We are led now, from language merely, to structure, to observe
the particularized dramatic expression, the actualization, of
this general narrative material, this "world."

Let us consider structure from the two points of view of
architectural and thematic development. The two are of course
interdependent, but we may see the novel more clearly, finally,
if we make the separation.

From an architectural point of view, *Emma* seems to consist
of four movements, or of four intermeshing blocks, each larger
than the preceding. Emma is always the focus for us, but her
own stature is altered as one block gives way to the next—that
is, she bulks less large in the whole action of each as one
follows upon another. The first block is the "Harriet Smith"
block, and here Emma's dimensions are nearly coextensive
with the block itself; this gives way to the Elton's block (and
that includes, of course, others); that, in turn, gives way to the
Frank Churchill-Jane Fairfax block; and that, finally, to the
Knightley block, where Emma is completely absorbed. John
Knightley observes at one point, "Your neighborhood is in-

creasing and you mix more with it." That is, of course, precisely what happens in the structure: an "increasing neighborhood" diminishes Emma. This development is perhaps best represented by the Coles' dinner party, where she finds herself in danger of exclusion and is herself alarmed, and it is completely dramatized in Frank Churchill's casual readiness to use —to abuse—her for his own purposes. Thus, as the plot becomes more intricate, and even as we view it through Emma eyes, she actually plays a less and less central, or relevant part in it.

Now on these blocks of increasing size we must imagine another figure, a cone, to represent Knightley. Its point would lie somewhere near the end of the first, the Harriet block, and through each of the following blocks it would widen, until, in the final block, it would be nearly coextensive with the limits of the block itself. It is important to see that the movement from block to block is accomplished not only by new elements in the action (the arrival of Mrs. Elton; of Jane Fairfax; the death of Mrs. Churchill) but by scenes between Emma and Mr. Knightley himself, scenes in which he usually upbraids her for an error of judgment and scenes out of which she emerges with an altered awareness, a dim alteration in the first, a slightly clearer alteration in the second and third, and at last, in the fourth, as full an awareness as she is capable of. The first of these is in Chapter 8, and the subject is Harriet; the second, Chapter 18, and the subject is Frank Churchill; the third, Chapter 33, the subject Jane Fairfax; and the last, Chapter 43, the subject Miss Bates. These scenes are debates between moral obstinacy and moral wisdom, and the first is slowly brought up to the proportion of the second. In the last scene, when Knightley takes Emma to task for her cruelty to Miss Bates, she fully recognizes and bitterly repents her fault. She *alters* at last: "could he *even* have seen into her heart," she thinks, "he would not, on this occasion, have found anything to reprove." Only then is she prepared to know that it is only Knightley that she can love, and with that the movement of awareness swells: "Every other part of her mind was disgust-

ing." And then, before his declaration, the movement comes
to rest:

> When it came to such a pitch as this, she was not able to re-
> frain from a start, or a heavy sigh, or even from walking about
> the room for a few seconds; and the only source whence anything
> like consolation or composure could be drawn, was in the resolu-
> tion of her own better conduct, and the hope that, however
> inferior in spirit and gaiety might be the following and every
> future winter of her life to the past, it would yet find her more
> rational, more acquainted with herself, and leave her less to re-
> gret when it were gone.

Thus we have a double movement in the architecture—the
diminution of Emma in the social scene, her reduction to her
proper place in the whole scale of value (which is her expia-
tion), and the growth of Emma in the moral scheme (which is
her enlargement). It is very beautiful.

Now most of this we are never told, and of Emma's diminution, not at all. We are made to experience this double development through the movement of the plot itself. This fact
calls attention to Jane Austen's method, and makes us ask what
her reasons were for developing it. The method consists of an
alternation of narration conducted almost always through the
heroine's eyes, with dramatic scenes illustrative of the narrative material. There is almost no direct statement of the significance of the material, and there is a minimum of reported
action. The significance of the material comes to us through
two chief sources: the dramatized scene itself, and the play of
irony through the narration. Of Jane Austen's skill in making
scene speak, I will say nothing, except to point out our awareness of the significance of Emma's silence—she says not a word
—in the scene in Chapter 12 where her sister is praising Jane
Fairfax and explaining why Jane and Emma had always
seemed to everyone to be perfectly suited for an equal friendship; and that later scene, in Chapter 21, where we are made
so acutely aware of the presence of the others and their several
emotions, as Miss Bates blunders along on the matter of how
some people had mistakenly felt that Mr. Elton might have

married a certain person—well, clearly, it is Miss Woodhouse herself, who is there, again stonily silent. Now just as the dramatic values of scene are left to speak for themselves, so the moral values are left, implicit *in* the scenes, not discussed through them.

Such a method, intermingling as it does dramatic scene with narrative observations of the heroine, requires from the author a constant irony that at all times transcends the ironic habit of mind of the heroine herself. Sometimes Jane Austen achieves this simply by seeming to accept the scene as the characters pretend that it was; as, for example, following on Emma's silence when Isabella praises Jane, the narrative proceeds: "This topic was discussed very happily, and others succeeded of similar moment, and passed away with similar harmony." Sometimes she achieves it through an unobtrusive verbal pointing, as: "Poor Mr. Woodhouse was silent from consternation; but everybody else had something to say; everybody was either surprised, or not surprised, and had some question to ask, or some comfort to offer." Could the triviality of the situation find a more effective underlining? On still other occasions, Jane Austen achieves this necessary irony simply by shifting her point of view a fraction away from the person who presumably holds it. This is shown nowhere more effectively than in the passage I have already cited, in which we begin with Emma's observation, then shift to that phrase, "the scale of vanity," which cannot possibly be hers, and then return at once to her.

> Emma perceived that her taste was not the only taste on which Mr. Weston depended, and felt that to be the favourite and intimate of a man who had so many intimates and confidantes, was not the very first distinction in the scale of vanity. She liked his open manners, but a little less of open-heartedness would have made him a higher character. General benevolence, but not general friendship, made a man what he ought to be. She could fancy such a man.

I am pressing this matter of the method of scene and the method of irony not only because it is through this method that the significance of the architectural structure of the work is brought home to us, that double movement I have described, but because it reveals an important fact about Jane Austen's relation to her audience, then and now, and because, unless we understand this relation, we cannot see as much as we should see in that thematic structure to which I will presently turn, or see at all that relationship of social and moral scale that is the heart of the book. Jane Austen was in an ambiguous situation in relation to her readers, a situation in which she was committed simultaneously to cherish and abominate her world. Within the framework of what is presumably a happy story, where everyone gets married off properly in the end, she must still make her comment, from her deepest moral evaluations, on the misery of this happiness. The texture of her style already has suggested that the world she pictures is hardly founded on the highest values. But this is not enough. She must besides develop a technique which could both reveal and conceal, that would give only as much as the reader wished to take. (That is why she can still be read in both the most frivolous and the most serious spirit.) Her problem—and perhaps this is the problem of every novelist of manners, at least if he is a satirist, who criticizes the society within which he yet wishes to remain and, indeed, whose best values are his own—her problem was to develop a novelistic technique that would at once conceal and reveal her strongest feelings, her basic observation of her heroine and her heroine's world, and that would express with sufficient clarity, if one looks at that technique closely, the ultimate values here involved.

For those who do not read while they run, the range of Jane Austen's irony, from the gentlest to the most corrosive, will suggest that she was perfectly able to see with absolute clarity the defects of the world she used. I will not trouble with the mild examples, but only with the gradation at the extreme:

"It was a delightful visit—perfect, in being much too short." And she leaned back in the corner to indulge her murmurs, or to reason them away; probably a little of both—such being the commonest process of a not ill-disposed mind.

Surely a mind that throws out observations such as these is not an entirely well-disposed one. But to go on—

> "I am persuaded that you can be as insincere as your neighbours, when it is necessary."

Still further: Emma on Miss Bates:

> ". . . and nobody is afraid of her—that is a great charm."

Consider next the bitter violence of the verb, in that comment on boarding schools, where young women are "*screwed* out of health and into vanity." And come last, to the extreme, an amazing irruption into this bland social surface of what has been called her "regulated hatred"—

> Miss Bates stood in the very worst predicament in the world for having much of the public favour; and she had no intellectual superiority to make atonement to herself, or *frighten those who might hate her into outward respect.*

Surely there is no failure here to judge the values of the social scale. We, in turn, are enabled to recognize these values, to judge the material, in other words, to place our evaluation upon it, not only by these oblique uses of irony, but by two other means: first, the dramatization of Emma's diminution in the community as we see more and more of it; second, by judging the real significance of her end.

The first, the dramatization of value, or moral scale, is achieved through what I have been calling "thematic structure," a structure that supports and unifies the architectural structure, the thematic integration of characters. Thematic structure exists, first of all, in the selection and disposal of characters around the heroine, and the relationship in moral traits which we are meant to observe between the heroine and the others. Emma is in many ways a charming heroine, bright and attractive and energetic, but Jane Austen never lets us forget that if she is superior to the Eltons, for example, the author (or, if you wish, Knightley) is superior to her. Emma's vanity is of no trivial kind. She is not "personally vain," Knightley tells us; "her vanity lies another way." It lies, for example, in her very charity. "Harriet would be loved as one to whom she could be useful. For Mrs. Weston there was nothing to be done; for Harriet everything." It is the vanity of giving, and brings to mind E. M. Forster's remark that, for many people indeed, it is better to receive than to give. It is the vanity, next, of power, for through the exercise of her charity, she succeeds in the imposition of her will. It is the vanity of abstract intellect. That Emma is capable of sound judgment is evident in her recognition of the real Elton even as she is urging him upon Harriet; it is evident again in her analysis of the real relation that probably pertains between Frank Churchill and his stepmother, even as she is herself about to fall in love with him. It is evident again in some of her self-studies, when, for example, after the Elton-Harriet fiasco, she resolves, in tears, that, since it is too late to be "simpleminded and ignorant," like Harriet, she will be at least "humble and discreet." In the next chapter she reveals herself incapable of acting on her own self-judgment, and Mr. Knightley again points up the discrepancy for us.

Emma: "He may have as strong a sense of what would be right as you can have, without being so equal, under particular circumstances, to act up to it."

Knightley: "Then it would not be so strong a sense. If it failed to produce equal exertion, it could not be an equal conviction."

Emma's intellectual judgments do not relate sufficiently to her conduct; in short, she is immoral. And we are not to be surprised when, rather early in the novel, she announces her own values: "those pleasantest feelings of our nature—eager curiosity and warm prepossession." The novel shows us the disastrous moral consequences of such insufficient standards.

This is Emma in her vanity. Let us observe, now, the kind of symbolic relationships in which her vanity is placed. First, of contrast, the contrast being with Miss Bates, and none in the novel more explicit:

Emma Woodhouse, handsome, clever and rich, with a comfortable home and happy disposition seemed to unite some of the best blessings of existence; and had lived nearly twenty-one years in the world with very little to distress her.

Ten pages later:

Miss Bates . . . a woman neither young, handsome, rich, nor married. Miss Bates stood in the very worst predicament in the world for having much of the public favour . . . and yet she was a happy woman.

That Emma unites with "some of the best blessings of existence," some of the worst possibilities of human society, is all too soon quite evident, but nowhere more evident than when she says of Miss Bates, "so silly, so satisfied, so smiling . . ."

The second kind of symbolic relationship is not contrasting but comparative, and is evident in Harriet and Mrs. Elton. Of Harriet we need only point out that she is a silly but harmless girl educated by Emma into exactly the same sort of miscalculations, only to be abused by Emma for her folly. The comparison with Mrs. Elton is more fully developed: Emma's judgment on the Coles, who are struggling to rise above the stigma of trade, is exactly duplicated by Mrs. Elton's judgment on a family living near Maple Grove, called Tupman: ". . . very lately settled there, and encumbered with many low connections, but giving themselves immense airs, and expecting to be on a footing with the old established families. . . . They came from Birmingham. . . . One has not great hopes for Birmingham." The analogy with Emma is detailed: Mrs. Elton, like Emma, has an almost aggressive determination to "do" for other people, and to ride over their wishes; on the "scale of vanity," she is precisely where we begin with Emma: "a vain woman, extremely well satisfied with herself, and thinking much of her own importance; that she meant to shine and be very superior; but with manners which had been formed in a bad school; pert and familiar; that all her notions were drawn from one set of people, and one style of living; that, if not foolish, she was ignorant . . ." And Emma makes this analysis—

Emma, who herself is "amused by such a picture of another set of being," the Martins; who broods on the inferior society of Highbury; who makes one test only, the class test, except when she judges creations of her own, like Harriet, and even Harriet's high-born antecedents, as Emma fancies them, are apparent in her face; Emma, whose manners at one point, at any rate, are not merely pert and familiar, but coldly cruel—a match, at least, for Mrs. Elton's.

The third kind of symbolic relationship is the contrasting-comparative kind that is evident in Jane Fairfax. This is a crucial relationship in the thematic structure. We are told that they are alike in many ways—age, station, accomplishments. They are alike, furthermore, in that Emma *thinks* of Jane as complacent and reserved, whereas we *know* Emma to be both. Her reserve with Jane Fairfax is complete from the beginning, and stony. Her complacency is nearly admitted: she "could not quarrel with herself"; "I cannot really change for the better." What a contrast, then, in actuality. Jane, whom we see through Emma's eyes as complacent, cold, tiresome, and in some ways rather disgusting, is, really, as much an antithesis to Emma as Miss Bates, and a much more difficult antithesis for Emma ever to deal with, to really admit. She is a woman capable of rash and improper behavior, a genuine commitment to passion, a woman torn by feeling, and feeling directed at an object not entirely worthy. She is hardly prudent. In short, she is quite different from what Emma sees, and quite different from what Emma is—all too complacent and perhaps really cold—and she stands in the novel as a kind of symbolic rebuke to Emma's emotional deficiencies, just as Knightley stands as a rebuke to her moral deficiencies. That Emma has emotional deficiencies is perhaps sufficiently apparent in her attachment to her father, and in her use of that attachment. Jane Fairfax is the blurred threat to Emma's complacency, the threat that Emma herself has never brought into focus in her own life and character, and at the end of the novel still has not, and so still has not achieved it for herself, or any radical reform of her qualities. They have merely moved on the scale.

So much for the heroine and the female characters. If we look now at the men, we can consider them as variations, or gradations, on the two traits, egotism and sociability, or "Candor," which is the positive virtue sought by Mr. Knightley. These characters run from Mr. Elton, the vain social snob, all egotism; through Frank Churchill, the man whose candor conceals a treacherous egotism; through Mr. Weston, so thoroughly amiable as to be nearly without judgment, and yet an egotist himself, the egotism of parenthood; to Mr. Knightley, who is the pivot, the middleman, moderate and sound, balanced and humane, neither an egotist nor a gadabout. From him, we shade off into his brother, the dour social egotist, to Mr. Woodhouse, the destructive (though comic, of course) malingering egotist.

Emma's relationships to them are revealing: she patronizes and then scorns Elton, of course; she "loves" Frank Churchill; she is fond of Weston; toward Knightley she holds a friendly animosity; she has tolerance for John; she adores her father. These relationships or emotional responses are Jane Austen's way of dramatizing Emma, of showing us her value. We see her through them, even as we are seeing them through her. It is a process of reciprocal illumination. And so in both the men and women, we come to see her above and beyond her presentation of herself, and at the same time, of course, we come to see the community at large through them—they represent Jane Austen's social "analysis," her breakdown of a community into its major traits, its two poles. If we study the bulking up at one end or the other of the scale, we can hardly conclude that the analysis is entirely friendly.

Thus we begin to see the real accomplishment of this objective technique, how deep it can go, how much subtle work it can do, how it defines its interpretations and analysis of the material, how it separates the material (which is trivial) and the effect (which is grave). Most remarkable, perhaps, how it holds together, makes one, the almost bland, comic tone, appropriate to the kind of society, too brittle for a severer tone, and a really bitter, sometimes acrid theme.

To define the theme completely we have to look closely at the real history of Emma. For all her superiority, Emma's values are really the values of the society she patronizes, and although she partially resolves her personal dilemma (hers really is a "profitable humiliation"), she *retains* those qualities: complacency, a kind of social cruelty, snobbery (Harriet must sink), and even greed (little Henry, who must inherit Donnell). Emma's self-study has always been partially mistaken; will it always be correct henceforth? Except for her final moment of awareness, her others have always exempted herself from judgment; can we believe that that is never to happen again? Does the final comment not come from Knightley, when Emma says, "Poor child! . . . what will become of her?" and he replies, "Nothing very bad. The fate of thousands. She will be disagreeable in infancy, and correct herself as she grows older. I am losing all my bitterness against spoilt children, my dearest Emma." The modification is minor. Does Jane Austen say less? Near the end she tells us:

Seldom, very seldom does complete truth belong to any human disclosure; seldom can it happen that something is not a little disguised, or a little mistaken; but where, as in this case, though the conduct is mistaken, the feelings are not, it may not be very material. Mr. Knightley could not impute to Emma a more relenting heart than she possessed or a heart more disposed to accept of his.

How severely does Jane Austen "chasten" Emma? "Do not physic them," says Isabella of her children; are we not left to "physic" Emma, to chasten her and her world together, with all necessary guidance from the style and the basic motives that analysis reveals in the work itself?

When we say that Emma is diminished at the end, as her world is, in a way, for us—the bright, easy society put in a real shade—we are really saying that she has been absorbed into that world, and has become inseparable from it. This observation suggests that we look again at the end of the novel. There is something apparently aimless and long-winded about it. Of

*Pride and Prejudice* the author said, "The work is rather too light, bright, and sparkling; it wants shade; it wants to be stretched out here and there, with a long chapter of sense, if it could be had." In *Pride and Prejudice* and *Sense and Sensibility*, Jane Austen's heroines were superior to their world. Then, in *Mansfield Park*, her dull Fanny was completely submissive to the conventional pieties of this same world, somewhat whitewashed. In *Emma*, Jane Austen seems to do what the remark about *Pride and Prejudice* aims at. Emma is finally nearly at the top of the moral scale, with Knightley, but the moral scale still has its relation to the social scale. The entire end of *Emma* is such a "shade" (even as it busily gets its characters happily married off, it is creating the shade, the moral shade, in which they will live) and the only justification for that long ending, once the Emma-Knightley arrangements have been made, is that it is needed there, as a kind of decrescendo into the social twilight that lies at the heart of the book. And so the end remains "open"—a question, in a way. It is Emma who at one point near the end exclaims, "I like everything decided and open"; everything here is at once decided and, in another sense, open.

How completely resolved are these strains of feeling? Emma and Jane, for example? Emma and Frank? How much "candor" is there? And how "happy" is this marriage, with Knightley having to move into old Mr. Woodhouse's establishment? Isn't it all, perhaps, a little superficial—not the writing but the self-avowals of the characters? A little perfunctory, as comedy may be, telling us thereby that this *is* comedy? One is reminded of the end of *Mansfield Park*:

> I purposefully abstain from dates on this occasion, that everyone may be at liberty to fix their own, aware that the cure of unconquerable passions, and the transfer of unchanging attachments, must vary as to time in different people. I only entreat everybody to believe that exactly at the time when it was quite natural that it should be so, and not a week earlier, Edmund did cease to care about Miss Crawford, and became as anxious to marry Fanny as Fanny herself could desire.

*Emma,* then, is a complex study of self-importance and egotism and malice, as these are absorbed from a society whose morality and values are derived from the economics of class; and a study, further, in the mitigation of these traits, as the heroine comes into partial self-recognition, and at the same time sinks more completely into that society. Just as with Elizabeth Bennet, her individual being, as she has discovered it, will make that society better, but it will not make it different. This is moral realism, and it shows nowhere more clearly than in the very end, when the pilfering of a poultry house is given us as the qualification of "the perfect happiness of the union." The irresolution of the book gives it its richness, and its tautness and precision of structure and style give it its clarity. The two together make it great.

We have not said enough about Knightley, and if we are to see Jane Austen's values as they positively underlie her drama, we must look at him. Only a little pompous, he is the humanely civilized man; it is he whose judgments move beyond class; only he seems to breathe deeply; only he, certainly, ventures out impervious to that "weather" that is always keeping the others in a state of alarm and inside their littleness; it is he who wants complete candor and no mystery; it is he who makes Jane Austen's demand that awareness and conduct be brought into the relationship which is morality. In the only unclear speech in the novel (a haunting speech, in Chapter 33) he observes the separation: "her own comparative littleness in action, if not in consciousness." This is likewise Jane Austen's demand, although she lets Emma speak it: "faith engaged . . . and manners so *very* disengaged." But if there were a complete congruity between profession and conduct, there would be no comedy in the world; and Jane Austen wants comedy.

That comedy was sufficient for her purposes she certainly knew, just as she knew the size of the world her comedy measures. John Knightley says, "Business, you know, may bring money, but friendship hardly does." Frank Churchill says, "I would have given worlds—all the worlds one ever has to give

—for another half-hour." And chiefly that phrase "a crowd in a little room," varied four times in a dozen lines:

> Emma demurred. "It would be a crowd—a sad crowd; and what could be worse than dancing without space to turn in? . . . Nothing can be further from pleasure than to be dancing in a crowd—and a crowd in a little room."

> "There is no denying it," he replied. "I agree with you exactly. A crowd in a little room—Miss Woodhouse, you have the art of giving pictures in a few words."

Miss Woodhouse has, in fact, given us a picture of Jane Austen's art. And it suggests that a narrow scene, like a good plot, is the occasion of pressure on the characters, to squeeze out their moral essence.

> Their being fixed, so absolutely fixed, in the same place, was bad for each, for all three. Not one of them had the power of removal, or of effecting any material change of society. They must encounter each other, and make the best of it.

And again:

> When she considered how peculiarly unlucky poor Mr. Elton was in being in the same room at once with the woman he had just married, the woman he had wanted to marry, and the woman whom he had been expected to marry, she must allow him to have the right to look as little wise . . . as could be.

The weather, so much a part of this book as of the others, is a double device for Jane Austen: it keeps these characters on the narrow social stage where they enact their moral drama; and it underlines, for us, the fact of their enclosure, their narrowness. It is only in Christmas weather, in the season of love, we are told, that everyone ventures boldly out. In Highbury, as elsewhere, it comes, alas, only once a year. We may conclude, then, that the scene may be narrow, the action trivial, the feelings (from the point of view of other kinds of novels) thin—but the condition is the human condition, and the problem is nothing less than original sin—the dry destructiveness of egotism. And so the novel, if one is pressed to say so, is really

about the narrowness of a wholly "secularized" life—in Eliot's
meaning—no prevailing spiritual awareness, no prevailing emotional fullness, no prevailing gravity except in the author's construction, in the character she allows to speak for her, in her
own oblique comment. We are reminded of all this in one of
the few metaphorical outbursts of the novel. Jane Fairfax, re-
signing herself to the life of a schoolteacher, is thrown into
the posture of religious renunciation:

> With the fortitude of a devoted novitiate, she had resolved at
> one-and-twenty to complete the sacrifice, and retire from all the
> pleasures of life, of rational intercourse, equal society, peace and
> hope, to penance and mortification for ever.

And her motive? The deplorable absence of a fortune!

# Jane Eyre

SIGMUND FREUD, discussing one of his earliest patients, Miss Lucie, a governess in the employ of a British manufacturer residing in Vienna in the 1880's, tells how as a result of the repression of her illicit feelings for her master, she developed an hysteric condition that showed itself in the loss of her sense of smell. The classic symptoms of this condition are more violent: paralysis, blindness, and so on.

Charlotte Brontë, like her creation, Jane Eyre, was a governess, and it is amusing to contemplate her counter-device, fifty years before Freud, whereby she so manipulates the plot of her novel that, while the governess retains her psychic health through the most fearsome tribulations, the master, Edward Fairfax Rochester, must be nearly de-manned—blinded and deprived of a hand in a holocaust that is as symbolic as it is real—before the governess can submit to what at least was his passion, and what remains, at least, his affection. The operations of conscience can be as transparently devious as the operations of ego.

English fiction is full of governesses, but perhaps none is so famous as plain little Jane Eyre, who vindicates the purity of her humble breed and at the same time releases and realizes a thousand of its gaudy dreams. One may hope that some day a not overly solemn social historian will undertake a study of the place of the governess in British culture. Victim and victimizer, her role has never been properly assessed. At the very center of every household of any distinction in nineteenth-century England, she is yet, and above all, the representative of the socially dispossessed. More frequently than not, her occupation was not of her choice: it was nearly the only possible employment for a respectable young woman without means and with some education and accomplishment. Once in the household, she occupied an uneasy place that was above that of the servants but distinctly below that of her employers. Living out her lonely spinsterhood in reveries limp or morbid, with children as her chief companions, the not infrequent object of their parents' abuse as of the children's disrespect and derision, she was yet the trustee of the intellectual and moral development of thousands of upper middle-class and aristocratic children in their most intensely formative years. Small wonder that she comes to play a prominent role in nineteenth-century fiction. Small wonder, too, that she should play it in the midst of such garish melodrama as we find in *Jane Eyre,* or in the midst of such chilling uncertainties as we find in Henry James's *The Turn of the Screw,* where we do not know if the ghosts are real and the governess is the benign protectress of innocence assailed by evil, or—as Edmund Wilson argued—if the ghosts are her hallucinations and she, suffering from the hysteria of Freud's Miss Lucie, and for the same reasons, is herself the mad agent of evil.[1] The pathos of the governess's position readily inverts itself in the mind into all the potentialities of the subtlest forms of malice, the social victim turned the moral victimizer, counterparts.

Without quite intending it, we have already suggested that there is some deep and critically inescapable connection between Charlotte Brontë's novel and her life and the life out of which her life came. From their early critical notices until now, the literary works of the Brontës have not only been looked at through the lens of biography but, often, have been treated as if they could be elucidated only through biography. And in a

[1] James's governess, in this interpretation, cannot, of course, be properly designated an hysteric in the sense that Freud used that term, but more desperately, a psychotic. I think that it should be argued that James thought of her as a witch, possessed, carrying evil with her and living in its ambience. ("What is a woman deprived but a witch?" asks Andrew Lytle in quite another connection in a preface to some fictions of his own.)

sense, Henry James to the contrary, they cannot be wholly elucidated without biographical help, in a very special sense, since
these works were, really, the substitutes for that life that the
Brontës were denied, and grew directly out of a fantasy life—
which has its literary record—that they lived instead. Yet as
long ago as 1905, in his lecture called "The Lesson of Balzac,"
Henry James complained of the biographical approach as follows:

> The romantic tradition of the Brontës, with posterity, has been
> still more essentially helped, I think, by a force independent
> of any one of their applied faculties—by the attendant image of
> their dreary, their tragic history, their loneliness and poverty of
> life. That picture has been made to hang before us as insistently
> as the vividest page of *Jane Eyre* or *Wuthering Heights*. If these
> things were "stories," as we say, and stories of a lively interest,
> the medium from which they sprang was above all in itself a
> story, such a story as has fairly elbowed out the rights of appre-
> ciation, as has come at last to impose itself as an expression of the
> power concerned. The personal position of the three sisters, of the
> two in particular, had been marked, in short, with so sharp an
> accent that this accent has become for us the very tone of their
> united production. It covers and supplants their matter, their
> spirit, their style, their talent, their taste; it embodies, really, the
> most complete intellectual muddle, if the term be not extravagant,
> ever achieved, on a literary question, by our wonderful public.
> The question has scarce indeed been accepted as belonging to
> literature at all. Literature is an objective, a projected result; it is
> life that is the unconscious, the agitated, the struggling, flounder-
> ing cause. But the fashion has been, in looking at the Brontës, so
> to confound the cause with the result that we cease to know, in
> the presence of such ecstasies, what we have hold of or what we
> are talking about. They represent, the ecstasies, the high-water
> mark of sentimental judgment.

Certainly; and James says it very well. The difference between
the unorganized excitements of life and the organized excitements of art is radical, and to confuse the two is not only to be
sentimental but also to risk critical absurdities. Yet the fact remains that no other works of literary art tremble so perilously

on the treacherous edge of the chaos of *fancied* experience as
the works of the Brontës, and, without confusing the two, life
and art, we are, to understand the *quality* of that art, forced
back once more to a consideration of the life.

To a brief consideration only, however, since that life is so
well known. There were six Brontë children, left motherless at
an early age with an aunt to bring them up and a considerably
tyrannical father to supervise the supervisor and her charges.
He was a parson in the isolated town of Haworth, and the
parsonage, like the crowded and gloomy old cemetery that it
looked out upon, stood open to the winds and rains that swept
off the Yorkshire moors. In 1824, all but the youngest of the
girls were sent to a school for clergymen's daughters at Cowan
Bridge (the Lowood of *Jane Eyre*). There, early in 1825, the
two oldest contracted illnesses that killed them, and the two
others were brought home. Charlotte was now the oldest child.
She had been born in 1816; her single brother, Patrick Branwell, in 1817; Emily Jane in 1818; Anne in 1820. With an age
span of only about four years between them, these children
inevitably formed a society of their own in the lonely parsonage; no other entertainment except reading proposed itself.
Their reading went without much supervision. Very early,
theirs became a literary society.

When, in 1826, Branwell's father brought him some wooden
soldiers, each of his sisters seized upon one as her own, and
around these figures the four of them then began to articulate
a joint daydream and to write it down in minute handwriting
in a series of tiny handmade books that, ultimately, contained
more words than all their combined mature publications. What
began as a childish impulse developed into an enormous and
enormously complicated fantasy. Whole cities, countries, con-
tinents were invented, their governments established, their histories written, and these were dominated by fantastic heroes,
heroines, villains, and villainesses. Ultimately, Emily and Anne
were to draw apart and develop their separate kingdom of
Gondal, and so Charlotte and Branwell were drawn together
to develop their kingdom of Angria. Branwell was largely oc-

cupied with Angrian military affairs; Charlotte chose for herself the hardly less spectacular and aggressive area of the passions. In the world she created, where attire was as rich and
lavish as emotion was riotous and loose, moral and imaginative
license ruled without interference from convention. Indeed,
license *was* the convention in Angria, and melodrama its mode
of expression.

For Charlotte, the recording of the daydream, if not the
dreaming of it, was broken off in 1831 when she was sent to
school at Roe Head; but she could return to the loom of her
fancy during her vacations, and, consistently again, when she
left the school in July of 1832. Then Angria flourished with a
vengeance for three years until, in 1835, she returned to Roe
Head as a teacher. Until the spring of 1838, when she left Roe
Head forever, she was able to write less even as the grip of the
dream took positive possession of her:

> Never shall I, Charlotte Brontë, forget what a voice of wild and
> wailing music now came thrillingly to my mind's, almost my
> body's ear, nor how distinctly I, sitting in the schoolroom at Roe
> Head, saw the Duke of Zamorna leaning against that obelisk. . . .
> I was quite gone. I had really, utterly, forgot where I was
> and all the gloom and cheerlessness of my situation. I felt myself
> breathing quick and short as I beheld the Duke lifting up his
> sable crest, which undulated as the plume of a hearse waves to
> the wind, and knew that music which sprang as mournfully tri-
> umphant as the scriptural verse,
>
> > O Grave, where is thy sting? O Death
> > where is thy Victory?
>
> was exciting him and quickening his ever-rapid pulse.

The Duke of Zamorna is, obviously, a stereotype out of the
Byronic tradition, and Lord Byron was indeed the swooning
young Charlotte's favorite poet. Under his influence she wrote
streams of verse in Byronic meters as well as all that prose on
Byronic subjects erratically enacted by *poupées fatales*. Under
an influence so facilely satanic, the young woman's imagination
slipped readily not only into the well-used Gothic moods but
also beyond, into the quite grossly grotesque. The extreme,

perhaps, is best represented by a work of 1834, in 20,000 words, called "A Leaf from an Unopened Volume," which Miss Fannie Ratchford, the authority on the Brontë juvenilia, describes as "a confused medley of intrigue, licentiousness, and fraternal hate, with illegitimate or disowned children, dwarfs, and Negroes playing leading parts." Yet in these extremities of unchecked fancy, this uninhibited but articulated reverie—and is it not remarkable that Charlotte and Branwell Brontë should habitually have referred to it as "the infernal world," or, better yet, "the world below"?—the shapes of the mature imagination were forming. The magnificently imperious Zamorna is the clear prototype of Rochester, and the burning, raging, disheveled Lady Zenobia Ellrington is the first form of Bertha Mason, Rochester's mad wife. There were others. In a story that she called "Caroline Vernon" we discover early versions of Adèle, Rochester's ward, and her mother, Céline Varens, his mistress; so we see in the early Ellen Hall the later Helen Burns. And there are others—the Reeds foreshadowed, Grace Poole, and so on—Angrians all. Most remarkable, however, is the appearance in this fantastic world of a plain, even drab little heroine called Elizabeth Hastings. She is the first form of the type of Jane Eyre, the first heroine to bear any resemblance to Charlotte Brontë herself. Under her commonplace exterior there breathes a noble, sensitive, high-spirited soul, and when it is observed by the until then impervious Sir William Percy, he proposes, like Rochester after him, that the girl become his mistress.

Charlotte Brontë herself was, of course, no longer a girl. She was a young woman in the England of Queen Victoria, a parson's daughter besides, and by no means entirely comfortable with these untamed flights of her fancy. At the end of 1839, when she was twenty-three years old, the voice of conscience spoke aloud:

> . . . I long to quit for a while that burning clime where we have sojourned so long—its skies aflame—the glow of sunset is always upon it—the mind would cease from excitement and turn now to a

cooler region where the dawn breaks grey and sober, and the coming day for a time at least is subdued by clouds.

Yet a certain habit of the imagination had been formed, and moving her characters into English scenes, giving them English names, as she now did, could not and did not alter either the kind of situations, or the exclamatory emotional atmosphere that they engendered, which that imagination was in the habit of conceiving.

Certain external events, however, stifled its continuing expression. In 1841 she went for a time to Rawdon where she was employed as a governess. Then, in 1842, when the Brontës developed the notion of opening a small school in the parsonage, she and Emily, in order to improve their languages, went to a school in Brussels that was kept by the wife of a Latin professor named Constantin Héger. Here, in 1843, she gave lessons in English and developed a hopeless attachment for the autocratic M. Héger, on the precise nature of which one can only speculate. Back at Haworth in 1844, her attempt to open a school ended abruptly when not one pupil came forward. It was the worst period of her life. Her sisters formed a kind of alliance of their own, Branwell was in disgrace, her aunt was dead, her father was blind and ill, her own eyesight was increasingly poor, her writing had been discouraged several times by persons whom she regarded as authorities. She was nearly thirty years old and there seemed to be nothing in her life at all.

The turn came in 1845. In that year she discovered a whole manuscript of Emily's secretly written poems and she persuaded her sisters that the three of them should bring out a volume of their verse under the pseudonyms of Currer, Ellis, and Acton Bell. Published at their own expense, the Bells' *Poems* fell without a splash or even a sound into the pool of the public in May 1846; exactly two copies were sold. Another literary project was, however, already under way before the *Poems* appeared: each of the three women had decided to write a novel.

Anne produced *Agnes Grey;* Emily, *Wuthering Heights;* Charlotte, *The Professor.* Using one of her favorite situations from the Angrian fantasy, dressing it up a bit with materials from her Brussels experience, but determined to bring Angria into the workaday world and to write of it in an appropriately stolid style, Charlotte wrote a lifeless, unpublishable work. But before the sixth publisher had declined it, Charlotte Brontë was well along with a second novel, and now, in style completely and in large part in subject, she renewed the febrile, romantic fashion that in its earlier forms had characterized her juvenilia. The book was accepted enthusiastically by the first publisher to read it, and it appeared on August 24, 1847, as "*Jane Eyre: An Autobiography,* edited by Currer Bell." It was an instant triumph and has remained one, especially with female readers, ever since. Why?

Its weaknesses are obvious and have long been observed. The action is pitted with implausibilities, indeed, absurdities. The account of the manners of an aristocratic life with which the author was unfamiliar is childish. The notion that a man can for years conceal a raging maniac in the attic of his house and keep even the servants ignorant of her presence there, especially since he is so unwise as to put her under the care of a gin-tippling attendant whose stupors permit her frequently to escape the attic and range cursing through the house, is truly ridiculous. To dress up one's hero in the skirts and shawls of an old gypsy fortuneteller and let him woo the heroine in that guise in his own house is to risk at least the loss of his Byronic austerity. To turn one's orphaned heroine out into the world alone, subject her to the most frightful physical and emotional ordeals, and then let her stumble up to a house one night only to discover that its inhabitants are cousins of whose existence she had not known, and then to let her inherit a fortune besides—this is to challenge the reader to throw the book aside as unworthy of serious attention. But the reader does not throw the book aside, not even when the whole plot turns on an act of mental telepathy that brings the protagonists to their bittersweet embrace at last. Nor does he do so through all the crudities of the characterization, which is sometimes as gross as that in the baldest melodrama: the unadulterated malignity of Mrs. Reed, the unadulterated goodness of Helen Burns, the unadulterated malice of Miss Ingram—these are only examples. He reads to the end, for somehow the whole of the novel is compelling and strong even though so much of it is composed of these silly, feeble parts.

Is it, one might ask, the total artistry of the structure, the whole organization so firm that it welds even the limpest materials together, holds even coincidence and miracle firmly in place? Hardly. The structure of *Jane Eyre* is nearly artless. It employs, to begin with, one of the oldest conventions in English fiction, a convention made famous by Defoe's *Moll Flanders* (in which Charlotte Brontë may have found her source for the telepathic episode)—the fiction that presents itself as fact, the memoir of a presumably real person. Charlotte Brontë called this not a novel but an autobiography; the "real" author was Jane Eyre herself, and Currer Bell was merely her editor. Like *Moll Flanders, Jane Eyre* is, within this convention, very loosely put together; in both, events are linked not causally but circumstantially. Things happen to happen, they do not *have* to happen. Both novels begin at the beginning, cover a good stretch of time through a series of rather disparate adventures, and arrive at last at their happy endings. When we put them side by side in this way, we can see that there are similarities beyond those of structure; different as the rogue, Moll Flanders, may be from the pure governess, Jane Eyre, they are yet alike in a basic fact: each is a woman alone, making her way in a hostile world and making that world submit to her ways.

The comparison can be pressed no further, for *Jane Eyre* does have certain organizing principles that give it the dramatic coherence of a novel, and one cannot say this of *Moll Flanders*. The action falls into four parts: the first ten chapters, which have to do with Jane's childhood and education, are introductory; the next seventeen chapters are concerned with her residence at Thornfield Hall, her developing love for its master, the collapse of their plans; the next eight chapters treat her flight, her life at Moor House and Morton, and the icy proposals of St. John Rivers; the final three chapters, returning her to Thornfield and a chastened Rochester, resolve the whole. The second and third sections are the heart of the book, and each of these is dominated by a male who symbolizes one of the two polar forces between which Jane's conflict is conducted. Rochester, licentious, remorseful, and handsomely ugly, is imperious physical passion; Rivers, chaste, self-righteous, and beautifully handsome, is equally imperious spiritual passion. Jane, who is independent will, refuses to accept either on his own terms: she will not be Rochester's mistress and she will not be Rivers's wife; Rochester cannot marry her and Rivers will not take her to India unless she marries him. The conflict is resolved when Jane returns to Thornfield and finds that it has been destroyed by a fire that killed Rochester's mad wife, who had been the legal barrier to marriage, and maimed Rochester himself in such a way as to suggest that it has subdued his rampant sexuality and thereby removed any ethical barrier. The conflicts here clearly represent Angrian extremities, and Richard Chase quite neatly referred to them as "myth domesticated." One could say, too, that *Jane Eyre* is fantasy rationalized.

Yet, important as it may be to know that the imagination that created Angria is likewise the imagination that created *Jane Eyre,* and interesting as it may be to see how nearly the situations and human types that struck the reverie of an adolescent girl are those that are still most prominent in the mind of the mature woman, one must yet recognize that we have transcended Angria. What in the early writings we must call fantasy we can here call vision. A number of things have happened to bring about the change.

Most important of these, perhaps, is the difference in characterization. If some of the minor characters are one-dimensional, the major characters are not. They are multi-faceted and of a certain complexity. Rochester is not only the Byronic *immoraliste;* he is also a landowner, a man with certain economic and social responsibilities, with humor to lighten his

*Ich-schmerz,* and tenderness to soften his pride. St. John Rivers
is likewise a complex conception: at once kindly and rigid,
turbulent within and frigid without, in love and unyielding, he
suffers from that spiritual pride that is the mark of the religious
fanatic and that can lead as readily to martyrdom as to acts of
inflexible cruelty. It is Jane Eyre herself, however, who represents Charlotte Brontë's triumph of characterization and who,
in fact, brings a new kind of heroine into English fiction. If we
think of her in relation to some of Jane Austen's heroines, for
example, they may seem more engaging and desirable, but it is
Jane Eyre who is motivated by desire itself. It is not only sexual
desire—although that, remarkably enough, is obviously working
through her conflicts—but a moral desire as well, and a moral
desire of a new kind that is based on the frank recognition of a
woman's need to find self-fulfillment in the world, in relations
with others, especially men. This need gives the novel a nearly
polemical bias:

> It is vain to say that human beings ought to be satisfied with
> tranquility; they must have action; and they will make it if they
> cannot find it. Millions are condemned to a stiller doom than
> mine, and millions are in silent revolt against their lot. Nobody
> knows how many rebellions besides political rebellions ferment
> in the masses of life which people earth. Women are supposed to
> be very calm generally: but women feel just as men feel; they
> need exercise for their faculties and a field for their efforts as
> much as their brothers do; they suffer from too rigid a restraint,
> too absolute a stagnation, precisely as men would suffer; and it is
> narrow-minded in their more privileged fellow-creatures to say
> that they ought to confine themselves to making puddings and
> knitting stockings, to playing on the piano and embroidering bags.
> It is thoughtless to condemn them, or laugh at them, if they
> seek to do more or learn more than custom has pronounced
> necessary for their sex.

Jane Eyre holds this view with *passion,* and passion is the key
to her character. It is above all a passionate sense of the right
of her own integrity to *be.* It breaks out first when, as a little
girl, she tells Mrs. Reed that she does not like her; it breaks out

most remarkably when, just before Rochester's proposal of marriage, she insists on her equality with him. It is the passion of Jane Eyre that imbues the whole novel—since it is all told from her point of view—and that animates those elements that give the whole its visionary quality. Similarly, it is the complexity that passion arouses in all these characters that gives the central ethical conflict a certain depth that enables us to take it seriously as we cannot take seriously the conflicts in Angria.

Another and hardly less important change lies in the fact that Angrian conflicts have been moved from imaginary lands of cloud into a real world, a world of social classes and institutions, no less than of natural landscapes. The presentation of manners may be naïve, but the observations on the injustices of charity schools, the hypocrisy of much religion, the cruelty of outmoded divorce laws, the vicious snobbery of a class system, are all sound, and they enter into what we have already called the polemical bias of the book. So while the novel is chiefly concerned with subjective conflicts of a sometimes nearly hysterical order, these are substantially located in a social texture that is objective and mundane.

If society as here presented is in general at odds with the heroine's subjective ambitions for self-realization, the natural settings are, rather, reflective of their immediate state; as in most dramatic poetry, natural phenomena are the external representatives of psychological conditions. Natural setting, then, provides a kind of tenuous symbolic substructure to the novel, not only heightening but expressing thematic conflict. This technique, perhaps quite unconscious, is particularly observable in Charlotte Brontë's use of vegetation, especially the priapean tree—dormant, blasted, blossoming.

In that long wintry season that was Jane Eyre's youth, trees are bare; the second sentence makes the announcement: "We had been wandering . . . in the leafless shrubbery an hour in the morning." In her reveries, little Jane decides that no magic is left in England, that the elves "were all gone out of England to some savage country where the woods were wilder and thicker." The morning is a long one. Gateshead is perpetual winter:

> . . . the shrubbery was quite still: the black frost reigned, un-broken by sun or breeze, through the grounds. I covered my head and arms with the skirt of my frock, and went out to walk in a part of the plantation which was quite sequestered: but I found no pleasure in the silent trees, the falling fir-cones, the congealed relics of autumn, russet leaves, swept by past winds in heaps, and now stiffened together.

Lowood School is little better:

> . . . these beds were assigned as gardens for the pupils to culti-vate, and each bed had an owner. When full of flowers they would doubtless look pretty; but now, at the latter end of Jan-uary, all was wintry blight and brown decay. I shuddered as I stood and looked round me . . .

As for the forest on the banks of the Lowood stream, "*that* showed only ranks of skeletons." With spring, as the time ap-proaches for Jane's departure for Thornfield, life blossoms with promise:

> and now vegetation matured with vigour; Lowood shook loose its tresses; it became all green, all flowery; its great elm, ash, and oak skeletons were restored to majestic life; woodland plants sprang up profusely in its recesses; unnumbered varieties of moss filled its hollows . . .

It is as if the terms are being set for the presentation of Roches-ter:

> "I have been green, too, Miss Eyre,—ay, grass green: not a more vernal tint freshens you now than once freshened me. My Spring is gone, however: but it has left me that French floweret on my hands; which, in some moods, I would fain be rid of. Not valuing now the root whence it sprang; having found that it was of a sort which nothing but gold dust could manure, I have but half a liking to the blossom . . ."

Nearly every important scene in the development of the pas-sion of Rochester and Jane Eyre takes place among trees—in an

orchard, an arbor, a woods, a "leafy enclosure." When Jane
returns from her visit to Gateshead, she finds Rochester seated
among roses, beside "a tall briar, shooting leafy and flowery
branches across the path," and shortly after, their first embrace
and his proposal of marriage take place among "trees laden
with ripening fruit," near a blossoming chestnut tree. But the
proposal is in fact bigamous, and if Jane does not know that,
nature seems to:

> But what had befallen the night? The moon was not yet set,
> and we were all in shadow: I could scarcely see my master's face,
> near as I was. And what ailed the chestnut tree? it writhed and
> groaned; while wind roared in the laurel walk, and came sweep-
> ing over us.

Next morning Jane learns that "the great horse-chestnut at the
bottom of the orchard had been struck by lightning in the
night, and half of it split away."

Just before the fatal marriage ceremony, Jane goes to the
orchard and enacts a scene that is preparatory to the end of
the novel:

> . . . I faced the wreck of the chestnut-tree; it stood up, black
> and riven: the trunk, split down the centre, gaped ghastly. The
> cloven halves were not broken from each other, for the firm base
> and strong roots kept them unsundered below; though community
> of vitality was destroyed—the sap could flow no more: their great
> boughs on each side were dead, and next winter's tempests would
> be sure to fell one or both to earth: as yet, however, they might
> be said to form one tree—a ruin, but an entire ruin.
>
> "You did right to hold fast to each other," I said: as if the
> monster-splinters were living things, and could hear me. "I think,
> scathed as you look, and charred and scorched, there must be a
> little sense of life in you yet: rising out of that adhesion at the
> faithful, honest roots: you will never have green leaves more—
> never more see birds making nests and singing idylls in your
> boughs; the time of pleasure and love is over with you: but you
> are not desolate: each of you has a comrade to sympathise with
> him in his decay." As I looked up at them, the moon appeared
> momentarily in that part of the sky which filled their fissure; her
> disk was blood-red, and half-overcast; she seemed to throw on me

one bewildered, dreary glance, and buried herself again instantly in the deep drift of cloud. The wind fell, for a second, round Thornfield; but far away over wood and water, poured a wild, melancholy wail: it was sad to listen to, and I ran off again.

When the marriage is halted, it is as if a "Christmas frost had come at midsummer . . . the woods which twelve hours since waved leafy and fragrant as groves between the tropics, now spread, waste, wild and white as pine-forests in wintry Norway. My hopes were all dead . . ."

During the unsatisfactory period at Moor House and Morton, trees and vegetation both tend to disappear, but when Jane at last seeks out the wounded Rochester, the arboreal imagery again becomes prominent. Ferndean, his house, is "deep buried in a wood,"

> . . . thick and dark grew the timber of the gloomy wood about it . . . the twilight of close-ranked trees. There was a grass-grown track descending the forest aisle, between hoar and knotty shafts and under branched arches . . . all was interwoven stem, columnar trunk, dense, summer foliage—no opening anywhere . . . at last my way opened, the trees thinned a little . . . the house—scarce, by this dim light, distinguishable from the trees . . . "Can there be life here?" I asked. Yes: life of some kind there was; for I heard a movement . . .

Blinded Rochester emerges, and he gropes for the trees with his sound arm. After their reunion, the whole import of this imagery is made explicit:

> "I am no better than the old lightning-struck chestnut-tree in Thornfield orchard," he remarked, ere long. "And what right would that ruin have to bid a budding woodbine cover its decay with freshness?"
>
> "You are no ruin, sir—no lightning-struck tree: you are green and vigorous. Plants will grow about your roots, whether you ask them or not, because they take delight in your bountiful shadow; and as they grow they will lean towards you, and wind round you, because your strength offers them so safe a prop." . . .
>
> . . . his old impetuosity was rising. "We must become one flesh without any delay, Jane . . ."

At last, "We entered the wood, and wended homeward." And the next, famous sentence: "Reader, I married him."

We have perhaps labored this documentation of a single but major strand of imagery in *Jane Eyre* to suggest that its basic organizing principle is like that of dramatic poetry rather than like that of conventionally realistic fiction. From this poetic strain comes its visionary quality and its sustained tone of agitation and excitement. In a realistic novel, much of the action would be intolerable, but in *Jane Eyre*, as it is written, the tone gives it all a visionary coherence and reality.

And from the beginning nearly all readers have been persuaded by it. The one denunciatory notice that it received was written because it had, in a little over a year, proved so persuasive to so many. When Charles Kingsley, in the *Quarterly Review*, a kind of "official" guardian of public taste, attacked it as ungodly and immoral, he was only saying, really, that something revolutionary had taken place in English fiction and, probably, in the social history of women. If Matthew Arnold was right when, in writing of another of Charlotte Brontë's novels, he complained that her "mind contains nothing but hunger, rebellion, and rage," he was saying, in effect—by the evidence of later literary history—that hunger, rebellion, and rage are adequate materials for the production of a novel that rose from daydream and mingles in a curious way the hope of individual fulfillment with a sense of doom.

The Brontës themselves were a doomed family, had always been doomed. Branwell, unaware that his sisters had each published a novel, died a drunkard's death in September of 1848. Emily took cold at her brother's funeral and died of tuberculosis in December. Anne died of the same disease in the following May. Charlotte lived to publish two more novels but died in pregnancy in March 1855, only nine months after her unenthusiastic marriage to her father's curate, a Reverend Nicholls.

> I am still very calm, very inexpectant. What I taste of happiness is of the soberest order. I trust to love my husband—I am grateful for his tender love to me. I believe him to be an affec-

tionate, a conscientious, a high-principled man, and if, with all this, I should yield to regrets, that fine talents, congenial tastes and thoughts are not added, it seems to me I should be most presumptuous and thankless.

It may be presumed that she never recovered from Edward Rochester.

# *The Good Soldier: A Tale of Passion*

LEARNING TO READ novels, we slowly learn to read ourselves. A few years ago, writing of Ford Madox Ford, Herbert Gorman said: "If he enlarged upon himself he was quite justified in doing so and it seems to me that the time has come now for somebody to enlarge upon him." I translate this remark to mean that the good novelist sees himself as the source of a subject that, when it has taken its form in his work, we may profitably examine because our analysis will bring it back to ourselves, perhaps to kiss us, more likely to slap us in the face, perhaps both—in any case, to tell us where *we* are. These are the fruits of criticism.

The time had indeed come, and today we are hearing again about Ford Madox Ford in a way that we have not heard of him for twenty years—for until recently he has had to survive as best he could in the person of Conrad's suspect collaborator and of that brilliant editor who said to the young D. H. Lawrence that his first novel had "every fault that the English novel can have" and that his second was "a rotten work of genius." The always present friend of many great, the abettor of many promising young, Ford was great in his own right, and now time indeed seems ready at last, as Herbert Gorman predicted that it would, to "weed out his own accomplishments."

He began work on *The Good Soldier* on his fortieth birthday —the seventeenth of December in 1913—and he himself thought that it was his first really serious effort in the novel. "I had never really tried to put into any novel of mine *all* that I knew about writing. I had written rather desultorily a number of books—a great number—but they had all been in the nature of *pastiches*, of pieces of rather precious writing, or of *tours de force*." This was to be the real thing, and it was; many years later he remarked of it that it was his "best book technically, unless you read the Tietjens books as one novel, in which case the whole design appears. But I think the Tietjens books will probably 'date' a good deal, whereas the other may—and indeed need—not." It need not have; it did not.

As in most great works of comic irony, the mechanical structure of *The Good Soldier* is controlled to a degree nothing less than taut, while the structure of meaning is almost blandly open, capable of limitless refractions. One may go further, perhaps, and say that the novel renews a major lesson of all classic art: from the very delimitation of form arises the exfoliation of theme. This, at any rate, is the fact about *The Good Soldier* that gives point to John Rodker's quip that "it is the finest French novel in the English language," which is to say that it has perfect clarity of surface and nearly mathematical poise, and—as an admirer would wish to extend the remark—a substance at once exact and richly enigmatic. As a novel, *The Good Soldier* is like a hall of mirrors, so constructed that, while one is always looking straight ahead at a perfectly solid surface, one is made to contemplate not the bright surface itself, but the bewildering maze of past circumstance and future consequence that—somewhat falsely—it contains. Or it is like some structure all of glass and brilliantly illuminated, from which one looks out upon a sable jungle and ragged darkness.

*The Good Soldier* carries the subtitle "A Tale of Passion," and the book's controlling irony lies in the fact that passionate situations are related by a narrator who is himself incapable of passion, sexual and moral alike. His is the true *accidia,* and so, from his opening absurdity: "This is the saddest story I have ever heard," on to the end and at every point, we are forced to ask: "How can we believe *him?* His must be exactly the *wrong* view." The fracture between the character of the event as we feel it to be and the character of the narrator as he reports the event to us is the essential irony, yet it is not in any way a simple one; for the narrator's view, as we soon discover, is not so much the wrong view as merely *a* view, although a special one. No simple inversion of statement can yield up the truth, for the truth is the maze, and, as we learn from what is perhaps the major theme of the book, appearances have their reality.

First of all, this novel is about the difference between convention and fact. The story consists of the narrator's attempt to adjust his reason to the shattering discovery that, in his most intimate relationships, he has, for nine years, mistaken the conventions of social behavior for the actual human fact. That he did not want it otherwise, that the deception was in effect self-induced, that he could not have lived at all with the actuality, is, for the moment, beside our point, although ultimately, for the attitude and the architecture of the novel, it is the whole point.

The narrator and his wife, Florence, are wealthy Americans; the friends with whom they are intimately concerned, Edward and Leonora Ashburnham, are wealthy English people. Together, these four seem to be the very bloom of international society; they are all, as the narrator repeatedly tells us, "good people," and the Ashburnhams are even that special kind of good people, "good county people." Florence is a little pathetic, because she suffers from heart trouble and must be protected against every shock and exposure. Leonora is perhaps a little strong-willed in the management of her domestic affairs, but these have been very trying and in their cause she has been altogether splendid and self-sacrificing, a noblewoman. Edward is nearly flawless:

> the fine soldier, the excellent landlord, the extraordinarily kind, careful, and industrious magistrate, the upright, honest, fair-dealing, fair-thinking, public character . . . the model of humanity, the hero, the athlete, the father of his country, the lawgiver.

For nine years these four have enjoyed an apparently placid and civilized friendship, visiting back and forth, meeting annually at Nauheim, where they take the seasonal hypochondriac baths, sharing in one another's interests and affairs. Then comes the tremendous, the stunning reversal: when illness proves to be a lusterless debauchery; domestic competence the maniacal will of the tigress, the egoistic composure of the serpent; heroic masculinity the most sentimental libertinism. And the narrator, charged at the end with the responsibility of caring for a little mad girl, Edward's last love, is left to relate his new knowledge of an exposed reality to his long untroubled faith in its appearance. Which he is not able to do, of course; as which of us could?

But are not these "realities," in effect, "appearances"? Are not the "facts" that the narrator discovers in themselves "conventions" of a sort? We are forced, at every point, to look back at this narrator, to scan his beguiling surprise, to measure the angle of refraction at which that veiled glance penetrates experience. He himself suggests that we are looking at events here as one looks at the image of a mirror in a mirror, at the box within the box within the box, the arch beyond the arch beyond the arch. All on one page we find these reversals:

> Upon my word, yes, our intimacy was like a minuet. . . . No, by God, it is false! It wasn't a minuet that we stepped; it was a prison—a prison full of screaming hysterics. . . . And yet I swear by the sacred name of my creator that it was true. It was true sunshine; the true music; the true plash of the fountains from the mouths of stone dolphins. For, if for me we were four people with the same tastes, with the same desires, acting—or, no, not acting—sitting here and there unanimously, isn't that the truth?

The appearance had its reality. How, then, does the "reality" suggest that it is something less—or more?

Why is Florence always "poor Florence" or "that poor wretch" or "that poor cuckoo"? Why the persistent denigration of tone? Why can Florence not be charged with something less trivial and vulgar than "making eyes at Edward"? The narrator has something to gain in Florence's loss, and that is a fragment of self-esteem. If Florence is a harlot, she is so, in part, because of her husband's fantastic failure, but if we can be persuaded of her calculated vice and of her nearly monstrous malice, her husband appears before us as the pathetic victim of life's ironic circumstance. What, again, is the meaning of the narrator's nearly phobic concern with Catholicism, or of the way in which his slurs at Leonora are justified by her attachment to that persuasion? This is a mind not quite in balance. And again, Leonora's loss is Edward's gain, and Edward's gain at last is the narrator's gain. For why are Florence's indiscretions crimes, and Edward's, with Florence, follies at worst, and at best true goodnesses of heart? Why, after his degradation, is Edward still "a fine fellow"? In every case, the "fact" is somewhere between the mere social convention and that different order of convention which the distorted understanding of the narrator imposes upon them.

Yet the good novelist does not let us rest here. These distortions are further revelations. Mirror illuminates mirror, each arch marks farther distances. Ford tells us that he suggested the title, *The Good Soldier*, "in hasty irony," when the publisher's objections to *The Saddest Story* became imperative; and while, under the circumstances of 1915, the new title must have seemed, for this novel and for this real soldier, Ford, peculiarly inappropriate, certainly uncongenial enough to cause the author understandable "horror," it is nevertheless very useful to readers today, so accustomed to war that the word "soldier" no longer carries its special force. The novel designates Edward as the good soldier, since Edward has seen Imperial service in India. For Edward the narrator has the strongest affection and his only forgiveness. Of him, he says:

> I guess that I myself, in my fainter way, come into the category of the passionate, of the headstrong, and the too-truthful. [This is his weirdest absurdity, the final, total blindness of infatuation, and self-infatuation.] For I can't conceal from myself the fact that I loved Edward Ashburnham—and that I love him because he was just myself. If I had had the courage and the virility and possibly also the physique of Edward Ashburnham I should, I fancy, have done much what he did. He seems to me like a large elder brother who took me out on several excursions and did many dashing things whilst I just watched him robbing the orchards, from a distance. And, you see, I am just as much of a sentimentalist as he was. . . .

Niggardly, niggardly half-truth!—for observe the impossible exceptions: courage, virility, physique! What sane man could except them? The narrator aspires to be "the good soldier," the conventionally fine fellow, yet has no expectation of ever being in the least like him in any but his most passive features, and these working not at the level of sexuality, as with Edward, but of malformed friendship. To understand the exact significance here, we must turn to another book.

In his dedicatory epistle in the 1927 edition Ford says that he hoped *The Good Soldier* would do in English something of the sort that Maupassant's *Fort comme la mort* did in French. The remark is suggestive in the structural terms that Ford must have had in mind; I wish, however, to call attention to what may be the most accidental connection of theme. Of one of his characters Maupassant says: "He was an old intellectual who might have been, perhaps, a good soldier, and who could never console himself for what he had not been."

The vicious consolations of failure form our narrator. "Men," said D. H. Lawrence, "men can suck the heady juice of exalted self-importance from the bitter weed of failure—failures are usually the most conceited of men." Thus at the end of the novel we have forgotten the named good soldier, and we look instead at the nominated one, the narrator himself. His consolations are small: attendance upon the ill, "seeing them through"—for twelve years his wife, for the rest of his life the mad girl whom he fancies he might have loved; yet they give him a function, at least. This is the bitter, paltry destiny that, he thinks, life has forced upon him; thus he need never see himself as bitter or as paltry—or, indeed, as even telling a story.

And thus we come to the final circles of meaning, and these, like ripples round a stone tossed into a pool, never stop. For, finally, *The Good Soldier* describes a world that is without moral point, a narrator who suffers from the madness of moral inertia.

You ask how it feels to be a deceived husband. Just heavens, I do not know. It feels just nothing at all. It is not hell, certainly it is not necessarily heaven. So I suppose it is the intermediate stage. What do they call it? Limbo.

*Accidia!* It is the dull hysteria of sloth that besets him, the sluggish insanity of defective love.

And, yes, from that day forward she always treated me and not Florence as if I were the invalid.

Why, even to me she had the air of being submissive—to me that not the youngest child will ever pay heed to. Yes, this is the saddest story. . . .

The saddest story? One may say this another way, and say the same thing. *The Good Soldier* is a comedy of humor, and the humor is phlegm.

It is in the comedy that Ford displays his great art. Irony, which makes no absolute commitments and can thus enjoy the advantage of many ambiguities of meaning and endless complexities of situation, is at the same time an evaluative mood, and, in a master, a sharp one. Perhaps the most astonishing achievement in this astonishing novel is the manner in which the author, while speaking through his simple, infatuated character, lets us know how to take his simplicity and his infatuation. This is comic genius. It shows, for example, in the characteristic figures, the rather simple-minded and, at the same time, grotesquely comic metaphors: a girl in a white dress in the dark is "like a phosphorescent fish in a cupboard"; Leonora glances at the narrator, and he feels "as if for a moment a lighthouse had looked at me"; Leonora, boxing the ears of one of Edward's little mistresses, "was just striking the face of an intolerable universe." Figures such as these, and they occur in abundance, are the main ingredient in Ford's tone, and they are the subtle supports of such broader statements as this:

I should marry Nancy if her reason were ever sufficiently restored to let her appreciate the meaning of the Anglican marriage service. But it is probable that her reason will never be sufficiently restored to let her appreciate the meaning of the Anglican marriage service. Therefore I cannot marry her, according to the law of the land.

This is a mode of comic revelation and evaluation less difficult, perhaps, than that which is evident in Ford's figures of speech, but to sustain it as he does, with never a rupture of intent, is the highest art.

Then there are the wonderfully comic events—little Mrs. Maidan dead in a trunk with her feet sticking out, as though a crocodile had caught her in its giant jaws, or the poor little mad girl saying to the narrator after weeks of silence: "Shuttlecocks!" There are the frequent moments when the author leads his characters to the most absurd anticlimaxes (as when, at the end of the fourth chapter, Leonora, in a frenzy of self-important drama, demands: "Don't you know that I'm an Irish Catholic?"), and then, with superb composure, Ford leads his *work* away from the pit of bathos into which his people have fallen. There is the incessant wit, of style and statement, the wittier for its deceptive clothing of pathos. And, most important in this catalogue of comic devices, there is the covering symbolism of illness: characters who fancy that they suffer from "hearts," who do suffer defective hearts not, as they would have us believe, in the physiological but in the moral sense, and who are told about by a character who has no heart at all, and hence no mind. "I never," he tells us with his habitually comic solemnity, "I never was a patient anywhere." To which we may add: only always, in the madhouse of the world.

Is *The Good Soldier*, perhaps, a novelist's novel? Ford thought that it was his best work, and his judgment was always the judgment of the craftsman. Certainly it can tell us more about the nature of the novel than most novels or books about them: the material under perfect control, the control resulting in the maximum meaning, the style precisely evaluating that meaning. But if it is a kind of archetype of the processes of fiction, if, that is to say, it can demonstrate his craft to the craftsman, then it can also help all of us to read. And is it not true that, once we learn how to read, even if then we do not live more wisely, we can at least begin to be aware of why we have not? *The Good Soldier*, like all great works, has the gift and power of remorse.

# PART THREE

# Women in Love

In Lawrence's little-read, brilliantly extended introduction to Maurice Magnus's *Memoirs of the Foreign Legion*, we encounter this passage:

> "Why!" I said. "Is it you?"
> "Yes," he replied. "A terrible thing has happened."
> He waited on the stairs, and I went down. Rather unwillingly, because I detest terrible things, and the people to whom they happen.

*The people to whom they happen.* Put this phrase beside an early exchange between Birkin and Gerald in *Women in Love:*

> "You think people should just do as they like."
> "I think they always do."

Put these two together, and we are at the very center of the startling development that the old idea that "character is fate" achieves in Lawrence, and particularly here, in *Women in Love.* If we consider this development in relation to uses of the same idea in earlier novels, we will see just how it is startling. Over a third of *The Portrait of a Lady,* for example, is "taken up with brushwork," according to Stephen Spender's mistaken reading, "that has nothing to do with the story." Really, James is painting in all the features of Isabel Archer's lovely, candid intelligence which is yet an intelligence where every virtue shades off into not, perhaps, a vice, but at least a false perception—all this so that we can recognize the inevitability of her renunciation of the right to ignorance once her education in corruption is completed, and she gains her moral freedom in the paradox of social slavery. This is among our finest demonstrations in fiction of the belief in the freedom of the will and the responsibilities of that freedom—a belief that necessarily selects for its emphasis the concept "character" from the whole phrase "character is fate." Take, now, Joseph Conrad's understanding of the proposition as it is implied by his title, *Chance,* and as this implication pervades all his novels. Chance is accident, and in accident lies opportunity, *that* kind of chance: determinism and free will, the will operating out from the ground that accident allows it. And here, of course, the emphasis falls upon "fate" in that whole phrase "character is fate." In Lawrence, the two terms become equivalents, the emphasis distributed with complete equality and balance, "Chance being at one with Choice at last," as Yeats succinctly said.

The new development in Lawrence is found most clearly in his theme of the victim who invites the victimizer, the murderee who invites the murderer. Because the equivalence of these terms had not previously been handled in fiction, and because of the extremity with which Lawrence felt the urgency of his interpretation for the modern world, the idea that we can and constantly do choose our fate, not only our social or our psychological fate, but our final fate, our *destiny,* choose life or death—because of the novelty of this interpretation in fiction and the extremity with which Lawrence felt it, he abandoned the kind of novel he had been writing and the kinds of novel that had been written by others, and attempted instead to write the novel as psychic drama. He first became aware of the alteration in his aims as he was writing *The Rainbow;* he became completely aware of it as he was writing *Women in Love.* The change can be seen in at least four ways:

First, characterization. The whole notion of character in fiction undergoes an alteration. He will now create more *essential* beings, will be concerned first of all not with the "ego" that interests the traditional novelist, but with the "primal forces" that are prior to "character."

I don't think the psychology is wrong, it is only that I have a different attitude to my characters, and that necessitates a different attitude in you, which you are not prepared to give. As for its being my cleverness which would pull the thing through— that sounds odd to me, for I don't think I am so very clever, in that way. I think the book is a bit futuristic—quite unconsciously so. But when I read Marinetti—"The profound intuitions of life added one to the other, word by word, according to their illogical conception, will give us the general lines of an intuitive physiology of matter"—I see something of what I am after. I translate him clumsily, and his Italian is often obfuscated—and I don't care about physiology of matter—but somehow—that which is physic —non-human, in humanity, is more interesting to me than the old-fashioned human element—which causes one to conceive a character in a certain moral scheme and make him consistent. The certain moral scheme is what I object to. In Turgenev, and in Tolstoi, and in Dostoevsky, the moral scheme into which all the characters fit—and it is nearly the same scheme—is, whatever the extraordinariness of the characters themselves, dull, old, dead. When Marinetti writes: "It is the solidity of a blade of steel that is interesting by itself, that is, the uncomprehending and inhuman alliance of its molecules in resistance to, let us say, a bullet. The heat of a piece of wood or iron is in fact more passionate, for us, than the laughter or tears of a woman"—then I know what he means. He is stupid, as an artist, contrasting the heat of the iron and the laugh of the woman. Because what is interesting in the laugh of the woman is the same as the binding of the molecules of steel or their action in heat: it is the inhuman will, call it physiology, or like Marinetti—physiology of matter, that fascinates me. I don't so much care about what the woman *feels*—in the ordinary usage of the word. That presumes an ego to feel with. I only care about what the woman *is*—what she is—inhumanly, physiologically, materially—according to the use of the word: but for me, what she *is* as a phenomenon (or as representing some greater, inhuman will), instead of what she feels according to the human conception. That is where the futurists are stupid. Instead of looking for the new human phenomenon, they will only look for the phenomena of the science of physics to be found in human beings. They are crassly stupid. But if anyone would give them eyes, they would pull the right apples off the tree, for their stomachs are true in appetite. You mustn't look in my novel for the old stable *ego* of the character. There is another ego, according to whose action the individual is unrecognizable, and passes through, as it were, allotropic states which it needs a deeper sense than any other we've been used to exercise, to discover are states of the same single radically unchanged element. (Like as diamond and coal are the same pure single element of carbon. The ordinary novel would trace the history of the diamond—but I say, "Diamond, what! This is carbon." And my diamond might be coal or soot, and my theme is carbon.) . . . Again, I say, don't look for the development of the novel to follow the lines of certain characters: the characters fall into the form of some other rhythmic form, as when one draws a fiddle-bow across a fine tray delicately sanded, and sand takes lines unknown. [*Letter to Edward Garnett, June 5, 1914.*]

In the novel itself, Birkin tells us that personalities are not very interesting, that there are only a few great ideas that animate all individuals: these are the basic elements, the carbon: life and death, the two possible allegiances. And these are the psychic engagements that the novelist wishes to explore, just as they are the elements beneath the social character that interest Birkin in forming his personal relationships:

He looked at her, to see if he felt that she was good-looking. "I don't *feel* that you're good-looking," he said.

"Not even attractive?" she mocked, bitingly.

He knitted his brows in sudden exasperation.

"Don't you see that it's not a question of visual appreciation in the least," he cried. "I don't *want* to see you. I've seen plenty of women, I'm sick and weary of seeing them. I want a woman I don't see."

"I'm sorry I can't oblige you by being invisible," she laughed.

"Yes," he said, "you are invisible to me, if you don't force me to be visually aware of you. But I don't want to see you or hear you."

"What did you ask me to tea for, then?" she mocked.

"I want to find you, where you don't know your own existence, the you that your common self denies utterly. But I don't want your good looks, and I don't want your womanly feelings, and I don't want your thoughts nor opinions nor your ideas—they are all bagatelles to me."

"You are very conceited, Monsieur," she mocked. . . . "I think you want to tell me you love me, and you go all this way round to do it."

"All right," he said, looking up with sudden exasperation. "Now go away then, and leave me alone. I don't want any more of your meretricious persiflage."

"Is it really persiflage?" she mocked, her face really relaxing into laughter.

This quotation is even more helpful than Lawrence's letter to an understanding of the change that has come over his intention since *Sons and Lovers*, and certainly it points to his new problem as a novelist. "I want to find you, where you don't know your own existence, the you that your common self denies utterly." And all the rest, all that attaches to the conscious, social character, is it, for a novelist, "really persiflage," "meretricious persiflage"? If it is, then the novel as it was written before Lawrence had been built on persiflage, since its generic character depends on the development of conflict out of social materials, and if we took Lawrence's letter with complete literalness, or Birkin's ambition as a true equivalent to the ambition of Lawrence, the novelist, he would be directed toward such a novelistic disaster as Virginia Woolf's *The Waves*, albeit in his terms. So we may say at once that in the novel, the *pure* psychic drama is an impossibility, and that we do not have that attempt here.

What we have, in fact, are several different orders of characterization, the orders that traditionally appear in the novel. We have a group of "free" characters, and a group of "bound" characters. The free characters are limited to four, the four who actively seek out their fate through the plot movement; the rest are all fixed in their social roles, and in rigid social scenes, and, except perhaps for Hermione and the elder Criches, are caricatures whose fate is sealed before the outset. These have all taken the way of death, and therefore they exist at the level of the social personality alone, and they are characterized by means of the familiar technique of caricature, maximum selection. But the free characters, the four, are compounded of a double drive, and it is here that the method of characterization is new and unfamiliar. They have their social existence and they have their psychic existence; the first is inevitably an expression of the second, but in the second lies their whole motivation. As two take the way of death, their social role becomes more and more important ("Civilized society is insane," reflects Constance Chatterley). And as the two others take the way of life, their social role becomes less important, ceases, in fact, to exist. This has been Birkin's ambition and struggle throughout, the need to isolate himself on the cliff of self-responsibility, outside society yet not outside human relationship.

> "If I find I can live sufficiently by myself," he continued, "I shall give up my work altogether. It has become dead to me. I don't believe in the humanity I pretend to be part of, I don't care a straw for the social ideals I live by, I hate the dying organic form of social mankind—so it can't be anything but trumpery, to work at education. I shall drop it as soon as I am clear enough—tomorrow perhaps—and be by myself."

> "What I want is a strange conjunction with you—" he said quietly; "—not meeting and mingling;—you are quite right:—but an equilibrium, a pure balance of two single beings:—as the stars balance each other."

The attempt is by no means an entire success, as the final pages of the novel make quite clear, and because of the nature of the attempt, the characterization of Birkin is not an entire success either. He, more exclusively than any of the others, embodies Lawrence's ambition to handle the carbon in character, his drama comes nearest to being the pure psychic drama, but for the very reason that his sufferings and his struggle have no social objectification and cannot have, he tends to elude us as a novelistic being. The contrast with Gerald is instructive.

The second large difference between *Women in Love* and the traditional novel is in the notion of structure. The book is to have no mechanical plot (or only the shadow of a mechanical plot), it is to have no "story" in the conventional sense; instead, it is developed in separate episodes, and these only sporadically developed as "scenes." Yet these are meant to form a pattern of psychic relationships ("the form of some other rhythmic form"), a pattern of psychic movement with a large *general* rhythm, but without the objective or rationalized frame of the old novel.

Because it does not have this rationalized frame, *Women in Love* gives a first impression of much greater looseness and even aimlessness than it actually has, and if we can begin reading it, not as what it begins by seeming—a realistic novel— but as a drama of primal compulsions, a psychic symbolization, it will be seen to have its own kind of coherence, its own kind of organized—indeed, highly and complexly organized—structural presentation of theme. It is a different kind of structure from Conrad's or James's or Hardy's, bearing, perhaps, a more immediate relationship to the art of dance than to the traditional art of fiction. As in dance, it develops through the shifting allegiances between the members, and the configuration of characters, their thematic signifying, is perhaps the strictest of all English novels.

The basic pattern is established at once: Gudrun feels drawn to Gerald; Ursula feels drawn to Birkin. Each of these males is presently seen in another relationship with females: Gerald with the Pussums, whom he destroys, as she wishes; Birkin with Hermione, who is determined to dominate him by force of her will. In the second chapter, Birkin enunciates the theme. There are no accidents, he says; death seeks death; individuation is life; between the two is a perilous balance. From this discussion emerges presently the double idea: of Will—victim and victimizer, and of Death, symbolized socially in the coal mines, intellectually in Bohemia, the two finally brought together in Loerke, the industrial artist; and of Being—wholeness of function, symbolized throughout the novel by the natural order—flowers, animals—and of Life.

Through this quartet of characters this theme will sound. We might glance at some of its variations. For it is of the essence of Lawrence's intuition that these two poles are not fixed or static; they are fluid forces in perpetual conflict, of dissolution and resolution; so that he creates a kind of psychical dialectic, and his relationships are not for a minute rigid. The pattern is fluid, as these two forces and their derivatives attract and repel.

Birkin and Hermione, for example, have had a long relationship; from its opiates to his being, Birkin is now feebly trying to detach himself; the conflict bursts into the open and Hermione beats him with a chunk of lapis. The next scene, the two girls at the railroad crossing and Gerald on his horse, demonstrates their allegiance, Gudrun's fascination, Ursula's horror at Gerald's cruel domination. Next, we find Birkin in a deathy mood still, and Ursula attracted by but resisting the "life" he offers, and it is in that resistance that she moves toward Hermione. The big scene of "The Water Party" clarifies issues momentarily: it is an experience of literal death, and it pushes both Gerald and Birkin, in their differing responses, toward their own destinies; the two women respond accordingly. In Chapter 15, which follows, Ursula yearns toward real death as an escape from a living death in society, and, being at death's door, not life's, she now hates Birkin. Birkin turns away, and in the next chapter, he invites Gerald to enter a pact of *Blutbrüderschaft*—a complete commitment, one to the other. Gerald declines this invitation, and in the next chapter, the great pivotal chapter, "The Industrial Magnate," we are reminded why. This is at once an interlude and a keystone, a projection of individual failure into the fabric of the social structure. The old man (impotent love) is here opposed to Gerald (abstract hate) and between them is the defeated will of the mother. This is a superb image of industrial society in its psychic terms, all its self-defeating pulls exposed. In industry, harmony becomes organization, and Gerald, as "God of the machine," "converted the industry into a new and terrible purity"—which is death itself. An immediate contrast with the mechanical image is found in the next chapter, "Rabbit," the image of the vital, wholly single, wholly self-possessed animal life. To Gerald and Gudrun, the creature is "mad," yet in their observation of it, they feel their own bond in some recognized "obscenity." Again, in this chain-like structure, a contrast follows.

The chapter called "Moony" shows us Ursula's conflict of despair and desire, to yield or to will; and Birkin's conflict between desire and destructiveness, in the elaborate moon image, reflected on the water, which he attempts to destroy. But like life, it persists in reasserting itself. The conclusion is Birkin's decision to propose marriage to Ursula, but the proposal is a fiasco, and once more he withdraws. Meanwhile, however, because the larger form of the "process" is working in both Ursula and Gudrun, through and above these variations, they draw apart, begin to feel their alienation. As they draw apart, Birkin once more turns to Gerald, having been denied by Ursula, and if we feel anything legitimate in the novel's purpose in the chapter called "Gladiatorial," we feel Lawrence's own sense of the desperateness of his psychic dialectic in this symbolic conflict. "Woman to Woman" is a counterpart of the chapter called "Man to Man" and shows us Ursula and Hermione in momentary allegiance against Birkin. Their climax comes in the chapter called "Excurse," in Birkin's self-recognition, and in the achievement of their "polarity" in relationship.

The other side of the story now develops contrariwise. In "Death and Love," the death of Gerald's father drives him to Gudrun, by way of the graveyard; he brings the clay of his father's new grave into her bedroom. This is love *as* death, and the process now need only resolve itself, as it quickly does. The four go abroad. Ursula and Birkin find the cold Alps uncongenial and leave; Gudrun pits her will against Gerald. She is on the way to becoming a Hermione, but because hers is the death-seeking, not the life-seeking antagonist, Gudrun wins: she kills him, which is also what he has sought. And the novel ends on the partial resolution found by Ursula and Birkin. It seems to say that they have found as much as can be expected by any two individuals unless more individuals will make their effort.

It is instructive to compare this fluid, dance-like movement with the characteristic structure of Thomas Hardy, as, for example, in *Jude the Obscure*. The scheme here is a kind of rigidly counterpointed interchange of character that Hardy much enjoyed. He begins with Jude and Arabella. Then he sets up Sue and Philotson. Then Jude and Sue reverse their roles, and at the end, they reverse them yet again, returning to thir original partners. It is like a folk-dance figure, and Hardy's interest is in making it come full circle; it is perfectly expressive of the iron morality that obsessed his imagination. "The certain moral scheme is what I object to," Lawrence declared, and referred, of course, not to Hardy, but to that social morality with which most novelists, including Hardy, have generally been concerned, and of which the traditional notion of plot is an expression. Lawrence wishes to explore a deeper life, a life that seethes and boils beneath institutions as it seethes and boils beneath "personalities."

This is the third great difference between *Women in Love* and other novels, the theme and subject themselves. The structure of the novel is so precisely and so richly expressive of this theme that, after even a cursory examination of the structure, little more need be said of theme. But we should observe how explicit Lawrence is in enunciating it. Halfway through the novel we come upon this exact anthithesis:

> Birkin thought of Gerald. He was one of those strange white wonderful demons from the north, fulfilled in the destructive frost mystery. And was he fated to pass away in this knowledge, this one process of frost-knowledge, death by perfect cold? Was he a messenger, an omen of the universal dissolution into whiteness and snow?
>
> Birkin was frightened. He was tired, too, when he had reached this length of speculation. Suddenly his strange, strained attention gave way, he could not attend to these mysteries any more. There was another way, the way of freedom. There was the paradisal entry into pure, single being, the individual soul taking precedence over love and desire for union, stronger than any pangs of emotion, a lovely state of free proud singleness, which accepted the obligation of the permanent connection with others, and with the other, submits to the yoke and leash of love, but never forfeits its own proud individual singleness, even while it loves and yields.

The relationships of the novel are founded on this opposition, on the idea of death and life and death-in-life; and the characters move entirely in terms of these two impulses, their conflicts and their embraces developing out of their allegiance to one or the other. Love is, of course, Lawrence's focus, since he wished to say that in modern life we use love for death-purposes more frequently than we do for life-purposes. ("The point about love is that we hate the word because we have vulgarised it. It ought to be prescribed, tabooed from utterance, for many years, till we get a new, better idea.") Lawrence's theme, as we have suggested, is dramatized in terms of a struggle between what he calls Will (which may be either sensual or "spiritual," a death impulse in either case) and Being, that integration of the total self which is life. Will is the integration of the drive of ego toward power, toward domination; it has its inverse in the desire to be overpowered, to be dominated, to yield everything to dissolution. Will is mechanical, and its symbol is therefore the machine; its historical and social embodiment is an industrial society that lives by war. Being is the integration of life forces in total and complete self-responsibility. Its historical embodiment lives in the future.

Lawrence had, of course, a conviction that the novel can still do what it has never done in the past. It is a conviction that follows upon his generally prophetic purpose. In the famous ninth chapter of *Lady Chatterley's Lover,* he says that the novel "can inform and lead into new places the flow of our sympathetic consciousness, and it can lead our sympathy away in recoil from things gone dead." The two elements here point to the two major technical developments in this novel: the concern with the future, with the smashing of dead patterns and the release of life into new ones, has a direct effect in the concept of structure and the use of structure that we have examined; the attempt to make a direct approach to our "sympathetic consciousness" has an immediate effect in Lawrence's sense of language and his use of language. The fourth difference, then, is in the style of *Women in Love,* and particularly in the visionary quality that is generated by the style.

An appeal to our "sympathetic consciousness" must be absolutely direct—as direct as music or dance. We must be made to *feel* this conflict not in our intellects but in our nerves, as it were, if it is to mean anything at all. Lawrence argues throughout, of course, but the only effective argument is in the direct presentation, which comes to us, if it does, through the style. This Lawrence seemed to know, since he deliberately attempts, first of all, a kind of incantatory prose through the use of repetition, a kind of drugged choral quality, which is perhaps what E. M. Forster had in mind when he said that Lawrence was the only modern novelist "in whom song predominates, who has the rapt bardic quality." It is Forster, too, who speaks of the achievement of Lawrence's style as the "irradiation of the universe and the objects that compose it." This would have to do with diction and figure rather than with rhythm, and we can perhaps see the intention in the high use of color, and in the resulting spectacular quality of the images and of the flitting scenes. ". . . through the man in the closed wagon Gudrun could see the whole scene spectacularly, isolated and momentary, like a vision isolated in eternity." This is a description of the best moments in the novel—scenes such as that where the whole party goes bathing:

The first to run across the lawn was the little Italian, small and like a cat, her white legs twinkling as she went, ducking slightly her head, that was tied in a gold silk kerchief. She tripped through the gate and down the grass, and stood, like a tiny figure of ivory and bronze, at the water's edge, having dropped off her towelling, watching the swans, which came up in surprise. Then out ran Miss Bradley, like a large, soft plum in her dark-blue suit. Then Gerald came, a scarlet silk kerchief round his loins, his towels over his arms. He seemed to flaunt himself a little in the sun, lingering and laughing, strolling easily, looking white but natural in his nakedness. Then came Sir Joshua, in an overcoat, and lastly Hermione, striking with stiff grace from out of a great mantle of purple silk, her head tied up in purple and gold. Handsome was her stiff, long body, her straight-stepping white legs, there was a static magnificence about her as she let the cloak float loosely away from her striding. She crossed the lawn like some strange memory, and passed slowly towards the water.

Attempts at this quality of the spectacular, of the hallucinated, are not always successful; certainly the three women dancing in Oriental costumes conveniently provided do not quite get into the convention that Lawrence is trying to develop, and the scene of Gudrun, doing her Dalcroze rhythms in the presence of the livestock, does not quite escape the ridiculous. Yet we must recognize, all through the novel, this attempt at the spectacular, the eternally isolated, which leads to the hallucinated effects, and throughout to the strangely irritating, compulsive character of dreams:

> She put her hand on the arm of her care-worn, sallow father and frothing her light draperies, proceeded over the eternal red carpet. Her father, mute and yellowish, his black beard making him look more care-worn, mounted the steps stiffly, as if his spirit were absent; but the laughing mist of the bride went along with him undiminished.
>
> And no bridegroom had arrived! It was intolerable for her. Ursula, her heart strained with anxiety, was watching the hill beyond; the white, descending road, that should give sight of him. There was a carriage. It was running. It had just come into sight. Yes, it was he. Ursula turned towards the bride and the people, and, from her place of vantage, gave an inarticulate cry. She wanted to warn them that he was coming. But her cry was inarticulate and inaudible, and she flushed deeply, between her desire and her wincing confusion.

To this development of style we should add the insistent contrast of the diction between the mechanical and the organic, and the attempt of the style to persuade us of the *force* inhering in all life. A third development of style is mentioned in Lawrence's own preface. "In point of style, fault is often found with the continual, slightly modified repetition. The only answer is that it is natural to the author; and that every natural crisis in emotion or passion or understanding comes from this pulsing, frictional to-and-fro which works up to culmination." The attempt to duplicate, in syntactical movement itself, the dialectical flow of the theme is perhaps a mistaken esthetic ambition, but we should observe it as part of Lawrence's particular kind of integrity as an artist.

The intention of *Women in Love* is so tremendous, so central to our lives, that we must for our own sakes make an effort to tolerate it. I say tolerate for the reason that I have known almost no readers who, on *first* reading, did not find it either opaque beyond endurance, or tiresome, or revolting. This has been the response even of readers who can agree with Lawrence when he in effect equates plot as we have known it with a morality that has lost its relevance, even its reality. Yet is it not the fact that the reason the novel is difficult to judge is that it will not accept the disciplines of plot but does not quite find some new limitation that will *contain* this material, so that we are repeatedly asked to love Lawrence the man in order to accept Lawrence the novelist? Scenes like that in which Birkin invites Gerald to be his blood brother, repulsive to our social sense, grotesque before our literary taste, simply say, "Take me at my own level of sincerity, of seriousness, and not at yours, and you will see that this is exactly right." And the question is whether a novelist has the right to impose himself to this extent on his reader, even when his reader is eager to accept as much as he can, even when his reader, like the present writer, cannot, after eight or ten readings of this novel, imagine being without it. It is possible that *Women in Love* attempts to do more than the novel as we know it and even as Lawrence developed it, itself knows how to do. This does not for a moment mean that the attempt must not be made. No novelist speaks more directly to us than Lawrence, and if we can't hear him, we are, I quite believe, lost. But he has not, in this book, found the whole way to speak. His attempt to move into the realm of psychic drama we can take seriously in a way that we cannot take the diluted attempt of Virginia Woolf; but can we always hear what Lawrence wants us to hear? The question is not whether he is *right;* the question is, What is a novel?

Judging *Women in Love* in its own terms as a single work, I should say that its success is partial; judging it as a step in a career, I should remove the qualification. It is perhaps the most important single work in Lawrence's formal education. If we follow him on from *Women in Love,* through the next really shattered books, and to the end, we will see that he took, finally, two ways: in his last two books, *Lady Chatterley's Lover* and *The Man Who Died,* both, in my view, very great books, he divided the intention that in *Women in Love* is one. In *Lady Chatterley,* he retrenches his claims a little—it is a novel in a solid and sustained social context, and it is a novel with a clear and happily developed plot, in which characters function fully and the author lets them speak for themselves; in *The Man Who Died,* he made an absolutely unqualified claim for the sanctity of the purely self-responsible individual human being, society not more than a shadowy threat outside the novel, and he gives us a real image of what he does not give us in Birkin, the wholly integrated man; but he writes in the form of the fable. And this is, perhaps, as far as we have gone with the novel.

For the novel always drags us back into the world, into circumstance. Conrad says that "the energy of evil is so much more forcible than the energy of good," and perhaps this is because in novels, at least, pure evil does not exist whereas there are those novelists who attempt to make pure good prevail. Those who read—those who can stay to read *Women in Love* to the last fifty pages—the death of Gerald in the snow and the grievous pathos of Birkin without him—those readers come, I think, upon fifty pages that have more power of a particular kind than any other fifty pages in any other English or American novel. It is what we might call the real Russian bang. But Gerald is not the saint, he is the sinner; he is—us; and as we can see in reading novels in some ways so different as *Middlemarch* and *The Wings of the Dove,* sinners—for the very reason that the novel as we have so far known it is a genre that deals with individuals in a social context—sinners it can save for art, but its saints are damned.

# Lady Chatterley's Lover

"LADY CHATTERLEY'S LOVER" came into being under the umbrella pines of an Italian wood where Lawrence liked to sit
writing beside a spring of San Eusebio, before the cave where
the saint had lived. The air was golden, wild flowers embroid-
ered the ground, nightingales sang to him. He wrote: "Civilized
society is insane." He had put himself at last as far as possible
"outside the made world" in order to deliver this last judgment
upon it, and yet, writing his condemnation of industrial society in the peace of this Tuscan *pinèta,* he was also closing
a circle.

As is known to all who read, D. H. Lawrence was born,
the son of a coal miner and a schoolteacher, in the village of
Eastwood in the English midlands of Nottinghamshire where
they edge on Derbyshire. What the life of that countryside was
like at the end of the last and the beginning of the present
century, and what Lawrence's youth, lived in that countryside,
was like, is best told in his novel *Sons and Lovers.* The background of that novel, as of his first, *The White Peacock,* is a
slow cultural convulsion about to reach its end, a convulsion
in which the ancient pastoralism of the yeoman way of life
yields to the new mechanization of the industrial way of life,
and in which, incidentally, a lovely landscape yields itself to
an iron horror. What was lovely and peaceful in that older
life and landscape was Lawrence's peculiar treasure; what was
ugly and new, his special anathema. Just before his death
(and very shortly after he had published *Lady Chatterley's
Lover*), as with a gasp of nearly desperate nostalgia, he wrote
to a boyhood friend, J. D. Chambers, the younger brother of

that girl "Miriam" who is at the center of the conflict in *Sons and Lovers.*

Dear David,—

I hardly recognized you as J. D.—and you must be a man now, instead of a thin little lad with very fair hair. Ugh, what a gap in time! it makes me feel scared.

Whatever I forget, I shall never forget the Haggs—I loved it so. I loved to come to you all, it really was a new life began in me there. The water-pippin by the door—those maiden-blush roses that Flower would lean over and eat and Trip floundering round. —And stewed figs for tea in winter, and in August green stewed apples. Do you still have them? Tell your mother I never forget, no matter where life carries us.—And does she still blush if somebody comes and finds her in a dirty white apron? Or doesn't she wear work-aprons any more? Oh, I'd love to be nineteen again, and coming up through the Warren and catching the first glimpse of the buildings. Then I'd sit on the sofa under the window, and we'd crowd round the little table to tea, in that tiny little kitchen I was so at home in.

*Son' tempi passati, cari miei! quanto cari, non saprete mai!*— I could never tell you in English how much it all meant to me, how I still feel about it.

If there is anything I can ever do for you, do tell me.—Because whatever else I am, I am somewhere still the same Bert who rushed with such joy to the Haggs.

This recollection is in sharp contrast to a fresher one that appears in the second version of *Lady Chatterley.* There, late in the novel, Lawrence has his lovers go to the Eastwood country; they meet in the church at Hucknall where "the pinch of dust that was Byron's heart" (Byron, "that fat lad"!) is enshrined, and they survey the old Lawrence landscape—Haggs Farm now deserted, Felley Mill still and abandoned, everything "dead as Nineveh," all life sacrificed to "coal and iron." This bitterly personal scene disappears from the final version of the novel, but here we have a comparable episode in the long motor trip that Constance Chatterley makes through Derbyshire:

The car ploughed uphill through the long squalid straggle of Tevershall, the blackened brick dwellings, the black slate roofs glistening their sharp edges, the mud black with coal-dust, the pavements wet and black. It was as if dismalness had soaked through and through everything. The utter negation of natural beauty, the utter negation of the gladness of life, the utter absence of the instinct for shapely beauty which every bird and beast has, the utter death of the human intuitive faculty was appalling. The stacks of soap in the grocers' shops, the rhubarb and lemons in the greengrocers'! The awful hats in the milliners'! All went by ugly, ugly, followed by the plaster-and-gilt horror of the cinema with its wet picture announcements. "A Woman's Love!" . . . Tevershall! That was Tevershall! Merrie England! Shakespeare's England! No, but the England of to-day, as Connie had realized since she had come to live in it. It was producing a new race of mankind, over-conscious in the money and social and political side, on the spontaneous, intuitive side dead, but dead. Half-corpses, all of them: but with a terrible insistent consciousness in the other half. There was something uncanny and underground about it all. It was an underworld. . . . This is history. One England blots out another.

Constance Chatterley's drive, we may assume, duplicates in fact and feeling a drive through the same countryside that Lawrence made in 1925. "Been motoring all over my well-known Derbyshire," he wrote mildly enough to Martin Secker. "But I can't look at the body of my past, the spirit seems to have flown." The Lawrences had been living above Taos and in Oaxaca; now they had paused in England on their way to Italy again. For a few months they settled at Spotorno (where Angelo Ravagli, the "Tenente" of Lawrence's letters, was their landlord). Lawrence was weary and felt no incentive to write a long book, but he did, during this period, write in its rough form the novelette, *The Virgin and the Gypsy*, which returns him to the English setting and is in some ways a thematic anticipation of *Lady Chatterley* as well. Then they moved south to Florence and the Villa Mirenda. In the summer of 1926 they made one more visit to England, and late in that year, after the composition of *Lady Chatterley* was well under

way, Lawrence wrote to Rolf Gardiner about this visit. In this
letter he tells Gardiner in explicit detail of the familiar land-
marks in Eastwood and its environs—the houses in which he
lived as a boy, Haggs Farm and Felley Mill and other places
that had figured prominently in the first half dozen novels and
in so many of his stories. "That's the country of my heart,"
he writes; but painfully, for he concludes as follows:

> I was at my sister's in September, and we drove round—I
> saw the miners—and pickets—and policemen—it was like a spear
> through one's heart. I tell you, we'd better buck up and do
> something for the England to come, for they've pushed the spear
> through the side of *my* England.

What he could do for "the England to come" was to write
*Lady Chatterley*, and we are reminded of a letter from as far
back as 1913:

> Pray to your gods for me that *Sons and Lovers* shall succeed.
> People should begin to take me seriously now. And I do so break
> my heart over England when I read the *New Machiavelli*. And I
> am so sure that only through the readjustment between men and
> women, and a making free and healthy of this sex, will she get
> out of her present atrophy. Oh, Lord, and if I don't "subdue my
> art to a metaphysic," as somebody very beautifully said of Hardy,
> I do write because I want folk—English folk—to alter, and have
> more sense.

Fourteen years after his death, his widow said of Lawrence
and *Lady Chatterley* and the English people, "he spoke out of
them and for them, there in Tuscany, where the different
culture of another race gave the impetus to his work."

Between the cottage on Walker Street in Eastwood, or Haggs
Farm outside it, and the Villa Mirenda outside Florence, lay
a long history. In that history, three items loom large: Lawrence's marriage to Frieda von Richthofen, the First World
War, and travels all over the globe. His marriage is one of the
most exploited subjects in our memoir literature, and all one
need say of it here is that, whatever stresses it may have undergone, it had more of blessedness, and that without that

blessedness, the lyrical portions of *Lady Chatterley*, which comprise a great hymn to true marriage, could not have been written. Lawrence's personal experiences in the war are the subject of the chapter called "The Nightmare" in the novel, *Kangaroo*, and the atmosphere of the war and of a war-made world hangs over all his works from 1916 on but is most prominent in the quality of that social world that threatens the lyrical world of *Lady Chatterley*, for Lawrence felt as early as 1916 what we all feel today, "the violence of the nightmare released now into the general air." The travels (southern and central Europe, the Far East, Australia, the United States and Mexico, Europe again) not only provided him with the series of settings through which his novels make their march and so lead him to their end at the Villa Mirenda, but also provided him with images of utopia (always smashed) that would give him the community relationship that he sometimes desperately felt he needed. It was only when he gave up that hope, and the programs that his novels sometimes developed out of that hope, that he could have come to rest in *Lady Chatterley*, where there is no program at all, only the inspired plea that the human being become what he already is, that is, human. The journey from the humanity and the inhumanity of his youth, to his discovery at the end of the essentially human as it could be defined in drama against that background—this is another circle that his last novel closes.

There were times in Lawrence's career when the whole beautiful line of it, as it was finally drawn, threatened to blow up completely. After the early autobiographical novel, *Sons and Lovers*, Lawrence wrote his two most complex works, *The Rainbow* and *Women in Love*. These were novels that attempted to seize directly on psychic reality. They end with regenerate heroes who have experienced visions of human felicity for which they can find no place either in this world or in the realistic convention of the novel. Then begins a period for which bitter, surely, is a mild word—bitter, galled, the withers wrung. And yet, in this period, when Lawrence tries to bring his characters into vital social relationships, we are at the center of the most fascinating and alarming elements in Lawrence, the artist.

*Aaron's Rod* (the novel that, in its first paragraph, announces the end of the war, the violence released now into the general air) was published in 1922, the year of Mussolini's *coup d'état; Kangaroo*, in 1923; *The Plumed Serpent*, in January 1926. Unable to see any but negative virtues (that is, vices) in democracy, which seemed to Lawrence a means of freeing the individual to mediocrity and a numbed anxiety only, he was still fairly desperate to find some means of satisfying what he himself called his "societal impulse" and of making his novels end positively in this world. So he turned to undemocratic ideas, a part of the violence released now; and in these three novels, in three different ways, tried them out to see if they would work either for the novel or for life. They did not. This is the imaginative test of theoretical abstraction, and Lawrence's greatness of mind shows in the necessity he felt to reject the abstraction when it would not work for the imagination. The first two of these novels are fragmentary, implosive structures because the author, while he cannot prove the abstraction right, is unwilling to let his story prove it wrong and so lets the story jar to a stop in negation. The third is a unified work because the lives of the characters, in the actualities of the plot, prove that the abstraction is merely abstract, that is, wrong, and the novel ends in its rejection.

*Aaron's Rod* presents Lawrence in the character of Lilly, who assures Aaron Sisson that he will not find himself until he finds a greater man to whom he can submit his partial individuality; but in the end, Lilly can produce no such leader, not even himself. In *Kangaroo*, Lawrence puts himself in Aaron's position, as the man who seeks the leader; but, confronted by the alternative of the socialist, Struthers, and the fascist, Kangaroo, the Lawrentian hero departs for America, where he hopes to find a more plausible choice. Then, in *The Plumed Serpent*, Lawrence tries still another device: he transforms his seeker into a woman, a jaded European who has severed her connections with her own social past and seeks fulfillment in Mexico through the leadership of two men who are trying to institutionalize a primitive religion which is not in the least unlike Lawrence's own religion of "the dark gods"; but it will not work. As the two leaders fail her, so she fails them, and discovers, with Lawrence, that there are two kinds of power: the power to dominate others, and the power to fulfill oneself. "The leader-cum-follower relationship is a bore," Lawrence wrote then, in a letter. "And the new relationship will be some sort of tenderness, sensitive, between men and men, and between men and women." *Lady Chatterley's Lover,* the last novel, was first to be called *Tenderness.*

This is the final Lawrence, the Lawrence who kicked out, although with a dragging reluctance, the hypothetical fragments that he had tried to shore against the world's ruin and his own, and who was determined to attempt still to be free in the actualities of human relationship. He was an artist who had gone through a purgatorial period that sought escapes from freedom, and then settled with small content and no complacency into the possible paradise that knows what freedom is, or at least where it begins. This is the paradise that is allowed to human life when human beings can recognize that after all the sweat for something else, for something either more or less, the value of life exists in the act of living; that living means full living, or the life of the full and not the partial self, the self that realizes its powers rather than the self that seeks power or submits to it. And this is, after all, the beginning of the true democracy, as it is of the true marriage, because it is total integration, and therefore makes possible the only creative spontaneity, even though that be in isolation, in an Italian wood.

2

The story of *Lady Chatterley's Lover* is among the simplest that Lawrence devised: Constance Chatterley, the frustated wife of an aristocratic mine owner who has been wounded in the war and left paralyzed and impotent, is drawn to his game-

keeper, the misanthropic son of a miner, becomes pregnant
by him, and hopes at the end of the book to be able to divorce
her husband and leave her class for a life with the other man.
Through all his career Lawrence had been concerned with the
general theme of this book—the violation or the fulfillment of
individuality in relationship—and many times he had handled
the theme in the concrete terms here presented where fulfillment involves the crossing either of class or cultural lines, and
often of both, where violation results from resisting this necessity. The familiar construction, then, is of a woman in a relatively superior social situation who is drawn to an "outsider"
(a man of lower social rank or a foreigner) and either resists
her impulse or yields to it. The two possibilities are embodied,
of course, and respectively, in the situation into which Lawrence was born and in the situation into which he married.
Inevitably, it became a favorite situation of his fiction.

Among the short stories, one might mention five as clear
illustrations: one of his juvenile works, *A Fragment of Stained
Glass*, deals with a medieval serf who flees his bondage with
a miller's daughter; in *The Daughters of the Vicar*, one daughter chooses to defy her family in order to marry a miner; in
*The Shades of Spring*, a Miriam-like girl reveals to her old,
poetic lover that a gamekeeper has taken his place; in *Mother
and Daughter*, the daughter chooses to upset her mother's
values and her own by committing the absurdity of going off
with an Armenian known to the mother as "the Turkish Delight"; in *None of That*, an enormously wealthy daughter of
the jazz age invites an involvement (to her destruction) with
a Mexican bullfighter.

Among the novelettes, one might again mention five. In
*The Fox*, a constrictive relationship between two girls is shat-
tered by the intrusion of a farmer-soldier and his passion for
one of them; in *The Ladybird*, an aristocratic Englishwoman
yields to a mysterious central European, Dionys Psanek; in
*St. Mawr*, Mrs. Witt and her daughter Lou are attracted by a
Welsh groom and a half-breed Navajo; in *The Princess*, a New
England virgin wishes to yield to a Mexican guide and dis-

covers only too late that she cannot truly yield; in *The Virgin and the Gypsy*, an English virgin yields to a gypsy.

From the ten novels, we can once more choose five, although the situation is omnipresent. There is *Lady Chatterley's Lover* itself. In *Sons and Lovers*, the parental situation is not only an obvious example but the archetype. In *The Lost Girl*, a middle-class English girl leaves the comforts (and depredations) of home for a rigorous life with an Italian peasant. In *The Plumed Serpent*, Kate Forrester, a refined European, yields (temporarily) to the intellectual leadership of one Mexican and the physical leadership of another. And in the very first novel, *The White Peacock*, the situation not only presents itself in the Lettie-George relationship, but a gamekeeper, Annable, appears briefly but volubly as the earliest version of Parkin-Mellors, the gamekeeper of the last novel.

Such a catalogue as this takes two risks: it suggests a limited imaginative range, and it seems to denigrate the subject by a tone of frivolity. Neither risk is serious, for the theme itself, however baldly one may state the situations that embody it, is pushed into every area that concerns us most seriously in this century. *Lady Chatterley's Lover*, like everything that Lawrence wrote, is an affirmation of life values as against the mechanization of human nature. This, his general subject matter, may be broken down into two major themes: the relation of men and women, and the relation of men and machines. In the works as they are written, the two are one, and his most subtle and penetrating perception, the knowledge that social and psychological conflicts are identical, is so firmly integrated in the structure of his books that it is almost foolhardy to speak of his having two themes when in fact he had one vision. But a vision has both a background and a foreground, and one may say, perhaps without distortion, that the men and machines relationship is the background, the man and woman relationship, the foreground. This division does not mean that the first determines the second, for it would be just as true to say that the second determines the first. They are, in fact, inextricable.

We might say that one provides the scene, and the other, the drama enacted on that scene.

Who *was* Annable? One must remind oneself of the British novel as it was in the year 1911 to recognize what an extraordinary figure he is, standing there so clearly from the beginning, in that first novel, written when Lawrence was a very young man. Whether he had some prototype in actuality we will probably never know, and it is of no importance that we should know; certainly he had none in fiction. What is important is simply to observe that he was uniquely *there*—there from the beginning in Lawrence's imagination as the figure who asserts that modern civilized society is insane, and who without compromise rejects it. Nothing that one might say of ideas of primitivism and of the natural man as these had been used in the writing of the two preceding centuries would in any way reduce his uniqueness.

> He was a man of one idea:—that all civilisation was the painted fungus of rottenness. He hated any sign of culture. I won his respect one afternoon when he found me trespassing in the woods because I was watching some maggots at work in a dead rabbit. That led us to a discussion of life. He was a thorough materialist —he scorned religion and all mysticism. He spent his days sleeping, making intricate traps for weasels and men, putting together a gun, or doing some amateur forestry, cutting down timber, splitting it in logs for use in the hall, and planting young trees. When he thought, he reflected on the decay of mankind—the decline of the human race into folly and weakness and rottenness. "Be a good animal, true to your animal instinct," was his motto. With all this, he was fundamentally very unhappy—and he made me also wretched.

Annable's difficulty is that he is not only an animal (as his name is not quite that word), but also a human being with a civilized experience behind him. The son of a prosperous father, he had been enrolled at Cambridge, had taken orders and served as curate to a fashionable rector, and had married (unhappily, in the end) a lady; yet now he lives in brutish squalor, amid a swarm of soiled children and a slatternly, illiterate woman, and strives not to lift his mind above these chosen circumstances. He does not manage to survive his choice. Yet he serves his function in providing a kind of choral emphasis in a novel that is concerned with the thinning out of human relationship amid a general deterioration of life. He serves no less to emphasize Lawrence's success in developing the character and situation of his last gamekeeper. His success with this figure is Lawrence's vindication of his crude attempt with Annable, just as it is the payment of his long-standing debt to the humanity of his own father. This is not so much a matter of psychological as it is of esthetic maturity; Lawrence had found precisely the way that he wished to speak. For if *Lady Chatterley's Lover* concludes a long thematic history, it concludes no less a history of forms.

Lawrence was, of course, three things: he was a man in search of a life; he was a prophet in search of a revelation; and he was an artist in search of a convention. The first formed the second, and the second created the problems of the third, but it is only the third, finally—or the third as containing the others—that we can with much profit consider in the name either of criticism or of thought.

In an enthusiastic book on Lawrence by an Anglican priest who writes under the name of Father Tiverton, we are shown that the spirit of Lawrence's work was not at all inimical to much that is central in Christian thought, and also that this spirit makes him the kind of artist that he is. And how simply Father Tiverton puts it! "He reached the point in imaginative being at which the preacher and the poet coincide, since the poem is the sermon." The *whole* poem, of course, or the *whole* story, or the *whole* novel, not any set of extractable words or scenes that exist only as a portion of those wholes. This primary axiom of all reading and all criticism applies nowhere more drastically than to *Lady Chatterley's Lover*.

To reach the point where the preacher and the poet coincide *formally* was not a simple matter. We have already observed something of Lawrence's intellectual progress, how, in novel after novel, the imaginative test qualifies the theoretical conviction. Thus Lawrence's mind constantly moved as each novel shrugged off its predecessor, at the same time that his techniques moved through a wide range of fascinating experimentation (still almost entirely unexamined by criticism) in his attempt to accommodate what was theoretically dear to him to the dearer forms of fiction. In both the broadest and the most special sense, Lawrence is first of all the artist: he gives primacy to the "living tissue" of imaginative experience, and his craft is constantly moving and moving always on a dynamic base.

All this is to say nothing at all about those sporadic bursts of "genius" ("A great genius, but no artist," runs the cliché) that even the unfriendliest critics grant, those "fitful and profound insights" that even Mr. Eliot, for example, finds it possible to allow; it is only to say that in the one important way that a man is an artist, Lawrence was an artist: that he knew where his real life was lived. Once this obvious matter can be established (and Father Tiverton went far in doing just that), we can begin to analyze the spurts of genius and their place in the whole art, or even, conceivably, to describe the constant artist.

Lawrence, the constant artist, made constant demands on the forms of fiction that had not been made in the past. "It is the way our sympathy flows and recoils that really determines our lives," he wrote in the ninth chapter of *Lady Chatterley's Lover*.

> And here lies the vast importance of the novel, properly handled. It can inform and lead into new places the flow of our sympathetic consciousness, and it can lead our sympathy away in recoil from things gone dead. Therefore, the novel, properly handled, can reveal the most secret places of life; for it is in the *passional* secret places of life above all, that the tide of sensitive awareness needs to ebb and flow, cleansing and freshening.

Among the "things gone dead" (and it is only one) is the conventionalized, the calcified ethic of Christianity, and it was Lawrence's belief that the human consciousness was capable of regeneration if only it could be led away from the rubble into "new places." ". . . for wide masses of people," John Lehmann wrote in 1947, in a plea for a renewal of "the world of love,"

> the Christian symbols as they have known them have ceased to be significant, and their desperate need is to find new symbols —even if those symbols should lead us back to a rediscovery of the central meaning of Christianity, restored through the discarding of outworn and corrupted images, and irrelevant accretions of fact.

Although Mr. Lehmann himself found the mass of Lawrence's symbols inadequate to this end, one can argue—and so Father Tiverton argued—that this attempt was precisely Lawrence's. His wish was to take the sacraments out of their merely institutional bindings and to reassert the sacramental nature of life itself.

> The old Church knew best the enduring needs of man, beyond the spasmodic needs of today and yesterday. . . . For centuries the mass of people lived in the rhythm, under the Church. And it is down in the mass that the roots of religion are eternal. When the mass of a people loses the religious rhythm, that people is dead, without hope. But Protestantism came and gave a great blow to the religious and ritualistic rhythm of the year, in human life. Non-conformity *almost* finished the deed. Now you have a poor, blind, disconnected people with nothing but politics and bank-holidays to satisfy the eternal human need of living in ritual adjustment to the cosmos in its revolutions. . . . Mankind has got to get back to the rhythm of the cosmos, and the permanence of marriage.

"I am a passionately religious man," Lawrence once said of himself, and when Father Tiverton comes to the concluding point in his discussion where he wishes to state the central fact about Lawrence's view and his art, he writes: "I should claim that one of the great virtues of Lawrence was his sense of the ISness rather than the OUGHTness of religion . . . he believed in his dark gods not because they 'worked,' but because they were true."

But how, in the realistic tradition of the British novel, was the artist to communicate the "ISness of religion"? Of the first three novels, where the content is suited to the realistic convention, *Sons and Lovers* is successful even though it is in that work that Lawrence discovers that what he wants his work to communicate is a more essential reality than "that hard, violent style full of sensation and presentation" (as Lawrence himself described it) was capable of. *The Rainbow* and *Women in Love* are his extended attempt at a form that will accomplish this end. The first begins as a traditional family chronicle and ends in a Blakean vision; the second consolidates the visionary and the hallucinatory effects of the first, and they dominate the whole. Neither is a novel in any traditional sense, not even a "psychological novel." They are psychic dramas in which primary human impulses rather than human personalities struggle and embrace, and they end with heroes who have made a journey of the soul and whose regeneration puts them beyond the conditions of that social world out of which the novel as we have known it has always come and in which it has always been rooted. In *Aaron's Rod* and *Kangaroo* the strenuous formal attempt is relinquished; these are rather rough chronicles of real journeys in which the soul's journey is *discussed* but in which no attempt is made to embody its destination in the drama. In *The Plumed Serpent,* an extremely ambitious work, the myth of the soul's journey coalesces with the primitive Mexican myth that the heroes are attempting to revitalize in Mexican political life and that makes up the bulk of the story; it ends with the European heroine's conclusion that the Mexican myth may be good for the Mexicans but that it is of small use to her, and she lapses back into the condition of her social world, saying, *"But I can fool them so they shan't find out."* She will take from them what is of use to her, for as long as may be.

In many of his short stories and in his short novels, Lawrence managed to maintain a realistic framework within which rich symbolic modulations that far transcend realism could be beautifully contained. In the shorter fiction, too, he could break into pure symbolic forms, as in *The Woman Who Rode Away,* or into splendid fable, as in *The Man Who Died.* But even as he managed more and more successfully to handle action that in itself was ritualistic and prose that was liturgical, the convention of the realistic novel could not be made wholly to yield. The progress from the first through the third version of *Lady Chatterley* is the history of an effort to make the events at once maximumly plausible in realistic terms and maximumly meaningful in psychic terms. The result is the third version which in itself finally forms one great symbol, so that one can easily remember it as one remembers a picture. In the background of this picture black machinery looms cruelly against a darkening sky; in the foreground, hemmed in and yet separate, stands a green wood; in the wood, two naked human beings dance.

### 3

The first *Lady Chatterley* is a relatively short, dark, and above all rough sketch written under the pall of recently experienced English gloom; the second, written just before or just after the Etruscan adventure, is much longer and leaps out of the dreariness of the first, with a strong infusion of lyric feeling and natural vitality that may derive from Lawrence's experience of the brilliantly sensuous tomb paintings at Tarquinia and elsewhere; the third, written after a hard and alarming illness, is about the same length as the second, but there is a sharpening of intellectual issues and a deepening of pathos. These are the large general changes, and if we add to them the fact that in each version as it succeeds an earlier, the treatment of the sexual act becomes more and more explicit, a development as necessary to the achievement of the four qualities just listed as it was to the full dramatization of Lawrence's theme, we have encompassed the major changes in tone and feeling. At the other end of the scale of revision are thousands of alterations in technical detail, and a systematic analysis of these changes would tell us a great deal about Lawrence the writer, but the place and time for such an analysis is a scholarly monograph that could best be published when all three texts of the novel are available to interested readers. Between these two extremes of revisionary method are a variety of changes in dramatic structure, many of which have been observed by E. W. Tedlock, Jr., in an appendix to his *The Frieda Lawrence Collection of D. H. Lawrence Manuscripts* (1948). It is in the interest of the present account to observe a few of these.

Lawrence's first problem in revision seems to have been to tell his story in such a way as to achieve maximum plausibility within the terms of his own aspiration: he had to make the love of the lady and the gamekeeper convincing, and he had also to give their love a chance for survival in the world as he saw it. If we follow the alterations in the character of the keeper, in the character of Constance, and finally, in the nature of the resolutions, we will be able to see how he achieved his end.

In all three versions, the gamekeeper (called Parkin in the first two, Mellors in the third) is a man of about forty, a miner's son who has misanthropically withdrawn from the industrial world into work in the wood. In the first and second versions, he is of medium height, with reddish-brown eyes and a shaggy mustache; in the third, he is taller, with blue eyes. In the first version he is physically strong; in the second, not so strong; in the third, sometimes rather frail. The Parkin of the first version speaks only in the vernacular; the second uses the Derbyshire dialect in scenes of affection and the king's English when he wishes; Mellors speaks more or less like the second Parkin but is capable of much more conceptual language. The Parkin of the first version has least motivation for his misanthropy but is the most violent in asserting it. He delights in trapping poachers and getting summonses for them; to Mellors, this is an unpleasant part of his work. Where Parkin is positively churlish with Constance, Mellors is ironical and mildly derisive. The first Parkin's motivation lies in a smashed marriage with a brutish woman; the second Parkin's motivation lies in the same marriage, but with a background of an awkward sexual trauma that unfits him for any other woman and yet does not fit her for him. In Mellors, the sexual background is amplified but the traumatic experience disappears: he has had love affairs with young women drawn exactly on the models of Miriam and the Helena of Lawrence's second and third novels—romantic, "spiritual" women who offended his manhood, and from these he had turned to the "common" girl, Bertha, whom he married, but who revealed at once a ferocious sexual will under the force of which the marriage passed swiftly into brutish deterioration. From this marriage, Mellors escaped into the world, and the world of gentlemen: he had become an officer's aide in India. Now, in his cottage, he has books that he can read and talk about, and he is Constance's equal in all but birth. The original Parkin is something of a clown as well as a boor:

> The skirts of his big coat flapped, his brown dog ran at his heels. He was once more going to take the world by the nose. . . . He strode with a grand sort of stride, baggy coat-tails flapping. The son of man goes forth to war! She smiled to herself grimly.

The second Parkin still has "a rather sticking-out brown moustache," but "his bearing had a military archness and resistance that was natural to him." Mellors has not only the military background itself, but, along with "a certain look of frailty," natural gentility, and when Constance sees him in town, "tall and slender, and so different, in a formal suit of thin dark cloth," she reflects that "he could go anywhere. He had a native breeding which was really much nicer than the cut-to-pattern class thing."

In Constance Chatterley, the changes are perhaps less drastic, but they are no less important to her motivation. In the first version, she has had a certain continental experience but it has hardly made her worldly; in the second version, she has had a continental education; in the third version, she has not only had a continental education but also a series of casual, "intellectual" love affairs before her marriage. She is still "a ruddy, country-looking girl with soft brown hair and a sturdy body, and slow movements, full of unused energy," but she is also a woman whose experience has equipped her to take the full measure of her world. Her marriage ruined by Clifford's physical incapacity, she has, in her third figuration, a casual postmarital affair (and is encouraged in this conduct by her friends, her father, even her husband). In the third version, Lawrence introduces the character of Michaelis, a successful, trivial playwright, to put Constance at the very center of the full emptiness of this social-intellectual world. This motivation is of first importance, for it places Mellors and Constance in precisely the same situation: an experienced man and woman, both disillusioned with their experience, both capable of a better experience. With the minimization of the class barrier between Connie and Mellors and the amplification of their similar sexual defeat, Lawrence achieves the psychological realism of the final version.

If they are ready for one another, they still face the problem of finding a world that is ready for them. As only a glance at the variation in the three endings will show, Lawrence had solved this problem only in part by the alterations that we have already observed. In the first version, where class barriers are strongest, and where Lawrence is still hoping for some social role for his characters, Parkin ends as a worker in a Sheffield steel mill and as the secretary of the local branch of the Communist party. Just before the end, after Constance is shown in an impossible scene in a worker's home, she and Parkin quarrel, and the likelihood of their finding any way out is small. In the final scene, she hopes to become his wife, simply his wife, living on his terms, sharing his interests, politics included; but our hope for her is small. In the second version, Parkin is no longer a political man and the Sheffield mills are an abomination to him; he plans to leave them for farm work. He is perhaps a little less unwilling to spend some of Connie's money in order to find a life for themselves, if she is so determined. The novel ends with his promising to "come to Italy" in her wake, when she needs him. But here Lawrence

has tried to write out the class barrier by fiat. While Constance
is visiting on the Continent, she has this revelation:

> Class is an anachronism. It finished in 1914. Nothing remains
> but a vast proletariat, including kings, aristocrats, squires, mil-
> lionaires and working-people, men and women alike. And then a
> few individuals who have not yet been proletarianised. . . .
>
> It was a great relief to her that that vague, yet very profound
> class-mistrust which had laid like a negating serpent at the bot-
> tom of her soul, was now gone. Vitally, organically, in the old
> organic sense of society, there were no more classes. That organic
> system had collapsed. So she need not have any class-mistrust
> of Parkin, and he need have none of her.

This discovery presumably frees them to live in the world as
it is, on their terms. The end of the second version is very
explicitly uninterested in any retreat to the colonies. It is the
world or nothing, this time. "To Connie, the wood where she
had known Parkin in the spring had become the image of
another world," but the implication is that she can make *that*
world bloom in this one, probably in Italy. On this subject,
Lawrence had taken his personal stand, and interested readers
should examine his *Autobiographical Sketch,* written at this
time and published posthumously in *Assorted Articles.* There
he writes:

> Class makes a gulf, across which all the best human flow is lost.
> It is not exactly the triumph of the middle classes that has made
> the deadness, but the triumph of the middle-class *thing* . . . the
> middle class is broad and shallow and passionless. Quite passion-
> less. At the best they substitute affection, which is the great mid-
> dle-class positive emotion. . . . Yet I find, here in Italy, for exam-
> ple, that I live in a certain silent contact with the peasants who
> work the land of this villa. I am not intimate with them . . . and
> they are not working for me; I am not their *padrone*. Yet it is
> they, really, who form my *ambiente*. . . . I don't expect them to
> make any millennium here on earth, neither now nor in the
> future. But I want to live near them, because their life still flows.

But Connie and Mellors are not Frieda and D. H. Lawrence,
and Lawrence has the dramatic tact to recognize as much in
the third version. While the entire implication (underlined by

the *rapport* that develops between Mellors and Connie's father) is that class is an anachronism, and that the moment we can make better assumptions about what we are in the potential human facts, this will be the first of many anachronisms to vanish from the actual social facts, Lawrence wisely allows the matter to remain in the realm of implication rather than forcing it to solve his dramatic problem. Again, with the question of marriage as it is versus marriage as it should be, the second version is as explicit as this:

> So it must be: a voyage apart, in the same direction. Grapple the two vessels together, lash them side by side, and the first storm will smash them to pieces. This is marriage, in the bad weather of modern civilisation. But leave the two vessels apart, to make their voyage to the same port, each according to its own skill and power, and an unseen life connects them, a magnetism which cannot be forced. And that is marriage as it will be, when this is broken down.

In the third version, the dramatic presentation of a true marriage is permitted to speak for itself, and the fact that this true marriage must exist in a wasteland leaves the end of the third version in some uncertainty, which is supremely right. The whole seems to slow down into a *decrescendo* as it begins to breathe out an uneasiness that is esthetically fine, among Lawrence's really great effects. Political affirmations (and some impossible scenes) vanish, both the earliest assertions of class war and the middle assertions of the absence of class, and the novel ends with a long letter from Mellors to Constance, written from a farm where he is working, as both characters await their divorces and Connie awaits her child. Mellors hopes to find a farm of his own, perhaps in Canada, where they can make their life; but he does not hope for more, and he is hardly bold in the hope he has.

> . . . what I live for now is for you and me to live together. I'm frightened, really. I feel the devil in the air, and he'll try to get us. Or not the devil, Mammon: which I think, after all, is only the mass-will of people, wanting money and hating life. Anyhow I feel great grasping white hands in the air, wanting to get hold

of the throat of anybody who tries to live, live beyond money, and squeeze the life out. There's a bad time coming! If things go on as they are, there's nothing lies in the future but death and destruction, for these industrial masses. I feel my inside turn to water sometimes, and there you are, going to have a child by me. But never mind. All the bad times that ever have been, haven't been able to blow the crocus out: not even the love of women. So they won't be able to blow out my wanting you, nor the little glow there is between you and me. We'll be together next year. A man has to fend and fettle for the best, and then trust in something beyond himself. You can't insure against the future, except by really believing in the best bit of you, and the power beyond it. So I believe in the little flame between us. For me now, it's the only thing in the world. I've got no friends, not inward friends. Only you.

Earlier in the novel, we encounter this exchange between the lovers:

"I would like to have all the rest of the world disappear," she said, "and live with you here."

"It won't disappear," he said.

They went almost in silence through the lovely wood. But they were together in a world of their own.

In the end, Lawrence permits them to meet the world as it is with the only armor that they have: the courage of their own tenderness. But the reader remembers, perhaps, for his comfort and theirs, the echoing promise of Clifford himself, meant with such an ironic difference and delivered in the cadences of the later T. S. Eliot, that "every parting means a meeting elsewhere. And every meeting is a new bondage."

If Lawrence's first problem in revision was to achieve maximum plausibility within the terms of his aspiration, his second problem was to achieve maximum meaning through the amplification of his symbols. If the first problem involved him primarily in the solid realities of a class situation, the second involved him in the modulations of psychic reality. The basic contrast between life-affirming and life-denying values, between "tenderness" and the "insentient iron world" is the sole subject of Lawrence's symbolic amplifications, and nearly any line of revision, no matter how minor, that we chose to follow through the three versions of his novel would demonstrate the swelling connotative richness with which this contrast is presented.

Perhaps the most obvious development over the three texts is Lawrence's increase in descriptions of both the mechanical world and the wood on the Chatterley estate, for this juxtaposition in the setting of the novel is the first symbolic form of the basic thematic contrast of the novel. It is developed until the new consciousness of the lovers is itself like a wood in flower, and the shrinking consciousness of Clifford is itself like a machine in gear.

> She was like a forest, like the dark interlacing of the oak wood, humming inaudibly with myriad unfolding buds. Meanwhile the birds of desire were asleep in the vast interlaced intricacy of her body.
>
> But Clifford's voice went on, clapping and gurgling with unusual sounds.

Hardly less obvious is Lawrence's development of two kinds of scene—the intimate sexual scenes between the lovers in the wood and the intellectual and abstract discussions (including discussions of sex) inside Wragby Hall. This development is important not only in that it dramatizes the two ways of life but more especially in that it presents symbolically two ways of conceiving life. Incidentally, one might observe that in his amplification of the Wragby scenes, Lawrence also benefits the dramatic force of his novel, for insofar as the character of Clifford undergoes changes through these revisions, the physical barrier between him and his wife, which was the only real barrier in the first version, takes on relative unimportance as the temperamental and intellectual barrier between them becomes much more important. Again, in this whole growth, one might observe that changes in characterization are likewise in symbolic support of the basic thematic contrast of the book, for as Constance, in the third version, grows into the mature woman with a consciousness like a flowering wood, so Clifford, at the very height of his industrial efficiency, sags into a horrible infantilism, and the whole relationship of Clifford and Mrs. Bolton becomes an enormously subtle trope of class relations. Finally, one might view the alterations in Lawrence's language, from text to text, as integral to his symbolic intentions, and the contrast in language between the two kinds of scene as absolutely primary to the whole esthetic purpose of the work. In the Hall, language is overintellectualized, abstract, polite, and cynical; in the wood, it is intuitive, concrete, coarse, and earthy. "We have no language for the feelings," Lawrence wrote in his essay, *The Novel and the Feelings*, "because our feelings do not even exist for us." In a novel which attempts to direct the consciousness to its source in the feelings, Lawrence necessarily employed the only language that English convention provides.

Whatever one may feel as to Lawrence's success, one cannot for a moment question the purity of his intention. Lawrence, who is perhaps the only important puritan in his generation, is eloquent and complete in his remarks on this novel in *A Propos of Lady Chatterley's Lover*. To those remarks one might add only a few observations that he made in other places. His purpose, he always asserted, was "to make the sex relation valid and precious, not shameful," and sex, he said, "means the whole of the relationship between man and woman." Given his intention, he could quite rightly say that "anybody who calls my novel a dirty sexual novel is a liar," and, "It'll infuriate *mean* people; but it will surely soothe decent ones."

With one friend, Lady Ottoline Morrell, who was apparently disturbed by the novel, he debated in calm protest:

> About *Lady C.*—you mustn't think I advocate perpetual sex. Far from it. Nothing nauseates me more than perpetual sex in and out of season. But I want, with *Lady C.*, to make an *adjustment in consciousness* to the basic physical realities. . . . God forbid that I should be taken as urging loose sex activity. There is a brief time for sex, and a long time when sex is out of place.

But when it is out of place as an activity there still should be the large and quiet space in the consciousness where it lives quiescent. Old people can have a lovely quiescent sort of sex, like apples, leaving the young quite free for *their* sort.

The basic physical realities have, as any thoughtful reading of this novel will reveal, enormous reverberations throughout the whole of life. The urgency for the modern world no less than the precise descriptive relevance of Lawrence's vision is constantly brought home to us by psychologists. Eric Fromm, for example, in *Escape from Freedom*, writes:

> The word "power" has a twofold meaning. One is the possession of power over somebody, the ability to dominate him; the other meaning is the possession of power to do something, to be able, to be potent. The latter meaning has nothing to do with domination; it expresses mastery in a sense of ability. If we speak of powerlessness we have this meaning in mind; we do not think of a person who is not able to dominate others, but of a person who is not able to do what he wants. Thus power can mean one of two things, *domination* or *potency*. Far from being identical, these two qualities are mutually exclusive. Impotence, using the term not only with regard to the sexual sphere but to all spheres of human potentialities, results in the sadistic striving for domination; to the extent to which an individual is potent, that is, able to realize his potentialities on the basis of freedom and integrity of his self, he does not need to dominate and is lacking the lust for power. Power, in the sense of domination, is the perversion of potency, just as sexual sadism is the perversion of sexual love.

In the second version of *Lady Chatterley*, Lawrence, in the poetic terms of his novel, made the same distinction when he spoke of the two "energies"—"the frictional, seething, resistant, explosive, blind sort" and "the other, forest energy, that was still and softly powerful, with tender, frail bud-tips and finger-ends full of awareness."

The pathos of Lawrence's novel arises from the tragedy of modern society. What is tragic is that we cannot feel our tragedy. We have slowly grown into a confusion of these terms, the two forms of power, and, in confusing them, we have left almost no room for the free creative functions of the man or woman who, lucky soul, possesses "integrity of self." The force of his novel probably lies in the degree of intensity with which his indictment of the world and the consequent solitude of his lovers suggest such larger meanings. Certainly it is these meanings that make these characters, in Edmund Wilson's word, "heroic," and that give them the epic quality that was felt by no less a poet than Yeats. "These two lovers," he wrote to his friend, Mrs. Shakespear—

> These two lovers the gamekeeper and his employer's wife each separated from their class by their love and by fate are poignant in their loneliness; the coarse language of the one accepted by both becomes a forlorn poetry, uniting their solitudes, something ancient humble and terrible.

Ancient, humble, and terrible. *Lady Chatterley's Lover* is all those; but it is also this: triumphant. Lawrence sings in his novel, like Stephen Spender in a short poem of twenty years later, our first and final hymn.

> Through man's love and woman's love
> Moons and tides move
> Which fuse those islands, lying face to face.
> Mixing in naked passion,
> Those who naked new life fashion
> Are themselves reborn in naked grace.

# Poste Restante: Lawrence as Traveler

POSTE RESTANTE!

So any knowing correspondent would have labeled the envelope of almost any letter he was addressing to D. H. Lawrence. *Poste restante*, or *Post-lagernd*, or *Hold until called for* —a half dozen languages, a dozen countries, but always the same admonition. How many postal clerks the world over must have observed it, wondered briefly or not wondered about the identity of the English mister, at last looked him in the face as they handed him his packet of accumulated mail, and then, once having seen this improbable addressee, thin and red and dusty and vivid, wondered about him indeed! Certainly the admonition on his letters was indispensable if the mail was by any chance to reach him. A paraphrased refrain of Lawrence's correspondence runs like this: *We are here . . . We leave to-morrow, write me at . . . Everything changed, we are still here . . . Tomorrow we may be off after all . . . We are still here . . . We are off at last, and in two days will be at . . . We have come here instead . . . We are leaving, I will send address.*

The most casual leafing through of Lawrence's letters, the unpublished together with the published, invokes at once a sense of the relentlessness of his itinerant life, and ten different leafings through would produce ten catalogues of travel in general like the following, each different from the others only as to details of place. In 1918 Lawrence wrote from England, "Frieda is pretty well—wondering what is to become of us. There are primroses in the wood and avenues of yellow hazel catkins, hanging like curtains." In 1920, from Taormina: "At the moment I feel I never want to see England again—if I

move, then further off, further off"; a few months later, from
the Abruzzi: "I feel all unstuck, as if I might drift anywhere";
and eighteen months after that, from Taormina again, "Our
great news is that we are going to Ceylon." Ceylon promptly
proved unsatisfactory: "Here we are on a ship again—somewhere in a very big blue choppy sea with flying fishes sprinting
out of the waves like winged drops, and a Catholic Spanish
priest playing Chopin at the piano—very well—and the boat
gently rolling. . . . We are going to Australia—Heaven knows
why . . ." Less than six months later, from Taos, New Mexico:
"We got here last week and since then I have been away motoring for five days into the Apache country to see an Apache
dance. It is a weird country, and I feel a great stranger still."
The stay in New Mexico and Mexico was to be long enough to
make of these places as much a home for Lawrence as any he
was to know after his native Nottinghamshire, and yet, in
1924, inevitably, he writes: "We are packing up to leave here
on Saturday. . . . It is time to go." England again, and then, in
late 1925, from Sportorno, south of Genoa, "We got here yes-
terday—it's lovely and sunny, with a blue sea, and I'm sitting
out on the balcony just above the sands, to write. Switzerland
was horrid—I don't like Switzerland anyhow—in slow rain and
snow. We shall find ourselves a villa here, I think, for the
time." The time was short, as usual, and presently they were
living outside Florence, and from there, in 1927, he wrote: "I
have put off coming to England. I just feel I don't want to
come north—feel a sort of migration instinct pushing me south
rather than north." But in the next year he wrote to Harry
Crosby from Switzerland, "I suppose we shall stay a week or
two, then perhaps move up the mountain a little higher—my
woful [sic] bronchials! How are you and where are you and
where are you going?" From the south of France less than a
year before his death, Lawrence could still write, "I wonder
where we shall ultimately settle! At the moment I feel very
undecided about everything. I shall send an address as soon
as I have one." And then in 1929 he had one, the last: "We
have got this little house on the sea for six months, so the

address is good. It is a rocky sea, very blue, with little islands way out, and mountains behind Toulon—still a touch of Homer, in the dawn—we like it—& it is good for my health . . ." But in less than six months the long, circling journey was over.

This odyssey that only death could end, as uneasy as it was adventurous, of the most restless spirit in a world that seems more stable than it is because his restlessness strides and flashes and flies across it—this odyssey, if we are to see it in its multiple and shifting details, demands an itinerary that is fixed at last in print; Lawrence's, more than any other modern literary life, should have a calendar.

The chief reason for this necessity is that all the time that Lawrence was moving, he was also writing, and the settings of his works follow upon the march of his feet. It is in no way surprising, of course, that a writer, and especially a novelist, should assimilate his travels in his works; but there is probably no other writer in literary history whose works responded so immediately to his geographical environment as Lawrence, and certainly there is no other modern writer to whose imagination "place" made such a direct and intense appeal, and in whose works, as a consequence, place usurps such a central role. Often it becomes the major character, as it were, Lawrence's arbiter, disposing of human destinies in accordance with the response that the human characters have made to itself, the non-human place. Or one may say that Lawrence's people discover their identities through their response to place, and that, having thus come upon their true selves, they mark out their fate and are able to pursue it to another place—factory or farm, city or country, north or south, England or Italy, Europe or America, death or life.

This catalogue of polarities should suggest what is in fact the one basic polarity that motivated Lawrence's attitude toward place and his use of it in his fiction. It was a polarity in which, as a child and a boy and a young man, his vision was daily educated, on which his imagination was forced to feed, and which finally formed the core of his intellectual view.

It is a polarity that founds itself on the distinction between natural place and natural place corrupted by unnatural circumstance. The early forms of the distinction are exact and simple: from his childhood on, landscape and the country were freedom, the industrial town and the city were mechanical slavery. An early novel like *Sons and Lovers* may be said to base its drama on values symbolized by the contradiction between flowers growing in the sunny fields and woods, and men working in the black depths of coal mines. In *The Intelligent Heart,* Harry T. Moore tells us that as a young schoolteacher Lawrence found only drawing and "nature study" congenial to him. The botanizing impulse throughout his poetry is evident from the start, and his novels from the beginning tended to organize themselves around the poles of place—civilized and wild, city and farm, mine and field. Industrialism, "the base forcing of human energy," almost inevitably made geography the first symbolic statement in anything he wrote, as, likewise, it was to drive him to the remote places of the world. War, the dehumanizing process of society in the destructive mass, always seemed to him a portion of the industrial process, and it is not accidental that Lawrence's hatred of industrial England seems to have reached its height during the war years when, in a letter to Catherine Carswell, he wrote, "I can't live in England. I can't stop any more. I shall die of foul inward poison. The vital atmosphere of the country is poisonous to an incredible degree: to me at least. I shall die in the fumes of their stench. But I *must* get out."

Thus, a polarity that began at the level of visual observation of place grows in the imagination into the difference between entities no smaller than war and peace themselves, and thus "place" can become a major symbol of distinction and judgment in Lawrence's great and sustained concern with "that sacrifice of life to circumstance which I most strongly disbelieve in." It was this sacrifice that made Lawrence sometimes rage in his work as it made him wander in his life, and there is merit in Mr. Moore's argument that there was an impersonality in this rage, that he was "a channel of rage . . . on behalf of life and growth." Lawrence himself said, "*I* won't have another war. . . . I am not one man, I am many, I am most."

At the outset, then, England provided the still coupled poles of place, and the earliest work invokes a kind of dream of an older England that is dying as it paints a dark picture of the new England that is death itself. The opening paragraph of Lawrence's first and very young novel, *The White Peacock*, strikes the note:

> I stood watching the shadowy fish slide through the gloom of the mill-pond. They were grey, descendants of the silvery things that had darted away from the monks, in the young days when the valley was lusty. The whole place was gathered in the musing of old age. The thick-piled trees on the far shore were too dark and sober to dally with the sun; the weeds stood crowded and motionless. Not even a little wind flickered the willows of the islets. The water lay softly, intensely still. Only the thin stream falling through the mill-race murmured to itself of the tumult of life which had once quickened the valley.

Lawrence's insights are still unanalyzed in this novel that is without any formal focus, and yet the suggestion seems clearly there in the picture of the ruined feudal farm, Strelley Mill overrun by rabbits, and in the picture of Annable, who has turned his back on society and lives by choice in primitive squalor, that the fault lies in civilization, that with the invasions of an industrial way of life and the end of that great, slow cultural convulsion which was the Industrial Revolution, human responses have split into warring dualities and have thinned out, sound human passions have been enervated as natural place has been devastated and corrupted.

In his next novel, *The Trespasser*, Lawrence presents two victims of these warring and debilitated responses and shows them fleeing from the dark city to the Isle of Wight, where, wrapped in the hot mists of the island, they make the belated attempt to heal themselves in a feverish, Wagnerian debauch that can only drive the war deeper and that kills one of them. This is a poor novel, but the major importance of the island to its structure as to its meaning foreshadows a major characteristic of the novels that are to come. It is in the next, *Sons and Lovers,* that Lawrence seems to push his initial intution about place and the opposition of kinds of place into their full cultural and psychological implications. His profound response to the natural world and his deep loathing for the unnatural things that are done to it now become articulate in this novel that opposes flower and farm and field to mine and machine and factory, creativeness and growth to mechanization and death, men and women struggling to live in wholeness to men and women determined to die in division.

It is in *Sons and Lovers,* appropriately, that we become aware of that element at the very heart of Lawrence's genius, the ability to convey the unique quality of physical experience that is so central to his power of communicating the spirit of places. This ability shows best in Lawrence's descriptions of non-human things, in his writing of animals, flowers, and grass, fish, birds, snakes—a genius for identifying and defining the individuated quality of life, the physical essences of things outside the personality, the not-me, the very *Ding an sich.* Some of Lawrence's poems, notably those in the volume called *Birds, Beasts, and Flowers,* reveal this ability in its most intense purity, but we see it flashing all through *Sons and Lovers,* in every natural description, and we begin to see how it will come to form the basis of Lawrence's sense of individual integrity and human relationships. At one point in the novel, when Paul Morel is sketching, Miriam asks, "Why do I like this so?"

> "Why *do* you?" he asked.
> "I don't know. It seems so true."
> "It's because—it's because there is scarcely any shadow in it; it's more shimmery, as if I'd painted the shimmering protoplasm in the leaves and everywhere, and not the stiffness of the shape. That seems dead to me. Only this shimmeriness is the real living. The shape is a dead crust. The shimmer is inside really."

The "shimmer," the "real living" in human individuals and relationships, in love no less than in place and natural forms,

Lawrence pursued above all else, and he was implying now, and would soon enough demonstrate explicitly, that the several varieties of reality are deeply interdependent. The corruptions of place and the corruptions of men are a single process, and with these corruptions, the "shimmer" is itself destroyed as place and men yield to the mechanical form, the "husk." Husks, chiefly, Lawrence believed, were modern men, deprived of vital connections with life outside themselves, ensnared in their partial and divisive and mechanized "personalities." To discover a place where the vital connections could be maintained intact was the motive of Lawrence's life as it increasingly becomes the motive of his heroes and heroines.

Before he had finished the final version of *Sons and Lovers,* Lawrence was already traveling and living outside England: the icy blue mountains and the black firs of Germany, the north, help to create the extraordinary, destructive atmosphere of an early story like "The Prussian Officer," and the lemon yellow air of the south, the sharp and yet somehow dreaming pathos of the first travel sketches in *Twilight in Italy.* In short, Lawrence had already started what was to grow into his vast and vastly various compendium of impressions, whether in essay, poem, story, or novel, of places all over the world, continuously supplemented until the very end of his life, and always written with his unique freshness and dash. But he was not yet, nor would he ever quite be, finished with England and the primary poles of place, together with their poles of value, that England meant to him.

The next novel, *The Rainbow,* is a slow and careful writing out of the whole long process of the transformation of the old England into the new, and a dramatization of the concomitant alteration in human functions. Perhaps no single passage in Lawrence communicates more fully his sense of the relation of place and character than that idyllic opening description of the old yeoman way of life in Britain:

> The Brangwens had lived for generations on the Marsh Farm, in the meadows where the Erewash twisted sluggishly through

alder trees, separating Derbyshire from Nottinghamshire. Two
miles away, a church-tower stood on a hill, the houses of the little
country town climbing assiduously up to it. Whenever one of the
Brangwens in the fields lifted his head from his work, he saw the
church-tower at Ilkeston in the empty sky. So that as he turned
again to the horizontal land, he was aware of something standing
above him and beyond him in the distance. . . . They felt the
rush of the sap in spring, they knew the wave which cannot
halt, but every year throws forward the seed to begetting, and,
falling back, leaves the young-born on the earth. They knew the
intercourse between heaven and earth, sunshine drawn into the
breast and bowels, the rain sucked up in the daytime, nakedness
that comes under the wind in autumn, showing the birds' nests no
longer worth hiding. Their life and interrelations were such; feeling the pulse and body of the soil, that opened to their furrow
for the grain, and became smooth and supple after their plough-
ing, and clung to their feet with a weight that pulled like desire,
lying hard and unresponsive when the crops were to be shorn
away. The young corn waved and was silken, and the lustre slid
along the limbs of the men who saw it. They took the udder of
the cows, the cows yielded milk and pulse against the hands of
men, the pulse of the blood of the teats of the cows beat into
the pulse of the men. They mounted their horses, and held life
between the grip of their knees, they harnessed their horses at
the wagon, and, with hand on the bridle-rings, drew the heaving
of the horses after their will.

From this initial condition of natural harmony between man
and his environment, the novel traces the disintegration of
both men and the environment, the dissolution of harmony, the
frenetic disintegration of life, and concludes with a visionary
challenge to new integration under still other circumstances of
place, yet to come. In *Women in Love*, a kind of sequel, we
observe two couples who are concerned to achieve the new
integration: one couple achieves it, the other does not, but the
solution no longer lies within England itself. In this novel,
England has become the full symbol of mechanization, and it is
the Continent that is opposed to it. On the Continent, the poles
of place once more become the north and the south, the icy

Alps and the golden Italian reaches of hill and flowering plain
and Renaissance city below.

> . . . as by a miracle she remembered that away beyond, below
> her, lay the dark fruitful earth, that towards the south there were
> stretches of land dark with orange trees and cypress, grey with
> olives, that ilex trees lifted wonderful plumy tufts in shadow
> against a blue sky. Miracle of miracles!—this utterly silent, frozen
> world of the mountain-tops was not universal! One might leave
> it and have done with it. One might go away.

One might go away! The theme of the life as of the works.
For two years now, while the Lawrences roamed the Italian
cities with their *pied à terre* a farmhouse clinging to the hills
over the sea at the edge of Taormina, Lawrence wrote two
more novels that played their variations on the theme. In *The
Lost Girl*, the heroine escapes the respectable stultifications of
commercialized Nottinghamshire by following an Italian peasant into the hard life of the Abruzzi. The hero of *Aaron's Rod*
leaves England for wanderings in Italy that are based on
Lawrence's own, seeking his fulfillment in place, and the work
is nearly as much travel book as it is novel. In the same period,
Lawrence produced his second genuine travel book, *Sea and
Sardinia*. As in *Twilight in Italy* he had seen industrial mechanization overcoming feudal Italy, so in his study of the vividly
dark island, so long isolated from the culture of continental
Europe, he sees Sardinia after it has been drawn into the
despoiling tensions of continental war. Place, in Lawrence's
account, is seldom presented without its cultural and even
sociological implications as Lawrence perceives them, and
these support his vivid descriptive gifts with an informal intellectual dimension that, even when, as in *Sea and Sardinia*,
he is writing with extreme casualness, gives them a permanent
seriousness. Or, if the implications are not directly cultural and
sociological, they are psychological, as in that most intense
evocation of all the places that he drew, the Sicilian landscape
in the story, "Sun," in which, through the sustained pressure of
an almost ferocious sensuosity, ritualistic rebirth is nearly accomplished; and accomplished through the power of place.

*Aaron's Rod* was a novel with political overtones: wandering through Italy, Aaron is also looking for a spiritual leader to whom he can submit his wounded individuality and be healed. Place becomes the political arena, and as, now, the Lawrencean wanderings themselves are flung out over wider areas in the world, travel and the search for spiritual rest are explicitly equated, in the work as in the life. The Australian novel, *Kangaroo,* which follows on the Sicilian period, is a novel of ideas that debates political alternatives for its Lawrencean hero, Richard Lovat Somers. On the raw edge of the world, at once sordid and primitive, corrupt in its abrupt modernity and at the same time inspiring in its continuity with a past forever unawakened, Australia is both exhilarating and terrifying to its hero, as Lawrence makes it to us. The actualization of the dark spirit of this continent on the underside of the world is as solid as the psychological and political judgments are ambiguous, and the spiritually reductive terrors of the one together with the elusive emotional and intellectual demands of the other give Somers no opportunity for genuine choice. He abandons both Australia and the socialist-fascist alternative, and, like Lawrence, leaves for America, where he hopes to find a less disturbing place and a more plausible choice. "One walks away to another place," Lawrence had written to Aldous Huxley seven or eight years earlier, "and life begins anew." And he had added—ominously, prophetically—"But it is a midge's life."

In the New Mexico–Mexico period that follows, the landscape and the cultures and the place-spirit all change, but the pattern of the work remains constant. In his third travel book, *Mornings in Mexico,* Lawrence gives us again his most explicit understanding of the full quality of the new world that absorbs him. In the fiction, place as such becomes more powerful than it has ever been as the arbiter of human fortunes. *St. Mawr* is the story of two Englishwomen, a mother and a daughter, who come to New Mexico to discover a life that will free them from the frustrating triviality of their social past, and in the end the daughter submits to the wild landscape itself, beyond humanity.

There's something else for me, mother. There's something else even that loves me and wants me. I can't tell you what it is. It's a spirit. And it's here, on this ranch. It's here, in this landscape. It's something more real to me than men are, and it soothes me, and it holds me up. I don't know what it is, definitely. It's something wild, that will hurt me sometimes and will wear me down sometimes. I know it. But it's something big, bigger than men, bigger than people, bigger than religion. It's something to do with wild America. And it's something to do with me. It's a mission to keep myself for the spirit that is wild, and has waited so long here: even waited for such as me. Now I've come! Now I'm here. Now I am where I want to be: with the spirit that wants me.—And that's how it is.

In the cruelly beautiful novelette, "The Princess," a frozen New England virgin makes a ritual journey, half-fearful, half-wishful, over New Mexican mountains, the symbolic barriers, to her destruction. In "The Woman Who Rode Away," which is a fable rather than a story and the center of which is, literally now, a ritual of sacrifice, a woman yields up her consciousness with her life to the consciousness and the life of the Indians whose religion is continuous with the spirit of the place to which she has come. In each, place triumphs.

*The Plumed Serpent,* the most ambitious work of this period, alters this pattern in some degree. Nowhere in the length and breadth of his work does Lawrence's prose communicate more fully or more glamorously the physical character of his setting, in all its rich singularity, than in this long novel, yet in the end, in part at least, the human will is more powerful than the spirit of the place. Once more the story concerns a European woman in search of her soul. Lawrence himself is still involved in the political ideas of the great leader that had occupied him in two previous novels. In the atmosphere of Mexican political life, these ideas find a more plausible embodiment than they have previously had, and the attempt of Lawrence's two leaders to replace the imposed Christian god and the Christian saints with the primitive Aztec gods, and to work this effort into the fabric of a larger political program, hardly seems fantastic. But for the European woman, Kate Leslie, as finally, for Lawrence, the solution is no solution at all. For that place and for those people who are native to it, some such challenge to the corruptions of Western civilization may be inevitable and even right; but it will solve nothing for the woman from Ireland, even less for the searching miner's son from Nottinghamshire. The future of Kate Leslie is not clear, either in place or time. For Lawrence, the future is clearly not in politics; he will settle for "tenderness," for the individual human relationship, for that whole lovely freedom in self-responsible conduct that was included in his sense of the word *insouciance*, a word he came to love above most others. And so—"It is time to go."

The circle nearly closes. It is time to go to Nottinghamshire. Two books come out of this otherwise ill-fated return. The first, *The Virgin and the Gypsy*, a kind of trial-run for the other, *Lady Chatterley's Lover*, sweeps out the old England with a flood, and gives the virgin life on the crest of it. It is a simple and unfinished story published posthumously, and it is not very interesting apart from the final novel, in which the whole judgment on England is at last delivered. The judgment is not very different from, only more maddened than, the judgment that was delivered in such an earlier novel as *Women in Love* or in such an elegy upon a dead culture as the story, "England, My England." We are back at the primary, coupled poles as, in *Lady Chatterley's Lover*, they are presented together again, coupled, the fulfilling and the destroying place.

The last writing was done in Italy, at the Villa Mirenda, a farmhouse outside Florence. There were not many places where even a simple insouciance was possible, but this was one where for a time it was.

There at the Mirenda, Frieda Lawrence recalled, Lawrence would go every morning into the nearby woods, settle himself next to a spring where a saint once meditated, look at the flowers and the birds at his feet, and remember that other place, England, while he wrote.

At the very end, he took this world of places that he had known into another world where the implications of "place" become more general than those immediately of this world. *The Man Who Died* is a fable of the resurrection; it is set in a hot Mediterranean country; the spirit becomes flesh, is connected with the beauties and pressures of place, as of society and of sex. Yet it is a fable—in the major sense, set in a place out of this world. *Etruscan Places*, which may be called the last of the travel books, is a re-creation in Lawrence's terms of an ideal society, colorful and brave and creative and, above all, insouciant. Stimulated by the wonderfully vivid paintings in tombs such as those at Tarquinia, Lawrence created in his Etruscan "place" the most living of all the societies that he had drawn. And the Etruscans, Lawrence discovered, put a little bronze ship of death on the tomb of their dead, symbol of the vessel that would carry them on further travels. And now mines disappear, machines disappear, science disappears, England disappears: only wind and sea and sails remain. Only that which is finally natural, only one last place . . .

> Now it is autumn and the falling fruit
> and the long journey towards oblivion.
>
> The apples falling like great drops of dew
> to bruise themselves an exit from themselves.
>
> And it is time to go, to bid farewell
> to one's own self, and find an exit
> from the fallen self.
>
> Have you built your ship of death, O have you?
> O build your ship of death, for you will need it.

How curious! And how to explain it, Lawrence's restlessness, if one had the temerity! In the last year of his life, he wrote to the Richard Aldingtons in the old, perpetual vein:

> . . . in the late autumn, let's really go somewhere. Would you go to Egypt if we went? We might find some way of doing it cheap —& there *are* quite nice modest pensions in Cairo. Let's go to Egypt in November, en quatre—& go sometimes & see the Dobrees, & go up the Nile and look at the desert and perhaps get

shot in Khartoum like General Gordon.—Frieda of course, woman-
like, pines for more islands—Majorca & Minorca—but I'm not keen
on islands. The other thing is the Mediterranean shore of Spain.
I'd like to go to Madrid to the Prado. But I *don't* want to stay in
the Mirenda this winter. . . . Have you got lots of flowers, beans
& carrots. We have phlox in a tiny fenced garden, & salad & a few
turnips & red currrants.

And only a month or two before his death he wrote to the
Huxleys from that last villa, less than a *pied à terre*, "Beau
Soleil" at Bandol,

> I am thankful for this unredeemedly modern and small Beau
> Soleil, taken for 6 months and no more, and am thankful to God
> to escape anything like a permanency. "Better fifty years of
> Europe than a cycle of Cathay." Well, I've had nearly fifty years
> of Europe, so I should rather try the cycle of Cathay.

The question forces itself: what, up to the bitter black end,
impelled him? But no answer comes; it lies in the still undefined history and character of our times.

There were superficial motives, of course. First, and for a
long time, Lawrence moved about because he was continually
looking for a place where he might conceivably establish that
ideal community, Rananim, as it was to be called, for which
he yearned over many years, that pre-Jeffersonian community
of congenial and creative and cooperative persons (many were
called but few chosen) who would make their own society, outside the destructive pressures of society at large. Second, Lawrence moved because of his health—first south, then north; to
the desert, then up into the mountains—always hoping for a
climate in which his bleeding lungs would heal, even while
he defied medical opinion and chose the place where he
thought that his spirit might find rest.

> I've been in bed this last week with bronchial haemorrhages—
> due, radically, to chagrin—though I was born bronchial—born in
> chagrin, too. But I'm better—shaky—shaky—and we're going to
> Austria tomorrow, D.V.—whoever D. may be—to the mountains.
> . . . Well here we are—got through on Thursday night in the

wagon-lit—not too tired and no bad consequences. I feel already much better. What with cool air, *a cool bed,* cool mountain water —it's like a new life. I never *would* have got well, down there in that heat in Tuscany. . . . It is such a mercy to be able to breathe and move. I take little walks to the country—and we sit by the river—the Drave—in the little town, under the clipped trees, very 18th-century German—Werther period. The river comes from the ice, and is very full and swift and pale and silent. It rather fascinates me . . .

And third, he moved about because he had an inexhaustible belief that somewhere a place would present itself that was in every way better than any other place he had known. In his writing, this place is finally discovered to be outside society but it is conceived in all of the most glowing colors of the natural world. Yet the last sentence of one of his last letters dies with his breath: "This place no good." It was time to move again.

He found no place where he could stay for long. But how much more beautiful and exciting and desirable, because of his vividly hopeful explorations of it, is this place where all the rest of us still are!

# Elmer Gantry: The Method of Half-Truths

LET US BEGIN with some quotations that are concerned with the conception of the novel as a social instrument. The two conceptions are opposed, but the author of each is led by his conception to conclude that because of it the novel is the most important literary form in the modern world, and *for* the modern world. The first is from D. H. Lawrence, and it is, I believe, a unique conception:

> It is the way our sympathy flows and recoils that really determines our lives. And here lies the vast importance of the novel, properly handled. It can inform and lead into new places the flow of our sympathetic consciousness, and it can lead our sympathy away in recoil from things gone dead. Therefore, the novel, properly handled, can reveal the most secret places of life: for it is in the *passional* secret places of life, above all, that the tide of sensitive awareness needs to ebb and flow, cleansing and freshening.
>
> But the novel, like gossip, can also excite spurious sympathies and recoils, mechanical and deadening to the psyche. The novel can glorify the most corrupt feelings, so long as they are *conventionally* "pure." Then the novel, like gossip, becomes at last vicious, and, like gossip, all the more vicious because it is always ostensibly on the side of the angels.

Lawrence's conception implies a novel that will admit us directly into the life-affirming activities of the integrated consciousness of his own ideal man; a novel that, concerned with the formed individual consciousness, re-forms ours; a novel that is not about society or the social character but that is ultimately indispensable to the health of both. We know whose

fiction he has in mind; we know, too, with what exasperation
he achieved the first term of his exalted ambition, the writing
itself, and how impossible it is to achieve the second, the
therapy.

Our second quotation is a commonplace in the annals of
American naturalism, and we could find it, in substance, in any
of a dozen writers. Frank Norris will serve. I quote first from
his essay, "The Responsibilities of the Novelist," an attack on
what he calls "lying novels," novels of sentiment and romance.

> Today is the day of the novel. In no other day and by no other
> vehicle is contemporaneous life so adequately expressed; and the
> critics of the twenty-second century, reviewing our times, striving
> to reconstruct our civilization, will look not to the painters, not
> to the architects nor dramatists, but to the novelists to find our
> idiosyncrasy. . . . If the novel . . . is popular it is popular with
> a reason, a vital, inherent reason; that is to say, it is essential . . .
> it is an instrument, a tool, a weapon, a vehicle. Public opinion is
> made no one can say how, by infinitesimal accretions, by a multi-
> tude of minutest elements. Lying novels, surely in this day and
> age of indiscriminate reading, contribute to this more than all
> other influences of present-day activity . . . The People have a
> right to the Truth as they have a right to life, liberty and the pur-
> suit of happiness. It is *not* right that they be exploited and de-
> ceived with false views of life, false characters, false sentiment,
> false morality, false history, false philosophy, false emotions,
> false heroism, false notions of self-sacrifice, false views of religion,
> of duty, of conduct and of manners.

And where do we find the truth-telling novel? In the novel
with a "purpose," as it is discussed in Norris's essay of that
name.

> Every novel must do one of three things—it must (1) tell some-
> thing, (2) show something, or (3) prove something. Some novels
> do all three of these. . . . The third, and what we hold to be the
> best class, proves something, draws conclusions from a whole
> congeries of forces, social tendencies, race impulses, devotes itself
> not to a study of men but of man. . . . Take this element from
> fiction, take from it the power and opportunity to prove that

injustice, crime and inequality do exist, and what is left? Just the amusing novels, the novels that entertain . . . the modern novel . . . may be a flippant paper-covered thing of swords and cloaks, to be carried on a railway journey and to be thrown out the window when read, together with the sucked oranges and peanut shells. Or it may be a great force, that works together with the pulpit and the universities for the good of the people, fearlessly proving that power is abused, that the strong grind the faces of the weak, that an evil tree is still growing in the midst of the garden, that undoing follows hard upon righteousness, that the course of Empire is not yet finished, and that the races of men have yet to work out their destiny in those great and terrible movements that crush and grind and rend asunder the pillars of the houses of the nation.

It is within this somewhat crude conception of "the novel with a purpose" that we are accustomed to place the novels that brought Sinclair Lewis his fame. Lewis himself was not content to have his work thus located. In a heavily playful refutation of the charge that he was "a raging reformer, an embittered satirist, a realist dreary as cold gravy," he said:

> I should have thought Brother Lewis was essentially a story-teller—just as naïve, excited, unselfconscious as the Arab story-tellers about the caravan fires seven hundred years ago, or as O. Henry in a hotel room on Twenty-third Street furiously turning out tales for dinner and red-ink money. In his stories Lewis does not happen to be amused only by the sea or by midnight encounters on the Avenue, but oftener by the adventure of the soul in religion and patriotism and social climbing. But they are essentially stories just the same.

The fact is that the novels we have in mind are not "essentially stories," that the "story" element is secondary and quite feebly managed; and that if they are not quite the "novel with a purpose" as Norris conceived it—motivated by an outraged sense of justice and executed with naturalistic fullness—their impulse is plainly the exposition of social folly. H. L. Mencken, some years after he had ceased to be a well-known literary critic, takes us to the center of Lewis's imaginative uniqueness

when, in 1945, he congratulates him on a poor novel called
*Cass Timberlane,* an exposure of the corruptions of marriage
in the middle class:

> I am not going to tell you that "Cass Timberlane" is com-
> parable to "Babbitt" or "Elmer Gantry" (all except the last
> 30,000 words, which you wrote in a state of liquor), but it seems
> to me to be the best thing you have done, and by long odds, since
> "Dodsworth." . . . In brief, a well-planned and well-executed
> book, with a fine surface. . . . The country swarms with subjects
> for your future researches. You did the vermin of the Coolidge
> era, but those of the Roosevelt and post-Roosevelt eras are still
> open—the rich radical, the bogus expert, the numskull news-
> paper proprietor (or editor), the career-jobholder, the lady
> publicist, the crooked (or, more usually, idiotic) labor leader,
> the press-agent, and so on. This, I believe, is your job, and you
> have been neglecting it long enough. There are plenty of writers
> of love stories and Freudian documents, though not many as good
> at it as you are, but there is only one real anatomist of the Amer-
> ican Kultur. I think it stinks, but whether it stinks or not is
> immaterial. It deserves to be done as you alone can do it.

The catalogue of social types is the significant item in this
letter. Each of these, with its implied section of social life in
the United States, could have become a Lewis novel. Some
already had. With Lewis, the subject, the social section, always came first; systematic research, sometimes conducted by
research assistants and carrying Lewis himself into "the field"
like any cultural anthropologist, followed; the story came last,
devised to carry home and usually limping under the burden
of data. If the result in some ways filled the Norris prescription for a novel of the contemporary social character, it was
still by no means a naturalistic product; at the same time,
precisely what was "new" in it was what D. H. Lawrence
called "dead," and he would have howled in outrage at the
complacency with which Lewis asserted that his stories described "the adventure of the soul in religion and patriotism."
For in the world of Sinclair Lewis there is no soul, and if a
soul were introduced into it, it would die on the instant.

The world of Sinclair Lewis rests upon two observations:
the standardization of manners in a business culture, and the
stultification of morals under middle-class convention. All his
critical observations are marshaled in support of these proposi-
tions, and his portrait of the middle class rests entirely upon
them. The proliferation of detail within these observations
gives them an apparent breadth, and his easy familiarity with
the manners—in Robert Cantwell's catalogue—of

> the small towns and square cities, the real-estate developments
> and restricted residential areas, the small business men, the coun-
> try doctors, the religious fakers, the clubwomen, the county office-
> holders, the village atheists and single-taxers, the schoolteachers,
> librarians, the windbags of the lower income groups, the crazy
> professors and the maddened, hyperthyroid, high-pressure sales-
> men—the main types of middle-class and lower-middle-class pro-
> vincial society, conspicuous now because he has identified them
> so thoroughly

—all this gives his observations an apparent richness and variety; yet in fact it is all there in support of the extremely limited
program. Similarly, his world is broken into many social sections—the small town, business ethics, medical science, evan-
gelical religion, marriage, the career woman, professional
philanthropy—and this is to name only those that come most
immediately to mind; but every section rests, again, on one or
both of the two primary principles. This is an extremely narrow and intellectually feeble perspective, but given the particular character of Lewis's achievement, its force paradoxically
rests upon its narrowness.

For its narrowness projects a very sharply defined image.
"Life dehumanized by indifference or enmity to all human
values—that is the keynote of both Gopher Prairie and Zenith,"
wrote T. K. Whipple nearly thirty years ago in what remains
one of the very few critical essays on Lewis.

> . . . nowhere does this animosity show itself more plainly than in
> hostility to truth and art. The creed of both towns is the philoso-
> phy of boosting, a hollow optimism and false cheeriness which
> leads directly to hypocrisy, as in making believe that business

knavery is social service. Toward ideas likely to break this bubble of pretense the people are bitterly opposed; toward new ideas they are lazily contemptuous; toward other ideas they are apathetic . . . intellectually both are cities of the dead, and in both, the dead are resolved that no one shall live.

Dead in the senses as they are in intellect and the affections, these people are horrible ciphers, empty of personality or individual consciousness, rigidly controlled by set social responses; and yet, being dead, together they do not form a society in any real sense, but only a group, a group which at once controls them and protects them from the horrors of their own emptiness. Their group activities, whether as families, as clubs, as friends, are travesties of that human interchange that makes for meaningful social activities: conversation is buffoonery, affection is noise, gaiety is pretense, business is brutal rush, religion is blasphemy. The end result is vacant social types in a nonsocial world. Quite brilliantly T. K. Whipple made and Maxwell Geismar developed the observation that *Babbitt* is set in Hell: "it is almost a perfectly conceived poetic vision of a perfectly . . . standardized hinterland."

Poetic, that is to say, in the sense that it *is* visionary, *not* documentary, so that nothing is either a lie or the truth. These are categories that have no relevance. Collecting his massive accumulations of social data with the naturalist's compulsiveness, Lewis creates a visual world and a world of manners that appear to be absolutely solid, absolutely concrete; but all that accumulation of data has from the outset been made to submit so severely to the selective strictures of two highly limited and limiting observations that what emerges in fact is an image and a criticism of middle-class society and not in the least a representation of it. A fragment blown into the proportions of the whole, it is a fantastic world dominated by monstrous parodies of human nature. Elmer Gantry, in his hypocrisy and self-deception, his brutal cruelty and fearful faith, his shallow optimism and wretched betrayals, his almost automatic identification of salvation and economic success, his loathing of all thought, his hatred of all human difference, his incapacity for any feelings but lust and fear and self-interest: in all this he carries to its extreme Sinclair Lewis's conception of the middle-class character. Both the paradox and the secret of such a creation lie in the fact that, except for the power of observation, the sensibility of the creator has few resources beyond those of the thing created, that Lewis's own intellectual and moral framework, and the framework of feeling, is extremely narrow, hardly wider than the material it contains. And the power of the creation, I would insist, lies in these limitations.

The limitations are so apparent that we need do little more than name them. As his conception of middle-class society is fragmentary, so his sense of history is vestigial. The characteristic widening of his shutter over social space does not qualify or alter the narrow social conception:

> Eight thousand radio-owners listening to Elmer Gantry—
> A bootlegger in his flat, coat off, exposing his pink silk shirt, his feet up on the table. . . . The house of a small-town doctor, with the neighbors come in to listen—the drugstore man, his fat wife, the bearded superintendent of schools. . . . Mrs. Sherman Reeves of Royal Ridge, wife of one of the richest young men in Zenith, listening in a black-and-gold dressing-gown, while she smoked a cigarette. . . . The captain of a schooner, out on Lake Michigan, hundreds of miles away, listening in his cabin. . . . The wife of a farmer in an Indiana valley, listening while her husband read the Sears-Roebuck catalogue and sniffed. . . . A retired railway conductor, very feeble, very religious. . . . A Catholic priest, in a hospital, chuckling a little. . . . A spinster school-teacher, mad with loneliness, worshiping Dr. Gantry's virile voice. . . . Forty people gathered in a country church too poor to have a pastor. . . . A stock actor in his dressing-room, fagged with an all-night rehearsal.
> All of them listening to the Rev. Dr. Elmer Gantry as he shouted . . .

Similarly, the characteristic extensions into time do not enrich the sense of history but merely provide broadly ironic contrasts that are analogically meaningless, both in the drama and in the intellectual framework:

So Elmer came, though tardily, to the Great Idea which was to revolutionize his life and bring him eternal and splendid fame.

That shabby Corsican artillery lieutenant and author, Bonaparte, first conceiving that he might be the ruler of Europe—Darwin seeing dimly the scheme of evolution—Paolo realizing that all of life was nothing but an irradiation of Francesca—Newton pondering on the falling apple—Paul of Tarsus comprehending that a certain small Jewish sect might be the new religion of the doubting Greeks and Romans—Keats beginning to write "The Eve of St. Agnes"—none of these men, transformed by a Great Idea from mediocrity to genius, was more remarkable than Elmer Gantry of Paris, Kansas, when he beheld the purpose for which the heavenly powers had been training him.

The characters of this world are aware of no tradition within which their lives are located; behind them lies no history except for the faintly heroic figure of a pioneer whose sacrifice their lives have made meaningless. And if the seat of this deficiency is in the imagination of the author, its result is the captive blankness of their existence, which is a large element in the egregious parody.

From an early if not very forcibly held socialist position, Sinclair Lewis, in his best novels, swung round to the antidemocratic views of H. L. Mencken; yet paradoxically, he had no values of his own (not even Mencken's vague Nietzscheanism) except those of the middle class that both were lampooning. The ambition to find in the East what is not available in the Midwest is always exposed as false; and when "the East" is pushed on to mean Europe, the same evaluation is made. The Midwest is shown as hopelessly narrow, yet somehow it is shown finally as the only sensible place to choose. Aristocrats are suspect if not phony; workmen tend to become shiftless mongrels; intellectuals and artists are irresponsible bohemians. The picture of middle-class provincialism is framed by a middle-class provincial view. "Russian Jews in London clothes," Lewis wrote in *Dodsworth*, "going to Italian restaurants with Greek waiters and African music." And again, if the deficiency in a sense of tradition and of history is the author's own, it contributes to the force of his image, for it permits his characters no escape. Always excepting the figures of Drs. Gottlieb and Arrowsmith, with their dedication to pure science, the dissident figures in Lewis's novels, the critics of this society, are permitted no realizable values toward which they or that society may aspire.

The feeblest characters in *Main Street,* and those most quickly routed, are the discontented. Carol Kennicott's vaporous values are the equivalent of that deeply sentimental strain in the author that led him as a young man to write in imitation of the early Tennyson and, as a man of over fifty, to say that "he, who has been labeled a 'satirist' and a 'realist,' is actually a romantic medievalist of the most incurable sort." Thus Carol:

> . . . a volume of Yeats on her knees. . . . Instantly she was released from the homely comfort of a prairie town. She was in the world of lonely things—the flutter of twilight linnets, the aching call of gulls along a shore to which the netted foam crept out of darkness, the island of Aengus and the elder gods and the eternal glories that never were, tall kings and women girdled with crusted gold, the woeful incessant chanting . . .

Thus the Babbitt who momentarily challenges Zenith does not so much present us with a scale of humane values that we can oppose to the inhumanity of the environment, as he presents us with all the insecurity on which Babbittry, or the environment, rests. The fact that there is never any real opposition of substantial values to "convention," or false values (as there is never any truly individual character to resist the social types), is what makes Lewis's world so blank and limits so drastically his social realism. In *Elmer Gantry* we do not have even these fitful glimmerings in the realm of reverie. This is a world of total death, of social monsters without shadow. It is, in my view and on rereading, the purest Lewis.

The publication of *Elmer Gantry* early in 1927 was not so much a literary event as it was a public scandal, and from the beginning, therefore, excitement took the place of criticism.

Preceded by the well-publicized "Strike me dead" episode, it called forth remarks like this from William Allen White: "Sinclair Lewis stood in the pulpit of a Kansas City church last spring and defied God to strike him dead. So far as Sinclair Lewis, the artist, is concerned in the book 'Elmer Gantry,' God took him at his word." Municipal bans extended from Kansas City to Camden; from Boston to Glasgow. Its initial printing of 140,000 copies was probably the largest to that date of any book in history, and the whole emphasis of the promotion campaign was on the *size* of the enterprise: the book was advertised on billboards; a publicity release from the publishers was headed "What it Means to Manufacture the First Edition of *Elmer Gantry*," and provided statistics on amounts of paper, thread, glue, board, cloth, and ink, both black and orange— black for the text, orange for the cover. (But then, as Lewis tells us in the novel, "Elmer was ever a lover of quantity.") In April of 1927, in a resolution supporting the Anti-Saloon League of New York State, the Rev. Dr. Otho F. Bartholow declared at the annual session of the New York East Conference, "The Methodist Church is cordially hated, not only by the class represented by Mr. Sinclair Lewis and the rum organizations, but also by every evil organization of every kind whatsoever," while, two weeks later, the graduating class of New York University voted Sinclair Lewis its favorite author. A news item in an Ohio newspaper ran as follows:

> Trouble in the home of Leo Roberts, general manager of the Roberts Coal and Supply Company, began when his wife brought home a copy of "Elmer Gantry" and he burned it as undesirable reading matter, according to Mrs. Roberts at a hearing Wednesday before Judge Bostwick of Probate Court, when Roberts was ordered to a private sanitarium for a short rest, after his wife, Mrs. Margaret Roberts, 1671 Franklin Park South, charged him with lunacy.

Literary appraisal seems to have been a quite secondary matter. Yet, if only because the images that Lewis projected came to play such a powerful role in the imagination both of America and of Europe, it is worth our time to analyze the method or lack of method that established them. Leslie Fiedler wrote as follows:

> . . . no one has succeeded since the age of Sinclair Lewis and Sherwood Anderson in seeing an actual American small town or a living member of the Kiwanis club. The gross pathos of Anderson or the journalistic thinness of Lewis is beside the point; for all of us, the real facts of experience have been replaced by Winesburg, Ohio and by Babbitt; myth or platitude, we have invented nothing to replace them.

How, then, did *he* invent them? What props up and holds in place that terrifying buffoon, Elmer Gantry—that "gladiator laughing at the comic distortion of his wounded opponent," as he sees himself; that "barytone solo turned into portly flesh," as Lewis shows him to us?

The primary fact in Lewis's method is the absence of conflict between genuine orders of value, and in *Elmer Gantry* this fact emerges most starkly.

In *Elmer Gantry*, any drama exists in the immediate victory of the worst over the weakest (who are the best), or in the conflict of the bad to survive among the worst: all is corrupt. In this extraordinarily full account of every form of religious decay, nothing is missing except all religion and all humanity. As there are no impediments to Elmer's barbarous rise from country boob to influential preacher, so there are no qualifications of the image of barbarity. On the very fringes of the narrative, among his scores of characters, Lewis permits a few shadowy figures of good to appear—Bruno Zechlin and Jim Lefferts, the amiable skeptics who are routed before they are permitted to enter the action; Andrew Pengilly, a humane preacher who asks the most striking question in the novel ("Mr. Gantry, why don't you believe in God?") but who himself no more enters the conflict than his question enters the intellectual context; and finally, Frank Shallard, who does come and go in the story, an honest human being, but one so weak that he presents no challenge to Elmer, serves only to illustrate the ruthlessness of Elmer's power.

In the novel, values can be realized only in action, and the action of *Elmer Gantry* is an entirely one-way affair. This is the inevitable consequence in structure of Lewis's method. Like most of Lewis's novels, *Elmer Gantry* is a loosely episodic chronicle, which suggests at once that there will be no sustained pressure of plot, no primary conflict about which all the action is organized and in which value will achieve a complex definition or in which the dramatization of at least two orders of value that conflict implies will be brought about. The chronicle breaks down into three large parts, each pretty nearly independent of the others. In each event Elmer's progress is colored and in two of them threatened by his relation with a woman, but from each Elmer emerges triumphant. The first part takes us through his Baptist education, his ordination, his first pulpit, and his escape from Lulu; the second takes us through his career as an evangelist with the fantastic Sharon Falconer; the third takes us through his experience of New Thought and his rise in Methodism, together with the decline of his marriage to Cleo and his escape from Hettie, who threatens to bring him to public ruin but who is herself routed as, in the final sentence, Elmer promises that "We shall yet make these United States a moral nation."

It should not be supposed that the frank prominence in *Elmer Gantry* of sexual appetite—a rare enough element in a Lewis novel—or the fact that it several times seems to threaten Elmer's otherwise unimpeded success, in any way provides the kind of dramatized counterpoint on the absence of which we are remarking, or that it in any way serves to introduce an element of human tenderness that qualifies Elmer's brutal nakedness. On the contrary, it is an integral part of his inhumanity and an integral part of the inhumanity of the religious environment within which he exists. Indeed, of all the forms of relationship that the novel presents, the sexual relation is most undilutedly brutish, and it is perhaps the chief element in that animus of revulsion that motivates the creation of this cloacal world and upon which I shall presently comment. Finally, its identification with the quality of Elmer's re-

ligious activity is made explicit in the climactically phantasma-
goric scene in which Sharon capitulates to Elmer before an
altar where she associates herself, in a ritual invocation, with
all goddesses of fertility.

"It is the hour! Blessed Virgin, Mother Hera, Mother Frigga,
Mother Ishtar, Mother Isis, dread Mother Astarte of the weaving
arms, it is thy priestess, it is she who after the blind centuries and
the groping years shall make it known to the world that ye are
one, and that in me are ye all revealed, and that in this revelation shall come peace and wisdom universal, the secret of the
spheres and the pit of understanding. Ye who have leaned over
me and on my lips pressed your immortal fingers, take this my
brother to your bosoms, open his eyes, release his pinioned spirit,
make him as the gods, that with me he may carry the revelation
for which a thousand thousand grievous years the world has
panted. . . .

"Ye veiled ones and ye bright ones—from caves forgotten, the
peaks of the future, the clanging today—join in me, lift up, receive
him, dread nameless ones; yea, lift us then, mystery on mystery,
sphere above sphere, dominion on dominion, to the very throne!

". . . O mystical rose, O lily most admirable, O wondrous
union; O St. Anna, Mother Immaculate, Demeter, Mother Benefi-
cent, Lakshmi, Mother Most Shining; behold, I am his and he
is yours and ye are mine!"

The extravagant absurdity of this scene is underlined by the
absence in it of any candid recognition of human need or of
human fulfillment. The travesty that it makes of both the sexual
and the religious experience is of course to be associated with
the temper of orgiastic evangelism with which the book is full.
Dramatically, however, it must be associated with such an
earlier scene, as homely as this one is horrendous, in which a
deaf old retired preacher and his wife are going to bed after
fifty years of marriage, and the whole of that experience of
fifty years is equated with an "old hoss."

They were nodding on either side of a radiator unheated for
months.

"All right, Emmy," piped the ancient.

"Say, Papa—Tell me: I've been thinking: If you were just a young man today would you go into the ministry?"

"Course I would! What an idea! Most glorious vocation young man could have. Idea! G'night, Emmy!"

But as his ancient wife sighingly removed her corsets, she complained, "Don't know as you would or not—if *I* was married to you—which ain't any too certain, a second time—and if I had anything to say about it!"

"Which *is* certain! Don't be foolish. Course I would."

"I don't know. Fifty years I had of it, and I never did get so I wa'n't just mad clear through when the ladies of the church came poking around, criticizing me for every little tidy I put on the chairs, and talking something terrible if I had a bonnet or a shawl that was the least mite tasty. ' 'Twant suitable for a minister's wife.' Drat 'em! And I always did like a bonnet with some nice bright colors. Oh, I've done a right smart of thinking about it. You always were a powerful preacher, but's I've told you—"

"You have!"

"—I never could make out how, if when you were in the pulpit you really knew so much about all these high and mighty and mysterious things, how it was when you got home you never knew enough, and you never could learn enough, to find the hammer or make a nice piece of cornbread or add up a column of figures twice alike or find Oberammergau on the map of Austria!"

"Germany, woman! I'm sleepy!"

"And all these years of having to pretend to be so good when we were just common folks all the time! Ain't you glad you can just be simple folks now?"

"Maybe it is restful. But that's not saying I wouldn't do it over again." The old man ruminated a long while. "I think I would. Anyway, no use discouraging these young people from entering the ministry. Somebody got to preach the gospel truth, ain't they?"

"I suppose so. Oh, dear. Fifty years since I married a preacher! And if I could still only be sure about the virgin birth! Now don't you go explaining! Laws, the number of times you've explained! I know it's true—it's in the Bible. If I could only *believe* it! But—

"I would of liked to had you try your hand at politics. If I

could of been, just once, to a senator's house, to a banquet or
something, just once, in a nice bright red dress with gold slippers,
I'd of been willing to go back to alpaca and scrubbing floors and
listening to you rehearsing your sermons, out in the stable, to that
old mare we had for so many years—oh, laws, how long is it she's
been dead now? Must be—yes, it's twenty-seven years—

"Why is it that it's only in religion that the things you got to
believe are agin all experience? Now drat it, don't you go and
quote that 'I believe because it *is* impossible' thing at me again!
Believe because it's impossible! Huh! Just like a minister!

"Oh, dear, I hope I don't live long enough to lose my faith.
Seems like the older I get, the less I'm excited over all these
preachers that talk about hell only they never saw it.

"Twenty-seven years! And we had that old hoss so long before
that. My how she could kick— Busted that buggy—"

They were both asleep.

The two scenes, the extravagantly repulsive and the devastatingly barren, supplement one another; they represent the extremes of the nightmare image of a world that, totally empty
of human value, monstrously, and without relief, parodies the
reality.

If the narrative method of loose chronicle, without sustained
dramatic conflict, is the primary means to this end, certain
orders of technical detail contribute no less and seem to me
entirely consistent with the imagination that is working through
the narrative method. It has been complained, for example,
that there is a coarsening of Lewis's style in this novel, and
that his view of the hinterland threatens to fall into a kind of
cracker-barrel stereotype. Both charges are true, but it can be
argued that both qualities make possible the kind of effect we
are trying to describe. *Elmer Gantry* is the noisiest novel in
American literature, the most *braying, guffawing, belching*
novel that we have, and it is its prose that sets this uproar
going; if we are to have a novel filled with jackasses and
jackals, let them, by all means, bray and guffaw. On the same
grounds, I would defend the "By crackee, by jiminy" crudities
of the physical environment within which this noise goes on,

this imbecilic articulateness, only pointing out in addition that
Lewis's old ability to invoke a concrete world—the smell of
Pullman car dust, the food at a church picnic, the contents of
the library of a small Methodist bishop—is still sufficiently in
force to cram full the outlines of his stereotypes. One can go
further. At each of his three climaxes, Lewis abdicates such
sense of the dramatic scene as he may have had and retreats
into melodrama: once to an inversion of the farmer's daughter
situation, once to a catastrophic fire, finally to a cops-and-rob-
bers treatment of some petty criminals who have attempted to
play the badger game on old Elmer. In each situation, through
bad timing, through a refusal to develop even a suggestion of
suspense, any potential human elements in the situation are
sacrificed to the melodramatic stereotype. And yet, out of this
very weakness, cumulatively, arises again the whole impression of bare brutality which is, after all, the essential social
observation. As the drama is only half realized, so the social
observation is only half true, but in its partiality resides such
force of which it is capable.

Most novels operate through a conflict, dramatized in a plot,
of social and individual interest, and the more sustained the
pressures of the plot, the more likely is the individual to be
forced into a position of new self-awareness, which prominently contains an awareness of his relation to his society. A
certain dynamic interchange has been at work, and the result
is that the historical forces which contain the individual's
experience have been personalized in his awareness. What is
most characteristic of the novels of Sinclair Lewis, and above
all of *Elmer Gantry,* is the fact that there are no such dynamics
of social action, that we are presented with a static, unper-
sonalized image—and that *there* lies its horror.

Elmer Gantry has perhaps one brief moment of honesty. He
has come to Sharon's fantastic home, he is looking out upon
the river, he fancies himself in love:

"Shen-an-doah!" he crooned.
Suddenly he was kneeling at the window, and for the first time

since he had forsaken Jim Lefferts and football and joyous ribald-
ry, his soul was free of all the wickedness which had daubed it
—oratorical ambitions, emotional orgasm, dead sayings of dull
seers, dogmas, and piety. The golden winding river drew him,
the sky uplifted him, and with outflung arms he prayed for de-
liverance from prayer.

"I've found her. Sharon. Oh, I'm not going on with this evangelistic bunk. Trapping idiots into holy monkey-shines! No, by
God, I'll be honest! I'll tuck her under my arm and go out and
fight. Business. Put it over. Build something big. And laugh, not
snivel and shake hands with church-members! I'll do it!"

Then and there his rebellion against himself ends, and after
that he knows nothing of self-recognition. This is about as
close to it as he can come:

"I'll have a good time with those folks," he reflected, in the
luxury of a taxicab. "Only, better be careful with old Rigg. He's
a shrewd bird, and he's onto me. . . . Now what do you mean?"
indignantly. "What do you mean by 'onto me'? There's nothing
to be onto! I refused a drink and a cigar, didn't I? I never cuss
except when I lose my temper, do I? I'm leading an absolutely
Christian life. And I'm bringing a whale of a lot more souls into
churches than any of these pussy-footing tin saints that're afraid
to laugh and jolly people. 'Onto me' nothing!"

A character so open to self-deception is not in a position to
estimate the forces that have made him so: to him, society is
given, accepted, used. Elmer Gantry was raised in an important if stultifying American tradition: the protestantism of the
hinterland; and Sinclair Lewis gives us a complete and devastating account of it that extends over four pages and from
which I now draw fragments, reluctantly omitting Lewis's sub-
stantiating body of detail:

The church and Sunday School at Elmer's village . . . had
nurtured in him a fear of religious machinery which he could
never lose. . . . That small pasty-white Baptist church had been
the center of all his emotions, aside from hell-raising, hunger,
sleepiness, and love. And even these emotions were represented
in the House of the Lord . . . the arts and the sentiments and

the sentimentalities—they were for Elmer perpetually associated only with the church . . . all the music which the boy Elmer had ever heard was in church . . . it provided all his painting and sculpture. . . . From the church came all his profounder philosophy . . . literary inspiration . . . here too the church had guided him. In Bible stories, in the words of the great hymns, in the anecdotes which the various preachers quoted, he had his only knowledge of literature. . . . The church, the Sunday School, the evangelistic orgy, choir-practise, raising the mortgage, the delights of funerals, the snickers in back pews or in the other room at weddings—they were . . . a mold of manners to Elmer. . . . Sunday School text cards . . . they gave him a taste for gaudy robes, for marble columns and the purple-broidered palaces of kings, which was later to be of value in quickly habituating himself to the more decorative homes of vice. . . . And always the three chairs that stood behind the pulpit, the intimidating stiff chairs of yellow plush and carved oak borders, which, he was uneasily sure, were waiting for the Father, the Son, and the Holy Ghost.

He had, in fact, got everything from the church and Sunday School, except, perhaps, any longing whatever for decency and kindness and reason.

And having neither decency nor kindness nor reason (as the novel contains no animated examples of these humane virtues), Elmer is necessarily unaware of the history in which he is involved.

That history, perhaps no larger than it is beautiful in our tradition, is nevertheless considerable, and Sinclair Lewis was aware of it even if, because he had no alternatives, he could not let his characters become so. (The tradition survives, of course: a Madison Avenue patina, extending from Washington, D.C., to Whittier, California, does not alter the motives of cynically opportunistic politicians; it merely moves boorish Elmer into gray flannel and the seat of power.) The whole brutally accurate conception of R. H. Tawney, which coupled business success and salvation, and then, in popular culture, began to pay dividends on the "saved" soul; the obvious connection between the Puritan repressions (I use Lewis's terms, not mine) and the orgiastic outbursts of middle-border evangelism; the Gospel of Service (made in Zenith) becoming the equivalent of the Gospels—all this is in the author's mind as he creates his characters, but the very nature of his creation prohibits it from in any way sharing his knowledge. The result is that the Lewis character cannot separate itself from the Lewis society; and this, in the dynamics of fiction, means that the Lewis character *has* no character apart from the society in which it is embedded, and that therefore the Lewis society is not a society at all, but a machine. And this is the moral, for criticism as for life today, of Lewis's novels, and especially of this one.

"All vital truth," said D. H. Lawrence, "contains the memory of all that for which it is not true." And Frank Norris, that infinitely simpler man, said, "You must be something more than a novelist if you can, something more than just a writer. There must be that nameless sixth sense or sensibility . . . the thing that does not enter into the work, but that is back of it. . . ." Here these two unlikely companions become companionable: both are asking for a certain reverberating largeness behind any concretely conceived situation if that situation is to echo back into the great caverns of the human condition. This quality, I think, even a partisan could not claim that Sinclair Lewis had. Quite justly, Robert Cantwell described him as one "who thought of his writing, not in terms of its momentary inspirations and the . . . pressure of living that played through him and upon him, but in terms of the accomplishment of a foreknown task"; and quite plausibly, Maxwell Geismar wrote that "Just as there is really no sense of vice in Lewis's literary world, there is no true sense of virtue. Just as there is practically no sense of human love in the whole range of Lewis's psychological values, and no sense of real hatred—there is no genuine sense of human freedom." Most of this indictment one may allow, but if we are speaking specifically of *Elmer Gantry*, we would wish to insist on two of the items that these descriptions deny him: "the pressure of living that played through him and upon him," and the "hatred."

*Elmer Gantry* is a work of almost pure revulsion. It seems to shudder and to shake with loathing of that which it describes. The very fact that the novelist must create the image of the thing he loathes, in order to express his loathing, points to the peculiar imaginative animus that motivates this novel. We can speculate about its sources: Lewis's own early evangelistic impulse, his dedication to the missionary field now turning in upon itself; the lonely, goofy boy at Oberlin, himself pushing the handles of a handcar (as Elmer Gantry does) to get to a rural Sunday School where, without conspicuous success, he doled out Bible stories; the poor fool of the hinterland at New Haven, who had never been given more by the hinterland than the dubious gift of deriding it, and therefore of having to love it. Perhaps such speculations are not much to the point. The point is only that in no novel does Sinclair Lewis more clearly announce his loathing of the social environment with which he is concerned, and in no novel does he make it more mandatory that we remain within the terrifying limits of that environment.

Sinclair Lewis is not unlike Elmer Gantry. The vicious circle in this picture exists, of course, in the fact that Elmer remakes society in precisely the terms that society has already made him. No one can break out; everyone, including the novelist, spins more madly in the mechanical orbit.

The novelist trapped in his own hallucination of the world as a trap: this seems to be the final observation that we can make. But it is not quite final. Finally, we are left with the hallucination of the novels themselves, with their monstrous images of what we both are and are not, their nearly fabulous counter-icons in our culture. They stand somewhere between the two conceptions of the novel with which we began: they tell us too much of why we are dead and not enough of how we can live to satisfy the prescription either of Lawrence or of Norris, deprived as they are of all that psychic affirmation that would meet the demands of the first, and of most of that social realism that would meet those of the second. But they have—for this very reason—their *own* quality. If that quality is of the half-truth, and the half-truth has moved back into our way of estimating our society, the judgment falls on us, on our own failure of observation and imagination. If we accept the half-truth for the fact, then the novel is indeed the most important literary instrument in and for our world; and we can only lament the inability, not of our novelists to provide the stimulus, but of ourselves to repel it, of our failure, in the sympathetic consciousness, to recoil from it. *Elmer Gantry* reminds us that we continue to embrace as fervently as we deny this horror that at least in part we are.

# Sinclair Lewis and His Critics

GENERALLY SPEAKING, the writings of Sinclair Lewis have almost never been the subject of serious criticism. Most of our best critics, when they have not ignored his work entirely, have assailed it for certain philistine attitudes that infected it, but either they did not analyze it as art, or they treated him as "a publicist in fiction" whose work cannot sustain that kind of analysis. Even the novels of the 1920's, which seemed to so many to mark Sinclair Lewis as the leading novelist in the United States, which aroused enormous controversy in their enormous audience and to which hundreds of thousands of lines of newsprint were devoted, suffered this fate.

The instance of Lewis's treatment in the pages of *Dial*, where the best American literary criticism was appearing in the 1920's, is instructive. *Main Street* (1920) and *Babbitt* (1922) were not regarded as important enough to deserve a full review and were dismissed peremptorily (even though the second was regarded as a better novel than the first) in one short paragraph under the heading "Briefer Comment." *Mantrap* (1926), one of the most absurd of Lewis's novels, received equal space. (Of this work the editors conjectured that Lewis had written it with one hand tied behind his back and they wished that his other hand might have been similarly incapacitated.) Only *Arrowsmith* (1925) received a full review, this by Robert Morss Lovett, who found the novel increasingly unbelievable once it had passed its middle. *Elmer Gantry* (1927) was ignored entirely. By the time that *Dodsworth* (1929) appeared, *Dial* was dead, but it may be assumed that the editors, so many of whom had themselves been expatriated esthetes, could hardly have found anything to sympathize with in this novel that satirized American artists abroad and gave its blessing to an American businessman.

Book reviewers (as opposed to critics) were another matter; from the first, they took Sinclair Lewis with considerable seriousness. At least three of the five novels that he published before *Main Street* were given the most respectful attention (the other two were frank hack work for which Lewis himself expected no praise). These novels—*Our Mr. Wrenn* (1914), *The Trail of the Hawk* (1915), and *The Job* (1917)—announced, for most reviewers, the appearance of a new and original talent on the American literary scene.

Sinclair Lewis had come to his maturity before 1914, the beginning of the First World War and the end of a period extending from the opening of the century when the prevailing intellectual view was committed to a critical but still happy optimism about the promise of American life, of democracy, and the middle class. At the same time, the American novel seemed to be written in two sharply opposing ways—with the alarming naturalism of a man like Theodore Dreiser on the one hand and with the sentimental gentility of the "Hoosier school"— most prominently, Booth Tarkington and Meredith Nicholson —on the other. Lewis's early novels were seen as important because they seemed to bridge this gap.

What the reviewers remarked in them was the unusual blending of "realism" and "romance." Realism meant a faithful depiction of the details of ordinary life and a willingness to come to grips with all that is not genteel in experience. Romance meant precisely that happy optimism about American life that characterized the prewar years, its adventurousness, its flexibility, its variety. It meant, too, the potentiality of adventure, even of heroism, in the lives of "little people"—an obscure clerk, a country boy, a village girl. So, each of Lewis's first three central characters illustrated the point: Mr. Wrenn, the timid little clerk who breaks out of his boresome routine for a European adventure and finds it with a cynical bohemian artist, Istra Nash, before he returns to New York and finds a more substantial woman for his wife; Carl Ericson, the country boy who becomes a famous aviator and marries a fashionable girl; Una Golden, the village girl who arrives in the city and, fighting all its hardships, becomes a successful career woman before she marries the bright young man of her dreams.

These novels are shot through with flashes of satire directed at certain American types and attitudes, but they are not primarily satirical. Yet, when these novels are viewed retrospectively, as they were by Maxwell Geismar in his essay on Sinclair Lewis in *The Last of the Provincials* (1947), they can be seen quite clearly to lay down not only the central themes of the later work, the chief pattern of action, and the ambiguous attitudes toward American culture, but also, in much of their detail, the satiric technique that was to make Lewis famous.

Nevertheless, *Main Street* broke in the literary atmosphere like an explosion, like something absolutely new and absolutely devastating, not only unlike anything that Sinclair Lewis had done before but unlike anything that anyone had done before. Neither of these assumptions was accurate. While the prevailing fictional view of the American village had presented it as friendly and good, there was a long if much less populous tradition in fiction that showed it as narrow and cruel. The difference is chiefly that these earlier critical novels were not, like *Main Street*, predominantly satirical. But that is also the chief difference between *Main Street* and Lewis's earlier novels. The pattern is identical—of a young person who finds herself in a stultifying environment, tries to reform and then break out of that environment, succeeds for a time, and then makes a necessary compromise with it. The optimism may be less gentle now, but it is still there. When H. L. Mencken, in his laudatory review of the book, remarked like so many others on the apparent reversal in Lewis, he was misled in part by his misreading of Lewis's attitude toward his heroine, Carol Kennicott.

Lewis by no means thought of "her superior culture" as "chiefly bogus," although certainly any reader today must so regard it. If she had to yield in the end to the taste of Gopher Prairie and of her kind but stodgy husband, Will, that, for Lewis, was the pathos of the novel. Although Will has the last word in the novel, it in fact ends in an impasse, and this impasse represents precisely the cultural ambiguities that Lewis could not resolve in his earlier novels and that Mr. Geismar has observed: his rather embarrassed admiration for "Eastern" culture and manners, and his inherent faith in "Western" simplicity and downright substantiality.

Yet he had, it is true, found his *métier* in the satirical treatment of American provincial life, and this vein he would continue to exploit. The pitch of the satire in *Babbitt* is much intensified, and this enabled H. L. Mencken once more to misplace the emphasis in his review, where he found only the kind of Babbitt that he wanted, not the kind that Lewis had shown, or not the whole kind. It was Rebecca West, rather, in her review, who observed the continuing strain of optimism, Babbitt's discontents with his environment, his sense of the promise of something better, something more fulfilling for the individual, less suffocating. It is "that something extra and above the logical treatment of its subject . . . which makes the work of art." For Mencken *Babbitt* was "a social document of a high order"; for Miss West, it was more nearly a kind of poem. And so, when Constance Rourke came to write of these two Lewis novels in *American Humor* (1931), she could quite correctly write of him as not simply a realist but as a "fabulist" —the creator of figures of archetypal stature. Inversely, Sherwood Anderson, whose own prose was in a murky way so much more explicitly "poetical" than Lewis's, found that it was exactly this extra dimension that was missing. However that question may ultimately be settled, the fact is that both terms, "Main Street" and "Babbitt," had become part of the international vocabulary, the United States had been "created" for the international mind, and Sinclair Lewis had established an international reputation.

The next novel, *Arrowsmith*, thoroughly consolidated that reputation and it quieted even his harshest critics. For here at

last Lewis had found a specific and realizable object in which
to locate his idealism and beside which he could pose his satire
in some sort of balance. Martin Arrowsmith, pursuing in his
laboratory what are presented as his lonely truths, was a new
kind of hero, scientific idealism a new subject, and scientific
individualism a new (and rather unscientific) perspective.
Sinclair Lewis was once again in the vanguard.

Reviewers and critics, English as well as American, were al-
most unanimous in asserting its superiority to *Main Street* and
*Babbitt,* and in basing the claim on esthetic grounds. *The
Atlantic Monthly* announced that Lewis was "no longer the
composer of superlative jazz. He has shown himself an artist,
sincere, powerful, restrained." Joseph Wood Krutch, in *The
Nation,* found it "better" because it was "essentially truer,"
and T. K. Whipple, in *New Republic,* took the same view; *The
New York Times,* in two different reviews, agreed, along with
Stuart Pratt Sherman of the New York *Herald Tribune,* who
none too lucidly found that the novel was "hot with the authen-
tic fire in which art and science are purified." "The humanity
of it outshines the science," declared the *Literary Review.*
Other reviewers thought that in its very attention to science it
had performed a tremendous "service." On these grounds, the
*Dial* made its historic exception for a Lewis novel when Robert
Morss Lovett declared that Sinclair Lewis had served "a public
cause which gives largeness of view and significance to *Arrowsmith.*"

Almost perversely, after the foolish interlude of *Mantrap,*
an adventure story, Lewis chose to fly in the face of all this
praise by publishing *Elmer Gantry,* his novel about the corruption of religious life in America. No novel in the history
of American literature outraged its audience so completely, and
very few novels in American literature had a larger immediate audience. The outrage was so intense that it extended to
threats of personal assault upon the author. It was the rare
critic, like Joseph Wood Krutch, who could see the novel in
some perspective and could see that it had some virtue. "*Elmer
Gantry* is as good as *Main Street* and *Babbitt,*" wrote Mr.

Krutch with critical sense and moderation, "and it is good in exactly the same way." Extremes were more characteristic of the reception of this novel. At one side of Mr. Krutch is H. L. Mencken, predictably ecstatic and shouting, "Voltaire! Voltaire! Not since Voltaire!" And at the other is the disappointed Rebecca West, for whom this satire fails because its chief character is unworthy of satire, because it seems to have been written on the assumption that "Voltaire would have got anywhere if he had spent his emotions on the pietistic errors of washerwomen in Brittany." Because *Elmer Gantry* aroused such hot feelings, it is probably the only one of Lewis's better novels that has been critically underestimated. In my own essay I have tried to write as dispassionately as Mr. Krutch, but, I fear, at much greater length.

In 1927 Sinclair Lewis was at his zenith, and at about this time extended surveys of his work began to appear, attempts at assessment of the whole of his work thus far. V. F. Parrington in his essay, "Our Own Diogenes" (1927), defines the nature of Lewis's satire, discusses his methods of gathering material, considers both his popularity and his unpopularity, and finds him rather harder on middle-class America than Lewis in fact was and would presently make very clear in his defense of Dodsworth. T. K. Whipple, whose fine essay of 1928 is a clear exception to the generalization with which this commentary began, did not make Parrington's error: he saw the complexity, the self-division in Lewis, the man, as clearly as he saw them in Lewis's novels; he saw what is lucid and valuable in these novels as well as he saw their limitations; he re-created the imaginative world of Sinclair Lewis with an artist's effectiveness; and he arrived at a final judgment with which, I believe, any dispassionate reader must agree. Walter Lippmann's essay of 1927 was an impressive piece of rhetoric, but it was written with a good deal more personal bias, even a kind of vindictiveness, than is to be found in the Whipple essay, and so it is critically less impressive. This is true even if one is inclined to agree with Mr. Lippmann that Sinclair Lewis, the man, had

never fully matured. The essay ends with speculations on what
subject Lewis will turn to next.

But what interests me is whether Mr. Lewis will reach maturity, or remain arrested in his adolescent rebellion. After *Arrowsmith* one would have said that he was beginning to be free of
that shapeless irritation and yearning which Carol Kennicott typi-
fies. But after *Elmer Gantry* one cannot be so sure. The hatreds
are turned inward, as if the effort to escape had failed and become morbid. There is some sort of crisis in this astonishing
career, which is not yet resolved.

Many readers of Lewis's next novel, *Dodsworth*, felt that this
was precisely what had happened—Lewis had matured at last,
mellowed. Here is a story that praised an American businessman and that saved its satire for cultural affectations and snobbery, for "Europeanized" corruptions of virtue and taste. The
American middle class was vindicated! At last the errant Lewis
had returned to his own! And while it is true enough that
Lewis's approval of Babbitry had never been so explicit before,
careful readers of Lewis's previous novels, even *Elmer Gantry*,
would not have been so deceived.

H. L. Mencken was, of course, disappointed, and gave the
novel only a kind of grudging praise, but most reviewers were
delighted with the book. Ford Madox Ford, that sensitive
British novelist, friend of Henry James whose own work
was so centrally concerned with the *Dodsworth* theme,
the American abroad, wrote enthusiastically of the "poetic"
quality of the novel and suggested that it might quite as well
have been called *Europa, an Epic*. Another fine English novelist, E. M. Forster, thought less well of it. Acknowledging
Lewis's superb photographic gift as he employed it in his
novels earlier in the 1920's, Forster said, "I persist in exclaiming, for what Mr. Lewis has done for myself and thousands of
others is to lodge a piece of a continent in our imagination."
But with *Elmer Gantry*, the photographic method had begun
to fail him, and with *Dodsworth*, the failure was complete.
"What has happened? What has changed the Greek Confec-
tionery Parlour at Gopher Prairie, where every decaying

banana mattered, to this spiritless general catalogue?" Mr. Forster concluded that photography was the art of a fresh, young man; Mr. Lewis was no longer young and he had no other resources. In this view, then, if Lewis had indeed matured, maturity was his disaster.

Yet it was indeed the fact that for thousands of Europeans, Lewis had created the image of America, and he had created it in the terms in which they wanted to believe—of a grossly materialistic, money-mad, smugly hypocritical, provincial civilization. It was not really surprising that in 1930 Sinclair Lewis should have been the first American writer to receive the Nobel prize. And the outraged Americans who regarded the award not as praise for American literature but as an insult to American culture were probably not entirely wrong. Yet it was praise for American literature, too, and not only for Lewis's novels but for a whole body of work that had throughout the 1920's developed a capacity for self-criticism that was new and that demonstrated that our writers, at least, were not chauvinists. For Europeans, Lewis had all along been the most effective of our social critics in the novel, and not only because he was the noisiest of them. He loved his country all the time that he scolded it, and this quality the Swedes, at least, found endearing in him, and for this quality, together with his humor, they praised him.

It was the climax of his career, of course, and from that high point a long descent lay ahead. He was to publish ten more novels of uneven quality, some very bad indeed and none as good as the five big novels of the 1920's. The immediate concern in critical America was not with Lewis's future but rather with an assessment of his past, and all over the United States the question that was being asked was whether Lewis deserved the great prize. Lewis Mumford's essay of 1931 is characteristic. It gives its subject due praise for the qualities that his best work showed, and it asserts that "on his literary merits, he would undoubtedly be one of the six or seven names that would come to mind as candidates for this prize." But it concludes that if the Swedish Academy had been capable of

recognizing the qualities that are "most precious and significant in contemporary American literature," it would have recognized Robert Frost.

A gap of a few years followed in Lewis's production. For
some time he had worked at the preliminary materials for a
novel about labor in the United States, and in the early 1930's
he devoted himself most intensively to this project, but he felt
that he could not yet write it, and even though he never quite
relinquished the idea, he never did write it. He began then to
write a whole series of novels about less complex (or at least,
for him, more manageable) social areas. Having recently married Dorothy Thompson, a career woman, he now wrote *Ann
Vickers* (1933), a novel about the career woman in the United
States who yearns to be a mere woman as well. Then followed
a poor novel about the hotel industry, *Work of Art* (1934), in
which the satire is directed against art (poor art, to be sure)
and the real art lies in the dream of a perfect hotel. Because
of Dorothy Thompson's interest, as a newspaperwoman, in the
developments in Hitler's Germany, Lewis next wrote *It Can't
Happen Here* (1935), a sensational novel about fascism in the
United States, and while the novel excited all readers of liberal
mind (for the threat of fascism in the mid-thirties seemed very
real), it in fact makes its appeal to the good old American
middle-of-the-road virtues as these are embodied in its hero,
Doremus Jessup, a small-town newspaper editor. Then, seeming to reverse himself once more, Lewis published *The Prodigal Parents* (1938), which was meant as a satiric exposé of
communist activity in the United States and which is unquestionably one of his feeblest efforts.

He was writing now with a kind of mechanical fury, and in
1936 it was this relentless grinding out of anything at all that
most impressed Robert Cantwell in his survey for the *New
Republic*. The famous Lewis "ear" is challenged in this essay
—is this really the way that Americans talk? Lewis is beginning to seem old-fashioned—he who had always been out in
front; and the essay already takes on the tone, as writing about
Lewis increasingly would, of elegiac assessment. When Lewis

found his substantial place in Alfred Kazin's brilliant history of modern American literature, *On Native Grounds* (1942), the extended analysis and the eminently fair judgment on the whole career and on Lewis's importance to American literature nearly suggest that the subject has already been dead for some time.

*Bethel Merriday* (1940), a novel about a young actress, had indeed suggested that at least the satiric novelist in Lewis was dead. While *Gideon Planish* (1943), a satiric attack on organized philanthropy and the activities of liberal "do-gooders," returned, in a crude way, to the old mode, it did little to support the old reputation. *Cass Timberlane* (1945), a novel about American marriage, is half-sentimental, half-splenetic, and one can understand why a lady like Diana Trilling, reviewing this book, should have found Lewis "the victim, so to speak, of his own divided heart." Most male reviewers felt rather differently. Edmund Wilson, for example, considering this novel, was impressed with the fact that Lewis was "one of the people in the literary field who do create interest and values, that he has still gone on working at this when many others have broken down or quit, and that he is, in fact, at his best—what I never quite believed before—one of the national poets." This judgment should be put beside the harsher view of Maxwell Geismar, who found Lewis now writing in "the land of Faery"— out of all touch with American realities.

In *Kingsblood Royal* (1947) he made his last strenuous effort to reenter them by addressing himself to the problem of the Negro minority in American life. The book aroused some excitement as a social document but none whatever as a literary performance, and even its social usefulness, it is now clear, was minimized by Lewis's mechanical oversimplification of what is, of course, one of the most complex, as well as one of the most pressing, issues in our national life. From this attempt to deal with the immediate present, Lewis retreated into the historical past of Minnesota. *The God-Seeker* (1949) is apparently the first part of what was finally projected as a trilogy about labor in the United States, but it is a wooden performance about which even Lewis's faithful publishers despaired.

His last novel, *World So Wide* (1951), was published posthumously. A thin attempt to write another *Dodsworth*, it is the final self-parody. As Malcolm Cowley wrote, his characters sound now "like survivors from a vanished world, like people just emerging from orphanages and prisons where they had listened for thirty years to nothing but tape recordings of Lewis novels."

It was a long and sad decline and it complicates the problem of making any final judgment. The patent weaknesses of the poor books highlight weaknesses already present but not so obvious in the great books, and the dimness of the final vision somehow casts in shadow their portions of brilliance. Yet, following in the steps of the few good critics who risked writing seriously about him (and now, in retrospect, they do not seem quite so few, although the fact remains that there is nothing from Eliot, from Levin or Pritchett or Mattheissen, from Brooks or Warren, from Tate or Ransom or Trilling or Rahv, and certainly nothing from the bearded old-young)—following the few who risked judgments, one must take the risk oneself.

Unquestionably, he helped us into the imagination of ourselves as did no other writer of the 1920's. What he helped us to imagine is a part of ourselves that we do not greatly admire and that, in some of its grossest features, we may indeed by now have outgrown. It was the very worst of our gawky adolescence that he showed us, with the chin weaker than it would finally be, the nose larger, the hands still hanging out of the sleeves, pimples all over the flushed face. Interestingly enough, Sinclair Lewis himself, one of the gawkiest adolescents of all time, always aspired to become an elegant man of the world. So, his fiction, without much more subtlety, tried to whip the most barbarous kind of American into the Lewis conception of culture. When his personal ambition failed, his novels fell back into a defense of the very barbarousness that he had always held onto as an ace in the hole. If the strategy was mistaken, and only marked the long falling off of his powers, he had, nevertheless, in his great years, not only made a personal fortune remarkable for an American literary man but he had also made his contribution to the fortunes of American literature. That treasure remains in our literary and cultural inheritance, remains both to enrich us and to remind us of our potential bankruptcy. At the very least, we must agree with T. K. Whipple's judgment that "Lewis is the most successful critic of American society because he is himself the best proof that his charges are just." In spite of all the bad writing, the lapses in taste and judgment, the sheer wilfulness of the whole career, we can only concur, too, with the observation of Joseph Wood Krutch that Lewis "recorded a reign of grotesque vulgarity which but for him would have left no record of itself because no one else could have adequately recorded it."

An involuntary achievement, perhaps, but not a small one. And if, besides, we can hope with Rebecca West that the very vitality that animates that vulgarity suggests the possibility of a more civilized future, we must thank Sinclair Lewis in large part among writers for pushing us toward it.

# Two Houses, Two Ways: The Florentine Villas of Lewis and Lawrence

Two NOVELISTS both chose more or less to close their worldly accounts near Florence; not in Florence, but in houses just outside it, looking down upon it from different hilltops—Sinclair Lewis's to the south, D. H. Lawrence's to the southwest. The pursuit of these two men, and of what remains of them in the memory of people still in Florence who knew them, leads in fascinatingly divergent directions, but perhaps nothing about them, not even their writing, is so diverse as the houses they lived in. These were, in reality, their last houses although neither died here; at the end each staggered away from Florence in the weary daze of his ultimate illness, Lewis for only a few months to the lakes and then to Rome, Lawrence, for less than two years, to wander uneasily and then to perch at Bandol and at last to die at Vence one day after he had been removed from a sanatorium called "Ad Astra."

Lewis's house was Villa La Costa. Having the American ear, attuned perhaps first of all to that question, *"Quanto costa?"* you are challenged even before you have seen the house by the unhappy accident of its name to consider its price, and relevant as this sullen intuition proves to be, the name is in fact as ordinary as "Elmwood" or "Lakeview," meaning only the house on the hillside. To reach it most directly, you leave Florence by the Porta Romana and the Viale del Poggio Imperiale, already ascending, and after a sharp, short jog to the left you are on the street you want, the Via del Pian dei Guillari. This is a narrow road that winds up between high, gray stone walls that shut from sight the estates behind them, and all that one sees are occasional heavy, closed gates, olive branches reaching out over the walls, their pale green leaves shimmering in the sunlight, and now and then the top of a towering grove of cypresses, blackly green against the brilliantly clear blue of the Italian sky in spring. Abruptly this road opens into a little country square, the Plain of the Jesters. Here, in the Renaissance and before, troops of traveling buffoons camped at night, for the ground levels out and the square lies at the center of a group of great, ancient houses where employment was certain. And very near here our latter-day jester lived out his jittery life in a very different kind of house.

You continue on out through the square by the same road, again between walls, and presently, after only a few meters, you are outside the walls of Number 124, Villa La Costa. There is the usual pull; the gates clang open; and you are confronted by two *carabinieri* in their dark blue uniforms with the broad, brilliantly red stripes down each leg, and by a young American military policeman in his lighter blue who emerges from a sentry box just inside the gate. Villa La Costa is now[1] occupied by the commanding officer of the Southern European arm of the Allied Air Forces, Lieutenant-General D. M. Schlatter, and his family. Mrs. Schlatter is a gracious Southerner who made this inspection easy.

The house presents not so much a formidable as a blank front, a glare of yellow plaster in the sunlight, with eight or ten windows that seem rather small in such a long expanse, and an enormous, arched oak door that, like a number of other doors in the house, you later learn, was appropriated by the owner from the storerooms of that great national monument in the city, the Palazzo Strozzi. Inside, such a rude assault is made upon the senses by the accumulated glitter of marble, gilt, dead white paint, glass, and crystal, that it is impossible, at once, to separate this general splendor into its parts. You are, you see, in a foyer as large as a moderately sized living room, your feet upon dark brown letters of marble laid in the beige marble of the floor, the letters forming the words PAX ET

_____
[1] 1953.

BONUM, and at the opposite end of the foyer, similar letters spell out that greeting you may already have observed over the northern gate of Siena, COR TIBI PANDIT. On both sides are expanses of glass, double sets of French doors set in heavy granite arches lined with oak arches. These doors, like all the windows in the house, consist of small leaded panes tinted in light pastel shades—blue, orchid, pink, yellow—and in the arch over each appears a crest of no significance in the history of Florence. PAX ET BONUM. This house was built in 1939, on the foundations of a modest but ancient villa, by a small official then in the Italian consulate at Madrid, and in its showy, shell-like opulence (the walls, under the burden of gilt, are very thin, so that the house rattles with human sounds) it shares with many another Italian monument of those years the atmosphere of minor and ephemeral officialdom on the loose, a truly horrendous taste. The Lewis rent in 1949–1950, when rents in Florence were still quite low, was $150 a month. Now, Villa La Costa is for sale: it can be had for fifty million lire, or about eighty thousand dollars.

The doors to the right open into a drawing room that, while it contains an elegant Strozzi mantelpiece, is nevertheless dominated by a flat and perfectly enormous modern portrait, perhaps five by six feet, of a lady associated with the owner's family, in ballroom dress. Here the relentlessness of marble under the feet is alleviated by rugs, and here stands an elderly servant who was attached to the house when Lewis had it. On the subject with which the world, alas, is most familiar, his drinking, she shows an engaging reticence, offering a few gently sad reflections that do not at all share the brutal tone of the obituary notices which the Florentine newspapers published with such energetic conviction. (*"Quando Arrivò a Firenze,"* read the headline in *La Nazione,* a highly respectable journal, *"Era Già un Uomo Finito,"* and then quoted with relish in its opening paragraph an anonymous friend who purportedly announced eighteen months before his death that *"Lewis è già morto"*—Lewis is already dead. The obituary itself was not so much the recognition of the passing of a distinguished man as it was a diatribe on the evils of drink—*"il vizio di bere"*—which, we are assured, broke up each of Lewis's three marriages, one more than in fact he had.) The old servant prefers another tone, and repeats over and over again that he was *gentilissimo, gentilissimo,* and ill, ill, ill. At La Costa, she says, he saw very few people, but every day he worked for long hours, on the terrace, in the tower, and he lived, she thought, in some great fear. In the management of the household he had small interest; she took her orders from the secretary. Knowing of Lewis's detailed interest in the management of some earlier houses—at Williamstown, where in his meticulous handwriting he had himself labeled the whole array of keys; at Duluth, where an itemized examination of various materials led to a smashing quarrel with his decorator—you begin to sense the lonely pathos and perhaps the terror of his butt-end days. This sense of pathos is not diminished if one considers another impression, from one of Lewis's new American acquaintances in Florence at that time, that he was enormously proud of La Costa and all its tinsel. Buried in his Baedeker, determined to master all the facts of art and architecture, history and hagiography in this city, he, who always had the sharpest eye for the human phony, yet felt—it is said—that in La Costa he had found the real thing, the truly elegant Italian establishment.

Beyond the drawing room is a commodious library that contains few books. At one end is an enormous fireplace so badly designed that a fire on the hearth merely pours smoke into the room; to use it at all, a small firebox on metal legs four or five feet high has been placed inside the great opening, to bring the fire near the draft. In the drawing room again, over excellent martinis, one can contemplate the kind of genius Lewis had for choosing to live in houses that were quite beyond the possibility of being shaken down into homes (the Williamstown house has been purchased by the Carmelite Order as a monastery), houses that, for all their richness, are somehow characterized by a gaunt impersonality; and the kind of genius he had, further, for losing friends, so that in the end he was surrounded by strangers (his last secretary was an employee of Cook's whom he had picked up as he contemplated the Giottos at Assisi), and badly painted portraits of ladies he did not know at all who were ready for a hypothetical dance with someone else.

Driven all his life, all over the world, from house to house, by his unmanageable restlessness, he was, perhaps, never at home, only always wishing to be. His first like his last novel is concerned with a hero who desires "the land of elsewhere," and then cannot abide it. The last hero goes to the American Church in Florence and longs for Colorado. "He knew then that he was unalterably an American; he knew what a special and mystical experience it is, for the American never really emigrates but only travels; perhaps travels for two or three generations but at the end is still marked with the gaunt image of Tecumseh." And how many Americans there are, how many American writers especially, who are as little at home out of the United States as they are in them! Certainly this gaudy villa, so near the Pian dei Guillari, was only another camp for a dark night.

On our way to the luncheon table, we cross the foyer into a sitting room about the size of the drawing room, with more white enameled walls and ornamental gilt embossments, a crystal chandelier large enough for a theater lobby, a white enameled grand piano that requires a ten-piece orchestra in white tuxedos and a singer like Ella Fitzgerald, another even larger portrait of a lady in yards and yards of extravagant chiffon gown, and, at one end of the room, most remarkable, a stairway that winds up to the higher floors. Its balusters and balustrade are made of Venetian spun glass in blue and milky white, and the stairs themselves are of that same slippery beige marble of which the floors are made. Small wonder that Lewis, with his famously ill-coordinated body, once came plummeting headlong down these stairs and that thereafter the owner boxed the balustrade in wood, and that at the bottom, Lewis's servants spread out all available rugs in the event of another fall! In this hard glitter, what heart had opened to him?

Beyond the blinding salon is a soberer, shadowed writing room, and then the pleasantly spacious dining room that opens out onto a capacious loggia overlooking the terraced, somber garden. We lunch beautifully on pheasant shot by the General in Germany, and the easy, amiable conversation permits us to reflect on those more melancholy meals that were served to Lewis at this table. A distinguished British woman of title whom Lewis met at a cocktail party just before he took La Costa has told me that, on this occasion, he devoted himself entirely to her and that, as soon as he had moved into the house, called to say that he wanted her to be his first dinner guest. She was a new acquaintance whom he tried to treat as though she were his oldest, dearest friend; and out of her great respect and great pity, she played his make-believe. (Perry Miller, in his brilliantly sympathetic *Atlantic* piece, "The Incorruptible Sinclair Lewis," has made the same point: "We perfected a little fiction between us that my wife and I, his newest friends, were his oldest and only friends.") With this British lady he took many drives into the country in his black Studebaker (this was his favorite relaxation—to drive out to some isolated country *trattoria* and, to understate, sample the wines), and with her he planned innumerable fascinating journeys abroad, with detailed itineraries, to be pursued as soon as he had recovered his health. Beginning in a kind of feverish exaltation, assisted by that nearly inexhaustible gift of verbal improvisation that never left him, he would build what she calls "fantastic paper castles." They would go here, there, and then on to that place; always different places, but always planned for with the same mounting excitement. They would have the most marvelous time! But he believed none of it, and at the pitch of his excitement, the paper castle suddenly fell apart in the air before him, and then he fell in upon himself, the long meager body collapsing in a hump on the table as he groaned, "Oh God, no man has ever been so miserable!" This misery, recollected in that brash, expensive house, is piercing, for it is the bright, cold house itself that makes one feel that he might well have been stating a quite simple truth.

Then there is Father Fosco Martinelli whose church, Santa Margherita a Montici, is just a few steps up beyond Villa La Costa. It is one of the oldest churches in the environs of the city and stands at the highest point of the hills that fall down to the valley of the Arno on one side, the valley of the Ema on the other. On the Arno side the slopes are covered with guide-book gardens cut out sharply by walls and hedges from scraggly olive groves; on the Ema side, the small, highly cultivated fields step down to the river and then rise up from it again, precisely, thriftily, as carefully tended as flowerbeds, and as different as it is agriculturally possible to be from the wanton spread of "wheat, a golden sea for miles about," of which Lewis liked to sing. Father Martinelli is a gravely handsome young man whose study is a rude, plastered cell. Behind the work table hangs a *certificato al patriota,* signed by Marshal Montgomery, that attests to his partisan activities, and he has published a small novel for youngsters about boys in the partisan movement—*I Romani Siamo Noi.* Propped up on top of a wardrobe is an unframed expressionist painting in oil that had been given to Lewis and that Lewis gave to him on the occasion when Father Martinelli was invited to dine at La Costa. It was one of those frequent, halfhearted gestures Lewis made in an attempt to come to know Italians, and like most, a failure. There was a little preliminary conversation in which Lewis ambiguously said that to be an artist, one really needed to learn to think in Italian. At the table, they talked of his work habits and of Italian writers, but Lewis was remote from the conversation, abstracted in gloom. After dinner he gave the priest the picture—Christ before the Sanhedrin—"as a remembrance of this evening," and sank into a chair. When Father Martinelli left, Lewis said, "Friend, friend, we will see each other often." They never saw each other again. Was he not interested in the Father's political views? "That evening he was interested in nothing. An inspiration was upon him."

One would have to search for a better example of the cultural barrier, for of inspiration there was unhappily very little at La Costa, but of drudgery, much. The gap that acquaintances could not fill, work might. We rise from the table and walk out in that loggia where, on fine days, Lewis did much of the writing on *World So Wide* and on those poems that he took to after this last novel. This is the north side of the house and lies entirely in deep shadow. We walk in the garden, contemplating the struggling box hedges, counting cypresses: there are seven. A gardener is raking over hard lumps of clay-ey earth. He says that this is where Lewis always walked, alone, in the shadows, back and forth, never on the sunny side of the house. And we are reminded of a prophetic passage in *Our Mr. Wrenn,* his first novel, published in 1915:

> . . . his loneliness shadowed him. Of that loneliness one could make many books; how it sat down with him; how he crouched in his chair, bespelled by it, till he violently rose and fled, with loneliness for companion in his flight. He was lonely. He sighed that he was "lonely as fits." Lonely—the word obsessed him. Doubtless he was a bit mad, as are all the isolated men who sit in distant lands longing for the voice of friendship.

But mainly he fled into work. Lewis finished *Main Street* on a certain day in 1920 "only by working eight hours a day, seven days in most weeks. . . . I never worked so hard, and never shall work so hard, again." But thirty years later, when he was about to die, he did. His secretary has written that he worked from nine to ten hours every day, and he told Father Martinelli that he got up at five and worked until seven, then had breakfast; at eight he was back at his desk and worked until eleven; at four in the afternoon he returned to it and worked until eight; and then, during the night, he would wake up and write some more. It was a kind of fury. In 1941, when Lewis was directing Jack Levin's play, *Good Neighbor,* he described "a working day which, extending from 6 A.M. to midnight, has kept me out of the more vigorous forms of dissipation." But it would seem that, at the end, work itself, more than drink or any other *vizio,* had become the most vigorous of all forms of dissipation, if by dissipation one happens to mean any drugging activity that helps us to forget the intolerable.

But there we are, on the terrace, remembering that (according to the secretary) Lewis had only three demands of a house: a place to work, decent servants' quarters, and a view. We study the view that lies beyond the falling hill: it is of the new, industrialized area of Florence, with none of the monuments that a Florentine would expect in a "view" except, at the extreme left, a section of the cupola of the Duomo; and yet, hideous as it is when you are near it, the new Florence is adequately far from Villa La Costa to look quite pretty, with its white and yellow planes in the sunlight. But the best thing in the view is quite near by, that Torre del Gallo on the site of which John Milton placed Galileo (". . . the sad Tuscan, who with Optic glass, Exalted, saw the Constellations pass . . ."), and where Lewis in that last novel he was writing located the villa of Sam Dodsworth, as if to have an old friend near him while he suffered in the higher splendor of La Costa. Father Martinelli says of their moment in the loggia, "To the left appeared the city lights; above, the stars." The observation seems important.

On bad days, Lewis worked in the tower. We mount those giddy stairs and pause for a moment on the second floor, where, in the large open hallway, a huge mirror in a floreated gilt frame doubles the vengeance on the eyes of white and gold and crystal-dripping chandelier, and then, as the stairs continue, we continue up into the square tower that juts up from the middle of the roof. It is a room about fifteen by fifteen feet, containing only a large work table and a few straight chairs, and entirely enclosed in long casement windows made up of hundreds of those tinted, leaded panes. Here, in full visual command of all his ancient surroundings, he finished his novel about Americans from a town called Newlife, uneasily attempting to make something of the old.

He could look, if he wished, straight north to Settignano, and on clear days, with ordinary field glasses, would probably

have been able to pick out the clock tower among the cypresses of I Tatti, the house of his old friend, Bernard Berenson. Why, in his last year, after the warmest association
beginning on that first day when, a friend of a dear friend,
Edith Wharton, he was brought to Berenson—why he let that
friendship lapse, too, is not clear. Nor is the situation made
clearer when we observe that in *World So Wide* Lewis at-
tributes to one of his shabbiest characters, an old fake of a
connoisseur, a remark that, according to the secretary, caused
Lewis to lose his temper at dinner one night at I Tatti; the
remark was that civilization ended with the fall of the Bas-
tille. All that one can be sure of is that if Berenson made this
remark, he made it out of his instinct for the remark that will
command a rise, which he got—twice. The juggling of values
in this story—Lewis's remembering it at all, then attributing it
to a mean character, then omitting entirely his own response
—all this suggests the self-reproach from which he was suffering. It is shown more simply in another anecdote. A brilliant
Florentine man of letters whose first name is Arturo has told
me, with a kind of humorous horror, that after their first meeting, Lewis called him Art—most insignificant, unless you can
hear a distinguished Florentine named Arturo and armed in
all the chilly pride of these people speak that nickname, "Art."
But then how pathetic it is to find, again in *World So Wide,*
the shabbiest American of all saying, "This is . . . Mrs. Baccio
. . . married to a fine young Italian businessman, friend of
mine, Art Baccio." And, in fact, as one tries to see clearly
through all that faintly tinted glass, one's emotion there in
Lewis's tower, his last writing place, is almost entirely the
emotion of pathos; for it is impossible not to juxtapose the
sentimental coziness of entirely fabricated feeling that characterizes the end of his last novel with the desperation of the
end of his life there in La Costa: the loneliness, the self-
reproach, the shadowed isolation amidst the garish splendor,
the desperate shame that kept him from people, especially
his true friends, and then always the destructive forgetting.

His Florentine doctor warned him: "You will die in the worst way; you will just go down a hole."

We think of this admonition as we go down to look at his bedroom, pausing to peer into two most un-Italian bathrooms, one apple green, one orchid, the two separated by a wall most of which consists of an aquarium where big goldfish sluggishly flaunt themselves. The room is large, but with all its new green and gold furniture in heavy imitation of the Rennaissance style it seems crowded. There is no rest from the gilt: on the doors, on the ceiling, on the fireplace, on the wide headboard of the bed. This is the bed on which Lewis's Florentine doctor first saw him. The occasion was a black, stormy night when he had suffered his initial heart attack, and the decanter on the bedside table contained not water but straight whisky. The doctor is the most fashionable in Florence, a cultivated man who buys pictures and reads widely, and who was more than merely respectfully aware of the great reputation of this new patient. He made it his personal rather than professional business to rehabilitate Sinclair Lewis, but it was a losing struggle. "Only gods and geniuses are as lonely as that man," he says, but then adds that this was a genius with a special problem. As is well known, Lewis suffered for most of his life from a violent form of acne that disfigured his face, and in his last years this ailment had become more acute, causing in Lewis a gnawing self-consciousness and shame that impelled him, at last, to cut himself off from the sight of others, especially others who knew him well. Two things spared him: drink, and the dizzying kind of dramatic improvisation into which he loved to throw himself. His gifts of mimicry were great, and his mind, like his memory, like his blue eyes, remained brilliant to the end (so say all his acquaintances), and with a kind of compulsive exaltation he spun out his verbal fantasies, his imitations, his imaginary travels, giving his listeners the sometimes uncomfortable feeling that he could not stop, until the effort reached its peak and suddenly collapsed completely. Then a deeper mood controlled him and sent him to his other solace, a mood that arose from what his doctor calls the "interior tragedy, a deep will to death, a real *cupio dissolvi*." We study the bed, and remind ourselves that he was a novelist who never wrote of death at all. Then outside a small white cloud moves, and the sunlight suddenly strikes into the room and dances with a frenzy on the glitter.

In April or May of 1926, D. H. Lawrence, who was careless about dating his letters, wrote to Dorothy Brett from a Lungarno *pensione* that "Perhaps now we shall take a little flat in the country here—outside Florence—for a couple of months, and I wander about to my Etruscans." How he found Villa Mirenda, isolated in the country beyond that ugly little town of Scandicci and the mere crossroads of Vingone, I have been unable to discover,[2] but to find it today is easy enough, since we have only to follow Lawrence's own directions.

> When is your sister Margaret coming out? [This to Rolf Gardiner.] Here we are—if nothing drives us away—so tell her to come and see us when she will. If she will walk out, then tram *No.* 16 from the Duomo to *Vingone* to the very terminus and dead end (½ hour). Then there's another 25 minutes' walk— straight ahead uphill from Vingone till you come to two cypresses, just beyond the house marked *Podere Nuovo.* Turn to the left there, and dip into the little valley. Our house is the square big box on top of the *poggio,* near the little church of San Paolo.

Why Lawrence wanted a house like Villa Mirenda is clear enough. Lawrence was suffering from the tubercular infection that killed him, and he should have been back on his ranch in Taos, but he could not bring himself to go back; England was out of the question, he found it so intolerable ("a kingdom, a tight and unsatisfactory one in which I should die outright if pinned to it"); he was not at work on a major effort, but he had interested himself in doing a series of

2 Edward Nehls, a more thorough man than I am, makes it clear in his *D. H. Lawrence: A Composite Biography*, III (1959), p. 59, that the Lawrences learned about the Villa Mirenda through Walter Wilkinson, soon to be a neighbor, who is mentioned later in this essay.

essays on Etruscan art and life, and the monuments of that civilization were scattered all over to the south and west of Florence; he wanted a particular kind of isolation, separation, loneliness; finally, he and Frieda needed a *pied à terre*, and they needed it cheaply: they rented Villa Mirenda (or their top half of it) for three thousand lire, which was then twenty-five pounds, or about $120 a year. They kept it for two years.

We do not take tram No. 16, but drive out through the Porta San Frediano, and then follow directions and the trolley tracks. Through the long narrow Via Scandicci, with its scaling walls off which posters peel almost as soon as they are pasted up, but on which they are nevertheless pasted in great number—out through this hazardous street we circumspectly ease the second-hand Morris Minor. It is a poor district, and the hazards are not provided by other cars, because there are few, but by the multitude of mule-drawn carts, bicycles, Vespas and Lambrettas, and, since it is a Sunday afternoon, half the Vespas are charging out into the country carrying hunters, their thick thighs splayed widely on the broad seats, their guns strapped to their backs, off to the tidy woods and fields to shoot the small birds, the larks and nightingales, for the markets and their own tables. Twenty-five years ago, when there must have been more birds in Italy than there are now, the hunters bothered Lawrence, who wrote to Aldous Huxley from Villa Mirenda, "Under cover of the mist, the Cacciatori are banging away—it's a wonder they don't blow one another to bits—but I suppose sparrow-shot is small dust. And it's Sunday, *sacra festa*."

Driving slowly, we peer into the dark one-room dwellings that open immediately upon the street and each of which houses at least one large family, many of them more than one. Here there are no great houses nor a long history to invite our speculation, but only, for block after block, the terrible evidence of the life of the European poor. Then at last the houses thin out, the solid walls of low buildings break up, we pass more rapidly through Vingone, and presently we see a square house painted orange, and under the paint we can still read the words *Podere Nuovo*. We decide to walk, park the car beyond the two cypresses, and proceed uphill. Now we are in open country, and the landscape is soft and still curiously precise, as only Tuscany can be, but the road is narrow, rutted, and covered with loose gravel, and, as bumblingly we climb, we wonder not only whether sister Margaret ever made it, but, aware of our own clumsy progress, remember also Lawrence's lines about inveterate motorists: ". . . the vibration of the motor-car has bruised their insensitive bottoms into rubber-like deadness." The Lawrences never had a car; they always walked, and not only on this rough road, but on every kind of road all over Europe.

The house is a great square block of whitish-gray stone that stands, like the typical farm villa of Tuscany, alone on its hill, its fields and vineyards falling away from it in all directions, and the matchstick dwellings of the *contadini* scattered here and there among the fields. Our gravel road climbs up toward it, then drops down again, then up once more, and at last we leave the road and climb up to the house by its own circuitous dirt path that brings us to a long, low, peasant house and an iron gate. A woman is spreading bits of laundry on stones in the sun, and we ask if this is Villa Mirenda. It is. Is there a dog? None but this, she tells us, and indicates a sleeping creature near her that has hardly lifted its ears at our approach. So we push open the gate and proceed. Near the great central door of the house, standing open, is a well—again, the characteristically Tuscan well, charming in its symmetry, a round gray stone cylinder perhaps six feet across and ten feet high, simply domed, with a small lion's head looking out in each of the four directions from the base of the dome. At the well is a young girl who is staring curiously at us as we approach. Is the owner at home? She turns her head and calls sharply to the open door, "*Zia! Zia!*" and in a moment her aunt, who is Signora Mirenda, appears, wiping her hands on her white apron. Then the explanations: who we are, why we are there, what we would like. "*Il gran scrittore inglese, Signor Lawrence . . . molto*

*tempo fa, venticinque anni fa . . . abitò qui?"* we stumble, half
convinced by her stern, questioning regard that we have
surely come to the wrong place in spite of those detailed
instructions. But the name of Lawrence brings recognition
and a smile; suddenly she understands us and bursts into a
string of *si, si, si's,* and calls her husband with a shout flung
over her shoulder. In a moment he appears in the doorway
behind her, and now she explains to him, and we are wel-
comed.

Signor Mirenda appears to be a moderately successful
farmer. He is wearing breeches and polished black boots to
his knees, a rough jacket, and a curiously high corduroy cap.
The boots are new and creak at every step, and the cap
remains on his head, inside the house and out, through the
entire time of our visit. He explains that the Lawrences used
a different entrance, and leads us around the house so that
we may enter as they did. How old is the house? *"Quattro-
cento,"* he replies, but that you do not take seriously, since
it is the answer that nearly every Italian gives when you ask
about the age of any structure, and you conclude that it is
more probably eighteenth or early nineteenth century. At
the front of the house are a wide green lawn and pleasant
trees and, in line with the door, a straight avenue of cypresses
that leads for perhaps a quarter of a mile downhill to the
house of the peasants who helped the Lawrences. The double
door, a handsome, arched affair painted dark green and standing at the head of five or six wide, stone steps, opens from the
inside, and Signora Mirenda appears again.

We enter a large, cool, rather dark room, entirely devoid
of furniture, and are startled by the walls, which are dec-
orated with evenly spaced, quite large, and very badly
painted murals of allegorical subjects, and for a moment we
wonder whether it is possible that Lawrence, who first took
seriously to painting in this house, could have exercised his
talent in these dubious studies of nymphs and clouds and
winged heroes. But no; they were painted, Signor Mirenda
says, by someone's mother—we cannot be sure whose. They

were here in the time of Lawrence? Ah, yes. We do not ask
what he thought of them, but go silently up a flight of rather
narrow wooden stairs to the second floor.

Now huge keys are produced. The flat is used by Signor
Mirenda's brother, but only in the summers, and it is differently furnished, but the rooms are of course the same. The
narrow hall in which we are standing divides the apartment
in two. Signor Mirenda unlocks one door and shows us into
a living room. The floors are of dull red brick. There is a
plain tile stove. The thick walls are plastered and scarcely
finished off with whitewash. The deep windows are barred
with iron grilles. (I have not inquired, but these grilles, which
appear so frequently in old Tuscan houses even on high windows, must have been a mode of protection against the more
ingenious of those bandits who thrived in such lively num-
bers in this part of Italy in past centuries.) The furniture is
moderately comfortable and scanty. Beyond this room are two
ample bedrooms, each containing a large dark bed, a chest, a
chair, little else. We remember how Lawrence described the
apartment in his *Letters*: "The rooms inside are big and rather
bare . . . spacious, rather nice, and very still. Life doesn't cost
much here. . . . I told you we'd fixed up the *salotto* nice and
warm, with matting and stove going and Vallombrosa chairs."
The description suits, except that the stove is cold and those
particular chairs do not seem to be here.

On the other side of the hall we see three more rooms. First,
the kitchen, with an enormous open fireplace that still serves
for cooking, the hearth raised about a foot from the floor, a
black kettle hanging from a hook over a neat pile of ashes.
Beyond the kitchen is a room for dining and intimate sitting,
and beyond that, another bedroom, smaller. And that is all.
Very simple, very plain, and although the rooms carry now
the musty air of shut-up places, we are vividly reminded of
Lawrence's preferences, of the things he loved and the things
he despised, and particularly of one of these as set down in
a poem written late in his life, perhaps here:

Some women live for the idiotic furniture of their houses,
some men live for the conceited furniture of their minds,
some only live for their emotional furnishing—

and it all amounts to the same thing, furniture,
usually in "suites."

The house speaks of him, and bears, in fact, an uncanny resemblance to another house of his that we had previously seen
and where he also lived for exactly two years—at the edge of
Taormina, where a vegetable garden grows just outside the
kitchen door and barnyard fowl energetically peck away on
the terraces.

Where did Lawrence work? In bad weather, in the *salotto,*
but in all good weather, either in the tower or in the woods.
From the narrow hall, we ascend by tight stairs to the tower.
It is not much more than six feet square, with two deep
romanesque arches open to all weather. The sun streams in,
and we look out through one arch to the valley of the Arno and
the whole miniature spectacle of Florence, every dome
and tower as clearly limned as in an old engraving, and to
the mountains beyond it, and immediately below to the vineyards and the olive groves and the small fields of grain that
belong to the Mirendas, and we watch two white bullocks
slowly moving up a field, and near a road, a flock of long-
legged, gray and black sheep munching grass under the supervision of a placid dog and a girl asleep in a ditch. From
the other arch, we look out at other villas on other hills, at
clumps of cypresses like omnipresent sentinels, and at the
spread of the *pinèta,* the pine woods, where Lawrence took
his daily walks and worked when he could. It is spring, and
everything is green and stands out with gemlike clarity, but
we remember Lawrence's reference in a letter written in
mistier autumn, to the yellow leaves dropping from the vines
against the barbarous red of sumac.

I begin to take some notes, and when the others thread
down the narrow stairs, I stay behind, for it is possible here,
high up and looking out and down, to feel a number of things

that Lawrence felt, chiefly his desire to be out of the social world, to make something positive of his loneliness. In one quarrel after another, he, too, had lost many friends, but he had retained those he wanted (*"Tu stai con me, lo so,"* he wrote to one of them from Villa Mirenda). Now, however, he did not want to see even them, and in this outlandish place he was quite safe. Few visitors came. An English couple living in a nearby villa came occasionally—the Wilkinsons, "sort of village arty people who went round with a puppet show, quite nice, and not at all intrusive." The Huxleys, who lived in nearby Forte dei Marmi, the Lawrences saw in this period, but not at Villa Mirenda. A daughter of Frieda Lawrence came once for a short stay. An occasional friend trekked out from Florence now and then, and the Lawrences went into Florence once or twice a week. But chiefly they had the peasants and themselves. One reason that they took the place was because it was "a region of *no* foreigners." Lawrence knew quite well what he was facing ("Have you built your ship of death, oh, have you?") and he was trying to face it. ". . . people don't mean much to me, especially casuals: them I'd rather be without," he wrote; and, "the Florence society is no menace." He did not want what he could have, and he could not have what he felt he needed.

I suffer badly from being so cut off. But what is one to do? One can't link up with the social unconscious. [This is a letter of August 1927 to Dr. Trigant Burrow.] At times, one is *forced* to be essentially a hermit. I don't want to be. But anything else is either a personal tussle, or a money tussle: sickening: except, of course, just for ordinary acquaintance, which remains acquaintance. One has no real human relations—that is so devastating.

Better to have no social relations at all than to have them and pretend that they are real! So he wrote disgustedly to Huxley of Beethoven, "always in love with somebody when he wasn't really, and wanting contacts when he didn't really —part of the crucifixion into isolated individuality—*poveri noi.*" Every future holds but one final fact, and what Law-

rence loved about Villa Mirenda was that it served to school
him in that ultimate isolation.

> I never know what people mean when they complain of
>     loneliness.
> To be alone is one of life's greatest delights, thinking
>     one's own thoughts,
> doing one's own little jobs, seeing the world beyond
> and feeling oneself uninterrupted in the rooted connection
> with the centre of all things.

In these bare quiet rooms, in this quiet country landscape,
the rooted connection might be found.

> There is nothing to save, now all is lost,
> but a tiny core of stillness in the heart
> like the eye of a violet.

Most of those many poems that Lawrence scribbled in his
notebooks toward the end of his life have no great interest as
poems, but, as I flatten my palms on the crusty gray walls of
his tower and look out toward his pine woods where just now
the violets are blooming, I feel their charge as facts.

He was ill much of the time, of course—with an illness that
could only be alleviated, not cured, and, in spite of his somewhat fantastic notions about sickness and health, about the
relation of physiology to temperament, he knew this fact,
and knew what he must expect. "My bronchials," is a kind of
refrain in the letters of these years. "I am itchy." But it was
worse than that: "I've been in bed the last eight days with
bronchial haemorrhage—and Dr. Giglioli!" It was this illness
quite as much as his native restlessness, his spirit of *andiamo*,
as he called it, that took the Lawrences away from Villa
Mirenda and the Florentine climate so frequently. Five or six
times in two years they left it for a month or two at a time
—for Switzerland, for Germany, for Austria, for Ravello, even
briefly for England—but always to return; and even when
they left it for good, it was the Mirenda that they hoped to
find in duplicate somewhere else. Yet their two years in Villa

Mirenda were punctuated with outbursts of dislike for Italy. "I've had a spell of loathing the Italian countryside altogether," Lawrence wrote to Earl Brewster, "and feeling that Italy is no place for a *man* to live in. I nearly decided to go off to Bavaria. But it all costs so much—and I think the discontent is inside me, and I'd better abide and wait a bit. But O miserere!—I've taken the house at least for six months more." In this mood, he could build up his own "paper castles," and with his own excitement.

> I *am* somehow bored by Italy, and when a place goes against my grain I'm never well in it. I do really think one is heaps better off in New Mexico—sometimes I pine for it. Let's go in spring— and you help me chop down trees and irrigate pasture on the ranch. I'm sure you'd be happier—if we were all there. After all one *moves*—and this deadening kind of hopeless-helplessness one has in Europe passes off. Let's all go in March, let's go. I'm sick of Here. . . . And let's make an exhibition of pictures in New York. What fun! For Easter, an exhibition of pictures in New York, then go west. We might afterwards sail to China and India from San Francisco—there's always that door out. Let's do it! Anything, anything to shake off this stupor and have a bit of fun in life, I'd even go to Hell, en route.

If illness and the image of a black ship lay under this restlessness, they also affected in a curious way Lawrence's attitude toward his work. A lethargic indifference, a weary kind of rest after all the high-strung battles, came over him.

> In the real summer [he wrote his British publisher] I always lose interest in literature and publications. The *cicadas* rattle away all day in the trees, the girls sing, cutting the corn with the sickles, the sheaves of wheat lie all the afternoon like people dead asleep in the heat. *E più non si frega.* I don't work, except at an occasional scrap of an article. I don't feel much like doing a book, of any sort. Why do any more books? There are so many, and such a small demand for what there are. So why add to the burden, and waste one's vitality over it. Because it costs one a lot of blood. Here we can live very modestly, and husband

our resources. It is as good as earning money, to have very small expenses. *Dunque—*

And to his agent: "I think perhaps it's a waste to write any more novels. I could probably live by little things. I mean in magazines." And yet, he did work, and under circumstances that few except Lawrence among modern writers could have found advantageous:

> We have come to the lying in the garden stage, and I go off into the woods to work, where the nightingales have a very gay time singing at me. They are very inquisitive and come nearer to watch me turn a page. They seem to love to see the pages turned.

The result of this kind of work was not only the articles that finally made up *Etruscan Places* (which called for a tour of cemeteries to the south and west in March and April of 1927, the essays themselves written rapidly in June when he was back at the Mirenda) but also the revision of all his poetry for the collected edition, that remarkable fable called *The Man Who Died,* a good deal of short work, and the three quite different versions of *Lady Chatterley's Lover,* all written here between February of 1927 and January of 1928. After that, Lawrence waited until June, when his queer friend Orioli, the Florentine bookseller and publisher, produced the private first edition, and then he left.

Downstairs, the others are standing in the doorway to a room off the big, shadowy hall. They are studying two plain chairs and a table, and Signora Mirenda explains that these belonged to the Lawrences, who gave them to the Mirendas when they left Scandicci. The Vallombrosa chairs! They are upright, walnut chairs with slim arms and straw seats, and this one, the signora continues, was his, and that, somewhat less comfortable with its single crosspiece in the center of the back, was hers. The room seems to be used for storage; on the floor, spread out on a large cane mat, are many lemons, and their fragrance fills the room.

The Mirendas invite us into their apartment, and we walk through rooms identical with those upstairs, through the kitchen with the same vast fireplace, and sit around the dining table with them. Signora Mirenda produces a decanter of white Chianti. Theirs? *Si, si.* ("They finished bringing in the grapes on Wednesday, so the whole place smells sourish, from the enormous vats of grapes downstairs, waiting to get a bit squashy, for the men to tread them out.") Now Signor Mirenda produces a photograph album and shows us a dim snapshot of the villa taken by Lawrence for them. Did the Lawrences have servants, we ask. They had the help of the *contadini,* but Lawrence liked to do the marketing himself, walking to and back from Scandicci, and he liked much to work around his house. He cooked, the signora says with a chuckle, and he washed the floors, he washed the clothes. He was very handy with the needle, and he turned his own shirt collars. He was *molto simpatico, molto, molto.* Was Signora Lawrence happy here? They do not know, but she cried much of the time. Did they quarrel? Was he cruel to her? Again, *"Non lo so,"* and the discreet Italian shrug. But he was very kind to the poor.

"The poor" must mean the peasants, of which there were twenty-seven on the place in the Lawrences' time. Lawrence has written in his letters how on each of their two Christmases at Villa Mirenda, they gave a party for all the *contadini,* with a tree brought in from the *pinèta,* presents for all the women and children, cigars for the men. Once, when they returned from Switzerland, all the peasants were "out to meet us, with primroses and violets and scarlet and purple anemones," and the peasants, say the Mirendas, enjoyed Lawrence's pictures and liked to watch him paint them. Lawrence pointed out that in this taste, they were rather different from the British magistrate who ordered the raid on the London gallery where the pictures were shown.

Somewhere in another room a radio begins to sputter over an Italian version of *I Want to Be Happy,* perhaps to the young girl we saw by the well, and it jars the easy flow of reminiscence to a stop. We ask whether we can walk to the wood, and the Mirendas take us on a sunny terrace on the south side of the house and point out the way. From a wicker rack on the wall of the house, Signora Mirenda takes a handful of figs ("great big figs that they call *fiori*") and offers them to us. We thank her and thank her husband, and they come to the door with us and wave as we go.

We take the path through the vineyard that stretches out beyond the well. A turkey puffs and swells at us, and spreads his feathers protectively between us and his unconcerned hens. Eating the figs, we pass the stream where, in warm weather, the Lawrences picnicked ("I can go about in shirt and trousers and sandals, and it's hot, and all relaxed"), and then walk over the fields for about a half mile and presently we are in the woods. They are deep and cool, the umbrella pines old and tall, with straight, thick trunks, and high above, their curious spread of branches. Nearer the ground grow bushier trees with very small dark leaves that one Italian has told me are "elms" (when you solicit this kind of information, most Italians would rather misinform you than tell you nothing at all), and under them and all over the ground is that whole array of spring flowers which Lawrence so liked to catalogue and describe: crocuses and grape hyacinth, primroses and violets, enormous purple anemones, and some heavypetaled chartreuse lilies that are strange to us. Here Lawrence once found a white orchid, but we find none; and here, in this most Italian wood, he imagined his English forest on the estate of Clifford Chatterley.

*Lady Chatterley's Lover,* like almost everything that Lawrence wrote, is a protest against the mechanization of human nature. At one point his heroine reflects that "civilized society is insane," and the novel opens with the assertion that "Ours is essentially a tragic age, so we refuse to take it tragically." This is a strange old wood to which Lawrence came every day: he had backed almost entirely out of society in order to give us this measure of it.

Then they moved again. ". . . at a certain point the business of the thistle is to roll and roll on the wind," he wrote about three months before they gave away their chairs and left for good. "We've given up the Villa Mirenda, and are once more wanderers in the wide, wide world." Much of what Lawrence wrote at Villa Mirenda was bitter, but the place seems to have preserved him from his final savagery of feeling. When, in his tower and in these woods, he worked over his many poems for the collected edition, he felt, he said, "like an autumn morning, a perfect maze of gossamer of rhythms and rhymes and loose lines floating in the air." It was only after he left that he was impelled to write the inscription for a hypothetical tombstone in Gsteig churchyard: "Departed this life, etc. etc.—*He was fed up!*"

Here in his woods the nightingales are singing like mad.

By the most direct route, Villa Mirenda is twenty kilometers or about twelve miles from Villa La Costa; in another measurement they are light-years apart. Yet they are perhaps not so far from each other as one is from the coal mines of Nottinghamshire, the other from the wheat fields around Sauk Centre, Minnesota. They were different men, Sinclair Lewis and D. H. Lawrence, very different writers, and they went by different routes to very different kinds of houses. And they were both a long way from home.

# PART FOUR

# The Burdens of Biography

MANY OF YOU KNOW the anecdote about Samuel Johnson and James Boswell in which Boswell, with his obsessive concern for the accumulation of more and more details of Johnson's life and character, was questioning a third person about Johnson in Johnson's presence, when Johnson suddenly thundered at him, "You have but two subjects, yourself and me. I am sick of both."

Let this anecdote serve as my text, and in a more special way than the exasperated Dr. Johnson intended, namely, that biography itself has two subjects, and two subjects only—the figure whose life is being re-created, of course, and the mind that is re-creating it, the scrutinizing biographer no less than the object of his scrutiny. Let me use it, too, to suggest that the largest burdens of biography are twofold: one, of course, on the man who has undertaken the work, responsibilities much more subtle than may at first appear and conceivably so enervating that he may well be tempted to throw up his hands and shout, "I'm sick of it"; the other on the ghost of the man who is not to be permitted the decent obscurity of death and who, seeing how he is being made to live, might well, had he a voice, shout, "I am sick of both!" And let me use this anecdote finally as a kind of warning, even as a request for forgiveness of what may well seem to be an exercise in egocentricity that goes far beyond Boswellian vanity. For I must be personal if I am to speak on this subject at all.

I spent some years in research for a biography and some more years in writing what proved to be a rather large book. I had not intended to speak directly about that book or of my experience in writing it. I had hoped to speak generally on biography as an art. I had written a biography but I had never read much about the nature of biography or how to write it. In preparation—as I thought—I have read a half dozen books, or more, on this subject, and I regret to say that I learned very little. It is difficult, but not impossible, to set up a definition of the novel more precise than E. M. Forster's quotation from the Frenchman, Chevalley, that a novel is "a fiction in prose of a certain extent." It is even more difficult to define biography, so various is it, or to set up rules for its composition, although this has been attempted. I am forced, for this reason, chiefly to posing some questions and then to answering them as well as I can from my own experience.

A writer of fiction, turning to biography, discovers the difference immediately (later, he will discover the similarities as well); as a writer of fiction he was a free man; as a biographer, he is writing in chains, as it were. As a writer of fiction, he invented his subject, even when he modeled it on real events and real people, and was free to handle it as he pleased; as a biographer, he is given his subject and is obliged to stay rigorously with its facts. This is, of course, a burden, but often, one discovers, a burden that it is a pleasure to carry. For facts can be surprisingly friendly, and they have, not infrequently, an eloquence, even a kind of poetry, that may well go far beyond the inventions of imagination.

I had thought, as I came to the end of my biography, that I would next write a short novel—a novel about Sinclair Lewis, no less, in which I could do some telescoping and some embroidering which the limits of biography did not allow, and also in which, with the happy disguises of fiction, I could use some episodes that my at least rudimentary sense of the power of legal restraints had not allowed. I gave up that idea. Almost simultaneously with the publication of my biography, a novel about Sinclair Lewis was published. It provided a sharply drawn picture of some of Lewis's most striking characteristics, but in its invented elements—chiefly, its

plot—it did not do so well. It is known that toward the end
of his life Lewis enjoyed the company of a young actress as
his mistress. She was a few years younger than the older of
Lewis's two sons, and in real life Lewis would try to amuse
her with the company of people of her own age, including
this son. But when now and then he urged the young man to
take her out for an evening, to dinner or to the films, he
complained to his mother: "I don't want to take her out.
She bores me." In the novel I have mentioned, the aging
novelist's son falls in love with the young woman, and when
in the climax of the story the father discovers the affair his
world at last crashes into total ruin. But the facts, while less
melodramatic, were much more interesting, certainly more
macabre. After the young woman left Lewis to marry a man
of roughly her age, Lewis decided to go abroad; but he
wanted a companion, and he invited a number of old friends
and a number of near strangers to travel with him. All refused. Then he turned to the young woman's mother, a plain,
inarticulate, simple New Jersey housewife, who accepted.
And Lewis, with his extraordinary gift for self-deception,
wrote back to his friends to say how graciously the Floren-
tines were receiving her. "Donna Caterina," they called her,
he said. But in the obituary columns of at least one Florentine
newspaper, she was referred to as *una vecchia gouvernante*—
an old governess. Here I am happy to be confined to the
pathos of fact.

Let me give you another and a much briefer illustration of
what I have called the friendliness of facts. Lewis died of
what we would call a heart attack; but in the official records
of the Roman hospital in which he died, the cause of his
death is given in another terminology, presumably a commonplace in the vocabulary of Italian medicine: *paralisi car-
diaca*. Could I possibly have invented it? Paralysis of the heart.
This, in its metaphorical significance, I had long before discovered was the very theme of Lewis's life and a major theme
of the whole book: his incapacity for love. Is this not poetry?
and more than that, magnificently, poetic justice?

There is then, first of all, the body of fact about one's subject. These details, if one is a responsible biographer, one ac-
cumulates with all the hoarding assiduity of a Boswell, the
most trivial along with the most striking. One *must* accumulate them all, or as many of them as can be retrieved from
moldering documents, for until one is in possession of them
all, one does not know two important things: one, what the
book is to be about; and two, what shape the book will have.
It is probable, however, that about halfway through the
process of accumulation one begins to have some sense of
each of these matters, since the accumulation is not made
according to chronology but in a hit-or-miss fashion as one
picks up scrap after scrap at whatever point it is offered. (For
my book, for example, my earliest extensive researches, because I happened to be living in Italy when I began, were
with the end of the Lewis life.) Italy, except for some newspaper accounts, did not provide much by way of documents,
but it contained the places where he lived—his Florentine
house, his last, gave me more eloquent facts than scores of
documents could have—and it contained besides a host of
living witnesses.

When one is writing the life of a person only recently dead,
living witnesses are, of course, an essential source of information. And one discovers all too soon the burden that such
evidence entails. Sometimes I wished that I had ten years
more, for in that time most of those people would have gone
away and I would no longer be confused by their conflicting
tales and would in fact be free to say what I wished about
*them.* Quite as often I despaired when, just as I was about
to get to an important informant, he *did* suddenly go away.

The first problem with living witnesses is simply human
vanity. It is natural enough that anyone who knows that he is
to appear in a book will wish to appear to the best advantage.
Inevitably, then, he will do one of two things, or both, when
he talks to the biographer: he will be exasperatingly reticent
or he will dress up the circumstances. Then there are those

who wish to be memorialized as having had a more important association with the subject than the facts will support.
Fortunately, if one has enough living witnesses, one can generally check the accuracy of one against the testimony of
another or of others. And often, of course, a letter, a scrap
of entry in a diary or a journal, a casual item in a newspaper,
a published reminiscence will turn up to provide the control
for which one is looking. This is not to say, of course, that
documents in themselves are to be trusted simply because
they are documents, even of the most personal kind. Leon Edel,
the biographer of Henry James, who has read some seven
thousand letters by James, tells us of the analytical scouring
he must do to get beyond the "mere twaddle of graciousness"
to the trustworthy kernel, if it is there at all. And Sinclair
Lewis, after he was famous but still writing his aged father
faithful weekly letters, mainly from Europe, enjoined his
young nephew, who read these letters with adolescent fascination, not to take them very seriously, that he wrote his
father only what his father wanted to hear. So documents,
too, must be checked against other documents, and back
against that talk from personal witnesses that may or may not
represent the truth.

A third kind of difficulty presented by living witnesses evi-
dences itself immediately when one is dealing with a personality like Sinclair Lewis's—at once so extreme in gregarious-
ness and so short in patience. The number of associates that
resulted from the first quality proposed an almost endless
round of interviews which I finally ended rather arbitrarily,
but I am not thinking of that problem so much as I am of
the hurt feelings that resulted from the second quality.
Lewis was like Richard Savage in at least one item in Johnson's life of that unhappy man:

> It was his peculiar happiness, that he scarcely ever found a
> stranger whom he did not leave a friend; but it must likewise be
> added that he had not often a friend long, without obliging him
> to become a stranger.

Hurt feelings lingering, even festering over the years, do not make for highly reliable testimony. One tends to come away with only the anger, the rancor, the wound—and beyond a certain point, these are not of much use to the biographer.

A more serious difficulty with living witnesses is the simple fallibility of human memory. I have told this anecdote before, but let me tell it again, because the general principle involved has again been amusingly illustrated, for me, since the publication of my book. Biography, as Bernard de Voto wrote, "is not concerned with the *must* but only with the *did*." Yet one soon finds, when writing the life of a man who gained great public prominence, that in many minds certain things *must* have happened even if they *did* not. A prominent man is, in many ways, a mythological man.

If Sinclair Lewis became the most famous man ever to have grown up in Sauk Centre, Minnesota, his youth there must have held the evidence, even if it was only belatedly observed. Thus, one of my witnesses, a contemporary of my subject, told me how, in June of 1902, graduating from the Sauk Centre High School in a class of seven, Sinclair Lewis, that baffled, awkward boy of seventeen, gave a brilliant valedictory address on the subject of "The Westward March of Empire." The subject was appropriate enough to the time, but the address itself was not appropriate to the academic circumstances of Harry Lewis. In this detail, the documentary control was easy enough to come by: the local newspaper under the proper date, which summarized the famous address and demonstrated quite clearly that it had been delivered, not by my subject, but by my informant himself. There is touching humility in this anecdote, but I fear only a rudimentary sense of history. On his graduation from a high school with a class that had three places of honor open to it, Sinclair Lewis was, for a change, completely silent.

This curious experience came back to my mind a few months ago when I had a letter of congratulation from my high-school English teacher in my sophomore year in the Sauk City (Wisconsin) High School—named after the same

Indian tribe, an almost interchangeable town with Sauk
Centre, Minnesota, but, it happens, a different one. She was
writing to congratulate me. She always knew that some day
I would be famous. (Let me say quickly that this is only *her*
view.) She supposed that I would not remember her (of
course, I do; did she not dismiss me from class for snickering
about a word in *Macbeth* for which Sauk City preferred a
euphemism?) She was always, she said, afraid of me, because
she felt that I knew so much more about the subject than
she did, and that I would expose her ignorance. I was the
"brightest boy in the school."

Ha! My academic record in Sauk City is no doubt quite as
available as was Sinclair Lewis's in Sauk Centre, but I have
no wish to examine it. I know what it was—highly undistinguished. And so was all my academic work until I was well
into graduate study. My undergraduate record, today, would
not admit me to any self-respecting graduate school, certainly
not that at Berkeley or Ann Arbor, probably not that of Harvard, where, as gawky as Sinclair Lewis at Yale, I mysteriously went.

This is all parenthesis, but not, I hope to indicate before I
finish, as gratuitously parenthetical as it may now appear.
And it leads me to the next point that I would like to raise:
who is the best biographer for a given subject?

Of all the living witnesses whom I approached, only four
declined to be of help. Two of these were men who had
known Lewis intimately and planned to write biographical
memoirs of their own; naturally, they did not wish to share
their material with me. A third was a man who had known
Lewis during a very large part of his life, had been Lewis's
editor for many years, but unfortunately was also the editor
of one of those first two men who planned to write his own
Lewis biography; naturally, his interests were with that book,
not with mine. The fourth was Lewis's last secretary, the man
with whom Lewis was living at the time of his death, the
man who, in the last years in Europe, managed his affairs.

His refusal to see me, made on the telephone in Rome, remains a mystery to me; but I am grateful to him, for his
refusal also enabled me to make something of a mystery of
him. Since he would not see me, I had to depend upon the
only available evidence for that association—hearsay. Much
of it came from interesting sources—Bernard Berenson, for
example, who declared to me, "I know a minor Central European adventurer when I see one." It is only in this part of the
book, I believe, the very end, and only because of the lacuna
which the obdurate ex-secretary provided, that my fictional
impulses necessarily came into play. They made for a nice
bit of implied melodrama and, I believe, for truth of its own
kind as well. And for once I was freed of the vexatious business of trying to force an informant to be truthful!

Now it is possible that those two men who had known
Lewis over a number of years, or even his editor, would have
written better biographies than mine. Samuel Johnson would
have thought so. The best biography, in his view, is written
by the subject himself; in other words, the best biography is
autobiography. Had Johnson had the interest to write his
autobiography, it would, I suspect, have been brief and in-
cisive and honest and masterly; but we can be certain that
it would not have given us that full-bodied portrait that the
patient drudgery of Boswell created in the great masterpiece
of all English biography. In the degree to which it would
have been shorter it would have been less true. Johnson was
a man of unusual self-knowledge, but he was also a man of
unusual reticence. Boswell's very naïveté gave him an advantage; so did his habit of garrulousness. And Johnson, we
should remind ourselves, was an exceptional man, fearful of a
number of things but never of contemplating his own nature.
Most men are. Certainly my subject was. He wrote many
autobiographical sketches, and all of them are inaccurate and
untrustworthy, deliberate softenings of what was harsh, deliberate alterations of fact for the sake of entertainment, confusions of fact, obfuscations—all in need of correction. One
of my informants has told me that, toward the end of his

life, Lewis spent many hours, usually in drunken rages, dictating fragments of his autobiography to her, all later to be assembled in a book. I have not been permitted to see her notes, if they exist, and until I am, I shall permit myself to doubt that they exist. Nothing in Sinclair Lewis's writings suggests that he could have been his own biographer.

I shall have something to say presently about the uses to which a writer's own works can be put by his biographer. At this point I wish only to point out the hazards. With a writer such as Sinclair Lewis, so little inclined toward candor with himself, it would be fatal to take with any literalness those fictional passages of his that do seem to arise from his immediate experience. Like Richard Savage, to whom I shall come in a moment, Lewis had mistaken preconceptions about the simple life but no gift for living it, yet he always yearned for a wilderness excursion. When his brother finally made such a trip into Saskatchewan possible, it began, for Lewis, as a series of drunken adventures and ended as a number of days so acutely uncomfortable that he abandoned the trip before it was half over and headed back for civilization. When he came to use the experience in fiction—in a melodramatic novel called *Mantrap*—the figure who corresponds to Lewis is the heroic and vindicated city man in the wilderness, and the novel provided a suitable film script for the talents of Clara Bow. In *Dodsworth*, which has commonly been read as an account of the decay of Lewis's first marriage, nothing can be trusted but the *feelings* of the hero for his first wife, and his *feelings* for the woman who was to become his second. But feelings are not precisely biographical fact. Alcohol was a grave problem for Lewis, who on untold occasions suffered the horrors of hangover and the acute pangs of guilt that go with that condition; but he almost never wrote about these matters. In one foolish story he began to, but soon turned the truly reported details into the mechanics of a tricky plot directed toward the kind of "happy ending" that he himself

was never to know. Never trust the author, said D. H. Lawrence. Trust the tale. Do not, he meant, believe the author
when he lectures us; believe only the conduct of the narrative itself, and the resolution of its values. If we follow this
sound advice with Sinclair Lewis, we arrive at one conclusion: self-deception.

After the subject himself, the best biographer was, Johnson
thought, a close friend, a man who had seen his subject in
the most intimate circumstances of his life over a long period,
who knew the accents of his talk, who knew his physical
habits, the way he walked, the way he behaved at table, the
way he laughed, the degree to which he permitted his sor-
rows to show. Again, one can only wonder.

Johnson himself, when he came to write the life of his
friend, Richard Savage, produced a work of art—he could not
do less; but did he, in a strict sense, produce a proper biography of Richard Savage? Had he known Savage less intimately, might he not have paused to question Savage's own
account of his birth and upbringing, found his friend not
the innocent victim of monstrous abuses but an unsuccessful
fraud, found his friend's supposed mother not the implausible fiend who has come down to us through the *Life*, but an
indiscreet woman unsuccessfully put upon by a small villain?
Recent scholarship suggests such miscalculations in Johnson's
narrative, and so, indeed, does the narrative itself on any close
inspection. Even Boswell, that glorious simpleton, had his
doubts about this much of the narrative. And it is all the
more surprising in that, at other points, Johnson could estimate his friend so ably. With what lovely irony he writes
when he tells us how Savage's friends, eager to remove him
from the threats of his debtors, arrange to ship him off to
the wilds of Wales. Savage, London-born and bred, familiar
only with the city, low life, and literature, had certain preconceptions about the country that Johnson was perfectly
capable of defining and enjoying:

. . . he had planned out a scheme of life for the country, of which he had no knowledge but from pastorals and songs. He imagined that he should be transported to scenes of flowery felicity, like those which one poet has reflected to another; and had projected a perpetual round of innocent pleasures, of which he suspected no interruption from pride, or ignorance, or brutality.

With these expectations he was so enchanted, that when he was once gently reproached by a friend for submitting to live upon a subscription, and advised rather by a resolute exertion of his abilities to support himself, he could not bear to debar himself from the happiness which was to be found in the calm of a cottage, or lose the opportunity of listening, without intermission, to the melody of the nightingale, which he believed was to be heard from every bramble, and which he did not fail to mention as a very important part of the happiness of a country life.

And yet, in spite of such perspicacity, the whole may very well be based on a miscalculation for the very reason that these men were intimates, had loved one another too much in life, too little, perhaps, in the imagination. There are deeper forms of intimacy than friendship.

Personal intimacy with one's subject would certainly have those advantages for the biographer that Johnson names, but does it not have certain disadvantages, too, and perhaps larger ones? Personal intimacy can readily lead to panegyric, which is not biography, for there are obligations to friendship even after one's friend is dead. Inversely, if hurt feelings are involved, it can lead to self-protective distortions and omissions, which are the chief faults of the first Mrs. Lewis's *roman à clef, Half a Loaf,* and her more recent biography of Lewis, *With Love from Gracie.* Personal intimacy, more significantly, may lead to mere memoir, which again is not proper biography, books of the "I Knew Him When" variety, or at least may permit intrusions of personal reminiscence which, if they do not decree the total shape, may yet throw the whole off balance (the only flaw in Andrew Turnbull's otherwise beautiful life of Scott Fitzgerald).

There is a further limitation: an intimate friend would almost certainly feel that he knew his subject to start with and
conclude that much plain drudgery in accumulating all that
detail, which a more impersonal biographer regards as essential to his enterprise, was not essential at all. For, believe me,
the first thing that a biographer must be is a drudge. I
wonder if either of those two men—one old and tired, the
other a very busy and highly successful foreign correspondent
—would, for example, have been willing to read through (and
take the full notes which are routine for a trained scholar)
Lewis's twenty-one novels, all but five of them of small literary worth and some of them almost unbelievably poor, let
alone track down in any number of different libraries the hun-
dred-odd stories, almost all of them worse than poor, which
Lewis published in the highly paying but also highly ephemeral national periodicals of large circulation. I cannot believe it. And yet I do believe, with Professor Pottle, that
among the obligations of a man who proposes to write a
*literary* biography one of the first is to read through the
complete works of his subject. And I will add a point that
Professor Pottle does not, I think, make: that he will find
that much of them he will have to read a second time, and
some a third and a fourth.

And all this for extra-literary purposes, for reasons that
have little to do with the literary worth of his subject's works.
I do not mean to suggest that a literary biographer is not
expected to deliver a literary judgment, indeed, a whole
series of them; of course he is, that is his ultimate obligation.
But even if the works are treated mainly as biographical
events (as I chose, on the whole, to treat Lewis's) they must
be read and analyzed, for in some important ways they are
the clue to and even the chart of the mind and being of his
subject. This is particularly the situation if the work is imaginative, and even if it is not generally autobiographical in the
usual sense (and Lewis's certainly was not), it is nevertheless
an autobiography of the spirit. Its lineaments are to be de-
tected in the situations and themes that recur, in repeated and

developing images, in certain character types that seem to haunt the author. Almost all of Sinclair Lewis's works, one discovers after a time, are built on the same general idea, of a character who is trying to escape from something restrictive into some kind of freedom. In the novels, the restrictions—convention, hypocrisy, injustice, institutions, et cetera —are metaphors, one finds at last, for a restriction that was unutterable for him in his life. For the second large theme of that life is Lewis's own frenetic and endless and impossible attempt to escape from the restrictions of his self into a freedom that does not exist.

We have gone beyond the drudge, who must accumulate, to the critic, who must analyze, and who is perceptive enough to see what is basically *there* in the work. The drudge alone could compile his material into a chronological catalogue, even a chronicle of sorts; but that is not proper biography. The critic alone, if he can see not only what is basically there in the work, but also how it threads its way through the whole mass of accumulated detail, will have moved toward the formal skeleton of a biography; but that is not yet proper biography either. No, now we need a third man, and you must forgive me for saying that he must be an artist, not only the man who can bring shape out of the mass but more especially the man who can give it living shape; and I do not mean only that he must make his subject live, but also that he must make him live in the reanimated history of his time, make him live in a living world. And now that we have come to the most interesting point, I too have reached the unutterable, the burden that is ineffable: I do not know how it is done. I can only hope that in some small way, perhaps, I did it.

We can talk about the shape if not about its animation. This brings us to the similarities with fiction, for biography, also, is a narrative art, and it seems probable that all the principles that pertain to fiction except for one—the free exercise of invention—pertain to proper biography. A novelist has his whole world of experience, real and imaginary, to draw from; how does he carve out of that limitless and undifferentiated mass the materials that fall into pattern in his beautiful, autonomous units? He has, of course, for each work, a theme, and his theme determines his selection of detail. The biographer finds his themes—the strains that seem most persistently to recur—in that mass of accumulated detail and selects from the mass accordingly. I am aware that some of my readers do not think that I selected drastically enough and others think that I did not select at all; the fact is that I did not, for example, report on every drunken rumpus, as one reviewer has complained, but only on, I suppose, some six or ten of them, whereas there must have been at least ten times ten and possibly one hundred times six of them. But if from my mention of six or ten, my exhausted reader has some sense of the exhausting intemperance to which Sinclair Lewis, in long stretches of his life, was addicted, I am at least partially vindicated: the reader, who carries the least burden, except perhaps on his pocketbook, has at least been made to suffer with my subject and with me. And while we are on intemperance and the problem of selection from the whole possible body of detail, may I remind you that it was only as recently as 1903, the year after Sinclair Lewis's inauspicious graduation from high school, that Sir Edmund Gosse arrived at the conclusion that the one horrendous fact about his subject which a biographer should under no circumstances reveal is his addiction to drink. If we were today to eliminate this phenomenon, what would the biographers of American writers have to write about?

For several centuries "the ethics of biography" (as Sir Edmund entitled his essay of 1903) was the subject of much discussion: what, in any body of accumulated detail, was clearly inadmissible by the biographer? Gibbon, in the eighteenth century, thought that everything was admissible, and so did Johnson except for one occasion when he reversed himself and opined that it was better to repress a detail than hurt the feelings of "a widow, a daughter, a brother, or a friend." In the nineteenth century, while biographies grew longer and longer, they tended to revert to their origins in England and become mere works of hagiography. Today, I believe, the problem of selection is not made more acute by what were once thought of as ethical considerations. One should write in anything that is true and relevant to one's themes—anything, that is, that will not bring us into court. In this sense, at least, therefore, the biographer today enjoys some of the freedom of the novelist, and he does not have to publish that famous and foolish disclaimer at the front of his book about how nothing in it has any relation whatever to any real person, now living or now dead.

Assume that our biographer has his several themes, those tensions or preoccupations or behavioral patterns that occur most frequently in the mass of the life, and that he can select his details accordingly. Like the novelist he faces a second step. All those themes must somehow be unified; the biographer, like the novelist, must find an appropriate emphasis, or general meaning. When I was about midway in my research, I decided that I would try to summarize Lewis's biography in a subtitle: *An American Life*. I had in mind at least a dozen things, not really separate but separable. I can mention a few. I saw Lewis's life, for instance, as representative of the curious social mobility of American life in general—the poor beginnings and the sudden, fantastic, uneasy success. I saw it more specifically as an extreme example of the fate of so many American writers—the quick supremacy and the long, dreary decline joined with an equally dreary debauchery. I began to see Lewis's life as peculiarly American in the very ambiguities that tore it apart—his love for his country, sometimes nearly chauvinistic, and his unhappy dislike of much of it. I might have borrowed a subtitle from Melville and called it *Sinclair Lewis: The Ambiguities*. Or *The Paradoxes*. For the very ambiguities of American life, those paradoxical polarities of an individualistic society which destroys individuality, an affluent society which does not permit mil-

lions of its citizens the merest decencies, a peace-loving society which does best in a wartime economy—all those ambiguities that engendered Lewis's ambiguous feelings about
his country are also represented in the profoundest ambiguities of his own character. And now perhaps you can see how
the biographer, subjective being, enters the objective facts.
For clearly I am talking like a novelist, talking about America
as it seems to me, and finding in the objective materials of a
single life facts that will support that view.

We have, then, some themes and what is meant to be a
unifying attitude. We must have, beyond these, a general
shape, or form, or rhythm—again, like the novel. Themes and
attitude, taking always into account the general chronology
of real events which in large part determined them, will in
turn determine this. The shape of my book seemed fairly
obvious long before I was into it very deeply—a general pattern of rise, climax, and frenzied fall, containing within it
many lesser patterns of rise-climax-fall, a few of them large.
And like the novelist, the biographer needs still another
element; he needs a plot, an element of persistent conflict
that will animate not only the subject himself but that pattern
which his life enacts, over and over in little, and once and
once only in the whole that it was. Here the facts of Lewis's
life were most obliging, and the central conflict (highlighted,
of course, by my own view of things) seemed clear enough;
first the quarrel of his environment with him, then his quarrel
with his environment, and that quarrel turning very early but
with slowly increasing intensity into his quarrel with himself
and his attempt to escape it, to escape the self.

I begin to sound like an amateur psychologist and for that
I am sorry, since I tried very hard in my book to avoid precisely that. A biographer, like any other civilized man, should
know about the developments of modern psychology, but I
do not think that he should write as if he were indeed a
psychoanalyst. Some of my reviewers wished that I had; they
wished that at some point I had said plainly, flatly, what was

*wrong* with Sinclair Lewis. It was precisely because I was unwilling to make such a statement that I made the book so long. I wanted to give the reader all the evidence that I coherently could which would permit him to say to himself what was wrong with Sinclair Lewis. But more than that, I wanted him to believe that Sinclair Lewis was a living man, and I wanted him to be moved by his life. I do not think that the jargon of psychoanalysis would have heightened either the comedy or the pathos of that life. A friend of mine, a psychoanalyst, has recently sent me a paper of hers on a phenomenon that she has observed and calls "the Pollyanna Paranoid." This is the person who conceives of an impossibly beautiful future which, when it does not develop, as it cannot, permits him to feel betrayed and persecuted. The concept can explain a good deal about Sinclair Lewis, if not everything. But I insist that the term would hardly have improved my prose.

And this is the final matter that I must touch upon, and probably the most important. Thomas Carlyle, I believe, said that a well-written life is a much rarer thing than a well-spent one. I do not know if my life of Lewis is well written, but I do know that I gave as much thought as a novelist does to the kind of prose that would be most appropriate to that subject, to the tone that my prose would strike. Recently I was invited to attempt a biography of Stephen Crane, and while I have still a good deal to learn about Crane's life (and hence of my relation to that subject) I know most of his writing, and already I am wondering what tone will be most appropriate to that subject. (I am thinking about something that I call to myself "*athletic* elegance.") But for the life of Sinclair Lewis, I decided, lived with so little dignity and so much fret and fury, and, on the literary side, producing so much loose and garrulous bulk, the tone must be casual—never exalted, seldom formal, but rather conversational, perhaps rambling a bit, frequently ironical, now and then a little snide. I wanted the reader to feel that I was talking to him,

or as if he were overhearing me as I talked to Sinclair Lewis,
saying in effect over and over, You did that . . . it was funny,
wasn't it . . . how did it go again? . . . why?

It was only after I was well into the book, accustomed to
that tone—or whatever tone it was that I achieved—that I
began to wonder about my relationship to Sinclair Lewis and
to begin to understand how much of that relationship was
making the substance of the book. Not the facts; they were
there. Not the themes; they were there. Not even the plot;
that was there. But the general attitude, the whole coloration,
because that was I, or rather, the two of us together. Here
we can differentiate between what goes into fiction (*I*, really),
and into history (*they*, really), and into biography (he *and*
I). For is not biography, when we reduce it to its essential
nature, simply—or complexly—the interpenetration of one
mind by another, and is this not, for all the apparent objectivity one may achieve, a considerably subjective operation? "History," said the great Theodor Mommsen, "is neither written nor made without love or hate." He could have
made that observation even more appropriately of biography.
In my relationship with Lewis, as I began to scrutinize it and
as it was revealing itself in my tone, there were both love and
hate, and there were also pity, shame, much impatience.
There were also self-love and self-hate and self-pity, and the
shame and the impatience were as much for myself as for him.

Why did I—first of all—and now we are at what is really
the beginning—why did I choose to write this life? It is true
that I was invited to write it, but surely I could have said no.
I believe now that from the outset I was challenged by what
I unconsciously felt to be a strange affinity, an affinity perhaps only demonstrated by the fact that my literary tastes,
as they matured, had moved about as far away from his as is
possible. There was, of course, the obvious affinity of our
beginnings—the same kind of raw small Midwestern towns,
probably much the same kind of inept and unsuccessful boys
in that particular man's world. But I discovered many more,

and many that were more subtle. Should I try to spell them out now I would be writing my autobiography, or even confession, and I have no such inclination. But I can give a hint or two: all the careless writing, all the ill-conceived ambitions, all the bad manners, all the irrational fits of temper, all the excesses of conduct, all the immature, lifelong frivolities and regrettable follies. That is a little of it. There is much more. And those of my critics who have complained of an imputed lack of sympathy with my subject might have said with equal accuracy and greater justice, with sharper perception certainly, and probably with more kindness, that I had refused to be self-indulgent.

Perhaps this is where the psychoanalyst is really needed—not in the biographer analyzing his subject, but beyond both of them, analyzing their symbiotic relationship. And it is perhaps this relationship that explains why one of those critics who complained of my want of sympathy—Mr. Irving Howe—found the book paradoxically moving, in spite of all my icy refusal to be moved.

Critics are not as wise as they sometimes sound and never as wise as they believe. I speak now as a critic, and a self-critic. My long conversation with Sinclair Lewis—my nine years' captivity with him, one witty journalist called it—taught me a good deal. As I learned about him with all his stubborn deficiency in self-knowledge, I believe that I gained in self-knowledge. I am not a better man, certainly, for having written his life; but I think that I am a wiser one. And I can only hope that my gratitude to him for that will lighten a little the onus of the life with which I have burdened him.

# PART FIVE

# Hamlin Garland

THREE OF THE ELEVEN STORIES in *Main-Travelled Roads* have
to do with the return of a man to the rural scenes of his youth
and young manhood. The return is not usually successful, but
his expectations are always high, and a first glimpse of the
land, which has such "majesty, breadth," reinforces the expectations.

> Mr. Howard McLane . . . gazed out upon it with dreaming
> eyes. It had a certain mysterious glamour to him; the lakes were
> cooler and brighter to his eye, the greens fresher, and the grain
> more golden than to anyone else, for he was coming back to it
> all after an absence of ten years. It was, besides, *his* West. He
> still took pride in being a Western man.

This passage is from the opening page of the story called
"Up the Coulee." Howard McLane is a successful actor, returning to Wisconsin from the East to visit his mother and his
brother. And while the land is rich and beautiful, he finds the
farms filthy and his mother and brother living in squalid,
grinding poverty. Out of a painful sense of guilt arising from
his neglect of them, McLane plans to buy back the old home-
stead for them and to assist his brother with money. But it is
too late.

> "Money can't give me a chance now."
> "What do you mean?"
> "I mean life ain't worth very much to me. I'm too old to take
> a new start. I'm a dead failure. I've come to the conclusion that
> life's a failure for ninety-nine per cent of us. You can't help me
> now. It's too late!"

The two men stood there, face to face, hands clasped, the one fair-skinned, full-lipped, handsome in his neat suit; the other tragic, somber in his softened mood, his large, long, rugged Scotch face bronzed with sun and scarred with wrinkles that had histories, like saber cuts on a veteran, the record of his battles.

There is no compromise here with the expectations that Howard McLane had brought with him.

In another story, "A Branch Road," another successful man returns, only to find his sweetheart of seven years before married to a brutal farmer, living in grimy drudgery, her fresh beauty utterly gone in a premature old age. He persuades her to flee with him into a completely new life.

The third story is different. In "God's Ravens," a young writer persuades his wife to leave the frustrating routines of the city with him and their children for the "native town— up among the Wisconsin hills." At first the villagers seem only crude and cold to them, "caricatures" of human beings, and the whole experiment seems to be the most dismal failure until the hero falls deathly ill. Then the village rallies round in a burst of neighborliness, restores him to health, and restores his faith in mankind and himself.

> "O God, let me live! It is so beautiful! O God, give me strength again! Keep me in the light of the sun! Let me see the green grass come and go!"

Now they know their neighbors for what they really are and know that they are living in "Friendship Village." Whether his neighbors can help the young man to a successful literary career is a question the story does not ask.

The third story, then, is a considerable sentimentalization of the facts as Hamlin Garland had himself experienced them. The third return forces the expectations to become the actualities that, for him, they never were. For the theme of the return to his rural past was, in large part, the theme of Garland's life.

Born on a farm near West Salem, Wisconsin, in 1860, young Garland was early initiated into the brutalities of dragging a living out of the rich but recalcitrant land of what was still essentially the American frontier. Following his family from failure to failure, first to Iowa and then to South Dakota, always enduring the same harsh and relentless drudgery that brought with it no rewards at all, he rebelled at last and in 1884 found himself in a little room in Boston where he read voraciously, began to write, and supported himself by teaching and lecturing.

Influenced by the realism of William Dean Howells and of the local colorists, his earliest work chose as its subject matter his prairie boyhood, with all its harshness and poverty. But there was also the spacious beauty of the prairies to remember, the memory of prairie sunsets to throw a rosy nimbus over the cruelty, and there was his own sense of guilt arising from what seemed to him his desertion of his parents, and especially of his mother. Three years after his arrival in Boston, he returned to the towns of his boyhood and to his parents in Dakota. Everything was even worse than he remembered.

Out of this visit came the stories that would ultimately make up *Main-Travelled Roads*.

> How poor and dull and sleepy and squalid it seemed! The one main street ended at the hillside at his left and stretched away to the north, between two rows of the usual village stores, unrelieved by a tree or a touch of beauty. An unpaved street, drab-colored, miserable, rotting wooden buildings, with the inevitable battlements—the same, only worse, was the town.

Surrounding the ugly little towns are the farms, raw and muddy, the scene of endless hardship, of an unremitting grind at the harshest labor, a daily physical struggle, as dogged as it is spiritless, for simple survival. And this atmosphere, whether of village or of farm, breeds not only boorishness but brutishness, as in the louts who invade the house of poor James Sanford, the ruined banker in "A 'Good Fellow's' Wife." But while Garland recognized that brutality and connivance and cold selfishness do exist in human nature, something instinctive in him made it impossible for him to accept these qualities as essential in human nature. The blame must lie elsewhere.

It lay, Garland felt, in some vague and amorphous entity called "the system." It is not surprising that his stories echo with his intense Boston reading in the scientific determinists, Herbert Spencer and Charles Darwin, and with the views of native radical movements such as Single Taxation and Populism, with which Garland had associated himself. In a story like "Under the Lion's Paw," Garland, the social critic, is as explicit as he can be in his attack on capitalism: here the power of capital triumphs over the effectiveness of work, and the pathos of the final situation is meant to vindicate "the labor theory of value." However dubious the economic facts of the story may seem today, they were real enough on the frontier then, and even if they had not been, the force of Garland's sympathy with the struggle of a human being to sustain himself and his family in an economic trap puts us quite willingly on his side of the issue.

Yet the fact is that the effect of the echoes of Garland's theories is sometimes to give his stories a curiously schoolmasterish tone, as if he is instructing some uninformed person in the anthropology of the frontier, lecturing him on sociological injustices while showing lantern slides of picturesque native habits.

> This scene, one of the jolliest and most sociable of the Western farm [he writes in "A Branch Road"], had a charm quite aside from human companionship. The beautiful yellow straw entering the cylinder; the clear yellow-brown wheat pulsing out at the side; the broken straw, chaff, and dust puffing out on the great stacker; the cheery whistling and calling of the driver; the keen, crisp air, and the bright sun somehow weirdly suggestive of the passage of time.

The paragraph is almost saved as it gets toward its end, and there are many passages in these stories, starting out in the same guidebook spirit, that are immediately assimilated into

the direct presentation of the scene, without this silly sense
of the "Eastern" audience. Some others are not. Garland,
after his few years in Boston, could commit the worst crimes
of the snob, i.e., the person who pretends to elegant experiences that he has in fact not had (". . . a new play to be
produced, or a new yachting trip, or a tour of Europe . . ."").
Such absurd appeals to gentility, in this cruel context, reach
their peak of absurdity, perhaps, when Howard McLane
dresses to work once more in the fields where he spent his
early years, and the reader is supposed to sympathize with
him in his miscalculation:

> He dressed himself hurriedly, in a négligé shirt with a windsor
> scarf, light-colored, serviceable trousers with a belt, russet shoes,
> and a tennis hat—a knockabout costume, he considered.

Small wonder that his brother in effect orders him out of
the field! And the reader wonders in such passages where
Garland, the social reformer, has gone.

It was not, in fact, through his theories that, in these stories,
Hamlin Garland's basic view of human nature most clearly
emerged. This view shows itself in two more positive ways,
one good, one generally bad.

The first way is his persistent avowal of the strength of the
individual will. In most of Garland's characters, there is a
general spirit of submission to the inevitable demands of the
world they have chosen, but this does not mean a necessary
submission to "fate" or to choices once made. Many of the
characters say with Agnes, in "A Branch Road," "It can't be
helped now, Will," and think, with him, "Life pushes us into
such things"; but they can turn, too, like Will, and say with
him that "It can be helped, Aggie," and then attempt what
until that moment had seemed the impossible.

It is this sense of the power of the individual will and
the resultant pride in independence and self-sufficiency that
make all the drudgery tolerable.

> "I consider myself a sight better 'n any man who lives on some-
> body else's hard work. I've never had a cent I didn't earn with

them hands." He held them up and broke into a grin. "Beauties, ain't they? But they never wore gloves that some other poor cuss earned." . . .

"Well, so I come West, just like a thousand other fellers, to get a start where the cussed European aristocracy hadn't got a holt on the people. I like it here—course I'd like the lakes an' meadows of Waupac better—but I'm my own boss, as I say, and I'm goin' to *stay* my own boss if I haf to live on crackers an' wheat coffee to do it; that's the kind of a hairpin I am."

And the journalist who is listening to this speech believes that he has heard uttered the grand credo "of the modern democrat against the aristocrat, against the idea of caste . . ."

This atom of humanity (how infinitesimal this drop in the ocean of humanity!) was feeling the nameless longing of expanding personality, and had already pierced the conventions of society, and declared as nil the laws of the land—laws that were survivals of hate and prejudice. He had exposed also the native spring of the emigrant by uttering the feeling that it is better to be an equal among peasants than a servant before nobles.

There are overtones here derived from Walt Whitman, whose poetry Garland admired, even though there is little of Whitman's romantic enthusiasm. Most often the individualism of Garland's characters shows itself in a nearly stubborn pride in self, sometimes in a paradoxically dogged pride. This is the motive of Haskins, for example, in "Under the Lion's Paw," where we read that "no slave in the Roman galleys could have toiled so frightfully and lived, for this man thought himself a free man," and so it is of the aging, exhausted veteran in "The Return of a Private"—returning from the Civil War to find his farm a shambles; "he was sick and emaciated, but his heroic soul did not quail. With the same courage with which he faced his southern march, he entered upon a still more hazardous future."

A certain softening in the harsh qualities in human nature is to be found too in Garland's occasional rather bitter humor, as in the two stories about the Ripleys. It occurs also in the general spirit of cooperation that pervades these char-

acters who, for all their flinty independence of spirit, assume
without question the necessity of assisting others to maintain
their independence. All this is true enough to the life that
Garland is describing, and it is effective in a literary sense.
It ceases to be effective only when Garland pushes it too
hard, when Garland the sentimentalist who, returning, hopes
to find things better than they can be, makes them so when
they are not. Thus, with the final sentence of "A Day's Pleasure," we tumble into a pit of bathos, and in "God's Ravens,"
into a welter of sentiment, and in "A 'Good Fellow's' Wife,"
into the script of a soap opera.

This sentimentalizing strain in Garland, which broadened
intolerably as he aged, is of particular interest because it is
at least apparently at odds with his theoretical ambitions.
These, developed in the essays that make up his book called
*Crumbling Idols* (1894), meant to extend the province of
Howells's realism, and, indeed, in order to distinguish his
own position from the somewhat simple notion of objective
reporting, he called it "veritism." The derivation of this word
from the Latin *veritas* is clear enough, but it is also, very probably, an acknowledgment of his debt to the Frenchman Eu-
gene Véron, of whose *Esthetics* Garland wrote: "This work
influenced me more than any other work on art. It entered
into all I thought and spoke and read for many years after it
fell into my hands about 1886."

Garland's veritism differs from Howells's realism chiefly in
its emphasis on impressionism, in its insistence that fiction
"develop a form based on the moment of experience, acutely
felt and immediately expressed," an insistence that urges the
centrality of the artist's individualistic vision, "one man facing certain facts and telling his individual relations to them."

> He aims to be perfectly truthful in his delineation of his rela-
> tion to life, but there is a tone, a color, which comes uncon-
> sciously into his utterances like the sobbing stir of the muted
> violins beneath the frank, clear song of the clarionet; and this
> tone is one of sorrow that the future halts so lamely in its ap-
> proach.

If this passage suggests a sanction for the strain of sentimentalization that we have observed, it also points to what
is most effective in Garland's writing, a strain of curious
poetry.

This quality is perhaps most immediately evident in the
contrast throughout these stories between the beauties of the
natural world and the rigors of human effort—as when Howard McLane, on a lovely country night, considers the barnyard where his brother is milking the fly-tortured cows. It is
evident, too, in an impressive cinematic quality of which
Garland is capable, when the details are camera-sharp but
the whole effect is of a painting.

> The man approached him, gazing intently at his face. "You
> are?" after a pause. "Well, I'm glad to see yeh, but I can't shake
> hands. That damned cow had laid down in the mud."
>
> They stood and looked at each other. Howard's cuffs, collar,
> and shirt, alien in their elegance, showed through the dusk, and
> a glint of light shot out from the jewel of his necktie, as the light
> from the house caught it at the right angle. As they gazed in
> silence at each other, Howard divined something of the hard,
> bitter feeling which came into Grant's heart as he stood there,
> ragged, ankle-deep in muck, his sleeves rolled up, a shapeless old
> straw hat on his head.
>
> The gleam of Howard's white hands angered him. When he
> spoke, it was in a hard, gruff tone, full of rebellion.

The camera-sharp detail, highlighting Garland's habitual gen-
eralizing diction, results frequently in scenes with a powerful
emotional charge. One thinks, for example, of the scene in
"Up the Coulee," where the worn, sober farm people sit
silently listening to the wild, sad music of William McTurg,
"his long beard sweeping the violin."

It is Garland's impressionistic method, too, that leads him
into certain unintended revelations, some discomforting, some
eloquent. His guilty attachment to his mother makes the
modern reader, who knows about incest, shudder with dis-
taste at the frequent intrusiveness of this unexamined theme.
There are many other examples of a curious autobiographical

naïveté. "The oldest boy ran a little ahead. He will never forget that figure, that face." This is at once Garland, the boy of six on the return of his father from the war, and Garland, writing at about thirty, in Boston. The intrusion of the present in a work of fictional reminiscence is startling.

Startling in quite another way, given Garland's proclivity for sentiment, is the emergence of what is almost certainly the most impressive subsidiary theme in the entire collection. This is the theme of the irrelevance of romantic love that is presented so forcibly in "Among the Corn Rows" and "The Creamery Man," and only a little less effectively in "A Branch Road," and again, still differently, in "A 'Good Fellow's Wife." In at least the first two of these stories and probably in the third it is as if Garland, totally disabused of illusions, were writing with the candid felicity of D. H. Lawrence.

This forcefulness enters effectively into many of the details of his prose style. The opening sentence of the opening story: "In the windless September dawn a voice went singing, a man's voice, singing a cheap and common air"—it could come from *The White Peacock*. Or, "In the farmhouse ahead of him a light was shining as he peered ahead, and his heart gave another painful movement"—*Sons and Lovers*. There are single words that point the effect, like the final word in this sentence: "Her powerful body had a superb swaying motion at the waist as she did this—a motion which affected Rob vaguely but *massively*," or, in "Mrs. Ripley's Trip," the ducks that "went *sprawling* down the wind."

Whole scenes, too, suggest the early Lawrence. There is that point in "A Branch Road," when, toward evening, the men are in the fields, the driver whistles like a peewee, and in the house the women are setting the table for supper. Or even more impressively, this passage:

> He hung for a long time over the railing, thinking of a vast number of things, mostly vague, flitting things, looking into the clear depths of the brook, and listening to the delicious liquid note of a blackbird swinging on the willow. Red lilies starred the

grass with fire, and goldenrod and chicory grew everywhere; purple and orange and yellow-green the prevailing tints.

Suddenly a water snake wriggled across the dark pool above the ford, and the minnows disappeared under the shadow of the bridge. Then Will sighed, lifted his head, and walked on. There seemed to be something prophetic in it, and he drew a long breath. That's the way his plans broke and faded away.

Human life does not move with the regularity of a clock. In living there are gaps and silences when the soul stands still in its flight through abysses—and then there come times of trial and times of struggle when we grow old without knowing it. Body and soul change appallingly. . . .

Overcome by the memories of the past, he flung himself down on the cool and shadowy bank, and gave himself up to the bittersweet reveries of a man returning to his boyhood's home. He was filled somehow with a strange and powerful feeling of the passage of time; with a vague feeling of the mystery and elusiveness of human life. The leaves whispered it overhead, the birds sang it in chorus with the insects, and far above, in the measureless spaces of sky, the hawk told it in the silence and majesty of his flight from cloud to cloud.

It was a feeling hardly to be expressed in words—one of those emotions whose springs lie far back in the brain. He lay so still, the chipmunks came curiously up to his very feet, only to scurry away when he stirred like a sleeper in pain.

One must, to be sure, to come across such passages as this, endure a good deal of bad writing, curiously inept lapses of taste and style, simple carelessness, some merely dogged narration, an excess of generalization at the expense of particularities. Often Garland was himself unable to recognize the point at which he might most effectively have withheld his pen; surely "The Return of a Private" would be more powerful if it ended with the sentence, "The voices at the well drop lower," instead of lumbering on through a dozen lines of generalization that end in the blatant, "They are fighting a hopeless battle, and must fight till God gives them furlough."

But Hamlin Garland's literary faults are well enough

known; it is his virtues that literary history of late has neglected to observe. Not one of our great exciting writers, and sometimes a plain boring one, he is nevertheless important in ways not merely historical. His stories are often moving in a peculiarly American way, in their allegiance to what we can only hope is a still persisting democratic trust, in their allegiance to a native locale that, for all its harshness, they cannot relinquish. And there is this underlying pathos of Garland's return to the idea of "return," which figured all through his life as well as all through these stories, the pathos of a man looking for something that is not there, that never was there, and finally, of the veritist for whom *veritas* was not enough, or too much.

# Conrad Aiken

## 1

RECENTLY A LETTER APPEARED in one of the literary reviews
that reminded its editors that we have in the United States
at least one writer who may still appropriately be called a
man of letters, and the name was Conrad Aiken. It is curious
how, year after year for more than four decades now, general
readers and editors alike have *had* to be reminded of that
name, which does indeed support an achievement that, in
its brilliant distinction and, more than that, in its scope, makes
Conrad Aiken so much more than a writer alone. He has the
range of the literary master: the beautiful bulk of his poetry
in all its formal splendor and variety; literary essays of pio-
neering quality; one of the most extraordinary autobiographies in the language; four novels, at least two of which—
*Great Circle* and *King Coffin*—must endure; a play; more
than forty short stories.

If the entire work of Conrad Aiken demonstrates this mas-
tery of a range possessed by few modern writers, the forty-
one short stories demonstrate a range of mood and method,
within the scope of the single form, that is almost as surprising; yet all of them, like the whole body of his work, are
stamped with the mark of his imagination, and could have
been written by Conrad Aiken alone.

In that complex imagination there is a prominent strain
of rather bemused irony that, when he gives it free rein, produces stories that are essentially comic, even rather light-
hearted, with a satiric edge that cuts into a human foible or

a paradox of personality or a turn of fate's screw, cuts deftly, delicately, without either the ritual air of major surgery or the thrust of passionate involvement. Such stories are "No, No, Go Not to Lethe," "The Necktie," "West End," "O How She Laughed!" and a good many others. They seem to say, with an air of the literary shrug, "Well, there it is. What do you think? Odd, isn't it?" Or, "Queer, isn't it, although surely he had it coming?" Or, "Amusing?" Yet even in these stories there is usually another strain, a note struck off from the taut strings of the stretched nerves, something sharp, shrill or somber, sinister, or mockingly morbid, an echo out of psychic chaos. Think only, for example, of that quite alarming hero of "No, No, Go Not to Lethe," whose ambition it is to enfold and paralyze others in the coils of his observation of them without ever himself becoming in the least involved. It is a comic story, but the laughter seems to come eerily up from the bottom of a very deep and a very old well.

This is, of course, the note that characterizes the most splendid and the best known of Conrad Aiken's short stories, those stories in which he moves from the mundane into the mysterious, into hysteria, horror, hallucination, phobia, compulsion, dream, death, and, more often than not, back again into the mundane. The sudden penetration into the shadows of consciousness, a veil surprisingly pulled back and dropped again, something beyond our perception perceived in it, a mythical beast suddenly gazing curiously up at us from the shrubbery at the end of our own well-kept garden: these are the gestures that are made by stories like "Silent Snow, Secret Snow" and "Mr. Arcularis" and many another. But let us consider one of the stories that is less well known.

"Life Isn't a Short Story" ought to be among the first documents in the demonstration materials of all people who profess to "teach" the writing of fiction, and among the instructional materials of all people who wish to learn to do it. It is about a story writer who "had run out of ideas; he had used them all; he was feeling as empty as a bath-tub and as blue as an oyster." This drudge of the imagination is having his breakfast—sitting in the window of a white-tiled restaurant, staring rather vacantly out into a busy city street, suddenly catching sight of a woman who might, if she were plumper, serve as the physical model for the woman in a story he is thinking about: for he isn't, after all, it seems, quite empty.

The story. The seed of the story had been planted in his mind as, passing through the lounge of a theater, he overheard phrases of a greeting—*"as I live and breathe!"* and *"in the flesh!"* I am alive and *you are alive;* these phrases translated themselves in his mind, and that, alive and not alive, was, he saw, the difference between life and a short story, even as he thought of his character, Gladys, a plump, commonplace creature who cannot tolerate such clichés, so plump and commonplace, any more readily than she can tolerate her simple and unrefined husband. So, sitting in the restaurant window, he imagines the proper town for Gladys to live in (Fitchburg, Massachusetts, seems right), imagines her apartment, imagines her story, which is the story of her intolerable marriage. Meanwhile, a horse-drawn laundry wagon has pulled up in front of the window, and the story writer's eye rests on the dejected horse, beaten by rain, while the story, through all its grimy fatalities, grows in his presumably disengaged, vacantly staring mind. When it reaches its climax, we know not only that the whole, dreary life of the street outside, bleary and rain-soaked, has been assimilated into the atmosphere of the life of Gladys and her husband, but we know also, as the writer does *not* know, any more than Gladys knows, that her poor old drone of a husband is the horse that pulls the laundry wagon. With their identification, the story is finished. Then we follow the horse up the street. "What did he think about, as he plodded from one dirty restaurant to another, one hotel to another, carrying towels? Probably nothing at all; certainly no such sentimental thing as a green meadow, nor anything so ridiculous as a story about living and breathing. It was enough, even if one was a slave, to live and breathe. For life, after all, isn't a short story."

Life isn't a short story because life, that spavined hack,

keeps going on its rounds and never meets a climax; but a
short story is life because, no matter where it may go all
through its middle, it begins in life and it ends there, and if
we look twice, we will see that, through that extraordinary
process of imaginative osmosis whereby the details of life are
lifted up into the pattern of art, its middle, too, is in large
part the street outside the real window. A story by Conrad
Aiken, in the characteristically fine middle, seems to rear up
on its hind legs and throw its head into white clouds and
among patterned stars, or it seems to race down into abysses
of peculiar horror and shrill alarm, but all the time, poor
creature (and the poor creatures that make it up), it is out
there in the street, stodgy in the rain.

> At the same time, there was the awful commonplaceness of the
> two phrases, the cheapness of them, the vulgarity—they were as
> old as the hills, and as worn; æons of weather and æons of hand-
> shake lay upon them; one witnessed, in the mere hearing of them,
> innumerable surprised greetings, innumerable mutual congratu-
> lations on the mere fact of being still alive. The human race
> seemed to extend itself backwards through them, in time, as
> along a road—if one pursued the thought one came eventually to
> a vision of two small apes peering at each other round the cheeks
> of a cocoanut and making a startled noise that sounded like
> "*yoicks!*" Or else, one simply saw, in the void, one star passing
> another, with no vocal interchange at all, nothing but a mutual
> exacerbation of heat. . . . It was very puzzling.

Puzzling, indeed, since it all starts in the lounge of the Or-
pheum, with a couple of portly blondes, and then at once
loops out into space and history and mystery and the perfect
terror of human experience as it plods through its generic
hysteria, most of the time not knowing where it is, whether
in the rainy street or in the stifled scream, when it is always
in fact in both.

This is a story by Conrad Aiken: a horror all wrapped in
an actuality, a fantasy all rooted and real, all rooted in a real
detail. "For the most part, this companion seemed to be nothing but a voice and a wing—an enormous jagged black wing,

soft and drooping like a bat's; he had noticed veins in it." *He had noticed veins in it.* If one could define the rhetorical mystery of this sentence, of this juxtaposition of the mad anatomy and the graphic physiology, one would probably have defined the effect of Mr. Aiken's fiction.

Just as the structure of these stories characteristically develops in the effort of the material to assert a reality beyond or below its mundane shape, so their drama characteristically arises within an individual mind as it struggles to break over the edge of its own limitations. This whole considerable body of fiction, long and short, has, for this reason, a central core of formal as well as psychological concern, an implicit, primary unity that marks it over and over as the product of this imagination and no other, as the work of this author. In one story, at least, the implicit becomes the explicit. "Gehenna" has as its protagonist an urban Everyman ("Smith, or Jones, or Robinson, or whatever his name happened to be") who reflects at the outset, "How easily . . . our little world can go to pieces! And incidentally, of course, the great world . . ." and then contemplates the imminence in the materials of consciousness of that disorganization of reality that is madness. But is that disorganization any less real than the organization which it has dispelled?

> In an instant it will be as if I had stepped through this bright cobweb of appearance on which I walk with such apparent security, and plunged into a chaos of my own; for that chaos will be as intimately and recognizably my own, with its Smith-like disorder, as the present world is my own, with its Smith-like order. Here will be all the appurtenances of my life, every like and dislike, every longing or revulsion, from the smallest to the greatest; all the umbrellas—so to speak—of my life, all the canceled postage stamps and burnt matches, the clipped fingernails, love letters, calendars, and sunrises; but all of them interchanged and become (by change) endowed with demonic power. At a step, I shall have fallen into a profound and perhaps termless Gehenna which will be everywhere nothing but Smith. Only to the name of Smith will the umbrella-winged demons of this chaos answer.

This possibility of the altered kaleidoscope of being and the further possibility of altering that kaleidoscope by an act of will fascinates Smith—or Jones or Robinson. "Perhaps I could achieve this gradually," he thinks, "and step by step, just as I pace to and fro across the four rugs from Persia which cover the floor; item by item I would tear down the majestic fiction which is at present myself and the world, and item by item build up another. Exactly as one can stare at a word until it becomes meaningless, I can begin to stare at the world." In his bathroom, he stares at a doorknob, and through a kind of self-hypnosis, he allows the process to get under way, only, at the last moment, through another effort of will, to rip himself out of this new prison that his consciousness is already building. He goes to bed and dreams of "a small glass aquarium, square, of the sort in which goldfish are kept."

> I observe without surprise that there is water in one half of it but not in the other. And in spite of the fact that there is no partition, this water holds itself upright in its own half of the tank, leaving the other half empty. More curious than this, however, is the marine organism which lies at the bottom of the water. It looks, at first glance, like a loaf of bread. But when I lean down to examine it closely, I see that it is alive, that it is sentient, and that it is trying to move. One end of it lies very close to that point at which the water ends and the air begins; and now I realize that the poor thing is trying, and trying desperately, to get into the air. Moreover, I see that this advancing surface is as if sliced off and raw; it is horribly sensitive; and suddenly, appalled, I realize that the whole thing is simply—consciousness. It is trying to escape from the medium out of which it was created. If only it could manage this—! But I know that it never will; it has already reached, with its agonized sentience, as far as it can; it stretches itself forward, with minute and pathetic convulsions, but in vain; and suddenly I am so horrified at the notion of a consciousness which is pure suffering, that I wake up. . . . The clocks are striking two.

It is at this margin, at this edge, where, without barrier, the water of daily human experience stands against the wall of air that is outside it—it is at this margin that Conrad Aiken's fiction is written. (His extraordinary novels develop and amazingly sustain the central concern of the stories.) And thus his fiction asks its great questions: "Was the North Star hung at the world's masthead only in order that on a certain day in a certain year an ugly wallpaper should be glued to the walls of this room?" Human tragedy exists because of the suffering that must inhere in a consciousness that can ask the question at all. It persists, with life itself, because the clocks in the city do strike, and with their reverberations, draw the invisible circles around that consciousness, saving it for its order, yes, but in the very act of saving it, re-committing it to an area within which questions must go on being asked.

We have, I think, no other body of fiction like this—so centrally coherent, its very coherence derived from a contemplation of the intransigence of that incoherence that lies scattered on all sides of us, and above and below, and, worst of all, within. But also best of all. For rationality would be a poor and shriveled thing if it did not have all that other to nourish no less than to alarm it. As life would be if it did not have the basic resources that can make it into art.

2

The experimental magazine *Wake,* intent on doing what it could by way of justice, dedicated a recent issue to the work of Aiken, and there appeared a passage from his then still unpublished autobiography *Ushant.* One expected a book of social prohibitions and defiances of those prohibitions: *You shan't!* and *I Will!*—society indifferent to and set against the poet, the poet rebellious. Yet *Ushant* is a very different kind of book, a work of the most extraordinarily sinuous, subjective affirmations: *I became; I am*—simply and magnificently that.

*Ushant,* the punning title—and the pun is there—is turned to us at almost all times with its positive face: That small island of rock off the coast of Brittany, Ile d'Ouessant, first sign to the sailor and the voyager that his ship is swinging

into the English Channel from the West, an island that looks
both ways.

The frame of this complicated "autobiographical narrative," or "essay," as the author engagingly calls it, is a voyage
to England on a barely converted troopship immediately
after World War II. It is only the most recent of the poet's
many voyages to England, and his dual relationship to England and America, to Europe and America, is, as in so many
of our autobiographies, a major theme. For "D," the initial
by which Conrad Aiken designates himself in this book
(which, like *The Education of Henry Adams,* is told in the
third person), for "D," Europe is a perpetual promise, a
vision of unimaginable discovery; yet all through his life it is
instructing him in a vision of the West, of America, and in
the end returns him to the West and to himself.

Conrad Aiken's autobiography seems to me one of the most
profoundly original documents to have come out of the
United States in many years, an almost stunning outpouring
of prose, an incredibly subtle reconstruction of "the soul's
landscape." It is difficult, even after three readings, to be
merely descriptive; but one can try.

Like Adams, Mr. Aiken rhetorically removes himself a little from the subject which is himself, but unlike Adams, he is
concerned not with the relationships of personality and institutions, but immediately with the psychic realities that
make up the "mystic equation: YOU." Personalities are concealed under fictitious names (one can guess at most, to be
sure) and all those valleys of shadow that Adams declined
to enter, Aiken plunges through as he continually goes out
and beyond the merely objective and social. His early loyal-
ties are divided between two places: Savannah on the one
hand, Massachusetts on the other. The half that is Savannah
is violently truncated when the young boy witnesses the mur-
der-suicide of his parents. Thereafter, he moves through all
the families of his New England relatives and of their antecedents, defining himself through them, separating his Self

at last from theirs, and always under the shadow of the mur-
dered, murderous past.

In this process, we see "D" at school in Concord, at Harvard, in the literary life of New York, Boston, and London
over thirty years. A different shadow, the long, thin shadow
of T. S. Eliot, falls across all these years, the shadow of a figure called "the Tsetse, the fabulously beautiful and sibylline
Tsetse," who was to perform the "office of creative response
. . . with an influence so close and consanguineous, or fraternal, as sometimes to be paralyzing, or eclipsing."

Unlike the Tsetse's is "D's" pursuit of his maturity:

> The thing, of course, was not to retreat, never to retreat: never
> to avoid . . . the full weight of awareness, and all that it brought,
> and above all never never to seek refuge from it in the comforting
> placebos of religious or mystical myth or dogma. The pressures
> would become, for some, too great to bear: the temptations, too,
> would be insidious. The security in conformity, in joining and
> belonging, was to prove to be too seductive for many a better
> mind than D's. Including that best of all, the Tsetse's.

So *Ushant* is, of course, the history of a rebel, but the rebellion is always against all those shutters over experience
that close the psyche from the self. If the many beautiful
pages that are concerned with the relationship of the identity
and its heredity are able to give us wonderful social portraits
of aunts and uncles, cousins and teachers, mistresses and
poets, give us handsomely rich evocations of "Rooms, Streets,
and Houses," their final interest is always their part in the
psychic pursuit. As nothing is ever merely social in this book,
so nothing is merely chronological. This is not so much "the
stream of life in which the stream of life we trace," as it is a
continually bubbling spring, and a spring that rises not from
one stratum alone, but from multistrata, and simultaneously.

So the intimate revelations, the impressive pages on the
birth of a poet, for whom experience becomes reality only
as it achieves form in language, and the consequences of the
persistent double compulsion of sex and art, and the history

of three marriages with many sexual asides, that search for "a more famous sleep"—all this, too, exists in the book only by its right as a portion of "the soul's landscape."

The result is a book of intensity and depth. In the end, it leaves us with the conviction that Conrad Aiken, with the weight of this experience but more particularly with his inimitably sensitive response to its pressure, saved from becoming a madman, had to become a great writer.

# Katherine Anne Porter

WITHOUT ANY VIOLENT ACT of generalization, we can state the central themes of Katherine Anne Porter's fiction in three enormous questions, and these happen to be the questions asked, in turn, by the three stories that make up the volume *Pale Horse, Pale Rider*. They may be put this way: What were we? What are we? What will we be? Or: From where did we come? Where are we at this moment? Where are we going? The individual in his past, his present, his future.

And put this way, we recognize, of course, that there are no other questions, really—that all literature, all humankind has always asked these questions and these alone. Being so basic, they can take infinitely various, endlessly specific forms. And the first quality that we are aware of in the fiction of Katherine Anne Porter is the absence of abstraction, its specificity, its immediacy, the richly individuating detail whether of persons, of situations, of scenes. It is precisely this tissue of observed, of felt, of living detail that gives the themes that we have abstracted their powerful emotional charge. Yet the abstraction can be made, and for the fullest understanding (the fullest feeling) perhaps must be made.

Taking many of Miss Porter's stories as his evidence, one critic has abstracted not a few themes but a whole thematic program, what he calls her "fictional philosophy."[1] It is perhaps better described as the grand plot that, taken together, the entire body of her work enacts.

The child is born into a world seemingly ordered and reasonable but it is in fact chaotic, ridiculous, and doubt-ridden ("The

[1] James William Johnson, "Another Look at Katherine Anne Porter," *Virginia Quarterly Review*, XXXVI, 4 (Autumn 1960).

Old Order"). He learns at an early age that he is an atomistic creature, often unloved ("The Downward Path"), and that the delightful spectacle of life masks fear, hatred, and bitterness ("The Circus"). He discovers that life and love must end in death ("The Grave," "The Fig Tree"). He must inevitably reject his heritage as lies and his family as hostile aliens ("Old Mortality"); but when he tries to substitute something else in their place, he is driven back by his own weaknesses to what he has been conditioned to ("Maria Concepcion," "Magic"). If he makes the break with the past and tries to replace the lost old love with a new, he is doomed to despair ("Pale Horse, Pale Rider"). If he tries to substitute another heritage for his own, he finds it full of evil ("The Leaning Tower"); or he discovers that he has lost his power to love through denying his own tradition ("Flowering Judas"). There is nothing for him to cling to but his desperate belief in his own courage and integrity ("Theft") and what little of love and certainty he has in life ("The Cracked Looking Glass"). But life is senselessly cruel ("He"), full of frustration and contention ("Rope," "That Tree," "A Day's Work"); and it ends in annihilation and the extinction of all hope ("The Jilting of Granny Weatherall"). Such is Miss Porter's fictional philosophy.

The second story in *Pale Horse, Pale Rider*, "Noon Wine," would have served as well for the final example in this brilliant analysis. And it may be fairly suggested that Miss Porter's only full-length novel, *Ship of Fools*, will, if we let one or another of the characters support one or another of the several themes, demonstrate this entire progress of motifs. The plot of this novel is neither more nor less than this journey from what we have been to what we will become.

But let us permit Miss Porter, the artist rather than the philosopher, to make the first qualification. In answer to certain questions about her craft and her beliefs, she wrote in part as follows in 1939:

> All my past is "usable," in the sense that my material consists of memory, legend, personal experience, and acquired knowledge. They combine in a constant process of re-creation. . . .
> My whole attempt has been to discover and understand human

motives, human feelings, to make a distillation of what human relations and experiences my mind has been able to absorb. I have never known an uninteresting human being, and I have never known two alike; there are broad classifications and deep similarities, but I am interested in the thumbprint. I am passionately involved with these individuals who populate all these enormous migrations, calamities; who fight wars and furnish life for the future; these beings without which, one by one, all the "broad movements of history" could never take place. One by one—as they were born.

"I have never known two alike" . . . "I am interested in the thumbprint" . . . "one by one"—it is this voice, insisting on the uniqueness of every individual, that we must heed before we observe that, taken all together, all the individualities do make the general human march.

In achieving her constant effects of particularity, nothing is more important, of course, than her own sharply remembered observations, and these go far back into her earliest years, into the place of her origin. In her surprisingly various literary production, in which so little is ever used twice, *place* is one exception—first the childhood place, then Mexico, then Germany, but above all, the childhood place, "the native land of my heart."

Katherine Anne Porter was born in 1890 in central Texas on a "small clear branch of the Colorado—full of colored pebbles—Indian Creek." (Note the pebbles, how she cannot resist the individuating detail!) It was "soft blackland farming country, full of fruits and flowers and birds, with good hunting and good fishing," and it "was peopled almost entirely by Southerners from Virginia, Tennessee, the Carolinas, Kentucky." Into this country was born not only Katherine Anne Porter but her fictional character, Miranda, a semi-autobiographical character certainly, who, like the one place that continues to appear in many of the stories, also appears in many of them. She is the central character in "Old Mortality," the little girl who grows up, and of "Pale Horse, Pale Rider," the young woman who, for the time being, she has become.

"Old Mortality" demonstrates the degree to which Miss Porter's is indeed a "usable past," for it is a story drawn not only from her own past, but, more importantly, depicts that past as immersed in another, the ancestral past, the romantic myth of a family tradition. The dead past, continuing to live in present memory, changes its character, becomes in effect a lie, and yet many members of the family are content to live in the lie, to define their present selves in terms of that altered past. One character, Miranda, is not, and the story is the account of her long effort to detach her self from the beguilements of the legend, to define her destiny as a separate thing from her heritage, to move out of the past into a clear present.

The story has three announced parts. In the first, the small child Miranda, hearing always the family version of the life of the beautiful, dead Aunt Amy and of the whole, heavily scented life of dashing gallantry and courtliness and style within which Amy presumably lived, already begins to detect the contradictions. How pathetic, how trivial even, are all those mementos of the dead Amy's life, over which Miranda's grandmother pores with nearly ritualistic fidelity, when one puts them beside her glowing memories! Above all, how dead! Her father asserts that there "were never any fat women in the family," but Miranda knows of several who were quite phenomenally fat. Already she knows that "this loyalty of their father's in the face of evidence contrary to his ideal had its springs in family feeling, and a love of legend that he shared with the others." And then there was all the talk about ravishing Cousin Molly Parrington, "an unnatural mother to her ugly daughter Eva, an old maid past forty while her mother was still the belle of the ball."

"Born when I was fifteen, you remember," Molly would say shamelessly, looking an old beau straight in the eye, both of them remembering that he had been best man at her first wedding when she was past twenty-one. "Everyone said I was like a little girl with her doll."

These were not malicious lies within which Miranda was growing up, only romantic ones, and all with their own charm and lyric melancholy and powerful invitation. But Miranda's life, unlike her elders', is not to be immured in them.

In the second part of the story she is two years older, ten. Now she is "immured" in a convent school with her sister, but the girls use the word, which they had found in romantic fiction, satirically. "It was no good at all trying to fit the stories to life, and they did not even try." Now, when their father takes them to the races in New Orleans, they meet the real Uncle Gabriel, the dead Amy's gallant, long-faithful suitor and finally, for her brief "tragic" marriage, her husband—"a vast bulging man with a red face and immense tan ragged mustaches fading into gray," a drunkard living in squalor with a hopeless, embittered wife. "Oh, what did grown-up people *mean* when they talked, anyway?" Any remaining illusions of romance are blown away, and Miranda, who decided that, because she would never be a great "beauty," she would be a jockey instead, now decides that she will not be a jockey after all.

In the eight-year interval between the second and the third part of the story, she had declared her independence emphatically by eloping with a man of whom her family could not approve. At eighteen, she is returning home for the funeral of Uncle Gabriel, and on the train she meets the embittered old maid, Cousin Eva, also returning. She listens to Cousin Eva's malicious account of Aunt Amy and of other "beauties" in that dead life.

"... she pretended not to know what marriage was about, but I know better. None of them had, and they didn't want to have, anything else to think about, and they didn't really know anything about that, so they simply festered inside—they festered—"

Miranda found herself deliberately watching a long procession of living corpses, festering women stepping gaily towards the charnel house, their corruption concealed under laces and flowers, their dead faces lifted smiling, and thought quite coldly, "Of course it was not like that. This is no more true than what I was told before, it's every bit as romantic."

Cousin Eva is even more hopelessly trapped in the past than the others, obsessively trapped. And as the story draws to an end, Miranda makes her resolve. She will commit her own mistakes, not theirs.

> She did not want any more ties with this house, she was going to leave it, and she was not going back to her husband's family either. She would have no more bonds that smothered her in love and hatred.

She will not be romantic with them, and she will not be romantic about herself. She will devote herself to knowing "the truth about what happens to me." But this promise she makes "in her hopefulness, her ignorance." She has moved into freedom through a degree of self-awareness, but the awareness is by no means complete. She is in the present, but the future, which she cannot know, is still ahead, as the present is forever tumbling into the past.

"Noon Wine" moves sharply out of the deceptively romantic world of "Old Mortality" into the squalid actualities of a run-down farm, but the country is the same. Any reader of this story who is also interested in the creative processes and especially in Miss Porter's, should read, too, her remarkable essay called "'Noon Wine': The Sources,"[2] in which she separates out of the texture of her childhood memories all the main elements of this story, which came to her at different times and about different people, and shows how they all then fell together into the unified pattern that makes this story, which tells for her a "truth" about life in that time, that place. And about life.

That larger truth is simply the fact, which Miranda did not yet know, that it is not easy, perhaps not possible, to know "the truth about what happens" to oneself.

[2] Published first in *The Yale Review* (Autumn 1956) but written especially for the revised edition (1959) of Brooks and Warren, *Understanding Fiction* (Appleton-Century-Crofts, Inc.).

But let us observe first what is observed before we come to contemplate that truth—Miss Porter's remarkable skill in moving into a kind of life that was not hers and into a point of view that was completely alien to her own, to Miranda's. The story is chiefly about Mr. Thompson, the slovenly farmer.

> He looked forward to the boys growing up soon; he was going to put them through the mill just as his own father had done with him when he was a boy; they were going to learn how to take hold and run the place right. He wasn't going to overdo it, but those two boys were going to earn their salt, or he'd know why. Great big lubbers sitting around whittling! Mr. Thompson sometimes grew quite enraged with them, when imagining their possible future, big lubbers sitting around whittling or thinking about fishing trips. Well, he'd put a stop to that, mighty damn quick.

This is Mr. Thompson "imagining" indeed, for the boys are still only wild youngsters, and it is he himself who spends his days "sitting around," in effect if not in actuality "whittling." He is projecting his easygoing present into an easygoing future. For the time he has been rescued in his farming by the presence of Mr. Helton, a stranger from the Dakotas who has turned up mysteriously and taken over the running of the farm. All goes well for nine years, until another stranger appears, a Mr. Hatch, and observe again the skill in pinning these alien creatures down in all their particularity.

> He wasn't exactly a fat man. He was more like a man who had been fat recently. His skin was baggy and his clothes were too big for him, and he somehow looked like a man who should be fat, ordinarily, but who might have just got over a spell of sickness. Mr. Thompson didn't take to his looks at all, he couldn't say why.

And the dialogue—Mr. Hatch, for example, telling about the single tune that Mr. Helton plays, day in and day out, year in and year out, on his harmonica:

> "Where I come from they sing it a lot. In North Dakota, they sing it. It says something about starting out in the morning feel-

ing so good you can't hardly stand it, so you drink up all your likker before noon. All the likker, y' understand, that you was saving for the noon lay-off. The words ain't much, but it's a pretty tune. It's a kind of drinking song." He sat there drooping a little, and Mr. Thompson didn't like his expression. It was a satisfied expression, but it was more like the cat that et the canary.

Mr. Helton, it develops, had escaped nine years before from an asylum for the criminally insane, and Mr. Hatch, having located him, has come to earn some easy money by returning him. The situation suddenly involves Mr. Thompson, who had had no such intention, in killing Mr. Hatch, and the rest of the story consists of his trying to persuade people that he did that only in defense of Mr. Helton, and in calling upon his wife, who had not witnessed the scene, to say that he was telling the truth. But the shame of these two people, of Mrs. Thompson for lying and of Mr. Thompson for finding himself inexplicably in a situation that "don't *look* right"—he had always justified his laziness through a curiously crippled code of what one can only call "decorum"—is overwhelming. Mr. Thompson finally knows that he is "a dead man," and in the last sentence of the story, he sees to it.

After all the easygoing years, the sudden unexpected *horror* of the present, the horror whose truth one could not know until one was inextricably *in* it, when it proves to be an absolute doom to which one's own nature, however trivially expressed before, now commits us: this is what the story is about. One man's present, the wine bottle empty and the time not yet noon.

"Pale Horse, Pale Rider" plays an interesting and complex variation on this theme. We return to Miranda, who is now twenty-four years old. She experiences death, too, but a necessary resurrection as well. The past is dead, says "Old Mortality," and the present moment may push us into death, says "Noon Wine," but death is inevitably the future, too, and therefore always with us. Only when we accept that awareness are we really free, only then do we know—perhaps, as with Miranda, dejectedly—that at last there is "time for everything."

This is again a story in three parts, like "Old Mortality," but the parts are not announced, are, rather, blurred in their outlines, and for necessary reasons in the material itself. What Miranda learns, essentially, is that the parts—the past, the present, the future—cannot be separated: one decrees another, backwards and forwards, and it is all therefore confused, dreamlike, feverish, trancelike, hallucinatory, all a mixture of the actual and the imagined, the real and the dreamed, the past and the future both flowing through a misconceived present.

Still, there are three stages in the story: Miranda, awakening from a dream half caught in childhood to her work in the present world at war, and her hope for Adam's alleviating love; then, sinking into her sickness, suffering her delirium in her bedroom, with Adam in and out; finally, her "death" in the hospital, her recovery, the knowledge of Adam's real death in the interim, her nostalgia for that moment when she was in "paradise," released from all bonds, and her grudging return to a present where all bonds would grip her again except for one—the bond of illusions.

Perhaps this story, so subtle and so complex that one is unwilling to try to take it apart in any detail, is really about the birth of an artist, the one who has suffered everything, including death, and comes back from it, disabused, all-knowing, or knowing at least all that we can know.

> Miranda looked about her with the covertly hostile eyes of an alien who does not like the country in which he finds himself, does not understand the language nor wish to learn it, does not mean to live there and yet is helpless, unable to leave it at his will. . . . "They will all be telling me again how good it is to be alive, they will say again they love me, they are glad I am living too, and what can I answer to that?" and her hardened, indifferent heart shuddered in despair at itself, because before it had been tender and capable of love.

She asks for some new accessories—"gauntlets" and a "walking stick of silvery wood with a silver knob" and a perfume called Bois d'Hiver, and other items suggestive of death and the death of the heart. But the heart has also made a great surge forward into understanding and feeling. She has lost Adam, the beautiful original innocent, and she is no longer any Miranda that we have known—certainly not Shakespeare's Miranda, that lovely innocent first observing humankind in her lovely illusory world; certainly not Miss Porter's first Miranda, less bedazzled as she may have been than Shakespeare's. The Miranda who emerges from "Pale Horse, Pale Rider" is Miss Porter herself, the artist, who will proceed to write these stories and others with that ultimate clarity—clairvoyance?—that only the true artist possesses. The artist must know everything—past, present, and future—and the true artist must know as much of that most difficult third member of the triad as it is given to men to know.

What Miss Porter makes me know, finally, is that with every present creation the artist dies into his past in order to bring forth another creation. That is why the artist makes us weep as we exult. Who else tells us anything else that is finally important?

# Carson McCullers and Truman Capote

IN ONE of his fascinating "essays for the left hand" called "Identity in the Modern Novel," Jerome S. Bruner makes a distinction between subjectivity and myth, or what he phrases as "subjectification and the demise of fate." He first speculated on this subject in an earlier essay, "Myth and Identity," which concludes as follows:

> . . . one may ask whether the rise of the novel as an art form, and particularly the subjectification of the novel since the middle of the nineteenth century, whether these do not symbolize the voyage into the interior that comes with the failure of prevailing myths to provide external models toward which one may aspire. For when the prevailing myths fail to fit the varieties of man's plight, frustration expresses itself first in mythoclasm and then in the lonely search for internal identity. . . . Perhaps the modern novel, in contrast to the myth, is the response to the internal anguish that can find no external constraint in myth, a form of internal map . . . the alternative to externalization in myth appears to be the internalization of the personal novel, the first a communal effort, the second the lone search for identity.

It is this proposal that is then amplified in the following essay, where Dr. Bruner writes that

> the psychological novel, in contrast to the myth, exists as a recognition of the distinction between subjective and objective. . . . The myth is objective, transcendental, timeless, moved by impulses beyond man to meet inhuman demands. In the objective verisimilitude of myth lies the triumph of its externalization of man's inner experience. With the novel and its interior monologues, the effort is to save the subjectivity, to use it as cause.

Carson McCullers and Truman Capote are among the most subjective of contemporary novelists, writers for whom the sensibility is almost the entire literary resource. Dr. Bruner's distinction may help us to understand how they use that sensibility, the ends to which they put subjectivity, and it may help us to distinguish in turn between them.

In the fiction of Carson McCullers[1] I believe that we can observe the effort to arrive at the objective externality of myth by placing the most extreme demands on that very subjectivity which is its opposite. The effort is not always successful and sometimes it is only partial, but, except for most of the short stories, her least impressive work, it is almost always there. Of these short stories, many of which abandon that Southern setting that is most congenial to her talent and, apparently, necessary to its fullest expression, only one approaches the amplitude of feeling in her longer fiction. That story, "A Tree. A Rock. A Cloud," tells of the early-morning meeting in an all-night café of an uncomprehending young paper boy and a shabby old transient who tries to describe the "science" of love to him— love, which must begin with the humblest of objects, a tree, a rock, a cloud. That the lesson is not communicated is of the essence. That the old man wanders out alone into the dawn of a loveless world is no less so.

"Why does anyone write at all?" Mrs. McCullers asked in the foreword to her commercially unsuccessful play, *The Square Root of Wonderful*, which is concerned with the same theme of universal love and lovelessness.

Why does anyone write at all? I suppose a writer writes out of some inward compulsion to transform his own experience (much of it unconscious) into the universal and symbolical. The themes the artist chooses are always deeply personal. I suppose my

[1] The manuscript of this book had gone to the publishers before the death of Carson McCullers. I could have changed the tenses of this essay in the galley proof to which I am adding this note. As a small gesture of regard for that great person, I want to retain the present tense.

central theme is the theme of spiritual isolation. Certainly I have always felt alone.

To transform the private insight into the universal truth—this is, of course, the axiomatic basis of all creative effort. But cannot it be conceived, too, in more particular terms as the inverse of the mythopoeic effort—where the private impulse finds its satisfying correlatives in the already formed universal statements—and yet conceivably arriving at something like the same end?

Spiritual isolation, universal alienation and loneliness—this is the given condition of the McCullers world. Then the effort to overcome it through communication, through love, and this in spite of the premonition felt from the start that no such resolution is possible. The anxious search for love in a loveless world and the recognition that one cannot hope—even if one wished it—to *be* loved, only *to* love, so that love is at least as much pain as it is benison. It is to do violence to the texture and feeling of Mrs. McCullers's work so to abstract the thematic core, and yet in at least one remarkable passage, itself abstract, she gives us a certain sanction for this procedure. The passage occurs rather early in *The Ballad of the Sad Café*:

> First of all, love is a joint experience between two persons—but the fact that it is a joint experience does not mean that it is a similar experience to the two people involved. There are the lover and the beloved, but these two come from different countries. Often the beloved is only a stimulus for all the stored-up love which has lain quiet within the lover for a long time hitherto. And somehow every lover knows this. He feels in his soul that his love is a solitary thing. He comes to know a new strange loneliness and it is this knowledge which makes him suffer. So there is only one thing for the lover to do. He must house his love within himself as best he can; he must create for himself a whole new inward world—a world intense and strange, complete in himself. Let it be added here that this lover about whom we speak need not necessarily be a young man saving for a wedding ring—this lover can be man, woman, child, or indeed any human creature on this earth.

Now, the beloved can also be of any description. The most outlandish people can be the stimulus for love. A man may be a
doddering great-grandfather and still love only a strange girl he
saw in the streets of Cheehaw one afternoon two decades past.
The preacher may love a fallen woman. The beloved may be
treacherous, greasy-headed, and given to evil habits. Yes, and the
lover may see this as clearly as anyone else—but that does not
affect the evolution of his love one whit. A most mediocre person
can be the object of a love which is wild, extravagant, and beautiful as the poison lilies of the swamp. A good man may be the
stimulus for a love both violent and debased, or a jabbering madman may bring about in the soul of someone a tender and simple
idyll. Therefore, the value and quality of any love is determined
solely by the lover himself.

It is for this reason that most of us would rather love than be
loved. Almost everyone wants to be the lover. And the curt truth
is that, in a deep secret way, the state of being beloved is intolerable to many. The beloved fears and hates the lover, and with
the best of reasons. For the lover is forever trying to strip bare
his beloved. The lover craves any possible relation with the beloved, even if this experience can cause him only pain.

It is a long passage, but its quotation here is justified in that it
is probably the passage in which Mrs. McCullers comes closest
to telling us explicitly what concerns her most.

Written some time after the publication of her first novel,
*The Heart Is a Lonely Hunter*, the passage might serve as epigraph for that novel, as its very title suggests. This novel, with
its many characters and its full easy evocation of the whole
dulled life of a Southern town in the years of the Depression,
has at its center a small group of characters, only five, who,
within the formless flow of the life around them, enact their
nearly mathematical parable.

The novel has three parts. The first introduces these five,
each with his obsession: the deaf mute, John Singer, whose life
center is its dedication to another mute, a gross Greek named
Antonapoulos, a half-wit who is presently incarcerated in an
insane asylum where Singer must henceforth visit him; Biff
Brannon, a café owner, obsessed with wonder; Jake Blount, a

drunken radical, obsessed with the cause of the workers; Dr.
Copeland, an educated Negro obsessed with the idea of justice
for his people; and Mick Kelly, an adolescent tomboy whose
obsession is music. At the end of the first part, each of these
four has turned to the first, Singer, a Christ figure, as the object
of his love, the source of understanding. Part Two develops
this dependence of these four on Singer, as each of them tries
to talk himself out of his solitude with the mute, each feeling
that "they wanted to tell each other things that had never been
told before." At the end of this central and longest part, Antonapoulos has died and Singer, in an empty world, shoots
himself. The third part, with Singer gone, shows us each of the
other four as he vanishes, so to speak, into his own solitude.

They are all characters doomed by a fated knowledge—"she
knew in the beginning that there was no good place"—even
though each of them struggles to communicate the burden of
his consciousness, wanders feverishly to find the "good place"
where isolation ceases. Their sealed fate is apparent in the fact
that they all turn to a deaf mute for communication, and that
he in turn finds the meaning of his life in his love for another
mute, who cannot understand him. For all the realistic detail
of the novel, it is at heart a parable that is suggested at once in
the legendary style. "In the town there were two mutes, and
they were always together," is the opening sentence. One
would probably find, on close examination, that such fairy tale-
like declarative sentences are the most frequently used throughout the book. At any rate, they give it its tone, and the elliptical
treatment of time underscores that tone:

> The town was in the middle of the deep South. The summers
> were long and the months of winter cold were very few. Nearly
> always the sky was a glassy, brilliant azure and the sun burned
> down riotously bright. Then the light, chill rains of November
> would come. . . . Often in the faces along the streets there was
> the desperate look of hunger and loneliness. . . .
> Then one day the Greek became ill. . . .

It is a tone appropriate to the retelling of an old myth, or to
the attempted construction of a new one: man, deranged by a

nearly cosmic loneliness, momentarily redeemed by his power
to love. "It was some good."

> All right!
> O.K.!
> Some good.

This quotation, the final reflection of Mick Kelly, suggests
that Mrs. McCullers infuses the general legendary tone with a
good deal of sharply reported vernacular talk and reflection
that is entirely appropriate to the social character of her people.
In the next novel, *Reflections in a Golden Eye,* there is almost
none of this, and the characters are both different and fewer in
number. Correspondingly, the story is much more tautly told,
the drama much more highly concentrated; and the quality of
fable, in fact, recedes. For here Mrs. McCullers has abandoned
her theme of love and loneliness, or rather, she has given us its
inversion, writing now of people whose self-engrossment, malice, contempt, or sheer stupidity have, for all their desperation,
put them outside the possibility of feeling either loneliness or
love. Theirs is a world of static rage and drugged destructiveness. Better that other world for all its pain.

This is not at all to say that one does not read this strange
short novel with engrossed interest. The setting is a Southern
army post in peacetime. Leonora Penderton, "a little feeble-
minded," feels nothing but contempt for her husband, Captain
Penderton, a homosexual in everything but practice, and is
having a meaningless sexual relationship with Major Langdon,
whose invalid wife, Alison, is "on the verge of actual lunacy"
and over the verge before the story ends. These four are set
against two young men. One is Anacleto, Alison's Philippine
houseboy, fantastic and comically elegant, whose devotion to
Alison never in any way qualifies the generally destructive
action. The other is Private Williams who becomes the unwit-
ting center of it. Mindless and unknown to thought, living by
animal instinct alone, he is fascinated by the accidental sight
of Leonora's naked body, and presently, night after night, he
lets himself silently into her house and kneels motionless beside

her bed, staring at her sleeping face. By day he serves as her groom, and in the atmosphere of the stables a situation like that in Lawrence's "The Prussian Officer" develops between him and the Captain. That unhappy half-man, like Lawrence's Hauptman, becomes obsessed with the young soldier's wholeness, at once enraged and enraptured, and when, one night, he finds him in his wife's bedroom, he shoots him and is himself thereby at last finished, "a broken and dissipated monk."

The title of the book derives from Anacleto's description of a water color he has been painting, of a peacock with an immense golden eye in which is reflected something tiny and grotesque. If the Lawrentian opposition, apparently intended, between the natural and the corrupt is not realized in this novel, that is perhaps because the static quality of the conception of the peacock's eye dominates the entire imaginative performance, with the young soldier somehow included in the grotesquerie. It is a dreadful world because his presence does not make it less negative: here there is no one to be redeemed, no love to deepen the loneliness.

We are not in any way echoing the old philistine demand that literature be "affirmative." At most, Mrs. McCullers's writing affirms little enough: *All right! O.K.! Some good.* It is, rather, a slackening of imaginative verve that is in question, as if the quality of the subject itself had somehow been injected into the presentation, frozen it. Mrs. McCullers once spoke of the "dimensions of a work of art" as being like "a flowering dream." That is as good a metaphorical account of her own successful work as one could find. And the trouble with *Reflections in a Golden Eye* is that the dream does not flower; we are trapped within its frightening rigidities, as we are in a horrid dream, before waking. All that is changed again in *The Member of the Wedding*.

In some "Notes on Writing" that she published in *Esquire* a few years ago, Mrs. McCullers began as follows:

When I was a child of about four, I was walking with my nurse past a convent. For once, the convent doors were open. And I saw the children eating ice-cream cones, playing on iron swings, and I watched, fascinated. I wanted to go in, but my nurse said no, I was not Catholic. The next day, the gate was shut. But, year by year, I thought of what was going on, of this wonderful party, where I was shut out. I wanted to climb the wall, but I was too little. I beat on the wall once, and I knew all the time that there was a marvelous party going on, but I couldn't get in.

This is the illusion by which Frankie Addams, the heroine of *Member of the Wedding*, lives, the illusion of a marvelous party going on somewhere that she must find and join.

Frankie Addams is not four but twelve years old when the novel opens. For a long time she had been "a member of nothing in the world," had become "an unjoined person," and in her yearning, pubescent loneliness, she lives in frenzied plans for flight from where she is to the discovery of some membership, some human connection, elsewhere. Then suddenly all her uncertain plans seem to find their actuality in the wedding of her older brother: she will become the *me* of their *we,* and the three of them will never separate. "She knew who she was and how she was going into the world."

So ends the first of the three parts of the book. But now, in fact, she knows less than ever who she is as, in the second part, she ceases to be Frankie and becomes F. Jasmine, or Miss F. Jasmine Addams, Esq. Her intensifying fantasies are always set against the anxious innocence of her six-year-old cousin, John Henry, not yet given to dreams, and the downright wisdom of Berenice, the Negro cook in the motherless household, experienced beyond the state of dreams. It is Berenice who, in this second part of the novel, tries to explain to Frankie how everyone is "caught" in himself, each in his own individuality, and how it is futile to try to break free of it. To that Frankie adds that one could say as well that everyone is "loose," by which she is trying to say that everyone is separate from everyone else, which is, of course, to say the same thing. But she believes that her separateness is about to be overcome and her freedom found.

Part Three begins after the disaster of the wedding, and

when, on the second page, she is named again, her name is Frances. She has settled at last into her own identity. When the book closes, she is a year older, she has a new best friend, John Henry has died, Berenice is leaving, the Addamses are moving to another house, and presently Frances will discover the nature of her identity. The materials necessary to that discovery she already possesses: the painful inevitability of separateness, the moderate mitigations to be found in love.

Less of a parable than *The Heart Is a Lonely Hunter*, *Member of the Wedding* manages, within the realistic tradition of the novel, to explore the same theme, and in doing so, with a quite wonderful blend of pathos and humor, overcomes the limitations of *Reflections in a Golden Eye*. With the novelette, *The Ballad of the Sad Café*, the theme remains the same but the method pushes farther away from social realism than anything she had yet written. It is probably her most successful work and attains most completely the objectification of myth.

The novelette is most properly named, for it does indeed share in most of the qualities of the traditional ballad except for the fact that it is not written in verse. The whole melodramatic action, the somehow depersonalized characters, the objective narration, the indifference to psychological as to social realism, the refusal to comment on even the most mysterious elements in the action, the frame in which the action is set (it begins and ends with a doomed, closed building inhabited by a haunted, crazed, and solitary figure), and the by now well-known legendary style, here much heightened—all this and more detailed matters of stylistic device and texture as well as more general matters such as the brooding, fated atmosphere of the work are characteristics familiar to us in the ballad form. In the prose version of this form, Mrs. McCullers's talent finds its completest consolidation.

The closed building, with its deranged inhabitant, Miss Amelia Evans, was once the only store in a desolate Southern town. Miss Amelia had been a huge, harsh, mannish creature who, at nineteen, married a handsome young man of dubious character named Marvin Macy, who had fallen hopelessly (and utterly improbably) in love with her. But she does not love him, refuses to consummate the marriage, and soon expels him from her establishment. For many years he is imprisoned for a subsequent crime. In the meantime, a grotesque hunchback named Lyman, claiming to be Amelia's cousin, has appeared, and he, quite as improbably, becomes the object of her love. She pampers him and he transforms the store into a café and the dead town into a lively community. This state of things continues happily until Macy returns and Lyman chooses him as the object of his love. The climax lies in a wrestling match between Amelia and Macy which she has nearly won when Lyman flings himself on her back and gives the advantage to Macy. Then Macy and Lyman destroy the café and flee the town together. Presently Miss Amelia boards the place up and incarcerates herself. The town falls back into its old death. "There is absolutely nothing to do in the town. . . . The soul rots with boredom. You might as well go down to the Forks Falls highway and listen to the chain gang." And so the story ends with an account of the twelve men on the chain gang, seven black and five white, singing. "Just twelve mortal men who are together." Together, of course, in their captivity.

*Some* good, one might add; but the pain is immeasurably greater. This is the familiar theme, but here it has achieved an esthetic logic in the presentation that is perhaps unique in Mrs. McCullers's longer work. The array of grotesque characters are perfectly suited to the fantastic action. The lover-beloved interchange is as patterned as a folk dance. The style is that of the fable or folk tale, and it gives universal validity to what is a highly private vision of the world, a vision for which the story itself is an extended metaphor, the symbolic objectification.

Mrs. McCullers's most recent novel is probably a falling away from her best work. Like *The Heart Is a Lonely Hunter, Clock Without Hands* is involved in public issues, but while the desolate sense of waste and human suffering that was evoked by the atmosphere of the Depression in the earlier novel was entirely appropriate to its general theme and, indeed, gave a special resonance to that theme, the public issues that enter *Clock Without Hands* are of a more specific and therefore more refractory kind.

Once more, the characters are few. There is J. F. Malone, an ordinary man, a pharmacist in a Southern town, who, at the age of forty, suddenly learns that he has only a very short time to live. He is man, alone, confronting his final destiny, and his story is moving. But it is ill-joined with the story of the second major character, a fanatical ex-congressman named Judge Fox Clane who is obsessed with the wild notion of redeeming Confederate currency and thus restoring the prestige and grandeur of the old South. This is the sort of grotesque character that Mrs. McCullers in earlier work had created with masterly authority, but here, where this absurd fanaticism is juxtaposed with the moral realities that suddenly confront Malone, and where the fanaticism itself is based on concrete contemporary social realities with which we are all most seriously concerned, the incongruities cannot be overcome. Nor are they much modified by the presence of two other characters, young boys both, one of them, Jester, the Judge's grandson, sensitive and sensible and, in his loneliness, reaching out for friendship with the other, a blue-eyed Negro, Sherman Pew, the Judge's amanuensis, so thwarted that he cannot accept friendship and lives in fantasy. Jester defies his grandfather and the town destroys Sherman with the Judge's support. The book ends as the Judge topples into final senility and Malone, after a redeeming act of conscience, falls into death. But somehow all these pieces have not fallen into the kind of meaningful pattern that is evident in almost everything else that Mrs. McCullers has written.

She has, except in rather oblique ways, abandoned the theme of love and loneliness, and the novel is therefore without the kind of lyric expansiveness with which that theme imbued her earlier work. Rather than pushing her materials in the direction of fable, she seems here to have attempted some sort of allegory, at once overrational and not at all clear, of the old and the new South. It is impossible for her not to interest us with anything she writes, and to charm us with her deft management of the comic-pathetic, which she does in this novel as in the others; yet there remains this disturbing disjunction between the half of her novel that is moving and the half that is confused and seems to belong somewhere else.

Truman Capote's talent is more urbane, more various, and more extravagant than Carson McCullers's, and his work has always seemed in danger of being overwhelmed by the stylish and the chic in a way that hers has not. Rereading his work one must conclude that this is a matter of personal reputation rather than of actual performance. The fact is that they are simply two different writers. Although their names are frequently coupled, the differences are greater than the similarities.

If Truman Capote is also a writer who comes from the South, he is not a "Southern writer" in the sense that Mrs. McCullers is: he is equally at home and perhaps even more at home in very different settings. The doctrine of love, as we have cited it in Mrs. McCullers's "A Tree. A Rock. A Cloud," and as we have quoted it from *Ballad of the Sad Café,* may seem alike, but they are given different interpretations. In Capote's *The Grass Harp,* the Judge speaks as follows:

> "We are speaking of love. A leaf, a handful of seed—begin with these, learn a little what it is to love. First, a leaf, a fall of rain, then someone to receive what a leaf has taught you, what a fall of rain has ripened. No easy process, understand; it could take a lifetime, it has mine, and still I've never mastered it—I only know how true it is: that love is a chain of love, as nature is a chain of life."

And later in the novel, Dolly recalls this speech:

> "Charlie said that love is a chain of love. I hope you listened and understood him. Because when you can love one thing," she held the blue egg as preciously as the Judge had held a leaf, "you can love another, and that is owning, that is something to live with. You can forgive everything."

The difference is that in the Capote world, love does make for communion and even community in a way that Mrs. McCullers can rarely permit. His is the gentler view, hers the more disabused. And if both like to write about children and grotesques, freaks and cripples and perverts, Mrs. McCullers seems to view them as representative of the human race whereas for Capote they are exemplars of a private world within the world at large, and of a private view. And finally, if both are novelists of sensibility, Mrs. McCullers's sensibility, as we have observed, expresses itself most fully in the objective forms of parable and fable, while Capote's sensibility moves in two different directions—into the most subjective drama of all, the psychic drama far below the level of reason, on the one hand, and, on the other, into objective social drama, often fanciful, and always indifferent to "social problems" in the usual sense. Close readers could probably find many minor similarities of detail (the crossed eyes of Miss Amelia Evans, for example, "exchanging with each other one long and secret gaze of grief," and the crossed eyes of Verena in *The Grass Harp,* peering "inward upon a stony vista"), but these make for no important similarity. In the end they are two quite different writers.

Rereading all of Truman Capote's writing,[2] we are perhaps surprised by the range of his mercurial talent, thinking of him still, as most readers do, as the strangely precocious youth from New Orleans, author of *Other Voices, Other Rooms.* His is, in fact, a prose of many moods, equally at ease—to name the extremes—in situations of dark and frightful nightmare, and of extravagant comedy. Perhaps the single constant quality of his prose is the sense of style and the emphasis that he himself places upon the importance of style. By style one means, of

[2] I have written a brief introduction to a selection of Truman Capote's writings. My views as expressed there are necessarily the same as those expressed here, since so little time had elapsed between the composition of that essay and this one, and I fear that my language, too, is often the same. When it is, I repeat it with the permission of Random House, Inc., publishers of *Selected Writings of Truman Capote* (1963).

course, not only the language as such but the body of detail precisely and freshly observed and the varieties of the speaking human voice accurately heard and quintessentially reported. (Here Capote's range is greater than Mrs. McCullers's: she is marvelous with the vernacular of children and of Negroes, but not particularly remarkable in reporting the speech of adult white urban characters; Capote, one feels, does not let any character talk unless he knows precisely *how* he talks, the very individual and individuating accents.) And the style changes, of course, with the changing subject matter, so that the variety is multiplied.

His earliest stories were written in what is frequently called the "Gothic" tradition or in the tradition of what Hawthorne meant by the word "romance" ("Hawthorne got us off to a fine start," Capote has said of style in the American short story), a tradition in which the subject matter is not confined to the limits of recognizable social experience but is free to shift continually and without transition or warning from the actual into the dream, from the real into the surreal, from the natural into the supernatural.

Over and over in these stories the central thematic concern shows itself to be with the idea of the *Doppelganger,* the alter ego, and the supernatural is, in fact, a kind of metaphor of the psychic world in which that other self, which we cannot ever confront in the active, diligent, and brightly lit social world, has its being. In general, these are stories about people who are lonely and without love, who are alone *because* they are without love, and who, in their isolated condition, come upon sinister, usually grotesque, often disgusting creatures with whom they are, in one way or another, ensnared and whom they are unable and usually unwilling to escape, for these creatures are their selves, discovered at last, and therefore their fate, which, once they have recognized it, they are necessarily committed to. And then, perhaps, they are free to love.

These stories, one feels certain, are written out of no systematic familiarity with modern psychological theories of the irrational ("I would not know a Freudian symbol as such,"

Capote has said, "if you put it to me") but directly out of the author's own experience of the irrational, his clutch on the remembered body of his own dreams and psychic frights. With a sometimes alarming immediacy they produce the most awful nighttime horrors of childhood, the hopelessness, the will-lessness, the ghastly mechanical compulsion of nightmare. One thinks sometimes almost entirely in pictorial terms when reading these stories, of some of the paintings of Fuseli, or Bosch, later, perhaps, of Max Ernst.

The analogy with such painters is useful only in that it is meant to suggest Capote's imaginative habit, in these stories, of direct presentation. Here there is no comment and, one feels, no previous speculation. These horrors are simply *there:* this is *it,* the stories say. In one of the earliest, "A Tree of Night," Kay, a pleasant ordinary girl on her way back to college from a funeral, is forced by two grotesques (who earn their living by re-enacting in public the burial and resurrection of Lazarus) with whom she is isolated on a train into a recognition of her own unconscious life and made at last to submit to it:

> Staring up into his hairless, vapid face, flushed brilliant by the lantern light, Kay knew of what she was afraid: it was a memory, a childish memory of terrors that once, long ago, had hovered above her like haunted limbs on a tree of night. Aunts, cooks, strangers—each eager to spin a tale or teach a rhyme of spooks and death, omens, spirits, demons. And always there had been the unfailing threat of the wizard man: stay close to the house, child, else a wizard man will snatch you and eat you alive! He lived everywhere, the wizard man, and everywhere was danger. At night, in bed, hear him tapping at the window? Listen!

The "wizard man," the bogyman of every childhood, that formless embodiment of every formless fear, the animated threat to every assumption of security—he takes many forms and, in these stories, is everywhere. He is that Mr. Revercomb in "Master Misery," who sucks the life out of others by seizing upon their dreams, and he is that Mr. Destronelli of "The Headless Hawk" who is disguised in nearly all the characters and yet is none of them, and his is the voice on the telephone in "Shut a Final Door," that voice of doom and fear which is also the hero's voice, Walter Ranney's, fleeing and unable to flee, as in the paralysis that overtakes us in our most wretched dreams.

"The Headless Hawk," the story that depends most completely on the nightmare mood and that explores it not only in a dream and in a fit of fever but also in strange dislocations that overtake the objective action, uses as its epigraph a passage from the Book of Job:

> They are of those that rebel against the light; they know not the ways thereof, nor abide in the paths thereof. In the dark they dig through houses, which they had marked for themselves in the daytime: they know not the light . . .

The central character is a young man named Vincent who, in his closest associations, can turn to maimed people alone, and these he must maim further if he is to preserve that self from the recognition of which, paradoxically, he is at the same time always fleeing. Now it is a deranged young girl known to him only by the initials D.J., who pursues him mutely; he accepts her, rejects her, and is pursued still. She in turn is haunted by a Mr. Destronelli, who appears in many guises, finally in Vincent himself. Presenting these mirrored and distorted relationships that evade all logic, the story depends probably more than any other on the disordered surrealistic imagery of the dream state and the hallucination, and by these means explores most explicitly the *Doppelganger* theme. In an extraordinary passage Vincent finds his other self, "old and horrid," clinging "spiderlike onto his back," and then, in a chaotic throng, he sees "that many are also saddled with malevolent semblances of themselves, outward embodiments of inner decay." But the theme is everywhere in these early stories—the hopeless flight from identity and the final recognition of it in the darkest depths of the self. It appears, in an inverse way, in "Master Misery," where another young girl, Sylvia, is systematically robbed of her dreams, and so is robbed finally of her very self.

". . . there was nothing left to steal." At the same time, the sinister figure who buys these dreams, a figure we are never permitted to see in this story which appears to be a kind of diabolic *Sacred Fount,* presumably enriches and even creates his self, and re-creates it.

The mood and method of these stories, if not so explicitly the alter-ego theme, find their fullest treatment in Capote's first novel, *Other Voices, Other Rooms.* Like a number of the stories, it begins in circumstances that are mundane enough as young Joel Knox is trying to get to an isolated place in the South where his father is; but very soon, as Joel finds himself in increasingly eerie circumstances, these enter the narrative method itself and more and more frantically he is spun about in the kaleidoscope of hallucination, and the reader with him. In search of his father, he is searching no less for someone who will love him: "Only how, how, could you say something so indefinite, so meaningless as this: God, let me be loved." (This is in rather sharp difference from Mrs. McCullers's characters, who are searching rather for someone to whom they can give their love.) Joel's father, when Joel is finally permitted to see him, is a paralyzed lunatic, and it is the decayed and elegantly sinister Cousin Randolph (the wizard man of the novel) who will love him, in his fashion, and force him to know himself. Thrust suddenly into this world of the sinister, the perverse, the lunatic, and the horrible, Joel makes an attempt to escape back into the sunnier world that he had left. But a deeper regression is in store for him. In the weird decay of the Cloud Hotel, in the final act of his initiation, he becomes at last what he is, and in this recognition there is relief and exhilaration and no regret.

Eight years after the publication of *Other Voices, Other Rooms,* having reread the novel, Capote said to an interviewer for *The Paris Review,* "I am a stranger to that book; the person who wrote it seems to have so little in common with my present self. Our mentalities, our interior temperatures are entirely different." That "interior temperature" was presumably already preparing for its alteration even when the nightmare mood was most upon him. In an early story like "Children on Their Birthdays," no less than in such later stories as "House of Flowers" and "A Christmas Memory," a very different mood asserts itself and, with it, a considerably different method.

These are stories about people who, inhabiting a private world of love, live peaceably with their selves, and are even capable—as in the instance of Miss Bobbit in "Children on Their Birthdays"—of transforming those around them. These characters dream still (". . . a man who doesn't dream is like a man who doesn't sweat: he stores up a lot of poison," says the Judge in *The Grass Harp*, which is the novel that explores most fully this more benign mood), but their dreams are gentle, even happy, with none of the violent turbulence and alarming exposures of the nightmare stories. The material of these stories exists among the realities of a recognizable social world, but because they do not concern themselves with "social problems" in any direct way and because the characters are, in one way or another, set apart from social realities, they are not bound by the limits of ordinary realism and maintain some of that freedom of fantasy and romance that is Capote's métier. Violence gives way here to pathos, even sentiment, and melodrama to comedy. In this mood, where pathos joins with comedy, the natural universe is transformed, too. A story like "The Headless Hawk" ends with jangling violence: ". . . it was as if the sky were a thunder-cracked mirror, for the rain fell between them like a curtain of splintered glass"; and this harsh image of sky and rain is characteristic of the treatment of nature, where all is gnarled and stark, deformed and submarine, in the earliest stories. But in "Children on Their Birthdays," for example, "it has been raining buoyant summer rain shot through with sun," and when the sun comes out at the end of the story, it brings "with it into the air all the sweetness of wisteria." For this more propitious world, Royal's "house of flowers" is the symbol, or the tree house in *The Grass Harp*.

This short novel has an air of the legendary which derives from at least two sources. One is the frame of the story, the idea of the grass harp, a field of dry grass over which the wind passes and speaks, "gathering, telling, a harp of voices remembering a story." The other is the remembered quality of the narrative, for the story is cast in the form of nostalgic reminiscence of a lost childhood, and the frequent interruptions of present time remind us over and over that Collin, the narrator, is reliving an idyl, or what, in retrospect, seems to have been idyllic.

Those famous landscapes of youth and woodland water—in after years how often, trailing through the cold rooms of museums, I stopped before such a picture, stood long haunted moments having it recall that gone scene, not as it was, a band of goose-fleshed children dabbling in an autumn creek but as the painting presented it, husky youths and wading water-diamonded girls; and I've wondered then, wonder now, how they fared, where they went in this world, that extraordinary family.

But the core of the story is real enough and not without a certain harshness.

A young boy—eleven when he arrives, sixteen when the story opens—comes to live with his father's two sisters, Verena and Dolly. Verena is hard, practical, loveless, formidably organized; Dolly is soft, gentle, affectionate, and a little dotty. The boy is, of course, attracted to Dollyheart, as she is called by her devoted friend, a Negro servant named Catherine; and the three of them work contentedly collecting herbs and roots for Dolly's secret remedy for dropsy. When Verena discovers that Dolly is, in fact, managing a considerably successful enterprise she decides to take it over and put it on a sound commercial basis, and she enlists the help of a sharp city character named Morris Ritz to help her. Dolly stubbornly refuses to yield up her secret formula and, when she is reproached for her general uselessness, she packs a few things together and, with Collin and Catherine, takes up her abode in a tree house on the edge of the field, the grass harp. There they are joined by two other dissident spirits, Judge Charlie Cool, retired and more or less expelled from his own house by his daughters-in-law, and an eighteen-year-old "loner" named Riley Henderson.

The rest of the novel has to do with the efforts of the conventional and indignant townspeople, under the leadership of Verena and a brutal sheriff, to force these five idiots back into sanity. When it develops that Morris Ritz has fleeced Verena and fled the town, she collapses, and so does the comic war that the village has been waging on the inhabitants of the tree. In a rainstorm, the broken Verena herself climbs into the tree, laments the perfidious Morris, and concludes: "it's too long to be alone, a lifetime. I walk through the house, nothing is mine: your pink room, your kitchen, the house is yours, and Catherine's too, I think. Only don't leave me, let me live with you. I'm feeling old, I want my sister." And they return to the house in the town.

But the tree-house episode has been the major demarcation in their lives, and the events of their lives are thought of as happening either before or after it. "Those few autumn days were a monument and a signpost." Their lives continue. Dolly does not marry the Judge, who has come to love her in the tree, but devotes herself to Verena and dies of a stroke.

> If in other ways he was a disappointed man, it was not because of Dolly, for I believe she became what he'd wanted, the one person in the world—to whom, as he'd described it, everything can be said. But when everything can be said perhaps there is nothing more to say.

Riley Henderson marries and becomes an industrious and respected citizen. Collin leaves the town to take up the study of law. Verena dies. But the grass harp goes on telling its story, and what it tells is that each of those eccentrics in the tree discovered there what he really was in himself. They discovered their separateness and their communion. "You're not yourself," Verena tells Dolly toward the end of the story, and Dolly replies, "You'd best look again: I am myself." The Judge has discovered what she is in herself and what he is when he calls her a "pagan," a "spirit"—

> someone not to be calculated by the eye alone. Spirits are accepters of life, they grant its differences—and consequently are

always in trouble. Myself, I should never have been a Judge; as such, I was too often on the wrong side: the law doesn't admit differences. . . . But ah, the energy we spend hiding from one another, afraid as we are of being identified. But here we are, identified: five fools in a tree. A great piece of luck provided we know how to use it: no longer any need to worry about the picture we present—free to find out who we truly are.

And if, as Collin later thinks, "No matter what passions compose them, all private worlds are good," it is because in the private world we find out who we truly are, and once we find that out, the novel seems to say, we can make the vulgar public world meet us on our own terms—or, if it will not, feel indifferent in our difference.

Capote's progression from the wholly private psychic world into the world of objective social realities continues. Isolating his characters still, but in a different way, and transforming the soft humor and the lyricism of these gentler stories and of *The Grass Harp* into high outrageous comedy, he moves into still another mood and possibly the one that suits him best. Holly Golightly of *Breakfast at Tiffany's* is self-sufficient, uncommitted to everything but her own need for freedom, a "wild thing."

"Never love a wild thing, Mr. Bell," Holly advised him. "That was Doc's mistake. He was always lugging home wild things. A hawk with a hurt wing. One time it was a full-grown bobcat with a broken leg. But you can't give your heart to a wild thing: the more you do, the stronger they get. Until they're strong enough to run into the woods. Or fly into a tree. Then a taller tree. Then the sky. That's how you'll end up, Mr. Bell. If you let yourself love a wild thing. You'll end up looking at the sky. . . . Good luck: and believe me, dearest Doc—it's better to look at the sky than live there. Such an empty place; so vague. Just a country where the thunder goes and things disappear."

This passage is not only the clue to the meaning of the whole story and to Holly's character, but it is also a prediction of the end of the story, and her end, as she too disappears in the sky.

So there is pathos still, of a sort, yet this choice is Holly's own, which modifies the pathos, and it is under any circumstances qualified by the lacquered manners of this brilliantly observed and re-created world of self-contained misfits and stylish eccentrics.

With this progression from the drama of the innermost terrors to what is basically a comedy of very special manners, and with his genuine gift for the observation of manners, it is not surprising that all the time that he has been publishing fiction, Capote has also been writing reportage. The travel sketches that make up his early book called *Local Color* are among the first of his attempts at reporting. Quite short, very pointed, they are at once highly personalized through the particularizing detail and at the same time without the intrusion of personal generalization. We are brought deftly, without fuss, into the objective heart of these places, and left there, immersed in the special quality of each.

From travel sketches, Capote moved on to a number of profiles of persons of public prominence, and of these, "The Duke in his Domain"—Marlon Brando in Japan, "just a young man sitting on a pile of candy"—is among the most successful. The quality of the place is evoked with the now expected skill, the necessary facts of Brando's enterprise in Kyoto are presented with journalistic grace, but it is the listening ear now that is most impressive as the characterization is set before us almost entirely through that speaking voice, ruminating through hours of muted self-inspection.

The high point of Truman Capote's reporting until now is *The Muses Are Heard*, surely one of the great satiric reports of our time, brilliant in its dead-pan presentation of a variety of very funny people in situations which, when they are not alarming, are hilariously wacky. So the reporting has moved, too, from places to people in places, from the lyric to the comic. And it will not stop there, one has reason to know. The narrator of *Breakfast at Tiffany's* speculates at one point as follows: "the average personality reshapes frequently, every few years even our bodies undergo a complete overhaul—desirable or not, it is a natural thing that we should change."

Truman Capote's personality is hardly average; but his literary personality, at least, has undergone constant, always refreshing change, and the substance of his work, as the social texture grows denser, has become more and more solid. The next change will become evident when he publishes the book at which he is now at work—*In Cold Blood*, the highly detailed and very compelling (a "cliff-hanger" without question) recreation of a brutal Kansas murder and its consequences. This may prove to be the most remarkable change of all and perhaps the most exciting achievement.[3]

It is, of course, his experience and discipline as a writer of fiction that make Capote the superb reporter that he is, and one wonders how his reporting will in turn modify his fiction when he takes it up again. Until then, we must rest with the observation of the way in which, beginning as an extreme example of the novelist of isolated sensibility, he has set that sensibility to work in the objective if offbeat, of course, materials of social reality. Inversely Carson McCullers has found the means to give her sensibility objective expression in literary forms that transcend social realities in approximations of myth.

---

[3] While writing this essay I was able to read in manuscript the half of *In Cold Blood* that was then finished. The brilliant promise of the part was of course spectacularly fulfilled in the whole, and this has been so widely acknowledged that it is unnecessary to say more about it here. Were I to do so, I would point out the extent to which this objective reporting depends on the techniques of fiction. Capote's phrase, "a nonfiction novel," tiresomely exploited as it was, nevertheless has genuine point.

# PART SIX

# Some Relationships: Gertrude Stein, Sherwood Anderson, F. Scott Fitzgerald, and Ernest Hemingway

THIS NARRATIVE begins in Baltimore, Maryland, in the year 1893. It could begin with equal propriety in a place called Clyde, Ohio, in 1896, when Sherwood Anderson first set out for Chicago, or at 481 Laurel Avenue, St. Paul, Minnesota, in the same year, or even in Oak Park, Illinois, two years later. But let it, for reasons of chronology, begin in Baltimore.

Leaving Baltimore for Radcliffe College is a young woman: Gertrude Stein. At Radcliffe she studied psychology with William James and performed laboratory experiments in automatic writing, among other phenomena, with Hugo Münsterberg. Upon the advice of James she proceeded to Johns Hopkins University to pursue an M.D. as the most suitable background for a professional psychologist. But she abandoned these studies for European travels with her brother Leo, and, fascinated by modern French painting, settled down permanently in Paris in the year 1903. There, with her brother, she became one of the first collectors of post-impressionist and cubist painting, and their establishment at 27 rue de Fleurus soon began to be famous.

She had, apparently, no focused literary ambitions, but she was widely read (her favorite novelists were Samuel Richardson, Anthony Trollope, and Henry James), and she had, in fact, during the winter of 1902–1903 started to write a novel more or less in imitation of James. The title of this work, *Quod Erat Demonstrandum,* indicates the scientific or at least the

mathematical bent of her mind, and the whole demonstrates
that she was perfectly able to write conventional, analytical
English, a fact that her more skeptical critics have not always
been ready to grant. She finished this short narrative in Paris
and then, apparently convinced that it was without merit, put
it away so thoroughly that it was forgotten for thirty years and
remained unpublished until five years after her death in 1946.

Alice B. Toklas forgot about that early effort (if she ever
knew of it) even more thoroughly than Gertrude herself: in
an interview of 1952, she declared that Gertrude Stein had
written nothing between her Radcliffe student compositions
and her first published book, *Three Lives,* and that until then
had had no literary ambitions at all.

> No, when it came upon her [Miss Toklas declared], it came
> upon her like this. She'd never made up her mind that she was
> going to be a writer, never expected to be one, and she started
> her writing by translating the—what is it, of Flaubert [*Tres
> contes*]. And then she started it . . . she did the first paragraph
> and said, "I'm not interested in somebody else's writing—I'm go-
> ing to do a story myself."

And that, she added, was in 1905.

It was probably a bit earlier, but no matter. It is true enough
that *Three Lives* took off from *Tres contes.* Of Flaubert's three
stories, the seminal one clearly was *Un coeur simple,* the story
of the naïve Félicité, a household drudge whose life consists
entirely in her dependence on the lives of others. Of her three
stories, two—"The Good Anna" and "The Gentle Lena"—are
about German-American servants. The third and most complicated story, and almost certainly the last to be written,
"Melanctha," is about a Negro girl.

The influence of Flaubert hardly extends beyond the example of humble characters as providing suitable material for
fiction and of the importance of style and *le mot juste*. But in
Gertrude Stein the conception of style and of its function was
to differ radically from Flaubert's. Style in Flaubert serves to
place the subject at an ironic distance through the detached

point of view of the narrator. Style in Gertrude Stein was to present the subject with the most direct immediacy and in what she came to call a "continuous present." On this conception she was not notably more lucid than she was on any other:

> . . . there was a constant recurring and beginning there was a marked direction in the direction of being in the present although naturally I had been accustomed to past present and future, and why, because the conception forming around me was a prolonged present . . . naturally I knew nothing of continuous present but it came naturally to me to make one, it was simple it was clear to me and nobody knew why it was done like that, I did not myself although naturally to me it was natural.

A more important influence than Flaubert in giving Gertrude Stein this direction was a portrait by Cézanne at which Gertrude Stein kept looking all through the composition of *Three Lives*. It is the portrait of Mme. Cézanne, dressed in blue, seated on a red chair, and it became Gertrude Stein's ambition to make the consciousness of her heroines, the very sense of their *existence*, as palpable, as immediately present as the figure on the wall. This was to be accomplished neither by details drawn from the external world around them, nor by subjective ruminations. These lives are lived in a city named Bridgepoint (presumably Baltimore), but a city so without specifying details that it could be any city anywhere. There are necessarily rooms and streets and occasional trees, but again, they are without any individuating quality, they are abstractions. There is a very simple narrative unfolding, but there is no plot, as there is no narrator. The language has been drained of all "poetic" qualities, of all those suggestive qualities that would release the reader's habits of association. It is language without connotation, almost entirely denotative, abstract.

> "There Anna didn't I tell you how it would all be? You see the spirit says so too. You must take the place with Miss Mathilda, that is what I told you was the best thing for you to do. We go out and see her where she lives to-night. Ain't you glad, Anna, that I took you to this place, so you know now what you will do?"

The simplest words, entirely colloquial words, words evoking
the dialect of the characters; the simplest kinds of sentences,
sentences almost entirely devoid of subordinating elements;
continual repetition; a kind of declarative bluntness: these
were to be the earmarks of the style. Through these and a
pronouncedly characterizing rhythm, she meant to make us
feel directly the movement of consciousness, the struggle of
these humble minds into their characteristic thoughts. And
through this style Gertrude Stein succeeded in divorcing her
characters and her stories from literary tradition, from any
literary language before her own.

The new style, and what it could accomplish in characterization and the presentation of psychological process, is everything. The stories, as stories, are nothing. The first and last are
much alike, portraits of human types. "The Good Anna" has
three parts. The first part presents Anna, as Donald Sutherland
points out, not "as a child or a young girl but in her full development, in a situation which gives full expression to her
typical kind of force, which is incessant managing will. The
first chapter gives her as the type of that" and nothing more.
The second and longest part gives her life through a series of
demonstrations and re-demonstrations in selected episodes of
her typical quality. The third part gives her death. "The Gentle
Lena," although shorter and slighter, is much the same except
that Lena is of another type. "Lena was patient, gentle, sweet
and german," and from these qualities the story takes on a
special tenderness that is absent in "The Good Anna."

The central story, "Melanctha," which is probably Gertrude
Stein's most important literary achievement, is somewhat different from and much more complex in intention than the other
two stories. Not of least importance is the fact that, as Carl
Van Vechten long ago pointed out, it is "perhaps the first
American story in which the Negro is regarded as a human
being and not as an object for condescending compassion or
derision." Once again, the story presents a central human type
and tells a life through selected moments or demonstrations.
More than that, now, although again through the style alone,

it attempts to trace the curve of a passion, its rise, its climax, its collapse, with all the shifts and modulations between dissension and reconciliation along the way. This is the center of the story and its *raison d'être*—the passion and its death between two persons of opposite type, a man named Jeff Campbell and the girl named Melanctha.

In her next book, Gertrude Stein was to base much on her declaration that all human beings can be reduced to two types, what she called the "attacking" type and the "resisting" type. In a sense, Anna and Lena have already suggested these two types. In "Melanctha," Jeff and Melanctha Herbert have moved much further in the direction of this distinction—Jeff as the slow, resisting kind, Melanctha as the swift, attacking kind. We read of them, "It was a struggle, sure to be going on always between them. It was a struggle that was as sure always to be going on between them, as their minds and hearts always were to have different ways of working." The conflict, however, is presented to us not explicitly, and not so much through dramatized scenes, as it would be in more conventional novelists, but through the endless repetition and modulated repetition of the sentences themselves. A sample:

"You are certainly a very good man, Dr. Campbell, I certainly do feel that more every day I see you. Dr. Campbell, I sure do want to be friends with a good man like you, now I know you. You certainly, Dr. Campbell, never do things like other men, that's always ugly for me. Tell me true, Dr. Campbell, how you feel about being always friends with me. I certainly do know, Dr. Campbell, you are a good man, and if you say you will be friends with me, you certainly never will go back on me, the way so many kinds of them do to every girl they ever get to like them. Tell me for true, Dr. Campbell, will you be friends with me."

The attempt here, the burden placed on language as such, is bold, sometimes exasperating, often successful. That this language has a certain veracity as dialect that some of us, Caucasians, may not detect, is borne out by the statement of the novelist, Richard Wright, who said that when he read aloud portions of "Melanctha" to a group of illiterate Negro workers, they roared with laughter not only at the comedy but in recognition of their own characteristic mode of speech. That, however, is not the point for us. One observes a certain dislocation of language that goes beyond that of the passage I quoted from "The Good Anna." There is a deliberate fracturing of normal syntax, a wrenching of idiom that is intended to call attention to the individual words through their very misplacement. Miss Stein is working toward her theory that words are plastic, that they are like cubes and ovoids and angles in painting, to be manipulated for their own sakes, that they have meaning apart from our general sense of meaning.

As soon as she had finished *Three Lives,* she set to work on her next book, an enormous tome to be called *The Making of Americans,* which was projected not only as a history of a family but (by the nature of her theory of human motives) a history of "everyone who ever was or is or will be living."

In this book certain tendencies already apparent in "Melanctha" are carried further. The characters are presented as isolated units; they have family connections, to be sure, but those connections are static, do nothing to determine their sense of their selves. The language is almost completely disembodied, divorced much more completely than before from any physical world or even physical details. If formerly her model was Cézanne and her ambition was a literary distortion of reality analogous to his painterly distortion, her model now is Picasso in his cubist phase and her ambition a literary plasticity divorced from narrative sequence and consequence and hence from literary meaning. She was trying to transform literature from a temporal into a purely spatial art, to use words for their own sake alone. Small wonder that the "monumental" work, as she called *The Making of Americans,* did not find a publisher for many years. This fact did not deter her. She pushed her efforts at total literary abstraction further and further in a whole series of shorter works.

When *Three Lives* was finished no publisher could be found for it, and finally, in 1910, she herself paid for its publication by an obscure New York firm that ordinarily published genealogies and historical works at their authors' expense. In 1912, her so-called "portraits" of Matisse and Picasso were published by the photographer, Alfred Stieglitz, in his periodical called *Camera Work.* In 1914 she published *Tender Buttons,* a collection of short pieces, with a nearly unknown New York publisher called Claire Marie, a firm devoted to "New Books for Exotic Tastes." The advance brochure described her as follows:

> She is a ship that flies no flag and she is outside the law of art, but she descends on every port and leaves a memory of her visits. . . . The last shackle is struck from context and collocation, and each unit of the sentence stands independent and has no commerce with its fellows. The effect produced on the first reading is something like terror . . .

And yet here and there in isolated spots these nearly unknown works began to find readers. Most of them assumed that she was either a madwoman or a fraud, but a few found that she had something serious to give them. Among these was an unpublished writer in Chicago named Sherwood Anderson. In 1914 he already knew *Three Lives* and had concluded, in his own words, that "it contained some of the best writing ever done by an American." Then his brother, a painter, significantly, brought him a copy of *Tender Buttons.* They read aloud from this strange work, and the brother said, "It gives words an oddly new intimate flavor and at the same time makes familiar words seem almost like strangers, doesn't it?" Sherwood Anderson concluded as follows:

> The loud guffaws of the general that must inevitably follow the bringing forward of more of her work do not irritate me but I would like it if writers, and particularly young writers, would come to understand a little what she is trying to do and what she is in my opinion doing.

"I always wanted to be historical, from almost a baby on, I felt that way about it," she wrote shortly before her death in 1946. She had, with these words of Anderson, in fact begun to become historical.

2

Of his life Sherwood Anderson always wished to construct
a parable, even a myth. It had various forms, but they all
sprang from a central action. The central action is this: on
November 27, 1912, a successful manufacturer in the town of
Elyria, Ohio, dreaming sometimes of becoming a great benev-
olent tycoon, chafing more often at the stultifying routines of
promotion and salesmanship, Sherwood Anderson, aged thirty-
six, walked out of his office and away from his wife and family
into the freedom of a wandering literary life, never to return
to business. " 'For the rest of my life I will be a servant to
[words] alone,' I whispered to myself as I went along a spur
of railroad track, over a bridge, out of a town and out of that
phase of my life."

It is a pretty fable that has considerable psychological
relevance to the lives of many modern American writers even
when its literal relevance is as slight as it was to the facts of
Anderson's life.

Sherwood Anderson was born in 1876, the third child of an
Ohio harness maker whose handicraft could not long compete
with rapidly developing mechanization. Forced out of his business, the father took to drink, spun out endless tales for anyone
who would listen, and became an itinerant sign and house
painter. The family moved from one Ohio town to another.
Young Anderson's education was always irregular and ceased
after one year of high school. His real education came to him
through the endless variety of odd jobs that filled his youth,
through the wisdom of laborers and Negroes and livery stable
hands and hangers-on, through race-track touts and trainers,
through tramps. When he was nineteen his mother died, his
father wandered off in his vague and irresponsible way, and the
family broke up.

Sherwood Anderson went from Clyde, Ohio, to Chicago to
become a laborer in a cold-storage warehouse until, desperately
bored with that merely dogged work, he enlisted in the
United States Army to fight in the Spanish-American War. His

company did not reach Cuba until four months after the armistice had been signed, so he saw no military action and was released from the army less than a year after his enlistment. Back in Clyde, Ohio, he worked for a while as a farm hand, and then, in September of 1899, dreaming of college education, he enrolled in the Wittenberg Academy in Springfield, Ohio, preparatory to enrolling in Wittenberg College, when he would have been twenty-four years old. Before he reached that age, he gave up the brief academic dream and returned to Chicago.

In the opening year of the twentieth century, significantly enough, Sherwood Anderson became an advertising man, and soon he was writing copy in which, very much in keeping with the times, he glorified what was then called the "adventure" of business. Always attractive to women, he married a girl above him in social station, moved to Cleveland where he became the president of a mail-order firm, and from there to Elyria, Ohio, where he presently bought a paint factory that produced something called "Roof-Fix." Wanting to "ennoble" that business activity which he had chosen as his own, he was at the same time writing what he called "lies" in his advertising copy. A conflict developed between his wish to succeed in the ordinary commercial world and his wish to escape into the imaginative world and into real writing.

He read a good deal, and it was probably now that he came across *Three Lives*. More and more he brooded about the character of the artist and about his situation in an industrial society. In about 1910, like Gertrude Stein when she gave up translating Flaubert, Anderson, having translated Stein, began to write short fiction of his own, and by 1912 he had written drafts of what would become his first two novels. At the same time, torn by conflict, he had taken to drink, turned from his wife to the comforts of loose women, and was neglecting his business, which suffered accordingly. If, in his later recollections, he was to say that he let people think he was a little mad so that his creditors would forgive him when he deserted his business, the fact is that he *was* a little mad. On November

27, 1912, that famous day of sudden rebellion and liberation, his nerves collapsed. Four days later, haggard, disheveled, and suffering from aphasia—a loss of the power of speech—he was found wandering around Cleveland in a daze and was hospitalized by the police. Late in December his wife brought him back to Elyria. In February 1913 he disposed of his business and left alone for Chicago to return to the servitude of advertising. He was now thirty-six years old, his marriage would last another two years (when he would marry a sculptress named Tennessee Mitchell), but he would continue in advertising for another ten years. So much for the fable!

When he was not in his office writing copy, still trying to make something good of a competitive life that he hated, he was working at his novels and at his queer, untutored short sketches. We must see him now as he described himself:

> My mind did a kind of jerking flop and after Miss Stein's book [*Tender Buttons*] had come into my hands I spent days going about with a tablet of paper in my pocket and making new and strange combinations of words. The result was I thought a new familiarity with the words of my own vocabulary. I became a little conscious where before I had been unconscious. Perhaps it was then I really fell in love with words, wanted to give each word I used every chance to show itself at its best.

He began to meet writers. Through his brother, Karl, the painter, he met Floyd Dell, and chiefly through him a whole circle of garrulous literary people including Ben Hecht, Carl Sandburg, sometimes Theodore Dreiser, and, presently, Margaret Anderson, who was to found *The Little Review* in Chicago in 1914 and there publish one of Anderson's first short stories. When Floyd Dell read the manuscript of Anderson's first novel, *Windy McPherson's Son*, he was enthusiastic and took it upon himself to find a publisher. After many rejections, it was published in 1916, and having given the publisher the conventional option on his next work, Anderson immediately produced the manuscript of that already written novel, *Marching Men*, which was published in 1917.

These novels, although they caused a considerable critical excitement as marking the appearance of an original genius, had small sales and were, in fact, poor novels. They are loose and sprawling works, without unity of theme or action, with sometimes comically unreal dialogue and with narrative and analytical passages written in long, straggling sentences that bear no relation to the style that Anderson presently would make his own. In the themes of *Windy McPherson's Son* there are hints of his future obsessions: the brooding boyhood in a drab Iowa town, the eccentric character of Windy drawn, Anderson said, after his own father, and above all, the criticism of the myth of business idealism and the assertion at the end of the novel of his own myth—the break with manufacturing into freedom, to "find truth." In *Marching Men,* a curious story about a mindless and militant brotherhood formed by workers under the leadership of one Beaut McGregor, intent on violence to free themselves from the routines of industrial slavery, both the inarticulate, somewhat Whitmanesque yearning for a bond between man and man and the aspiration to freedom, however ill defined, suggest characteristic future themes. It is less easy to see the future Anderson at his best in the volume of inchoate poems called *Mid-American Chants,* published in 1918.

But all the time, from 1913 on, Anderson was working toward something quite different from these books—his masterpiece, *Winesburg, Ohio,* published in 1919. A number of separate pieces from this work appeared in *The Little Review* and elsewhere between 1916 and the year of book publication, and these seemed to be autonomous if rather amorphous narrative entities. Only when the book as a whole was published was its overall design and significance to appear.

The book comes directly out of the life of Anderson's boyhood in small Ohio towns, and the central character, who appears in most of the separate parts, George Willard, is drawn after Anderson in his late adolescence. Without explication of any sort, the book somehow evokes the dying end of an agrarian culture as it slips over into industrial culture. It evokes, too, the intellectual climate of that late nineteenth-century mid-America in which Anderson grew up: the world that had fostered the heroic individualism of men like Abraham Lincoln and Mark Twain; the atmosphere that encouraged the atheism of a man like Robert Ingersoll, the rhetoric of William Jennings Bryan, the "grass roots" stir of such a political movement as the Populist Party; the era that brings to an end gas-lit streets, wooden sidewalks and the cracker barrel, the flourishing village saloon, thriving village eccentrics.

All this was the inheritance of Sherwood Anderson, and within all this he had observed, and was still observing in Chicago, the character of individuals. But how to use this material? He was not happy with the more or less conventional novel form that he had already twice attempted. He was no more happy with the prevailing fashions in the short story, either in the formal sense (the contrived melodrama of Poe, for example, or the slick machinery of O. Henry) or in the conventional interpretation of village life (the sentimental romanticism of Booth Tarkington and other writers of the Hoosier School). He had himself observed the pathos, the suffocation of hope and dream in small-town characters, the flight into eccentricity and neurosis, the cruelty no less than the comedy. And in form he wanted something loose and impressionistic and without the contrivance of "plot" that would permit him to get under the surface of manners and character, into the secret life, and into what he felt was the soft, warm flow that, taken together, all the secret lives made into life itself. "A man keeps thinking of his own life," he was later to write. ". . . life itself is a loose, flowing thing. There are no plot stories in life."

He had heard talk of Sigmund Freud and psychoanalysis in bohemian Chicago, and this helped him. He was reading or was about to read the fiction of D. H. Lawrence, and this would help him, too. But above all he had the example of Gertrude Stein's *Three Lives*. It may very well have been this example that urged on him the notion of the plotless, flowing story that would put nothing between the reader and the directly presented contours of the buried life itself. And it was she, of course, who helped him most precisely to discover the language that he now knew he wanted to use—the colloquial language of Mark Twain, of everyday America, of country roads and village streets; but more than that, the naïveté of manner engendered by the simplest words, the simplest, least sophisticated of syntactical forms, the constant repetition.

Finally, it was *Three Lives* that encouraged a habit of plainness, a certain bareness even in content itself—a kind of concentration on essentials and the elimination of all else, so that his characters are divested of "their incidentals," as Edmund Wilson called them—"their furniture, their houses, their clothes, their ordinary social relations."

Anderson many times acknowledged his debt to her, perhaps never so explicitly as in 1934 when he replied to an article in *The Atlantic* by the Harvard psychologist, B. F. Skinner, who had concluded that Gertrude Stein's was automatic writing. Anderson wrote:

> This matter of writing, the use of words in writing, is an odd affair. How much Miss Stein has taught all of us. . . .
>
> This nonsense about automatic writing. All good writing is, in a sense, automatic. It is and it isn't. . . . There is something stored within that flows out . . .
>
> Stein is great because she is a releaser of talent. She is a pathfinder. She has been a great, a tremendous influence among writers because she has dared, in the face of ridicule and misunderstanding, to try to awaken in all of us who write a new feeling for words. She has done it.

And on another occasion he said that she had released in him the "stored" thing, the other, the "automatic" man, the "wordman."

Yet she could not, in spite of all this, help him in the larger problem of unity and form. This problem was not solved until 1915, when he read Edgar Lee Masters's long poem, *The Spoon River Anthology,* that collection of voices of about two hundred and fifty dead people, all buried in the cemetery of a single Midwest town, each speaking out the essential truth of his secret life, and many of these characters reappearing in the reflections of many of the others. As Masters had done it in free verse, so Anderson would do it in prose, and with two important additional elements of unification.

Like Masters, he would give a certain unity to the separate stories of his twenty-two characters through the common background of the town, Winesburg. As the stories progressed, characters would keep reappearing; someone who had been a minor figure in one story would presently emerge as the major figure in another, and so on, until a whole sense of the community would emerge. Then he would employ a single narrator, George Willard, who would himself appear in many of the stories and would finally climax the whole. While the other characters would come to George in the dumb expectation that he could somehow understand and perhaps tell their stories, their stories would also be like gifts to him, gifts that would help him grow until, at the end, he was mature and made the characteristic gesture of flight into freedom. And Anderson would have one further means of unification—a theory embodied in the opening section, a prelude called "The Book of the Grotesque."

A grotesque is formed, Anderson tells us, when an individual seizes on some single truth from the whole body of truths and tries to live by that alone. A single truth, a single wish, a single memory, a single obsessive ambition that distorts the self even as it compels it—these are the motivations of Sherwood Anderson's grotesques. But what is probably a further consequence of these motivations is perhaps more important than the grotesques themselves: in their single pursuits, the characters isolate themselves from one another, and in their isolation, they are at once lonely and mute. Everyone in this world seems to grope helplessly toward everyone else, but no one can communicate with anyone else—or only with the artist-reporter, George Willard. And that, as Anderson came to understand it, is the function of the artist: to absorb the lives of others into himself, and himself to become those others and their lives.

As a totality, as a book, that is, *Winesburg, Ohio* is the height of Anderson's achievement. Taken singly, however, none of its separate pieces is as good as any of a half dozen or more truly separate short stories that he was to write then and later—stories like "The Egg" and "I Want to Know Why" from *The Triumph of the Egg* (1921), "I'm a Fool" and "The Man Who Became a Woman" from *Horses and Men* (1923), and "A Meeting South" and "Death in the Woods" from the final volume of stories, called *Death in the Woods* (1933). Grotesques still appear in all of them; and perhaps Anderson's masterpiece of grotesquery is the father in "The Egg," the chicken farmer who collects and preserves in alcohol deformed chickens that could not live and whose own frenzied frustrations are symbolized by his failure to do tricks with eggs. Loneliness and isolation continue to be the condition of the characters, whether grotesques or adolescent boys such as the heroes of "I Want to Know Why" and "I'm a Fool"—both modeled on the young Anderson himself. The style continues much the same—the slightly hesitant, slightly repetitious, and considerably rhythmical prose that bases itself so clearly on the spoken American language, sometimes, indeed, as in "I'm a Fool" and "I Want to Know Why," becoming the dialect itself, as it had been earlier used by Mark Twain in *Huckleberry Finn* and elsewhere, and later by Gertrude Stein.

Whatever similarities Anderson's later stories may bear to the slighter sketches of *Winesburg, Ohio,* it is neverless in their fuller embodiment that we can best see why Sherwood Anderson was a revolutionary force in the American short story, why he in turn became a model for younger writers, and why the short story was the form most suited to the full expression of his talent. These later stories, like the Winesburg pieces, seemed to contemporary readers to be a new victory for realism, and in a sense they were. It was in that light, certainly, that Theodore Dreiser and H. L. Mencken, for example, read and praised them. These stories seemed to close their eyes to nothing, to gloss over nothing, neither the brutalities of men nor the beauty of animals. Their relatively candid concern with the sexual relationship and with sexual motivations and repressions, their implied criticism of a society that frustrates individuality and of an individualism that creates a society of hermits, their accurate report of such physical detail as they employ and of a certain range in the speaking voice—all this and more made Anderson seem to be the champion of realism both in subject matter and in method. Yet when we put stories like "The Egg" or "I Want to Know Why" beside the work of such a realist as Stephen Crane or such a naturalist as Theodore Dreiser, we see readily enough that, with their impressionistic method, the first story is more nearly a fable and the second more nearly a poetic lamentation than either is a conventionally realistic or naturalistic report. Anderson's important observations are at once under the surface of manners and transcendent of the surface of society.

The short story was perfectly calculated to articulate those glimpses—and glimpses rather than sustained vision they were; James Joyce's word, "epiphany," is not inappropriate to Anderson's gift—those glimpses into the secret, inarticulate life that was his special province. Yet over and over he would attempt the longer form of the novel where, over and over, he would lose his imaginative grip on his materials.

Even before *Winesburg, Ohio* was published, Anderson began his next novel, *Poor White*. Finished and published in 1920, it is probably his best attempt in the form, but still much less satisfactory than the best of the stories. Bringing to it what he had learned about style in *Winesburg, Ohio* and hoping again to accommodate a certain "looseness" of structure by making the community itself the unifying center (the explicit theme now is the transformation of an agrarian to an industrial way of life), the narrative focus shifts so frequently and so drastically that the total is not "a new looseness" but a thematic confusion. Of this novel, Anderson himself said that "the town was really the hero of the book. . . . What happened to the town was, I thought, more important than what happened to the people of the town." But a town, after all, is made up of its people, as a novel is made up of its characters. If the people do not live, there is no town; if the characters do not live, the novel cannot. The hero of *Poor White*, Hugh McVey, begins like a boy out of the Winesburg stories, but as he grows up he becomes an implausible mechanical genius and inventor (this without any training at all) and an equally implausible husband. The characterization, like the plot, disintegrates in incoherence.

By the time that *Poor White* was published, Anderson had several times attempted to escape Chicago (and his second wife) by trips to New York and to various parts of the South. In the East he made new and important literary friends—Van Wyck Brooks, Waldo Frank, Ring Lardner, Paul Rosenfeld, Alfred Stieglitz—all of whom were enthusiastically responsive to his writing; but his books did not yet bring him an income adequate to free him from advertising once and for all, and in the winter of 1920–1921, he was still writing copy in Chicago. In the summer of 1921, he escaped once more when his friend, Paul Rosenfeld, invited the Andersons to go to Europe with him.

In Paris, in that summer, the momentous meeting with Gertrude Stein at last came about when Sylvia Beach, the owner of the *avant garde* American bookshop, Shakespeare and Company, wrote Miss Stein to ask if she could bring him to 27 rue de Fleurus. "He is so anxious to know you for he says you have influenced him ever so much & that you stand as such a great master of words." Of the meeting Gertrude Stein herself wrote in *The Autobiography of Alice B. Toklas:*

. . . Gertrude Stein was moved and pleased as she has very rarely been. Gertrude Stein was in those days a little bitter, all her unpublished manuscripts, and no hope of publication or serious recognition. Sherwood Anderson came and quite simply and directly as is his way told her what he thought of her work and what it had meant to him in his development. He told it to her then and what was even rarer he told it in print immediately after. Gertrude Stein and Sherwood Anderson have always been the best of friends but I do not believe even he realises how much his visit meant to her. It was he who thereupon wrote the introduction to Geography and Plays.

In that little essay, which was to be published in the next year, he said that he found her "a woman of striking vigor, a subtle and powerful mind, a discrimination in the arts such as I have found in no other American born man or woman, and a charmingly brilliant conversationalist." Then he tried to say what her work was doing:

> There is a thing one might call "the extension of the province of art" one wants to achieve. One works with words and one would like words that have a taste on the lips, that have a perfume to the nostrils, rattling words one can throw into a box and shake, making a sharp, jingling sound, words that, when seen on the printed page, have a distinct arresting effect upon the eye, words that when they jump out from under the pen one may feel with the fingers as one might caress the cheeks of his beloved.

And he conjectured that her work might in the end prove to be "the most lasting and important" in that literary generation.

After Paris, Chicago was too dreary for Anderson to bear. Even those Chicago writers who were his friends, and who were to have brought about that literary renaissance that had somehow fizzled, now seemed less than glamorous. In the summer of 1922, Anderson at last broke for good with advertising, with Chicago, and with his second wife. In the meantime, he had become acquainted with one younger Chicago writer, not of that older group nor really of any group, who had impressed him more than any of his friends and who, in turn, had been impressed by the Anderson short stories. To his sometime friend, F. Scott Fitzgerald, this young man was later to say that *Winesburg, Ohio* had been his first model. On December 3, 1921, Anderson wrote a letter of introduction to his new friend, Gertrude Stein, for the unknown young writer on his way to Paris. He said:

> I am writing this note to make you acquainted with my friend Ernest Hemingway, who with Mrs. Hemingway is going to Paris to live. . . . Mr. Hemingway is an American writer instinctively

in touch with everything worth-while going on here, and I know you will find Mr. and Mrs. Hemingway delightful people to know.

## 3

Ernest Hemingway, although a Midwesterner too, had, nevertheless, a background very different from Anderson's. He was born in the respectable middle-class Chicago suburb of Oak Park in 1899, the son of a doctor who loved the out-of-doors, and of a rather pious, domineering mother who dressed him for a long time in girl's clothes. Herself a singer, she had ambitions to make a musician of him, but the boy resisted her influence and turned to his father. The most important experiences of his boyhood were not in fact to take place in stuffily genteel Oak Park but in the northern Michigan woods where the Hemingways spent their summers and where the father and son enjoyed hunting and fishing together. All the skills of the outdoors the father, who knows how demandingly, taught his son.

The young Hemingway was a high-school athlete. Much later he was to remark that his athletic activities were a very different matter from Scott Fitzgerald's frustrating *ambition* to be an athlete. "I had no ambition nor choice. At Oak Park if you could play football you had to play it." Athletics, at any rate, did not interfere with what was his apparently early ambition to be a writer. He published short stories in the high-school literary magazine and in the high-school newspaper he published sketches in imitation of the vernacular style of Ring Lardner, just then establishing his reputation as a sharply satirical journalist through a column he published in the Chicago *Tribune*. When Hemingway was graduated from high school in 1917, he had developed still another ambition more consuming than any other, and that was to enlist in the armed forces and get into the war in Europe. His father forbade that, and the young man chafed through his last summer in northern Michigan. Then, in the autumn of 1917, he went to Kansas

City to become a reporter on the Kansas City *Star*. He was eighteen years old and his formal education was over.

His early journalistic experience was to be of considerable importance to the writer that Ernest Hemingway was to become, of much more importance than he could possibly have known during his seven months' employment in Kansas City when his most urgent wish was still of a quite unliterary kind. In April 1918 he managed at last to get into the war as an honorary lieutenant in the Red Cross ambulance corps serving on the Italian front. His service was dramatically brief: on July 8 he was severely wounded by the explosion of an Austrian mortar shell, and the next three months he spent in a hospital in Milan. Nothing more important than this wounding was ever to happen to him. The brief experience of war was to come prominently into his early fiction, but more specifically, a wound was to become the central symbol of nearly everything he was to write, and the consequences of a wound his persistent thematic preoccupation.

He returned to Oak Park and to Chicago, spent the remainder of the summer and the autumn in northern Michigan, trying to write, went to Canada to work on the Toronto *Star Weekly* for the first half of 1920, and then, back in Chicago, accepted employment, like Sherwood Anderson, in an advertising firm. In his spare time he loitered about gymnasiums, boxing and watching boxers, and tried to write short stories and poems. He roomed in an apartment with a number of other people who earned their living by writing and presently, through one of them, he met Anderson. Already intimately familiar with Anderson's stories, much of whose material was drawn from the same areas of life as Hemingway's would be, he was quietly attentive to everything the older man said whenever they were together. Anderson himself is said to have known at once that he had met a young man who was going to become an important writer, and while he never claimed to have influenced him profoundly or even at all (but surely Hemingway's early story, "My Old Man," is simply his version of Anderson's story, "I Want to Know Why"), the example of

Anderson's success, at least, was a powerful incentive to the still unpublished, struggling Hemingway. His style was to develop into a tighter, more concentrated, and more lucid instrument than Anderson's, and it would develop its own character, but in diction and in rhythm it looks back to Anderson, and one could quote passages from each that might have been written by either. Both men thought of Mark Twain as the great model (in a moment of exaggeration Hemingway later said that *all* American literature came from *Huckleberry Finn*), and the older man had already accepted, as the younger soon would accept, the tutelage of the same contemporary, Gertrude Stein.

The famous remark that she would presently make to Hemingway—"You are all a lost generation"—marks the most important difference between Hemingway and Anderson. In a long letter to his son, Robert, written in November 1929, Anderson tried to explain the difference between their generations, the difference between men who were formed before the World War and men who were largely formed by it. The rebellion of the older generation of American writers, of men like Anderson, was against the repressive conventions of American life, but they still believed in American life and they still sought their values in its democratic promises. The war ended those conventions at a blow, and the younger generation, men like Hemingway, had really nothing to rebel against and found little in American life that they could believe in. In Chicago, Hemingway grew increasingly cynical about America and about his employment in particular—and with reason, he soon discovered, for his employer was in fact committing an enormous fraud in his enterprise. The young Hemingway now wanted to get out of America.

Early in the autumn of 1921 he married a young woman as eager to go abroad as he was. Later that fall he was ceremoniously reminded of the European experience he had already had when he was presented with Italy's Medaglia d'Argento al Valore Militare and with the Croce ad Merito di Guerra. Then suddenly the opportunity came. He was offered employment as a roving correspondent for the Toronto *Star*. Anderson had his farewell glimpse of him on the night before he left. Hemingway had packed all the canned food from his kitchen into a knapsack and brought it to Anderson. "That was a nice idea," Anderson wrote in his *Memoirs*, "bringing thus to a fellow scribbler the food he had to abandon. . . . I remember his coming up the stairs, a magnificent broad-shouldered man, shouting as he came."

Soon afterward Anderson went South and lived for a time in New Orleans. There he became acquainted with the staff of a literary periodical called the *Double-Dealer*, and it was perhaps through his intercession that the editors accepted two totally undistinguished works, a prose sketch and a poem, by Ernest Hemingway—his first creative publications. That they bear no resemblance whatever to the Hemingway we know today suggests that the young man still had a good deal to learn about his craft.

Bohemian Paris in the early 1920's was the scene of a good deal of dissension, petty gossip, trivial jealousies and rivalries, secret malice and open name-calling, and much of this can be localized in the Stein establishment at 27 rue de Fleurus. *Testimony Against Gertrude Stein* was to be the title of a work later put together by a group of her ex-friends, chiefly painters, and she herself was to say, "Quarreling is to me very interesting." Hemingway very soon presented himself to her.

> I remember very well the impression I had of Hemingway that first afternoon [she later wrote]. He was an extraordinarily good-looking young man, twenty-three years old . . . rather foreign looking, with passionately interested, rather than interesting eyes. He sat in front of Gertrude Stein and listened and looked.
>
> They talked then, and more and more, a great deal together. He asked her to come and spend an evening in their apartment and look at his work. . . . We spent the evening there and he and Gertrude Stein went over all the writing he had done up to that time. He had begun the novel that it was inevitable he would begin and there were the little poems afterwards printed by McAlmon in the Contact Edition. Gertrude Stein rather liked

the poems, they were direct, Kiplingesque, but the novel she found wanting. There is a great deal of description in this, she said, and not particularly good description. Begin over again and concentrate, she said.

That was the first advice: compress, concentrate. And Hemingway, wisely, took her advice in good part. "Gertrude Stein and me are just like brothers, and we see a lot of her," he wrote to Anderson. And, "We love Gertrude Stein." She enjoyed walking with him and talking about writing, his writing, her writing, and writing in general. She was not always, one might point out, so open to young American writers; of Glenway Wescott she said quite maliciously after a first meeting that he had a certain syrup but it did not pour. Hemingway was more fortunate, and her advice that he pursue as prose ideals precision, selectivity, the utmost economy was the best possible antidote he could have had to the kind of diffuse evocativeness that characterized the stories of Anderson. A certain *secco* quality and a certain hardness were the traits that came from her advice and her example.

Although Hemingway, on principle, did not believe that it was good for a writer to mingle very much with other writers, now in Paris he was seeing other American writers besides Gertrude Stein. There was Max Eastman, for example, with whom, some years later, Hemingway was to have a much publicized physical encounter over a slighting observation of Eastman's that related Hemingway's prose with the hair on his chest. There was John dos Passos, whose wife was a friend of Hadley, the first Mrs. Hemingway. There was Donald Ogden Stewart, who was to be Hemingway's companion at the bullfights at Pamplona and who was to become the prototype of Bill Gorton in *The Sun Also Rises*. There was Harold Loeb, in Europe to establish his little magazine *Broom* (for which he now waited on Gertrude Stein) and who was to become the prototype of the abused Robert Cohn in the same novel. But none of these was as important to him in any real sense as Gertrude Stein.

It was she who urged him to give up his newspaper work if he could; she suggested that it damaged his serious work by encouraging a false kind of immediacy and by draining away his material, and this, he said much later, "was the best advice she gave me." He had hardly met her when he told Anderson that "this goddamn newspaper stuff is ruining me," and later he told her, "You ruined me as a journalist last winter. Have been no good since." Yet the fact is that his brief career as a journalist was of importance to his long career as a writer. Immediately now, as a roving correspondent, he was traveling all over Europe and the Near East and thus broadening the scope of his subject matter. Nearly all of the brief vignettes that form the inter-chapters of his second book, *In Our Time*, are derived directly from his newspaper experience. These sketches were written in August 1923, and before his first published book, *Three Stories & Ten Poems*.

The arrangements for the publication of this little work were made at Rapallo, where Hemingway stopped to visit Ezra Pound early in 1923 and where he encountered Robert Mc-Almon, who owned the Contact Publishing Company, a small expatriate press in France. McAlmon remembered later that Hemingway was talking about Anderson and Stein and that he told McAlmon that he had lost most of his manuscripts in a train theft but that he still had a few stories and poems. The poems are negligible, but the stories—"My Old Man," "Out of Season," and "Up in Michigan"—announced the appearance of a brilliant talent as well as the debt that talent owed to two older writers. At just about the time that book appeared, Hemingway completed the manuscript of his second work, which was the first, or European version, of the work then published as *in our time*. This version contained only about two thirds of the vignettes and none of the longer stories that would appear in the American version, *In Our Time*, 1925; it was, indeed, little more than a pamphlet, but the vignettes of that first version show a considerable development in style, and the double influence of cablese reporting and the lessons of Gertrude Stein.

In the summer of 1923 Hemingway appeared at Gertrude Stein's one day and after many hours of lingering on at last blurted out that he was too young to be a father; but a father he was to be. In August, largely because of the unborn infant, the Hemingways returned to Toronto and to full employment on the *Star* for what was supposed to be two years. But Hemingway's relationships with at least one of his superiors were impossible, and the stay lasted only four months, after which they returned to Paris with the new baby, and Hemingway was finished with journalism as a career.

In Toronto Hemingway read in a literary column in the New York *Tribune* that the columnist had been told by Edmund Wilson of "some amusing stuff by Ernest Hemingway in the new issue of the *Little Review*." These were six of the brief vignettes that were to appear later in *in our time*. Hemingway now wrote Wilson and sent him a copy of *Three Stories & Ten Poems*, which Wilson acknowledged. In his reply Hemingway wrote:

> No I don't think My Old Man derives from Anderson. It is about a boy and his father and race-horses. Sherwood has written about boys and horses. But very differently. It derives from boys and horses. Anderson derives from boys and horses. I don't think they're anything alike. I know I wasn't inspired by him.

This is a considerably incoherent protest. It continues:

> I know him pretty well but have not seen him for several years. His work seems to have gone to hell, perhaps from people in New York telling him too much how good he was. Functions of criticism. I am very fond of him. He has written good stories.

Then, in response to Wilson's promise to give *Three Stories & Ten Poems* a notice in the *Dial*, Hemingway suggested that he wait for *in our time* and review the two little books together. Wilson obliged, and what resulted in the *Dial* for October 1924 was "Mr. Hemingway's Dry-Points." Wilson was as astute then as he was to be later:

> . . . his prose is of the first distinction. He must be counted as the only American writer but one—Mr. Sherwood Anderson—who has

felt the genius of Gertrude Stein's *Three Lives* and has evidently been influenced by it. Indeed, Miss Stein, Mr. Anderson and Mr. Hemingway may now be said to form a school by themselves. The characteristic of this school is a naïveté of language, often passing into the colloquialism of the character dealt with, which serves actually to convey profound emotions and complex states of mind. It is a distinctively American development in prose . . . which has artistically justified itself at its best as a limpid shaft into deep waters.

He compared Hemingway's vignettes with the lithographs of Goya and observed that *in our time* had "more artistic dignity than anything else about the period of the war that has as yet been written by an American."

The observations on the influence of Gertrude Stein were to be extended in Wilson's essay on Stein published in *Axel's Castle* six years later. They may have annoyed Hemingway, but surely the accolade pleased him. At any rate, it was because of his great admiration for Hemingway in these early works that Edmund Wilson, at about this time, urged his friend, the successful young novelist, F. Scott Fitzgerald, to look up the still little-known but very gifted younger man when Fitzgerald next got to Paris.

4

Sherwood Anderson's work "seems to have gone to hell," said Hemingway in 1923. In 1922 Anderson had at last fled business and Chicago, more or less on the heels of Hemingway. His major work was probably finished when finally he won his freedom. He left his second wife and presently married a third, and there was to be one more after her. Now, in 1922, he was quite appropriately working on a novel called *Many Marriages*. This story dealt with the familiar theme of a businessman's attempt to escape routine, including the routine of matrimony. Anderson was wandering about in the South and in and out of literary New York. At the height of his fame, he was meeting many other writers, among them a phenomenally successful young man from Minnesota named F. Scott Fitzgerald. Fitzgerald thought Anderson's a "brilliant and almost inimitable prose style," but these two men, temperamentally so different, were never to have the kind of close association that, briefly, Anderson and Hemingway had enjoyed in Chicago, and that Hemingway and Fitzgerald would briefly but much more intimately enjoy in Paris.

Yet while Hemingway thought that Anderson's work had deplorably deteriorated, it was Fitzgerald who thought that it had achieved a new distinction. He agreed to review *Many Marriages*, and found it to be "the full flowering of Anderson's personality." This could be taken as a damaging observation, but it was not so intended. To Anderson he wrote afterwards as follows:

> I liked *Many Marriages* much more fully than I could express in that review—It stays with me still. It's a haunting book and, it seems to me, ahead of *Poor White* and even of the two books of short stories.

Why, one wonders. He shared Anderson's pleasure in the work and company of Ring Lardner (Lardner and Fitzgerald, at about this time, were reading *Three Lives* together), and he had a proper recognition of Anderson's best work (in 1924 he wrote his publisher to say that "despite Anderson, the short story is at its lowest ebb as an art form"), and presently he said that Anderson's talent was only for the short story, not for the novel at all. Yet he was somehow swept away by that poor thing, *Many Marriages*, and read it in one day.

F. Scott Fitzgerald was born in 1896. His father was the somewhat shiftless descendant of an old American line; his mother was the daughter of an Irish immigrant. On one side was "breeding" and failure, on the other, money but not enough of it. To this situation Fitzgerald was later to attribute his inferiority complex, and to it he should have attributed his fascination with the very rich and with social success. Still, a good-looking boy of charm and social grace, he got along well enough with the privileged young people he most ad-

mired even though his family always lived on the periphery
of the best neighborhoods in St. Paul, Minnesota, and in rather
shabby circumstances. He began to write in the St. Paul Academy and continued to write at the Newman Academy, where
he finished his secondary school education, and was admitted
to Princeton, with the dream of being a football player, in
1913. He was unable to realize his athletic ambition because of
his slight physique and he never quite recovered from this boy-
ish disappointment, but he threw himself into other college
activities, literary and theatrical, and he was elected to a top
social club. A romantic young man, the social world of Princeton seemed to him glamorous and all-important. His academic
work was undistinguished. In his junior year, when illness further retarded his already limping studies, he dropped out of
Princeton for the rest of the year and was put on probation.
When he returned, his interests were more serious and so were
his friends. These now included T. K. Whipple, who was to
become a distinguished critic and literary historian; John Peale
Bishop, later a fine critic, poet, and fiction writer; and Edmund
Wilson.

Fitzgerald had known Wilson before his separation from
Princeton. Indeed it was Wilson, associated with the student
periodical, the Nassau *Lit,* who encouraged him to submit his
manuscripts to the magazine and who, in 1915, after correct-
ing Fitzgerald's spelling (always bad) and tightening up his
prose, accepted for publication both a story and a play. He
was graduated before Fitzgerald and, setting himself up as a
bachelor in New York, he became the younger man's ideal of
the metropolitan man of letters. In that capacity, he presently
introduced Fitzgerald to George Jean Nathan and so was responsible, in a sense, for Fitzgerald's first commercial sale to
the Nathan-Mencken magazine, *Smart Set.* He advised him
about his work throughout his life, was often severe in his
criticism and impatient with Fitzgerald's frivolities, and even
when the men did not see one another for long stretches of
time, he was always hovering in the background of Fitzgerald's

mind, his "intellectual conscience," as Fitzgerald himself was
to call him.

He almost always took Wilson's admonitions and advice with
utmost seriousness; only once did he lose his patience, when he
wrote, "You are always wrong—but always with the most correct possible reasons." And to that he quickly added, "This
statement is merely acrocritical, hypothetical, diabolical, metaphorical."

Finally, after Fitzgerald's death, it was Wilson who put together his first collection of posthumous work in the volume
called *The Crack-Up* and who pieced together the fragments
of the unfinished final novel, *The Last Tycoon*.

All through Fitzgerald's last winter and spring at Princeton,
students were going off to the war. Fitzgerald applied for a
commission in the army, received it, and left Princeton for
Fort Leavenworth in November of 1917. He did not get abroad
but was transferred from training camp to training camp while
he worked at a novel. Called *The Romantic Egotist,* it was
declined by Charles Scribner's Sons in August of 1918. In the
next month, at an officers' dance at Camp Sheridan, the young
man met a girl, Zelda Sayre, a Montgomery, Alabama, belle
with whom he fell painfully in love.

Discharged from the army early in 1919, he went to New
York to earn enough money to persuade Zelda Sayre to marry
him. Gertrude Stein never worked for an advertising agency,
which is almost certainly a loss in the history of advertising;
but of our quartette, Fitzgerald now was the third of this group
who went into advertising, and at a very small salary. When,
by the summer of 1919, he began to understand that this work
would never make his marriage possible, he gave up his job,
returned to St. Paul, and thoroughly replanned and rewrote
his manuscript, *The Romantic Egotist.* It became his first novel,
*This Side of Paradise.* Scribner's accepted it, and when it was
published in March of 1920, it proved to be a sensation. The
"jazz age" had found its definition.

Cynical, witty, overwritten, very romantic, *This Side of Paradise* is the story of Amory Blaine at preparatory school and Princeton, a brilliant and somewhat erratic young man, the college leader and athlete that Fitzgerald himself was not. There is one love in his life, the girl Rosalind, but she, believing that she cannot be happy without money, marries another man who has it. And the novel ends with the announcement of "a new generation dedicated more than the last to the fear of poverty and the worship of success; grown up to find all Gods dead, all wars fought, all faiths in man shaken. . . ." It is "the lost generation," and it was Gertrude Stein, much impressed with this novel, who said that it "really created for the public the new generation." Sinclair Lewis, another phenomenal success of that year, 1920, with his *Main Street,* announced that "in Scott Fitzgerald we have an author who will be the equal of any European," and Fitzgerald wrote to Lewis to say that *Main Street* was now his favorite novel, replacing *The Damnation of Theron Ware* by Harold Frederic. Glenway Wescott, who was later to say of Scott Fitzgerald, "He was our darling, our genius, our fool," would also say that

> *This Side of Paradise* haunted the decade like a song, popular but perfect. It hung over an entire youth-movement like a banner, somewhat discolored and wind-worn now [1941]; the wind has lapsed out of it. But a book which college boys really read is a rare thing, not to be dismissed idly or in a moment of severe sophistication.

Severity came from Fitzgerald's friend, Wilson, who wrote the author that "it would all be better if you would tighten up your artistic conscience and pay a little more attention to form," and who, in reviewing the novel, announced that it "has almost every fault and deficiency that a novel can possibly have," including imitation of "an inferior model." To the author he gave two pieces of advice: one, that he cultivate "a universal irony" which would prevent him from taking a character like his fatuous hero so seriously; and two, to read "something other than contemporary British novelists" like Compton

Mackenzie, whose *Sinister Street* had been Fitzgerald's "inferior model."

Before the novel's publication, Fitzgerald, who, half the time, was behaving like one of his own characters in crazy, drunken carousing, was in the other half writing short stories, good and bad, with abandon, and selling them to magazines, chiefly *The Saturday Evening Post*, at about $1000 each, often more. His success was sudden and unexpectedly splendid. *This Side of Paradise* made him famous and gave Princeton a new reputation as a frenzied pleasure dome. Miss Sayre married him in April. A spectacular, champagne-drenched marriage and an extraordinary literary career were simultaneously launched, everything about both, for the moment, glittering and golden. Neither Anderson nor Hemingway had yet escaped from Chicago.

In New York, with money now, very popular, the dazzling young Fitzgeralds tried to realize their romantic dream of success and happiness through endless parties, and for a time it was, indeed, fun. This life, with its night-club glitter, its atmosphere of great, beautiful ballrooms, its irrepressible and irresponsible youthfulness, is evoked in story after story that Fitzgerald was writing in his sober hours and which he collected in two books, *Flappers and Philosophers* (1920) and *Tales of the Jazz Age* (1922). But where was it to lead them? The answer is contained in his next novel, the title of which in itself contains it: *The Beautiful and Damned* of 1922 is not so much an autobiographical novel as it is a prophecy of autobiography.

Anthony Patch and Gloria, his girl and then his wife, are Scott and Zelda Fitzgerald on the road to ruin. Thinking of themselves as utterly liberated from all conventional bondage, they are in fact painfully immature—and Fitzgerald did not seem to know this. Sensation, romance, wealth, a hedonistic happiness are their aims, as drinking bouts and wild parties are the substance of the action. Into this novel Fitzgerald did manage to infuse a certain heavy irony, yet the fact is that he had hardly come closer to the kind of tone that could properly evaluate his material even as he was displaying it.

With *The Beautiful and Damned* finished, the Fitzgeralds had a brief and frantic fling in Europe, and then, disappointed in their travels and depressed, they returned to the United States, where they took a house in St. Paul. Fitzgerald wrote his publisher to say:

> Loafing puts me in this particularly obnoxious and abominable gloom. My 3rd novel, if I ever write another, will I am sure be black as death with gloom. I should like to sit down with ½ a dozen chosen companions and drink myself to death but I am sick alike of life, liquor and literature. If it wasn't for Zelda I think I'd disappear out of sight. . . .

Zelda presently gave birth to their only child, a girl named Frances. And Fitzgerald did, in fact, work very hard.

He wrote a play, *The Vegetable*, which, when it finally found a producer in 1923, was unsuccessful. And they moved East again, now to Long Island, and gave great parties and drove recklessly in and out of Manhattan even as Fitzgerald was writing that novel about great parties and reckless drives that would be *The Great Gatsby*. This work was interrupted by a burst of story writing necessary to clear them of their debts, and that accomplished, they went again to Europe, now with the partially completed novel. In October of 1924 he sent his first version of it to his publishers from France, where he had just met Ernest Hemingway.

## 5

When the Hemingways returned to Paris early in 1924, Ford Madox Ford was editing the *transatlantic review* in the small office of Three Mountains Press, the establishment of Hemingway's friend William Bird. Hemingway had met Bird, an amateur publisher like McAlmon, at the Genoa Economic Conference in 1922, and he had sent him to Ezra Pound for manuscript suggestions; Pound proposed a series of six books to appear over six months, and one of these was to be the first *in our time*. Now Hemingway at Pound's persuasion went to work for Ford as his editorial assistant, and almost the first thing he did was to convince Ford that he should publish Gertrude Stein's *The Making of Americans,* nine installments of which were to appear in *transatlantic.*

The Hemingways had gone at once on their return to Gertrude Stein with plans for the baptism of their infant, nicknamed "Bumby." Alice B. Toklas and Gertrude Stein were to be his godmothers.

> We were all born of different religions and most of us were not practicing any, so it was rather difficult to know in what church the baby could be baptised. We spent a great deal of time that winter, all of us, discussing the matter. Finally it was decided that it should be baptised episcopalian and episcopalian it was . . . in the beginning we were active god-parents . . . In the meantime the god-child's father was very earnestly at work making himself a writer.

He continued to seek Gertrude Stein's opinion and criticism of his work, but he was also exposing himself to her influence in a different way. When it developed that there was no copy of *The Making of Americans* that the printer could use, Hemingway volunteered to type a new copy.

> Hemingway did it all. He copied the manuscript and corrected the proof. Correcting proof is, as I have said before, like dusting, you learn the values of the thing as no reading suffices to teach it to you. In correcting these proofs Hemingway learned a great deal and he admired all that he learned. It was at this time that he wrote to Gertrude Stein saying that it was she who had done the work in writing The Making of Americans and he and all his had but to devote their lives to seeing that it was published.

Certainly he was submitting to the most intimate possible kind of exposure to her prose, consolidating, as it were, the influence she had already exercised on him as it was to show in his book of sketches, the first *in our time,* published by Bird in March of 1924.

Gertrude Stein credited Alice B. Toklas with having first told Hemingway about bullfighting. Be that as it may, it was in this summer that he had his initial experience of bullfighting when he went to Pamplona with Donald Ogden Stewart and others. In the autumn, after his return to Paris, he met Scott Fitzgerald, and for Fitzgerald this became the most important and in some ways the most ominous literary relationship of his life.

It was Hemingway who, in the following spring, would bring Fitzgerald to Gertrude Stein, but already in 1924 Fitzgerald was writing to Max Perkins, his editor at Scribner's, urging him to bring out *The Making of Americans* as important "original" work. Almost simultaneously, he was urging Perkins to seize upon Ernest Hemingway, whom he described as "the real thing." Glenway Wescott remembers meeting Fitzgerald on the Riviera at about this time and being astonished by the one-man Hemingway campaign that Fitzgerald was conducting.

> What could I do to help launch Hemingway? Why didn't I write a laudatory essay on him? With this questioning, Fitzgerald now and then impatiently grasped and shook my elbow. . . . He not only said but, I believe, honestly felt that Hemingway was inimitably, essentially superior [to both of us]. From the moment Hemingway began to appear in print, perhaps it did not matter what he himself produced or failed to produce. He felt free to write just for profit, and to live for fun, if possible. Hemingway could be entrusted with the graver responsibilities and higher rewards such as glory, immortality. This extreme of admiration— this excuse for a morbid belittlement and abandonment of himself—was bad for Fitzgerald, I imagine.

Wescott did not write the "laudatory essay" that Fitzgerald proposed, but Fitzgerald himself presently wrote one, a review of the American edition of *In Our Time*, in which he said that "many of us . . . have felt a sort of renewal of excitement at these stories wherein Ernest Hemingway turns a corner into the street." And he made an interesting juxtaposition when he observed that only Gertrude Stein's "Melanctha" and Sherwood Anderson's "The Egg" could compare with Hemingway's "Big Two-Hearted River" in achievement.

Charles Scribner's Sons did not publish *In Our Time* because faithful Sherwood Anderson had also been pressing his publishers, Boni and Liveright, on Hemingway's behalf, and Horace Liveright got to Hemingway first. *In Our Time* has further connections with Anderson than this bit of publishing history.

Like *Winesburg, Ohio,* it is a group of related short stories which must be read as a whole if the total impact of the book is to be felt. Like *Winesburg,* too, it has a central character, Nick Adams, modeled after the author in his youth and young manhood, who appears, if not in all the stories, at least throughout, and who, in the course of the book, like George Willard, comes into his maturity, such as it is. The stories in which he does not actually appear are, one must assume, observations made by Nick Adams as he advances into this maturity. Unlike *Winesburg,* the stories of *In Our Time* are interspersed with brief vignettes about war, bullfighting, and journalism. Each of these recounts in the sparsest prose, without any commentary, events of brutal violence, and they include one which recounts the wounding of Nick Adams in the war. Ezra Pound once spoke of Hemingway's "self-hardening process"—the deliberate exposure of himself to suffering, ugly sights, the spectacle of convulsive death, and so on. These vignettes are examples of this "hardening process." Brutal violence, they assert, is the characteristic of our time; and a mute, apparent indifference, grim and tight-lipped, they seem to assert, is the only possible attitude that one can take toward the brutal violence of our time. This is the Hemingway attitude, and the attitude of Hemingway's hero.

In the stories proper, we begin with Nick Adams as a small boy in Michigan, introduced to violence, to death, to sex, to the multiple pains and perplexities of his initiation into life. All this violence is brought to its climax in his battle wounds. At the end of the book, in "Big Two-Hearted River," he returns to Michigan, about twenty years old, and in this remarkable story that seems on first reading to be little more than an almost monotonously detailed report of two days in which Nick, alone, makes his camp on the river and fishes it for trout, we are given the man he has become.

He is not a well man. He is a man who has suffered not only physically but deeply in his spirit. He must occupy himself in physical acts so that his mind does not revert to the climax of his suffering or to the steps of lesser suffering that led to it. He must exhaust himself or he cannot sleep, and when he does sleep, he often has bad dreams.

After he was wounded, he made his famous "separate peace":

> Nick sat against the wall of the church where they had dragged him to be clear of machine gun fire in the street. Both legs stuck out awkwardly. He had been hit in the spine. His face was sweaty and dirty. The sun shone on his face. The day was very hot. Rinaldi, big backed, his equipment sprawling, lay face downward against the wall. Nick looked straight ahead brilliantly. The pink wall of the house opposite had fallen out from the roof, and an iron bedstead hung twisted toward the street. Two Austrian dead lay in the rubble in the shade of the house. Up the street were other dead. Things were getting forward in the town. It was going well. Stretcher bearers would be along any time now. Nick turned his head and looked down at Rinaldi. "Senta Rinaldi; senta. You and me we've made a separate peace." Rinaldi lay still in the sun, breathing with difficulty. "We're not patriots." Nick turned his head away, smiling sweatily. Rinaldi was a disappointing audience.

He made "a separate peace" with the enemy and went a little insane. Now, symbolically, he makes his tent and gets into it. "He was there, in the good place" where he could keep his separate peace. And next day, again symbolically, he does not fish in the fearsome swamp into which the river flows, as he keeps his mind above that swamplike state into which it had fallen in his wartime trauma. Physically active, solitary, cut off from society, without either self-pity or hope, forever wounded, he will *endure* life, and only that.

This is the Hemingway hero and his famous "code," living by his "guts" alone, which is to say with "grace under pressure." He will appear in various guises throughout the rest of

Hemingway's work except for his very next book, which is a sport, a merciless parody of a successful book by his mentor, Sherwood Anderson. What happened next between these two hardly supports the epithets in Ernest Walsh's review of *In Our Time* in his periodical, *This Quarter:* "the shyest and proudest and sweetest smelling story-teller of my reading."

When Carl Van Vechten wrote to Gertrude Stein in 1923, saying "now that you have Imitators & Disciples!" he was no doubt thinking of both Hemingway and Anderson. But Hemingway felt presently that it was time to detach himself from both. The Stein influence in the early *Three Stories* and *In Our Time* is clear enough. One does not mean that he did not have qualities of his own. ". . . selectivity, precision, uncompromising economy, deep emotional clarification"—to list them as Charles Fenton did in his book on Hemingway's "apprenticeship"—are all there in his newspaper writing, but they are never there together. In the stories they come together and take on their special power. And this, in part at least, he owes to Gertrude Stein. "Her method," he wrote to Edmund Wilson, "is invaluable for analyzing anything or making notes on a person or a place." The "method" involved not only simple language and simple sentence forms, but repetition and the organization of paragraphs in terms of repetition. The Hemingway style of 1924 finds in these terms its very skeleton. Yet in 1952 Hemingway was to say, "I was always working by myself years before I met Ezra or Gertrude," which he no doubt was, and he told how he knew from the beginning the importance of "sensations," how he would go home from the boxing gymnasium in Chicago and write the sensations down. And, of course, his powers of sensuous observation and response were his own, yet we are reminded again of his praise of Gertrude Stein's "method"—"invaluable for analyzing anything or making notes on a person or place."

And at that time he could be open with her about his debt. In August of 1924, when he was working hard for her financial and publishing interests with *the transatlantic,* the continuing

existence of which was being threatened, he took occasion to
write the following:

> I have finished two long short stories, one of them not much
> good, and the other very good and finished the long one I
> worked on before I went to Spain where I'm trying to do the
> country like Cézanne and having a hell of a time and sometimes
> getting it a little bit. It is about 100 pages long and nothing
> happens and the country is swell, I made it all up, so I see it all
> and part of it comes out the way it ought to, it is swell about the
> fish, but isn't writing a hard job though?
>
> It used to be easy before I met you. I certainly was bad, gosh,
> I'm awfully bad now but it's a different kind of bad. . . .

This is a rare humility. Would that he had preserved a touch
of it!

Anderson was always as naïve as that—but, for all his rather
foppish vanity, he was also always more generous. In these
years, he was at work on his *A Story Teller's Story*, and in 1923
he wrote to Gertrude Stein to tell her how he was trying to
write an acknowledgment of her importance to him in that
book. The book was published in 1924, and, taking up Edmund Wilson's suggestion from the *Dial* that Anderson, Hemingway, and Stein formed a school, the editors of *Ex Libris*, a
publication of the American Library in Paris, asked both Hemingway and Stein to review it in successive columns. Both
agreed. Gertrude Stein said that Anderson was one of four
American men of letters (the others were Cooper, Twain, and
Howells) who had what she called "essential intelligence"—
a profound misjudgment, surely, and one that we can contrast
with Fitzgerald's sounder view that Anderson was "a man of
scarcely any ideas at all" but "the possessor of a brilliant and
almost inimitable style"—and she concluded by saying that certain parts of this book were "without any equal in quality in
anything that has been done up to this time by any one writing
to-day." Ernest Hemingway nearly matched her in his praise:

> There are very beautiful places in the book, as good writing
> as Sherwood Anderson has done and that means considerably

better than any other American writer has done. . . . He is a
very great writer. . . .

In another year he could not have brought himself to such a
generous gesture.

In the next spring, however, he did bring Scott Fitzgerald
to Gertrude Stein. Fitzgerald's novel, *The Great Gatsby*, had
just been published, and he arrived with a presentation copy.

Probably Fitzgerald's most flawless novel, Edmund Wilson's
every admonition fully mastered, it was a good deal more than
what Fitzgerald called it to his editor—"a consciously artistic
achievement"—although it was unquestionably that too. This
is certainly the point at which Fitzgerald's talent was most
fully consolidated and the point, too, at which all his themes
and interests achieved their fullest synthesis. Here is the romantic dream of an impossibly glamorous existence, the frenetic, even orgiastic attempt to make it real, the corruption that
underlies its approximation, the sense of disaster that pervades it, and the disaster in which it ends. Here, too, is that
constant concern of Fitzgerald's with "the very rich," about
which Hemingway liked to tease him. In a joking letter re-
ferring to his still unpublished *The Sun Also Rises*, Hemingway wrote, "I have tried to follow the outline and spirit of the
Great Gatsby but I feel I have failed somewhat because of
never having been on Long Island. . . . The action all takes
place in Newport, R. I."

"The very rich are different from you and me." When Fitzgerald made that observation to Hemingway, it is said, Hemingway replied, "Yes, they have more money." But for Fitzgerald, as for Jay Gatsby, the poor boy who has been made
rich by bootlegging and crime but who has not been able to
enter the world of those who were born to riches, there is a
greater difference.

> "She's got an indiscreet voice," I remarked. "It's full of—" I
> hesitated.
> "Her voice is full of money," [Gatsby] said suddenly.
> That was it. I'd never understood before. It was full of money

—that was the inexhaustible charm that rose and fell in it, the jingle of it, the cymbals' song of it. . . .

The romance of money! But there is also the reality of it. Nick Carraway, the narrator, thinks:

> I couldn't forgive him or like him, but I saw what he had done was, to him, entirely justified. It was all very careless and confused. They were careless people, Tom and Daisy—they smashed up things and creatures and then retreated back into their money on their vast carelessness, or whatever it was that kept them together, and let other people clean up the mess they had made. . . .
>
> I shook hands with him; it seemed silly not to, for I felt suddenly as if I were talking to a child. Then he went into the jewelry store to buy a pearl necklace—or perhaps only a pair of cuff buttons—rid of my provincial squeamishness forever.

This young narrator, Nick Carraway, who has come from the Middle West to be an Easterner—for him, finally, the Middle West comes to represent simplicity and innocence, and the East, complexity and corruption. Fitzgerald's use of Carraway is an act of technical brilliance, for it enabled him to put a certain objective distance between himself and the subject matter that was in itself so fascinating for him. At his best— and certainly here in *The Great Gatsby*—Fitzgerald manages to do two things simultaneously as he had not managed in his two earlier novels: to make us feel, along with him, the Circean charm and glamour and romance of the careless world of the very rich; and at the same time to judge it. When his stories fail, it is because the second element is missing, and when it is, the first is somehow shoddy and unreal. When they succeed, when these two elements are held in balance, he is among our greatest novelists of manners. Perhaps Fitzgerald himself recognized this necessary balance of a double thing in novels when he made his famous observation later that "the test of a first-rate intelligence is the ability to hold two opposed ideas in the mind at the same time, and still retain the ability to function." It is, one might say, rather, the test of a first-rate

novelistic imagination, and it was very probably this particular imaginative achievement that led T. S. Eliot to write the
author of *The Great Gatsby* that "it seems to me to be the first
step that American fiction has taken since Henry James. . . ."

At just about the point at which *The Great Gatsby* was published, Fitzgerald began work on one of his finest short stories,
"The Rich Boy," which occupied him for most of the summer
of 1925. In this story he addressed himself directly to the matter of "the very rich," and the subtle revelation that the story
makes through the character of Anson Hunter and that a summary such as this can only debase, is that not only does their
"carelessness" serve to be sometimes brutally destructive of
others, but that their ease and pride and self-sufficiency prevent their own fulfillment in human relationships, numb the
capacity for love, make personal commitment impossible. Once
again Fitzgerald managed—as he repeatedly would—the double imaginative act of making us feel, with his peculiar eloquence of style, the charged charm of a certain way of life,
and demonstrating to us its rather terrible fatality. Many other
fine stories in *All the Sad Young Men,* the volume in which
"The Rich Boy" appeared in the next year, 1926, perform the
same feat. This is all the more remarkable in that now, in the
mid-twenties, Fitzgerald himself more and more succumbed
to the gaudy pleasures of that world which would at last
destroy him. His first letter to Ernest Hemingway was an
apology for drunken conduct:

> I was quite ashamed. . . . However it is only fair to say that
> the deplorable man who entered your apartment Saturday morn-
> ing was *not* me but a man named Johnston who has often been
> mistaken for me.

But he was a great success at 27 rue de Fleurus.

## 6

Gertrude Stein liked him, and she liked his writing. She
irritated Hemingway when she argued that Sherwood Ander-

son "had a genius for using the sentence to convey a direct emotion," one of the few Americans who did, and then she added that Fitzgerald was another. To him she wrote about *The Great Gatsby:*

> The next good thing is that you write naturally in sentences and that too is a comfort. You write naturally in sentences and one can read all of them and that among other things is a comfort. . . . My belief in This Side of Paradise was alright. This is as good a book and different and older and that is what one does, one does not get better but different and older and that is always a pleasure.

In his reply, Fitzgerald thanked her, referred to himself as "a very second-rate person compared to first-rate people" such as she, and told her how eager he was to get a copy of *The Making of Americans* "and learn something from it and imitate things out of it which I shall doubtless do." That Fitzgerald was ever very seriously influenced by Gertrude Stein may certainly be questioned, but his problem as a stylist was always to objectify and tie down a kind of floating lyricism in a solid texture of language, and of this problem her own dry work, by way of opposite, could at least remind him.

So, for that matter, could Hemingway's style, a more difficult prose to resist. The two were seeing each other very frequently, exchanging manuscripts, advising one another. Hemingway let Fitzgerald read an early version of *The Sun Also Rises* and Fitzgerald let Hemingway see the manuscript of "The Rich Boy." About ten years later, Fitzgerald was to say that he did not let Hemingway's "infectious style" influence him, but the influence is in fact apparent in precisely that story, "The Rich Boy," and again in certain scenes of *Tender Is the Night.* And he did, in 1934, write Hemingway as follows:

> There are pieces and paragraphs of your work that I read over and over—in fact, I stopped myself doing it for a year and a half because I was afraid that your particular rhythms were going to creep in on mine by a process of infiltration.

In spite of the praise of men like Eliot, *The Great Gatsby* was not the success that Fitzgerald had hoped for, and a long period of uncertainty about his own quality was about to set in. One afternoon, his birthday, he declared to Gertrude Stein that it was "tragic" that he had turned thirty. "What is to become of me? What am I to do?" Alice B. Toklas reports him as lamenting.

> And Gertrude told him that he should not worry, that he had been writing like a man of thirty for many years. She told him that he would go home and write a greater novel than he ever had.

Gertrude Stein said that while there was now a lot of talk about Fitzgerald's drinking, he was always sober with her. A report to her from Antibes, made by her friend, René Crevel, is less complaisant. A "curious and poor fellow," he called him. "A boy." And Hemingway gives us this metaphorical (one supposes) glimpse of him:

> It was at this point in the story, reader, that Mr. F. Scott Fitzgerald came to our home one afternoon, and after remaining for quite a while suddenly sat down in the fireplace and would not (or was it could not, reader?) get up and let the fire burn something else so as to keep the room warm.

That quotation comes from Hemingway's next book, called *The Torrents of Spring*, published in 1926, a short and in itself unimportant work that nevertheless leads to one of the most curious episodes in modern American literary history.

In July of 1925, Sherwood Anderson had written Gertrude Stein to say that he had finished a new novel, *Dark Laughter*, and in the same letter he told her of the "crackerjack" blurb, characteristically lavish in its generosity, that he had written for the dust wrapper of *In Our Time*. A few weeks later he wrote his publisher with the request that he send a copy of *Dark Laughter* to Hemingway. He was writing from New Orleans, where he had met and was befriending still another aspiring young writer, William Faulkner, whose first novel, *Soldiers' Pay*, he was urging upon his publisher, who indeed brought it out. (There was a kind of prologue here to the Hemingway drama, for in only a little more than half a year, Anderson, while still working in Faulkner's interests, was writing that same publisher to say that Faulkner had been "so nasty to me personally that I don't want to write him myself. . . .") There was, however, the compensatory fact that *Dark Laughter* was a commercial success, his first.

It did little to rescue his sliding reputation. Fitzgerald had already announced to his editor that Anderson was "a short story writer only," and in a letter of October 1925, in which he asked, "Isn't Ernest Hemingway's book fine?" he also asked, "Isn't Anderson's new book *lousy?*" The questions were just even if one of the men involved hardly was.

*Dark Laughter* today reads like a parody of the greater Anderson. This is the story of one John Stockton, a Chicago reporter who changes his name to Bruce Dudley and, in imitation of the old Anderson myth, walks out of his job, out of his marriage, out of Chicago in search of the free life of unhampered adventure and self-fulfillment. He works his way down the Mississippi, reflecting on Mark Twain and the river world of Huckleberry Finn, and contrasts it with the modern industrial era in which men's physical lives have been reduced to mechanized routine and their emotional lives to a shallow, nervous trickle. He takes a factory job in a town called Old Harbor, Indiana, becomes a gardener for the owner's wife, then becomes her lover, and at last takes her away from her husband, to go who knows where? The book, taking some hints from Gertrude Stein's "Melanctha" and more than mere hints from a mythology popular among Caucasians in the United States, rests on the supposed contrast between the rich and easy sensuality of Negroes and the anemic sterility and emotional rigidity of whites, white joylessness versus their dark laughter.

This novel was published by Boni and Liveright, who through Anderson's efforts had also published *In Our Time*. Fitzgerald had been continuing his campaign for Hemingway with his editor at Scribner's, but Hemingway's next novel was under option to Liveright, and Max Perkins at Scribner's could hardly do anything about *The Sun Also Rises,* the first draft of which was finished, while that option held. Fitzgerald was also praising John Dos Passos to him, and especially his new novel, *Manhattan Transfer,* and it was in fact after an evening with Dos Passos, spent largely in discussing *Dark Laughter,* that Hemingway wrote *The Torrents of Spring.* He wrote it, he said later, "to cool out" after the intense effort of *The Sun Also Rises.*

No intensity of effort went into the *The Torrents,* a *jeu d'esprit* that Hemingway took (he said) ten days to write and almost certainly none to rewrite. In an undergraduate way, it is fairly funny. Set in Petoskey, Michigan, it substitutes American Indians for Anderson's Negroes, and reduces both to absurdities. It imitates Anderson's loose construction, his questioning style, the adolescent romanticism and mooning of his principal characters, the cozy tone of chat with the reader to which Anderson was given, and, like Anderson at his loosest, throws in anything that occurs to the writer, no matter how irrelevant.

Hemingway was frequently with Gertrude Stein at this time. "He used to recount to Gertrude Stein the conversations that he afterwards used in The Sun Also Rises," she wrote later, "and they talked endlessly about the character of Harold Loeb." He entitled the fourth part of *The Torrents* "The Passing of a Great Race and the Making and Marring of Americans." *The Making of Americans* was published in McAlmon's edition in the spring of 1926, just before *The Torrents.* Anderson wrote to thank Gertrude Stein for his copy and said that he kept it on his desk, to "steal from it." He praised Hemingway's story, "The Undefeated"—"a beautiful story, beautifully done. Lordy but that man can write"—which had appeared in *This Quarter.* Then the unexpected blow fell.

When *The Torrents of Spring* was submitted to Horace Liveright, that unhappy man could only decline to publish it since it treated his own stellar author so outrageously. To Fitzgerald Hemingway wrote, "I have known all along that they could not and would not be able to publish it as it makes a bum out of their present ace and best seller Anderson. Now in tenth printing. I did not, however, have that in mind in any way when I wrote it." Perhaps not. But the fact is that the refusal released him from his contract, as Fitzgerald was quick to report to Perkins, and Scribner's then accepted and published the book.

Hemingway sent Anderson a copy together with what he called "an all-right letter." Anderson did not think so. He described it in his *Memoirs* as "certainly the most self-conscious and probably the most completely patronizing letter ever written."

> He spoke of the book as something fatal to me. He had, he said, written it on an impulse. . . . It was intended to bring to an end, once and for all, the notion that there was any worth in my own work. This, he said, was a thing he had hated doing, because of his personal regard for me, and he had done it in the interest of literature. Literature, I was to understand, was bigger than either of us.
>
> There was something in the letter that was gigantic. It was a kind of funeral oration delivered over my grave. It was so raw, so pretentious, so patronizing that in a repellent way it was amusing, but I was filled with wonder. Just what I said to him, in return, I don't remember. It was something to the effect that I thought it foolish that we writers should devote our time to the attempt to kill each other off. In the letter he had used a prize-fighting term, speaking of the knockout blow he had given me, and in my answer I think I did say that I had always thought of myself as a pretty good middleweight and I doubted *his* ever being able to make the heavyweight class.

In that winter, Anderson was in Paris, and in response to the urging of a common friend, Ralph Church, Hemingway kept promising that he would go to see the injured man. To Perkins, Hemingway wrote: "Sherwood Anderson is in Paris and we had two fine afternoons together. . . . He was not at all sore about *Torrents* and we had a fine time."

Anderson's recollection was quite different:

It came to my last day in Paris and I was sitting in my room, having packed. Church had told him of my plan to depart and there was a sudden knock on the door of my hotel room, and there Hemingway was.

He stood in the doorway.

"How about a drink?" he said, and I followed him down a stairway and across a street.

We went into a small bar.

"What will you have?"

"Beer."

"And you?"

"A beer."

"Well, here's how."

"Here's how."

He turned and walked rapidly away. He had, I dare say, proved his sportsmanship to himself.

And to his friend, Paul Rosenfeld, Anderson wrote a few months later that "it made me pretty sick seeing Hemingway this winter. . . ."

Whether out of loyalty to Anderson, or out of irritation at finding her name in the undignified context of Hemingway's burlesque, or out of both, or conceivably out of some quite other, perhaps fancied injury, Gertrude Stein now turned against Hemingway, too. One day Mrs. Hemingway arrived at the studio with her child, to chat a bit, as was her custom; but she was met at the door by a cold Alice who announced that Gertrude could not see her. Mrs. Hemingway—she would cease to be Mrs. Hemingway quite soon—never knew what had happened, and Hemingway never talked about the break. Gertrude Stein's own account, in *The Autobiography*, is famous, undocumented, and not always very clear:

Gertrude Stein and Sherwood Anderson are very funny on the subject of Hemingway. The last time that Sherwood was in Paris they often talked about him. Hemingway had been formed by the two of them and they were both a little proud and a little ashamed of the work of their minds. . . . They admitted that Hemingway was yellow, he is, Gertrude Stein insisted, just like the flat-boat men on the Mississippi river as described by Mark

Twain. But what a book, they both agreed, would be the real
story of Hemingway, not those he writes but the confessions of
the real Ernest Hemingway. It would be for another audience
than the audience Hemingway now has [1933] but it would be
very wonderful. And then they both agreed that they have a
weakness for Hemingway because he is such a good pupil. . . .
it is so flattering to have a pupil who does it without understanding it, in other words he takes training and anybody who
takes training is a favourite pupil. They both admit it to be a
weakness. . . . But what a story that of the real Hem, and one
he should tell himself but alas he never will. After all, as he himself once murmured, there is the career, the career.

This is all very much without relation to anything that we
know about Hemingway except for the feelings he had hurt in
Anderson and the irritation he had aroused in Stein. After all,
quarreling to her was very interesting. A few years later, a
young American novelist, one Bravig Imbs, wrote to her as
follows:

> I remember you said once that all the young men went away,
> and I wondered at your statement, for I could not believe it
> possible. Perhaps the young men should go away for their own
> sakes, but I do not feel or care to be one of them.

Perhaps it was the right time for the young man, Hemingway,
to go away, brutally as he may have done it. Anderson's hurt
bewilderment did not prevent him, through the remainder of
his life, from appreciating Hemingway's literary achievements,
and Hemingway continued to have meetings with Gertrude
Stein. But the publication of *The Torrents of Spring* nevertheless made some sort of watershed. Anderson's friendship with
Hemingway was at an end. Stein's friendship with him would
never really be a friendship again. For Hemingway, the writing of his silly parody was an act by which he exorcised an influence, and perhaps two; his next book would show that he
could stand up as his own man, even if on at least two graves.
With this metaphor Gertrude Stein would presently plague him
when, in an amiable conversation, she charged him with having "killed a great many of his rivals and put them under the

sod." Hemingway protested; he said that he had killed only one man in his writing, and that was a bad man who deserved to be killed.

That man was not Sherwood Anderson, and *The Torrents of Spring* did not, to use the Hemingway rhetoric, knock him out. The best Anderson still stands and the best of his antagonist still stands at least in part because of him.

And in part, too, because of Gertrude Stein. Hemingway was late in taking his revenge on her. Not until *A Moveable Feast*, 1964, did he publish that presumed recollection of overhearing the vocal sounds that accompanied a horrid Lesbian debauch in her Parisian flat, to which he had been inadvertently admitted.

7

Although Anderson had finally written a successful book, his work continued to decline. He became a country newspaper editor in Virginia[1] and he turned his interest to the influence of machines on American life and to the situation of the American worker in the industrial South. In 1930, writing to Ralph Church, he praised Hemingway's "fine novel," *A Farewell to Arms*, deplored Sinclair Lewis (whose view of American life he had always found false and deadly), and declared that he himself occasionally still wrote "a pretty good short story." And indeed he did; but his major efforts now went into a number of works of semi-autobiography such as *A Story Teller's Story*, into impressionistic essays, and into two more novels, *Beyond Desire* and *Kit Brandon*, which reveal no significant extension of his thematic interests even when labor became his subject matter, and certainly no greater control of his material. Like many another writer, he flirted with left-wing politics during the depression years in the 1930's, but Anderson was no man to

[1] In 1927 Anderson bought two weekly newspapers in the town of Marion, the *Marion Democrat* and the *Smyth County News*. A generous selection of his not very interesting editorial contributions have recently been published by Ray Lewis White under the title, *Return to Winesburg*, for the University of North Carolina Press.

commit himself to the disciplines of party politics. Even after he had his farm in Virginia, he continued to be a wanderer, yearning always for some freedom that his individuality was never quite satisfied it had found. During the last twenty years of his life, when he was more or less free to serve words alone at last, he became in many ways his own legend. Yet that legend was suitable, somehow, only to an older, more expansive America. Symbolically enough, his death occurred on a journey. No less symbolic was the cause of his death: peritonitis brought about by a colored toothpick that he had swallowed while eating *hors d'oeuvres* at a cocktail party.

In the mid-twenties, his lost friend, Ernest Hemingway, began to create his own legend. The rather shy, retiring youth was gone forever. The devil-may-care, somehow bittersweet expatriate who fought bulls and studied the ritual of bullfighting, the athlete who boxed and sometimes brawled, the big-game hunter and the deep-sea fisherman, the war-lover who turned up on every front in every war, the lover of women (he too had four wives, one, in Fitzgerald's theory, for each major novel) whose heroines are always the same submissive dream figure in different guises, the adventurer miraculously rescued from a variety of physical catastrophes, and finally that "Papa" whose best friend was Marlene Dietrich, known to him both as "Daughter" and "the Kraut." The legend was in large part true but it was partial, and omitting Hemingway, the fine writer, it omitted the most important fact about him and the fact that the legend tended to obscure.

If 1925 saw the appearance of one great American novel in *Gatsby*, 1926 saw another in *The Sun Also Rises*. This novel of the lost generation in Paris and Spain, with its wounded hero, Jake Barnes, and its bitterly gallant, unobtainable heroine, Brett Ashley, is not only Hemingway at his purest but perhaps the classic of postwar American fiction. Here Hemingway's prose has been distilled to its essence; here the code of endurance amidst fatality achieves its clearest definition; here the flicker of satire plays most effectively over the pathos; and here the style is the perfect expression of the subject, the attitude, the man himself.

The novel was extraordinarily influential. Not only did Hemingway's attitude and style find countless imitators among writers a little younger than he, but the entirety created an image of conduct for a generation just a little younger than his. This was perhaps not a part of Hemingway's intention at all, for later he would always protest that the quotation from Gertrude Stein (which she had first heard uttered by a garage mechanic in the south of France) was in fact mistaken, that one could not speak abstractly of a "generation," and that he intended to refute her observation by putting below it on the inscription page the well-known passage from Ecclesiastes which provided him with his title. This protest would seem again to be only a part of Hemingway's insistence on independence, for the Biblical passage is not so much a refutation of Stein as it is an instrument that gives perspective to the dilemma of these war-torn people living with desperate abandon in a world that offers them no values.

Like Fitzgerald, Hemingway alternated his novels with books of short stories. The former brought out *All the Sad Young Men* in 1926, the latter brought out *Men Without Women* in 1927; and in their correspondence they joked about a work called *All the Sad Young Men Without Women*. But the joking mood was soon to cease for Fitzgerald. In the summer of 1925 he had started a new novel, about matricide, to be called *Our Type,* but the small sales of *The Great Gatsby* forced him to abandon it and to write short stories, many of them glib and poor, for *The Saturday Evening Post* and its substantial checks. He hoped to have the novel finished by December of 1926, but refractory material, the constant interruption to write the shorter things he despised, and a life of ever greater dissipation in Paris and on the Riviera successfully militated against that plan. Then followed two and a half years —from the end of 1926 to June of 1929—of nearly complete inability to move the novel ahead. With Zelda nervously ill and given to increasingly antic behavior and Fitzgerald himself nearly a physical ruin, they suddenly abandoned Europe at the end of 1926 and began the year 1927 with Fitzgerald's first employment in Hollywood. There things were hardly quieter, and after a few months they bought a serene house called Ellerslie outside of Wilmington, Delaware, and hoped for peace and productivity. The hope was vain.

Edmund Wilson, who was still Fitzgerald's father image but of whom he had seen little during his European years, came once to visit them in the country and gives us his recollection of "the literary life of a period in which nonsense and inspiration, reckless idealism and childish irresponsibility, were mingled in so queer a way." In his account of the Fitzgeralds' characteristically frenetic and erratic behavior, he says:

> He had now gone on to tackle a subject that might well have taxed Dostoevsky, and he was eventually to find it beyond him. It must have been a psychological "block" as well as the invincible compulsion to live like a millionaire that led him even more than usual to interrupt his serious work and turn out stories for the commercial magazines. . . . I had always felt that he was expecting me to point a finger at him and say, "What has become of that novel?" It was his own artistic conscience that accused him, but this was beginning to make our meetings uncomfortable, for any inquiry about his work was likely to bring a sharp retort.

He was beginning to feel uneasy about Ernest Hemingway, too —Hemingway whom he was presently to call his "literary conscience"—and in 1928, writing to his editor and pretending good progress on the novel, he said, "Remember novel is confidential, even to Ernest." Called now *The World's Fair*, the novel was not progressing at all.

As their marriage had grown older, Zelda Fitzgerald had developed stronger and stronger competitive feelings about her husband, and now she decided that she must study ballet and become a professional dancer. Chiefly for that purpose they returned to Paris in the summer of 1928, and, in spite of pretenses to his agent, and perhaps to himself, he did no work at all. They returned to Ellerslie in the autumn, and still the work dragged.

In that spring and summer, Ernest Hemingway was in the United States. He began to write his next novel in Key West, Florida, and finished it in Wyoming, and then, for the next six months, back in Paris, he rewrote it. Serialization in *Scribner's* magazine began in May of 1929, and he continued to revise on the periodical galleys. It is said that the end of the novel was rewritten seventeen times.

In December, during the period of revision, Hemingway's father committed suicide in Oak Park, Illinois. There is not much on record as to the son's response, but we can make some inferences from the attitude of his hero in *For Whom the Bell Tolls*, Robert Jordan, whose father was also a suicide and who reflects,

> Anyone has a right to do it. But it isn't a good thing to do. I understand it, but I do not approve of it. . . . But you do understand it? Sure, I understand it but. Yes, but. You have to be awfully occupied with yourself to do a thing like that. . . . I'll never forget how sick it made me the first time I knew he was a *cobarde*. Go on, say it in English. Coward. . . . He wasn't any son of a bitch, though. He was just a coward and that was the worst luck any man could have. Because if he wasn't a coward he would have stood up to that woman and not let her bully him.

To Maxwell Perkins, Hemingway wrote, "I feel terrible and sick." One wonders how he felt when "that woman," his mother, sent him as a gift the pistol that his father had used, and why she did that. However distressing these circumstances were, they apparently did not seriously hamper the completion of his novel, which was in the hands of Maxwell Perkins by April 1, 1929.

In March of 1929 the Fitzgeralds had once more arrived in Europe, this time to remain until September of 1931. Living much of the time on the Riviera, the scene of *Tender Is the Night*, he began the novel again with quite another conception. This was to be the transitional stage between the unyielding first conception and the version that would finally emerge.

The spring and summer of 1929 the Fitzgeralds spent in Paris, and there, presently, Morley Callaghan, a young Cana-

dian writer whom Hemingway had known in Toronto, looked
them up. Callaghan found that, while Hemingway had given
Fitzgerald a manuscript of *A Farewell to Arms,* he was nevertheless avoiding him as a drunken nuisance who was married
to a "crazy" woman, and he asked Callaghan not to give Fitzgerald his address. Callaghan had been a boxer in college, and
now he became Hemingway's sparring partner at the gymnasium that he frequented. Finally, Fitzgerald did discover the
Hemingways' apartment and one afternoon he came along to
the gymnasium with the other two. They asked him to act as
timekeeper. Without intending it, Callaghan knocked Hemingway to the floor, and Fitzgerald, appalled, exclaimed that he
had let the round run one minute overtime. Hemingway was
enraged and accused Fitzgerald of having wanted to see him
knocked down, and then stalked off to the showers in a fury.
Fitzgerald was hurt and crestfallen, but when Hemingway returned, he made no apologies and all three pretended that
nothing had happened.

Callaghan had other occasions on which to observe the phenomenon of Hemingway's having to be the "champ." Although
Hemingway was derisive about Fitzgerald's inability to get on
with his novel and about the stories he turned out for the *Post,*
his attitude may well have been part of the "champ" complex.
In a letter to a hypothetical young writer that Hemingway
published later, he said that a writer "should have read everything so he knows what he has to beat."

Later, too, he is supposed to have said to the novelist,
Josephine Herbst, "But my writing is nothing. My boxing is
everything"—as though he were Oscar Wilde saying, "I have
put my genius into my life, only my talent into my works"!
The source material for the legend, after all, was manufac-
tured in the life. One can only wonder how a man of Fitzgerald's sensitivity could have taken this man, *as* man, so seriously, and why he should have used him, of all people, as the
agent of his own self-flagellation and debasement. Within
weeks after the boxing incident, Fitzgerald wrote him from
Cannes as follows:

Just taken another chapter to typist's and it's left me in a terrible mood of depression as to whether it's any good or not. In 2½ months I've been here I've written 20,000 words on it and one short story, which is superb for me of late years. I've paid for it with the usual nervous depressions and such drinking manners as the lowest bistro (bistrot?) boy would scorn. My latest tendency is to collapse about 11:00 and, with the tears flowing from my eyes or the gin rising to their level and leaking over, tell interested friends or acquaintances that I haven't a friend in the world and likewise care for nobody, generally including Zelda, and often implying current company—after which current company tend to become less current and I wake up in strange rooms in strange palaces. The rest of the time I stay alone working or trying to work or brooding or reading detective stories—and realizing that anyone in my state of mind, who has in addition never been able to hold his tongue, is pretty poor company. But when drunk I make them all pay and pay and pay. . . .

I have no possible right to send you this gloomy letter. Really if I didn't feel rather better with one thing or another I couldn't have written it. Here's a last flicker of the old cheap pride: the *Post* now pays the old whore $4000 a screw. But now it's because she's mastered the 40 positions—in her youth one was enough.

That letter was written in the month that saw the publication of *A Farewell to Arms*, the novel that Fitzgerald thought so beautiful that he felt impelled to read aloud from his manuscript copy to Morley Callaghan. And it is, to be sure, with its subtle play of symbols in the development of its counterpoint, Hemingway's most successfully structured novel. It is a novel of doom, perhaps even of tragic doom, the war novel that gives us the background of *The Sun Also Rises*. Frederic Henry, the hero, is a lieutenant in the Ambulance Corps of the Italian Army. He is disastrously wounded, makes his "separate peace," and flees with his lovely nurse, Catherine Barkley, who dies in childbirth. He is left with nothing at all, like Jake Barnes, and can only, like the Hemingway hero always, enact the ritual of endurance.

Physical activity, whether to keep from thinking or not, was as important to Hemingway as to his heroes, and in two works of non-fiction he gave extended treatment to two of the forms of physical activity that interested him most. *Death in the Afternoon* (1932) is about bullfighting, literary matters, and death; *The Green Hills of Africa* (1935) is about big-game hunting, literary matters, and death. These are among Hemingway's lesser works, but, revealing as they do a man of bias and prejudice as well as of daring and courage, they are important to an understanding of a not entirely engaging literary personality. (Sherwood Anderson, who also in the end became a Scribner's author, felt as he read *The Green Hills of Africa* that "it leaves a curious bad taste.")

In the first of these books, Hemingway explicated those literary principles that *A Farewell to Arms,* perhaps more clearly than any other of his novels, demonstrated. There is, first of all, the dedication to absolute clarity and directness of statement, qualities that will permit no "faking," as he calls it. Next, there is the conception of prose as "architecture," of conscious building in the modern manner, with clean lines and no frills or decoration. Next, there is the insistence on selection of detail on a basis of experience and knowledge derived from experience:

> If a writer of prose knows enough about what he is writing about he may omit things that he knows and the reader, if the writer is writing truly enough, will have a feeling of those things as strongly as though the writer had stated them. The dignity of movement of an ice-berg is due to only one-eighth of its being above water. A writer who omits things because he does not know them only makes hollow places in his writing.

And finally, there is that urgent sense of putting down only what really happened, of creating the sense and feel of "the way things were."

In *Death in the Afternoon,* which begins by telling how Gertrude Stein and Alice B. Toklas showed him photographs of themselves at the bullfights in Spain, he was still friendly to those ladies. But when *The Green Hills of Africa* was written, Gertrude Stein had published *The Autobiography of Alice B.*

*Toklas* (which was, of course, her autobiography, not Alice's),
with its damaging references to Hemingway; and what he has
to say about the lady is not friendly. He is conversing with his
second wife:

> ". . . he doesn't have to read books written by some female
> he's tried to help get published saying how he's yellow."
> "She's just jealous and malicious. You never should have
> helped her. Some people never forgive that."
> "It's a damned shame, though, with all that talent gone to
> malice and nonsense and self-praise. It's a god-damned shame,
> really. It's a shame you never knew her before she went to pot.
> You know a funny thing; she never could write dialogue. It was
> terrible. She learned how to do it from my stuff and used it in
> that book. She had never written like that before. She never
> could forgive learning that and she was afraid people would no-
> tice it, where she'd learned it, so she had to attack me. It's a
> funny racket, really. But I swear she was damned nice before
> she got ambitious. You would have liked her then, really."
> "Maybe, but I don't think so. . . ."

Anderson, writing to Ralph Church, tried to understand Hemingway's problem as it appeared to him in what he called this
"lousy book," and one wonders what he thought of certain
passages in which Hemingway speculated on the fate of
American writers, passages that must have involved for Anderson a degree, at least, of self-recognition.

> . . . You see we make our writers into something very strange.
> . . . We destroy them in many ways. First, economically. They
> make money. It is only by hazard that a writer makes money
> eventually. Then our writers when they have made some money
> increase their standard of living and they are caught. They have
> to write to keep up their establishments, their wives, and so on,
> and they write slop. It is slop not on purpose but because it is
> hurried. Because they write when there is nothing to say or no
> water in the well. Because they are ambitious. Then, once they
> have betrayed themselves, they justify it and you get more slop.
> Or else they read the critics. If they believe the critics when they
> say they are great then they must believe them when they say they
> are rotten and they lose confidence. At present, we have two good

writers who cannot write because they have lost confidence through reading critics. If they wrote, sometimes it would be good and sometimes not so good and sometimes it would be quite bad, but the good would get out. But they have read the critics and they must write masterpieces. The masterpieces the critics said they wrote. They weren't masterpieces, of course. They were just quite good books. So now they cannot write at all. The critics have made them impotent. . . .

He may have been thinking of Sherwood Anderson; he was certainly thinking of Scott Fitzgerald.

In April 1930 Zelda Fitzgerald suffered a complete mental collapse and spent nearly a year in a Swiss sanatarium. The diagnosis was schizophrenia, and the possibility of her recovery was slight. All work on Fitzgerald's novel now came to a stop, and it did not seriously begin again until 1932, but even during his sad time in Switzerland, he could think of others. He wrote Maxwell Perkins enthusiastically, for example, about Thomas Wolfe, whose *Look Homeward, Angel* had been published in the autumn of the previous year:

> All the world seems to end up in this flat and antiseptic smelling land—with an overlay of flowers. Tom Wolfe is the only man I've met here who isn't sick or hasn't sickness to deal with. You have a great find in him—what he'll do is incalculable. He has a deeper culture than Ernest and more vitality, if he is slightly less of a poet that goes with the immense surface he wants to cover. Also he lacks Ernest's quality of a stick hardened in the fire—he is more susceptible to the world. John Bishop told me he needed advice about cutting, etc., but after reading his book I thought that was nonsense. He strikes me as a man who should be let alone as to length, if he has to be published in five volumes. I liked him enormously.

Zelda Fitzgerald, after a time, seemed somewhat better, and there were to be occasional spells of partial recovery throughout her life. They returned to the United States and once more went to Hollywood to try to get out of debt. And if there was no progress on the novel through all of 1931, that year did see the publication of one of Fitzgerald's most moving stories, a kind of preparation for *Tender Is the Night*, called "Babylon Revisited."

This is the story of Charles Wales, an alcoholic who is permitting himself only one drink a day, returned to Paris to try to obtain the custody of his daughter, who has been made a ward of Wales's dead wife's sister because of his past irresponsibility. Wales reflects:

> "I spoiled this city for myself. I didn't realize it, but the days came along one after another, and then two years were gone, and everything was gone, and I was gone."
>
> He was thirty-five . . .

Fitzgerald, too, was thirty-five, and the emotions of the story —the sense of waste, even of devastation, and of hope that, while the past was irredeemable, something might yet be made of the future—were likewise his. So is the recognition of fact. He thinks of "the effort and ingenuity of Montmarte"—

> All the catering to vice and waste was on an utterly childish scale, and he suddenly realized the meaning of the word "dissipate"—to dissipate into thin air; to make nothing out of something. In the little hours of the night every move from place to place was an enormous human jump, an increase of paying for the privilege of slower and slower motion.

This is all very interesting, as Gertrude Stein would have said. Fitzgerald's wife was now, in a most profound sense, "dead" to him. He had not lost his daughter, but he well might if he continued to live as he did. He had not put himself on one drink a day, but he should have. He was, however, looking straight into the realities of his life, which is to say that he was mature. And his prose had become much more direct than it had ever been: the emotions are real and complex, and they need not be supported by that lyrical vocabulary on which, in his earlier work, he had so much depended when the feeling in the fiction was lighter.

In the last decade of his life, as it would prove to be, he wrote some other very good stories, along with the trash: "Crazy Sunday," derived from his 1931 experience of Hollywood and paying his respects to the film producer, Irving Thalberg, who was to be the prototype of the hero of his final attempt at a novel; "An Alcoholic Case," looking at himself at his worst through the eyes of an outsider; "The Long Way Out," looking at poor Zelda in her madness with kindly, injured eyes; and "The Lost Decade," which evokes the period, much more than a weekend, when he "was taken drunk . . . every-which-way drunk." Not all of these and other similar stories were published in his lifetime, but many of them were, and they were all equally candid in their self-revelation just as they were all equally devoid of self-pity. He did not worry about the inferences of his public. All the more curious that he continued to worry about the inferences of one member of it, Ernest Hemingway. "Don't tell Ernest or anyone," he was still enjoining his editor. "Don't tell Ernest or anyone—let them think what they want—you're the only one whose ever consistently felt faith in me anyhow." It is not only the suspicion that is pathetic, or the sense of inferiority, but rather simply the constant awareness of the figure of Hemingway lurking out there.

Hemingway's attitude toward Zelda Fitzgerald did not help matters. While Fitzgerald was in Hollywood, her father died, and in January of 1932 she suffered another breakdown. She was taken to Baltimore for treatment, and there presently Fitzgerald took another house, this one inappropriately called La Paix. In one period of relative lucidity, she had completed a novel, *Save Me the Waltz*, which Scribner's was to publish, and of this novel Fitzgerald wrote as follows to Perkins:

> You haven't been in the publishing business over twenty years without noticing the streaks of smallness in very large personalities. Ernest told me once he would "never publish a book in the same season with me," meaning it would lead to ill-feeling. I advise you, if he is in New York (and always granting you like Zelda's book), *do not praise it, or even talk about it to him!* The finer the thing he has written, the more he'll expect your entire allegiance to it as this is one of the few pleasures, rich and full and new, he'll get out of it. I know this, and I think you do too

and probably there's no use warning you. There is no possible
conflict between the books but there has always been a subtle
struggle between Ernest and Zelda, and any apposition might
have curiously grave consequences—curious, that is, to un-jealous
men like you and me.

He was quite right in his feelings, and not very much later
Hemingway was to be brutally plain about that not so subtle
struggle:

> Of all people on earth you need discipline in your work and
> instead you marry someone who is jealous of your work, wants
> to compete with you and ruins you. It's not as simple as that and
> I thought Zelda was crazy the first time I met her and you com-
> plicated it even more by being in love with her and, of course,
> you're a rummy.

The breakdown of Zelda Fitzgerald had one possible value for
him: it gave him the third and final conception of his next
novel, *Tender Is the Night,* and once he had seized upon it,
the novel began to move and to grow. The new conception
seemed to begin to become a book just at the point at which
he felt most lost. "Five years have rolled away from me and
I can't decide exactly who I am, if anyone. . . ." His life was
a nightmare, with liquor necessary to work, and work necessary if he was to live. Still, he was writing. In April of 1932
he thanked Gertrude Stein for sending him a copy of her
new book:

> Whenever I sit down to write I think of the line that you drew
> for me and told me that my next book should be that thick. So
> many of your memorable remarks come often to my head, and
> they seem to survive in a way that very little current wisdom
> does.

And he told her that, reading her book, he was "learning a lot
as we all do from you." How thick a line she had drawn when
she told him that his next book would be his best, we cannot
know; *Tender Is the Night* did turn out to be his thickest book,
and in some ways it is indeed his best.

He interrupted the writing of it in the autumn of 1933 to

compose a prose elegy to his dead friend, Ring Lardner. Earlier
in that year, in one of his "Don't tell Ernest" admonitions, he
had said that "I am *his* alcoholic just like Ring is mine." He
may have been contrasting their qualities when he ended his
memorial piece as follows:

> A great and good American is dead. Let us not obscure him
> by the flowers, but walk up and look at that fine medallion, all
> abraded by sorrows that perhaps we are not equipped to under-
> stand. Ring made no enemies, because he was kind, and to many
> millions he gave release and delight.

Sherwood Anderson, who had published an appreciation of
Lardner eleven years before, wrote to compliment him. "That
was a swell piece you wrote about Ring Lardner." Edmund
Wilson thought that he had overestimated the literary importance of his friend, but a new young writer, John O'Hara,
wrote to say that if Fitzgerald "had never written another line,
'Ring' would have been writing career enough for anyone."
Ring Lardner had been much in Fitzgerald's mind as he drew
the character of Abe North in *Tender Is the Night*. Almost finished when 1933 came to an end, it was published in April of
1934. Hemingway had some reservations, but he could nevertheless write to say, "You are twice as good now as at the time
you think you were so marvellous."

Just before the publication of that novel, when he was urging his editor to respect all his last-minute revisions, Fitzgerald recalled a conversation with Hemingway.

> After all, Max, I am a plodder. One time I had a talk with
> Ernest Hemingway, and I told him, against all the logic that was
> then current, that I was the tortoise and he was the hare, and
> that's the truth of the matter, that everything that I have ever
> attained has been through long and persistent struggle while it is
> Ernest who has a touch of genius which enables him to bring off
> extraordinary things with facility. I have a facility for being
> cheap, if I wanted to indulge in that . . . but when I decided to
> be a serious man, I tried to struggle over every point until I
> have made myself into a slow moving behemoth. . . .

If there is any accuracy in the analogy, then the tortoise had made an extraordinary and wholly unnatural leap in *Tender Is the Night*, where there is no hint of plodding but always of brilliance, and a full and rich brilliance that was beyond Hemingway. Always sensitive to the "awful pull toward him" that Hemingway exerted, Fitzgerald warned himself to avoid any imitation lest his own style be corrupted, and the echoes of Hemingway, while they are no doubt there, are few and well assimilated in his own melodies.

Writing again to Maxwell Perkins, shortly after the publication of his novel, he was commenting on a story by Thomas Wolfe:

> I thought it was perfectly beautiful and it had a subtlety often absent from his work, an intense poetry rather akin to Ernest (though naturally you won't tell Tom that because he wouldn't take it as a compliment). What family resemblance there is between we three as writers is the attempt that crops up in our fiction from time to time to recapture the exact feel of a moment in time and space, exemplified by people rather than by things— that is, an attempt at what Wordsworth was trying to do rather than what Keats did with such magnificent ease, an attempt at a mature memory of a deep experience.

It was Keats, of course, in "Ode to the Nightingale," that poem of illusory flight from reality and return, of thrilling beauty and disenchantment, a poem that Fitzgerald had read countless times and could not read without finding tears in his eyes— it was that poem that gave him his title, and it is not surprising that it should now be in his mind.

Writing Thomas Wolfe later he was still thinking of *Tender Is the Night* and the problems of composition it had presented to him.

> The novel of selected incidents has this to be said: that the great writer like Flaubert has consciously left out the stuff that Bill or Joe (in his case, Zola) will come along and say presently. He will say only the things that he alone sees. So *Madame Bovary* becomes eternal while Zola already rocks with age. . . .

Once he had said that his next novel after *Gatsby* would be "something really NEW in form, idea, structure—the model for the age that Joyce and Stein are searching for, that Conrad didn't find." It was an enormous ambition and one may doubt that *Tender Is the Night* achieved it. Whether it "becomes eternal" remains to be seen, but that it has endured until now with ever increasing prestige is a fact of literary history. Hemingway was quite right when he said to Perkins some time after its publication, "A strange thing is that in retrospect his *Tender Is the Night* gets better and better."

Much more complex than *The Great Gatsby*, the new novel, in spite of the tortured circumstances of its composition, is probably Fitzgerald's greatest achievement. A story of "emotional bankruptcy," it depicts not only the dissolution of a life but of a way of life. It is a story of breakdowns. The hero, Dick Diver, an ambitious and charming young man who wants to become the best doctor in the world, marries Nicole Warren, his patient, in part to help her recover from her breakdown. The large action of the novel shows Nicole's slow recovery of health and the discovery of an identity, at which point she abandons Dick, and, contrapuntally, his slow disenchantment, disintegration, and final loss of identity, at which point he disappears, in the literal sense of *dissipation* on which Fitzgerald had remarked: something turning into nothing. Breakdowns in the self, then, but also in marriages, in friendships, even in a way of life. It is the elegy of the 1920's, the allegory of the dream that Fitzgerald himself tried to make of reality and the dissipation of that dream. It is, quite simply, one of the most moving novels in all American fiction. And the reviews were lukewarm, obtuse, the sales trivial. It was Fitzgerald's greatest defeat.

We have mentioned the character called Abe North, drawn after Fitzgerald's friend, Ring Lardner. As Lardner, failing to fulfill his own literary promise, took to drink, bitterness, and early death, so Abe North, a musician who "after a brilliant and precocious start had composed nothing for seven years," takes to drink, an acid bitterness, and invites an early, brutal death. Lardner became the figure that Fitzgerald feared he might become and it is not surprising that the character of North, for whose breakdown there is no very specific motivation beyond a "natural declension of the soul," is drawn both with the sympathy that comes from self-identification and with the clarity that comes from self-recognition.

Ernest Hemingway objected to Fitzgerald's technique of "composite" characterization—combining some qualities of one real person with those of another to make a fictional character. (Dick Diver, for example, combines the most attractive qualities of himself and of Gerald Murphy, a wealthy Riviera friend of both Hemingway and Fitzgerald.) Fitzgerald suggested that perhaps Hemingway was without sufficient detachment from these particular cases to construct a general literary principle. A second technical point that, he said, might interest Hemingway has to do with the end of *Tender Is the Night*. The two of them, five years earlier, had had long discussions about the proper ending of *A Farewell to Arms*. Hemingway argued for a slow fade-out, a kind of non-dramatic summarizing; Fitzgerald wanted a staccato dramatic end. Hemingway acceded and wrote such an end; and later Fitzgerald decided that he had been wrong, and when he came to write the end of *Tender Is the Night*, it was to be the other kind, a dying fall, one of the most beautiful decrescendos in modern fiction:

> In the last letter she had from him he told her that he was practising in Geneva, New York, and she got the impression that he had settled down with someone to keep house for him. She looked up Geneva in an atlas and found it was in the heart of the Finger Lakes section and considered a pleasant place. Perhaps, so she liked to think, his career was biding its time . . . ; his latest note was postmarked from Hornell, New York, which is some distance from Geneva and a very small town; in any case he is almost certainly in that section of the country, in one town or another.

A very fine ending—and a prediction of almost exactly what was presently to happen to Fitzgerald himself.

His wife now incurably insane, Fitzgerald managed one

more collection of short stories (*Taps at Reveille*, 1935), but really, the remaining years of his life were all downhill. In February, March, and April of 1936 he published in *Esquire* the three pieces that make "The Crack-Up," a beautiful and moving confession; without a hint of self-pity, it is one of the most extraordinary self-revelations in literature. "Of course all life is a process of breaking down," it begins, and then with perfect candor tells a wide public of his breakdown. It is in the second of these pieces that he names Wilson as his "intellectual conscience" and indicates, without naming, Hemingway as his "artistic conscience." It is in the third that he asks the shattering question, "why I had become identified with the objects of my horror or compassion," and ends with despairing self-appraisal:

> . . . so that life will never be very pleasant again, and the sign *Cave Canem* is hung permanently just above my door. I will try to be a correct animal though, and if you throw me a bone with enough meat on it I may even lick your hand.

Those of his friends who responded—Wilson, Dos Passos, Hemingway, to name three—were appalled, disgusted, rigid in their want of admiration, let alone of pity. There is no record of Gertrude Stein's response.

## 8

Life had taken an amusing turn for her: she became a best-seller. In 1933 she fulfilled her earliest literary ambition when her book *The Autobiography of Alice B. Toklas* was serialized by *The Atlantic Monthly*, which until then had been impervious to her merits. The *Autobiography* was a new kind of writing for her, to be sure, and Americans found it vastly entertaining, even as a few of her literary friends found it painful. Sherwood Anderson wrote her to say that he was "a bit sorry and so on the night after that number [of *The Atlantic*] when you took such big patches of skin off Hemmy with your delicately held knife," but Hemmy did not, at this point, indicate his hurt. The success of the book led to Gertrude Stein's famous lecture tour of the United States in 1934. Interviewed upon her disembarkment, she allowed that Shakespeare, Trollope, and Flaubert had influenced her and that she had always felt affection for Ernest Hemingway.

As far as one knows, Hemingway paid no attention to her tour. She did meet some older writing friends. Scott Fitzgerald had urged her to spend with them any time that she might have in Baltimore when she lectured there, and she did go to the Fitzgeralds' house on Christmas Eve. She talked, that evening, on one of her favorite subjects, sentences. Sentences must not have bad plumbing—they "must not leak." That wisdom was the last that she could give him, for she was never to see him again.

In New Orleans, as she continued her progress, she saw Sherwood Anderson, who brought her oranges, "wonderful oranges, very sweet and very juicy, not at all like the oranges we had had in France," and that was the last time that she saw him.

Her tour was a great success, a true *succes fou,* and she had no way of knowing that, as far as two of her three favorite American writers were concerned, it was also a funeral. She did not see Hemingway on this tour, but she saw him at least twice, later, in Paris. He had not yet had the time or the opportunity to retaliate for the remarks that she had made about him in that very successful book that had made her lecture tour in the United States a possibility and then such a triumph.

## 9

Sherwood Anderson had said of *The Green Hills of Africa,* published in 1935, that "it leaves a curious bad taste." Some of Hemingway's fiction leaves the same "curious bad taste." This is when his personality obtrudes upon his material, or when the material is not sufficiently objectified. The stories of *Winner Take Nothing,* which was published in 1933, are—with the possible exception of the autobiographical "Fathers and Sons" —still free of this taint, and the volume does contain some of his most justly celebrated stories. Generally speaking, the short stories became more and more impressive, reaching their climax, perhaps, in those two of 1936, "The Short Happy Life of Francis Macomber" and "The Snows of Kilimanjaro."

Both stories derive from Hemingway's African experience, which he had already written about in the *Green Hills* of the year before. The first is probably the better story, but the second tells us more about Hemingway's literary attitudes. This is the story of a writer who is dying of gangrene on a safari and who is remembering all the experiences for stories he has never written and, now, will never write. He is married to a very rich woman for whom he feels only indifference, ". . . this good, this rich bitch, this kindly caretaker and destroyer of his talent." But "Nonsense" he immediately adds, and recognizes that he himself has betrayed his artistic conscience:

> Why should he blame this woman because she kept him well? He had destroyed his talent by not using it, by betrayals of himself and what he believed in, by drinking so much that he blunted the edge of his perceptions, by laziness, by sloth, and by snobbery, by pride and by prejudice, by hook and by crook.

It is almost as if, in the character of this writer, Hemingway has combined certain qualities and experiences of his own with his image of Scott Fitzgerald, and as if, in order to throw the reader off the track of that inference, he mentions Fitzgerald by name.

> The rich were dull and they drank too much, or they played too much backgammon. They were dull and they were repetitious. He remembered poor Scott Fitzgerald and his romantic awe of them and how he had started a story once that began, "The rich are different from you and me." And how some one had said to Scott, Yes, they have more money. But that was not humorous to Scott. He thought they were a special glamorous race and when he found out they weren't it wrecked him just as much as any other thing that wrecked him.

Fitzgerald, so depressed about himself ("I wish I had those great masses of manuscript stored away like Wolfe and Hemlngway but this goose is beginning to be pretty thoroughly plucked I am afraid") and already so elegiac about his friendship with Hemingway (". . . we will never again see very much of each other") had just published the "Crack-Up" essays in *Esquire* when Hemingway's story appeared in the same magazine. Fitzgerald was understandably shocked and hurt. "I don't think I can ever forgive him," he said to Sheilah Graham a few years later. "That was hitting me when I was down." And in his notebooks he made this entry: "Ernest—until we began trying to walk over each other with cleats." To Hemingway he wrote this letter:

> Please lay off me in print. If I choose to write de profundis sometimes ["The Crack-Up"] it doesn't mean I want friends praying aloud over my corpse. No doubt you meant it kindly but it cost me a night's sleep. And when you incorporate it (the story) in a book would you mind cutting my name?
>
> It's a fine story—one of your best—even though the "Poor Scott Fitzgerald, etc." rather spoiled it for me.
>
> Ever your friend,<br>Scott
>
> Riches have *never* fascinated me, unless combined with the greatest charm and distinction.

Hemingway justified his use of Fitzgerald's name by the fact that he had exposed his private life so "shamelessly" in *Esquire;* "he felt that it was sort of an open season for me," but he agreed to change the name when the story appeared again, and ever since we have read of "poor Julian," not of "poor Scott." And Fitzgerald wrote to a friend, "He is quite as nervously broken down as I am but it manifests itself in different ways. His inclination is toward megalomania and mine toward melancholy."

To Maxwell Perkins Fitzgerald wrote as follows:

> I wrote Ernest about that story of his, asking him in the most measured terms not to use my name in future pieces of fiction. He wrote me back a crazy letter, telling me about what a great Writer he was and how much he loved his children, but yielding the point—"If I should outlive him—" which he doubted. To have

answered it would have been like fooling with a lit firecracker.

Somehow I love that man, no matter what he says or does, but just one more crack and I think I would have to throw my weight with the gang and lay him. No one could ever hurt him in his first books but he has completely lost his head and the duller he gets about it, the more he is like a punch-drunk pug fighting himself in the movies.

"The gang?"—critics who felt that Hemingway was deteriorating, not to mention friends and ex-friends. Sherwood Anderson, for example, was writing a friend about him:

> . . . there is too much talk of style. In the end the style is the man. I keep wondering why the man feels life as he does. It is as though he saw it always as rather ugly. "People have it in for me. All right. I'll go for them." There is the desire always to kill. Stein says that it is because he cannot bear the thought of any other men as artists, that he wants to occupy the entire field.
>
> There is this sharp difference between the man and, say, Wolfe or Faulkner. They may write of terrible happenings, but you feel always an inner sympathy with the fact of life itself.

Yet Anderson was a little like Fitzgerald in his *consciousness* of Hemingway. When he wrote Gertrude Stein about his attempts at deep-sea fishing in the Gulf of Mexico, he added the quick, "Don't tell Hemingway." Gertrude Stein herself had a late and accidental meeting with Hemingway in Paris presently which she thought worth reporting to Carl Van Vechten. He, in turn, was sure that the meeting "will result in literature ON BOTH SIDES. I can't wait to see what you write about this." But the encounter threw off no literary sparks.

And Fitzgerald himself? Within a year he had met Hemingway again and told him that "it was fine to see you so well and full of life," wishing that they "could meet more often. I don't feel I know you at all." But his letter to Perkins, with its metaphor of the "punch-drunk pug," suggests that he knew what was happening to him, almost as though he had read his still-unwritten next novel.

In the 1930's the Hemingways had moved to Key West, Flor-

ida, and out of the Florida experience came the novel *To Have
and Have Not* in 1937. Like Anderson, Hemingway, observing
the America of the depression years, was briefly pushed toward
the political left, and this novel is an attempt to vindicate the
"outlaw" hero, Harry Morgan, for whom society makes an honest living impossible, and to denounce the decadent rich. Harry
Morgan's chief virtue seems to be his sexual prowess, which is
hardly an adequate basis for a critique of the class system. But
the novel is not really meant as serious criticism of capitalism;
it seems rather to be the outlet for a large reservoir of spleen
that had been aroused in Hemingway by a certain kind of
visitor to Florida, and the spleen poisons the book, which is a
fragmentary performance, unsatisfactory both in structure and
in style.

The final wisdom of Harry Morgan, as he lies dying, is that
no man can go it alone, that no man is an island. It is this
wisdom that provides the theme for Hemingway's next novel,
*For Whom the Bell Tolls*, published in 1940. A novel about
the Spanish Civil War, in which Hemingway was deeply involved both personally and professionally (it impelled him to
write his single play, *The Fifth Column* of 1938), it is different
from his other fiction in that his hero, although he must die
for it, is committed to a cause. The novel attempts an epic
scale unlike any other book that Hemingway published, and
while it has many wonderful scenes and some magnificently
realized Spanish characters, the whole does not sustain the
heroic intention. In the sexual encounters especially, one feels
again that the personality of the author has been imposed upon
the personality of Robert Jordan, the hero; and then Jordan
becomes slightly absurd, and the style falters into bathos, and
the tragic subject invites a smile. Symbolic of the major fault
of the book is this single sentence, which takes off from Gertrude Stein's famous "A rose is a rose is a rose":

> "An onion is an onion is an onion," Robert Jordan said cheerily
> and, he thought, a stone is a stein is a rock is a boulder is a
> pebble."

*For Whom the Bell Tolls,* which is certainly Hemingway's most *important* novel if not his *best,* should be seen in the whole framework of his career up until 1940.

What was for long the sign of his work—the tension between subject matter and style, between the themes of violence and the perfectly controlled prose—has gone. He was extraordinary among modern prose writers for exactly this reason, that he pressed his style into the service of his subject matter in this special way: the style was the immediate representation of the moral attitude of the author toward his material, it objectified the author's values, and thus in itself was comment in writing otherwise unhampered by comment. When, however, the subject matter began to change—from violent experience itself to the expressed evaluation of violence—the manner began to change. The separation seems to take place in the story about Kilimanjaro, but it is in the novel *To Have and Have Not* that the fumbling transition is clearest. The first third of the book is good narrative in the old manner; but as Hemingway lets himself into the theme proper, the book begins to break down, and the end is a debacle, the noisy collapse of a style and technique simply unable to support the matter. Before, the style in itself was moral comment; with a change in moral attitude, that style was necessarily disrupted. In *For Whom the Bell Tolls,* a new style, less brilliant but more flexible, attempts to integrate itself.

*The Sun Also Rises* was a representation of the life that Hemingway lived and enjoyed and out of which his values came. The characters in this novel—without belief, without relation to a cultural or national past, without ideological relation to the future—submerge themselves in extravagant sensation and view life as a losing game, a sport like bullfighting which, while it is more nearly tragedy than sport because death is inevitable, is interesting only if it observes strict rules. Hemingway epitomized this matter when in an author's note he once said, "I've known some very wonderful people who even though they were going directly to the grave . . . managed to put up a very fine performance en route." This "fine performance" is the sporting attitude, and it is dramatized in the gesture of Lady Brett when she gives up her lover: "You know I feel rather damned good, Jake, . . . it makes one feel rather good deciding not to be a bitch. . . . It's sort of what we have instead of God." Jake has himself observed that morality is what makes you feel good afterwards. Brett feels "rather damned good" because she has behaved according to the tenets of that negative morality, that emphasis on the "performance en route," the *manner* of living, which the group has substituted for belief.

The preoccupation with bullfighting is not accidental; bullfighting is at once the most violent and the most stylized of sports. Its entire excitement depends on the degree to which the matador exposes himself to death *within the rules*. It disregards consequences, regards performance. Both are important. Courage, or unconcern for disaster, is a moral virtue: the best bullfighter works closest to the horns; the best man disregards present and impending catastrophe. Syphilis, the occupational disease of bullfighters, "of all people who lead lives in which a disregard of consequences dominates," is nearly commended. A blundering display of courage, however, is absurd: the matador should "increase the amount of the danger of death"

> within the rules provided for his protection . . . it is to his credit if he does something that he knows how to do in a highly dangerous but still geometrically possible manner. It is to his discredit if he runs danger through ignorance, through disregard of the fundamental rules. . . .

Courage stylized, *style,* then, matters finally, and the experienced spectator looks for this; "what they seek is honesty and true, not tricked, emotion and always classicism and the purity of execution of all the suertes, and . . . they want no sweetening." Since the performance is a matter of the fighter's honor, bullfighting is a *moral* art, and style a *moral* matter. In *The Sun Also Rises,* Romero, who "fakes" nothing in the fight, who has "the old thing, the holding of his purity of line through the maximum of exposure," is the one character who makes the others feel fine: he is the representation of artistic, hence of moral, excellence.

As T. S. Eliot could say that a High Mass "well performed" was for him the consummation of drama because the stylization of its ritual permitted the juncture of the divine and the human, so Hemingway argued that the consummation of tragedy for him was in the bullfight because its stylization permitted exposure of the greatest discipline to the greatest danger.

All this carried directly over into Hemingway's concept of prose and into his own prose. The definition of morality and Brett's dramatization of it; the important counterpoint between danger and performance; the concept of art as moral insofar as its style is "honest" or "true" or "pure"—this complex is translated as follows:

> It is much more difficult than poetry. . . . It can be written, *without tricks* and *without cheating. With nothing that will go bad afterwards* . . . First, there must be talent. . . . Then there must be discipline, the discipline of Flaubert. . . . Then there must be . . . an *absolute conscience* as unchanging as the standard meter in Paris, to prevent *faking*.

The style that made Hemingway famous—with its ascetic suppression of ornament and figure, its insistence on the objective and the unreflective (for good fighters do not talk), its habit of understatement (or sportsmen boast), the directness and the brevity of its syntactical constructions, its muscularity, the sharpness of its staccato and repetitive effects, "the purity of its line under the maximum of exposure," that is, its continued poise under the weight of event or feeling—this style is an exact transfiguration of Hemingway's moral attitude toward a peculiarly violent and chaotic experience. His style, in effect, is what he had instead of God—"God" came in a brief but genuine political commitment.

The position taken at that time by Edmund Wilson in *The Atlantic Monthly* was, I think, mistaken. He argued that Hemingway's political persuasion was no persuasion at all but a simple transfer of the desire to kill: from kudu to fascist. I believe that the motive of *For Whom the Bell Tolls* was an honest sense of man's dignity and worth, an awareness of the necessity of man's freedom, a nearly poetic realization of man's *collective* virtues. If the individual vanishes in the political whole, he vanishes precisely to defend his dignity, his freedom, his virtue; hence the superb importance of the political whole. This novel is not, of course, a *War and Peace*, a *Dynasts;* it is realistic, political, and deeply partisan. The defects of characterization are the conventional defects of partisan novels, in which personalities always threaten to vanish in abstractions, as, half the time, the woman Pilar becomes a Spanish Gaea, Robert Jordan any vaguely attractive young American, and Maria that perfect sexual creature of the private Hemingway mythology. As in so many partisan novels, too, it is the minor characters, who bear no burden but their own, who are excellent: Sordo, the good old man Anselmo, the insane Marty, the politically exhausted Pablo, this last a magnificent portrait, and perhaps as many as a dozen more. About their cause, which is his, Hemingway wrote with a zealot's passion. And the old mold was as useless to him—as meaningless—as the old insistence on the individual's isolation, on the private pursuit of his pleasures, and on the exercise of his wholly private virtues. If the early books pled for sporting conduct on violent occasions, this book pleads the moral necessity of political violence. A different thing; indeed, a different writer.

Here is none of the grace of *The Sun Also Rises,* none of the precise perfection of stories such as "A Clean, Well-Lighted Place." The severe compression of the old work gives way to nearly complete relaxation. The first effect of this relaxation is evident in the pace of the narrative itself, which is leisurely. The second effect is in the fullness of detail, which Hemingway's sentences can suddenly accommodate. The third effect is the one we have noted, the intrusion of the author's personality where it is alien. The final effect is in the sentences themselves, which employ a wide variety of cadences, short and long, truncated and sinuous, bare or copious—as they are needed. This syntactical loosening up is excessive. Understatement is gone and overstatement too often replaces it; we are reminded of Hemingway's own remark about the dignity of icebergs. The older objectivity of style held the narrative in check in a way that this narrative is not held in check; and to this fact we may attribute many long passages of reflection not particularly well written and not necessary to the story, long reveries which the younger Hemingway would not have permitted. This easy method of exposition is a technical device which the older style made a luxury; here it is everywhere, and largely wasted.

Thus we gain and lose. Because it is a story based on different values, it could not have been told in the older style. If the new style sprawls sometimes, sometimes even snores a little in the sun, we should tell ourselves that moral seriousness and the best manners are possibly not always compatible. If Hemingway, under changing historical circumstances, could not maintain the moral seriousness that the Spanish conflict aroused in him, that does not mean that for that brief time it was not there.

*For Whom the Bell Tolls* was an enormous success. Where Fitzgerald had been stupidly attacked for writing about frivolous people in an urgent and earnest time, Hemingway was praised for seriously committing himself to a just cause in a tragic time. Fitzgerald's last letter to Hemingway, dated November 8, 1940, was written to congratulate him on that "great success" and on the book. "I'm going to read the whole thing again." He hardly had time to do that.

## 10

". . . it is gloomy to see how few things I really care about when I see clearly," Fitzgerald wrote in 1937, after years of lingering in the neighborhood of those sanatariums to which his wife was successively committed, and just before he went once more to Hollywood, looking for work. "I don't care much where I am any more," he wrote to Gerald Murphy, "nor expect very much from places. . . . I am writing a picture called *Infidelity* for Joan Crawford. Writing for her is difficult."

He was writing some things of his own, as well. In 1934 he had started—and he worked at this project off and on for the rest of his life—a fantastically ill-conceived novel to be called *The Count of Darkness*. Set in the ninth and tenth centuries, this novel was to have as its hero a daring young man named Phillipe who would play a part in the founding of France and in the consolidation of feudalism. Fitzgerald's plan was that "it shall be the story of Ernest" and his hope that "just as Stendhal's portrait of a Byronic man made *Le Rouge et* [*le*] *Noir* so couldn't *my* portrait of Ernest as Phillipe make the real modern man." It is not surprising that those portions of this work that he finished are among the least satisfactory pieces of writing he ever did. It is surprising that he should have so misjudged his own talent and performance. Generally, his powers of self-appraisal were strong. If anything, he underestimated the achievement of *Tender Is the Night*. Now, eighteen years later, he wrote of *This Side of Paradise* that it was "one of the funniest books since *Dorian Gray* in its utter spuriousness." He was writing and publishing a series of stories about a Hollywood character named Pat Hobby, who was what in his worst moments Fitzgerald saw himself becoming— a subject serious enough, surely, yet he knew that these stories were trash. All his life he had worried about his hack writing and now at the end of his life he was still making in substance a remark that he first made in 1924: "I now get 2000 a story and they grow worse and worse and my ambition is to get where I need write no more but only novels."

He was treated like a hack writer by producers, he was nearly forgotten by the public, thought by some to be dead, at most a dim figure lost in the now legendary twenties. Then there was the defection of friends, the hardest fate. When Thomas Wolfe turned against his editor, Maxwell Perkins, who had devoted untold time and thought and patience to his novels, and the mean-spirited portrait of him as Foxhall Edwards, nicknamed "The Fox," appeared in *You Can't Go Home*

*Again,* Fitzgerald saw an analogy with "Ernest's sharp turn against me." He probably had Hemingway in mind when he wrote in "The Crack-Up" that "I didn't have the two top things: great animal magnetism or money. I had the two second things though: good looks and intelligence. So I always got the top girl." He was thinking of Hemingway explicitly now when he wrote: "I talk with the authority of failure—Ernest with the authority of success. We could never sit across the same table again."

Gertrude Stein's title, *Before the Flowers of Friendship Faded Friendship Faded,* might well have come to his mind, for Hemingway was not alone.

> It's funny what a friend is—Ernest's crack in "The Snows," poor John Bishop's article in the *Virginia Quarterly* (a nice return for ten years of trying to set him up in a literary way) and Harold's [his agent's] sudden desertion at the wrong time, have made them something less than friends. Once I believed in friendship, believed I *could* (if I didn't always) make people happy and it was more fun than anything. Now even that seems like a vaudevillian's cheap dream of heaven, a vast minstrel show in which one is the perpetual Bones.

And thinking of his whole career in eclipse, he could only add to that letter, "But to die, so completely and unjustly after having given so much!" And to his wife: ". . . but my God I am a forgotten man."

Small wonder that after a considerable period of considerable abstinence he took again to drink. The story of his disastrous attempt to write a scenario with Budd Schulberg about Dartmouth College and its Winter Carnival is told in fictional form in Schulberg's novel, *The Disenchanted,* and again in the play of that name, written by Schulberg and Harvey Breit. He was rescued by the Hollywood columnist, Sheilah Graham, and he had, at the end of his life, at least his love for her, and hers for him. He began to make notes for and write fragments of still another novel. This, after his death, Edmund Wilson was to put together as *The Last Tycoon.* Had he lived to finish it, it would almost certainly have been our one great novel about Hollywood.

In her book, *College of One*, Sheila Graham tells of Fitzgerald's odd habit of making lists. In the last year of his life, he made such a list of his meetings with Hemingway. Curiously, he had forgotten the earliest meetings. The list is as follows:

| | |
|---|---|
| March — Aug '25 | Paris |
| Oct '25 — Feb '26 | Paris |
| Apr '26 — Oct '26 | Riviera |

One Day in October '28

| | |
|---|---|
| Apr '29 — June '29 | Paris |

Three or four meetings in Autumn [?] 1929

| | |
|---|---|
| One meeting in Oct 1931 | Two years |
| One meeting in 1933 | Two years |
| One meeting in 1937 | Two years |
| | Three years |

4 Times in 11 years

Four times in eleven years (1929–1940). Not *really* friends since '26

In November of 1940 he had a serious heart attack. He stopped drinking. But on December 21 he had a second attack, and that fatal.

Sherwood Anderson had always brooded about the situation of the artist in America. In his *Memoirs*, which he at this time was straining to finish, he tried once more to define the problem for himself. What was it, in America, that destroyed its writers, or drove them to destroy themselves? Hemingway had already published his speculations on the question: "Politics, women, drink, money, ambition." Anderson, who had also suffered at Hemingway's pen, was like Fitzgerald in that, wounded as he may have been, he maintained his regard for Hemingway, the writer. In 1938 he had defended *To Have and Have Not* when it was threatened with censorship and called the author "a great writer." Now, after Fitzgerald's death, he brought the two together in a letter to Gertrude Stein: "I dare say you have heard of Hemingway's huge success with his new book and of the sudden death of Scott Fitzgerald. I guess poor Scott has had a rather rough time. . . ." And within six weeks, in 1941, Anderson himself was dead.

Almost immediately after his death, Fitzgerald's reputation took an upward turn. Stephen Vincent Benét, a casual acquaintance at most, wrote: "You can take off your hats now, gentlemen, and I think perhaps you had better. This is not a legend, this is a reputation—and, seen in perspective, it may well be one of the most secure reputations of our time."

A little later Edmund Wilson, writing to Gertrude Stein, made a comparative judgment: "I think you are right: that he had the constructive gift that Hemingway doesn't have at all —& I feel sure that some of his work will last." She herself wrote to her friend, W. G. Rogers, "Poor Fitzgerald I would have liked to have done something for him in memoriam, the three out of that old time together whom I really care for were Sherwood, Hemingway and Fitzgerald."

"That old time"! We are reminded that Fitzgerald's career began just as one world war came to an end and that it ended just as another began. Did anyone in the years between speak more eloquently for them than he? Did Hemingway?

He survived to participate in that Second World War, and after he arrived in Paris in the vanguard of the Fourth Infantry Division of the First Army to liberate the bar of the Ritz Hotel he had one more encounter with Gertrude Stein: "There wasn't a hell of a lot of time then and so I just told her I had always loved her and she said she loved me too which was, I think, the truth from both of us."

Charity was never Hemingway's long suit. Twenty years after Fitzgerald's death he could express only contempt for him. To a feature writer for *Holiday* magazine he said in 1960, "Fitzgerald was soft." Soft—that greatest of crimes in the masculine book! We do not know how he responded when

Gertrude Stein died in 1946, but in a *Paris Review* interview of 1958 he was still declaring that she learned to write dialogue from him. What dialogue?

11

Hemingway had not finished with Fitzgerald. In the posthumous *A Moveable Feast*, he includes a number of anecdotal sketches about him. One, about the trip to Lyons, is quite funny and probably fairly accurate and only a little patronizing. Another, "A Matter of Measurements," about the size of Fitzgerald's penis and his worry over the matter, whether or not it is an invention, makes Hemingway himself sound much more adolescent than Fitzgerald. "Tell me truly," Hemingway has Fitzgerald saying at least twice, in this expression that is so characteristically Hemingway's own, so little Fitzgerald's. That weird nonsense about male statues in the Louvre ("Have you ever seen anything in here except the Mona Lisa?") and the huddled instruction, not so very expert, in the techniques of sexual intercourse—all this suggests that we are unwillingly overhearing a couple of boys behind a barn. And this was Hemingway at the age of sixty, writing about Fitzgerald who had been dead for more than twenty years!

A literary judgment appears as an epigraph to the first of these sketches:

> His talent was as natural as the pattern that was made by the dust on a butterfly's wings. At one time he understood it no more than the butterfly did and he did not know when it was brushed or marred. Later he became conscious of his damaged wings and of their construction and he learned to think and could not fly anymore because the love of flight was gone and he could only remember when it had been effortless.

It is a curious passage because, while Fitzgerald's literary career from the beginning had been a mixture of serious with shabby work, the novels, which were always serious, steadily improved, one after the other, so that there is a real possibility that the last one, the one that he did not live to finish, might have been the best of all. The quotation suggests that Hemingway was either unable or unwilling to understand the talent of his friend.

For all the temperamental difference between Scott Fitzgerald and Ernest Hemingway, and for all the difference in style and conception of fiction, there were resemblances. These have been examined and summarized in *F. Scott Fitzgerald and His Contemporaries,* by William Goldhurst. He argues persuasively that they treated the same three basic themes of "the alien outsider, the modern aggressive and destructive woman, the ruined writer," and the final analysis seems to suggest that while Fitzgerald in large part resisted the influence of Hemingway's style, Hemingway made no effort to resist the influence of Fitzgerald's treatment of these themes.

They shared, besides, a certain quality that Fitzgerald had himself pointed out—that determination to communicate to their readers the feel of actuality in experience, the sense of "the way it was." And even in his later writings one can say of Hemingway that this quality at least is present still, even when it is threatened by that other quality that we have observed, the intrusions of a bullying personality.

This problem plagues the only full-length novel that Hemingway published after the Second World War, *Across the River and into the Trees* of 1950. It is possible that the old pattern of the wounded hero who returns to the scene of his wounding for a kind of ritualistic exorcism is worn rather thin. It is possible that the lovely young heroine, the Contessa Renata, is too much an old man's fancy to be real. It is possible that Colonel Cantwell is too much like Hemingway himself (they were both fifty years old), or too directly a transcription of his dream of himself, his legend. The old habit of burying his literary fellows continues in this novel, but now in a totally gratuitous way in the savage portrait of poor old exhausted Sinclair Lewis drinking with his companion in Harry's Bar in Venice. Sinclair Lewis had been the first American writer to win the Nobel Prize in 1930. That honor did not come to Hemingway until 1953. *Across the River and into the Trees* has many other flaws. Yet there are those readers who argue that the true Hemingway *aficionado* can be tested by his response to this book, that if he does not think it great his entire judgment of Hemingway is suspect. In his review of this novel, John O'Hara, only one of the scores of younger writers who have been influenced by Hemingway in style, in attitude, in the conception of fictional form, began by saying that Hemingway was "the most important, the outstanding author out of the millions of writers who have lived since 1616," i.e., since the death of William Shakespeare.

Many other readers, less certain in their judgment, were reassured by Hemingway's next book and last fictional publication, the extended short story or novelette called *The Old Man and the Sea* which has been said to be only a small part of a much longer work of fiction still to be published. The short work stands by itself and seemed fine to many. It contained, for example, no women—only an old man and a boy and a large fish. And the athletic performance of the heroic old man was precisely as gratifying as the esthetic performance of the perhaps heroically aging novelist. The point was the same as ever: winner take nothing.

During most of these later years, Hemingway lived in Cuba, and he continued his life of adventures and misadventures. No man surely survived so many catastrophes in which the odds were all on the side of death. It was almost as if he had been selected by the gods to be their darling. And that he did have courage is beyond doubt. Yet in the end he had to reconsider his definition of that word.

While he was apparently sympathetic to the Castro regime in Cuba, his brief period of political commitment was long over, and he left Cuba in 1960 for his ranch in Idaho. One is reminded of the end of the story, "Fathers and Sons," where Nick Adams's young son, who had been brought up in France but is now with his father on the ranch in the West, asks, "Why do we never go to pray at the tomb of my grandfather?"

and Nick explains that they live at a great distance from it. The dialogue continues:

> "I hope we won't live somewhere so that I can never go to pray at your tomb when you are dead."
> "We'll have to arrange that."
> "Don't you think we might all be buried at a convenient place? We could all be buried in France. That would be fine."
> "I don't want to be buried in France," Nick said.
> "Well, then, we'll have to get some convenient place in America. Couldn't we all be buried out at the ranch?"
> "That's an idea."

And he was.

Hemingway was ill, losing weight, and spent a long time under observation in the Mayo Clinic in Rochester, Minnesota. Then early one morning the silence of the Idaho ranch house was shattered by the blast of a double-barreled shotgun. The entire world was shaken, and not alone by the death of the man but by the very force of the drama. One hopes that in the last moments he forgave his father. ". . . *cobarde*. Go on, say it in English."

He had himself long before written his own epitaph when, in *Death in the Afternoon,* he said,

> Madame, all stories, if continued far enough, end in death, and he is no true story teller who would keep that from you. Especially do all stories of monogamy end in death, and your man who is monogamous while he often lives most happily, dies in the most lonely fashion. There is no lonelier man in death, except the suicide. . . .

With the end of this man, a legend had been rounded out, brought to its end with a stunning symmetry. And do not these lives, taken together, suggest that American writers, American writing, in fact do share some fated symmetry?

# PART SEVEN

# The World We Imagine: Notes on the Creative Act and Its Function

THE CREATIVE PROCESS is the process whereby order is brought out of disorder, form out of chaos. That is why James Joyce was being only very literal rather than heretical when he insisted on the artist's role as God-like. For as God brought the universe out of chaos and ancient night, so the artist brings his creative work out of the chaos of his subjective life and out of the disorder of the world. But there is order in the world as well as disorder, and particularly the order of all that has been created before any new creation; and there is *some* order in the subjective life as well, if only that impulse, striated through it, that impels a particular order to emerge. *"Spur in Treibsand"*—trace in the shifting sand: this is the conception of consciousness held by the painter Kokoschka. We can, if we wish, take this figure of speech in its most intense and heightened significance as representative of the creative impulse itself, as that striation through the flow of subjectivity that will fulfill itself in created objectification. And the created object, every truly creative act, transcends in one degree or another both forms of order, the order of the world and the potential order within the subjective life, is new, goes beyond what has been. This is not in the least to say that it is *better*, only that it is *itself*, and therefore, in one way or another, perhaps in many ways, different. The bringing of order out of relative disorder and the emergence of the new over the old, over all that has been before—these are probably the two basic facts about creativity.

Men have speculated since ancient times on the power that is prior to and activates the creative impulse. Such speculations are interesting enough but probably vain because they are ultimately undemonstrable. Ancient and later romantic theories of divine fire, of the sudden infusion in the creative mind of a power from without or above, theories of inspiration in the literal sense of being breathed *into,* conceits such as that of the poetic soul like a harp upon which the wind blows—all these are probably only metaphors for a mystery that eludes rational inquiry because in itself it is non-rational. It is because the first movements of the creative impulse toward the created object are non-rational that many writers have assured us that the work was accomplished automatically, somnambulistically, as if under hypnosis, in a state of trance. From these assertions one can only suppose that the intensity of creative concentration may seem to induce such states or states analogous to them, but that is not at all to say that such states are necessary to the beginning of creation or that creation will begin if they are induced.

There are more mundane speculations. There is, for example, D. H. Lawrence's belief that the motive force lies in a psychic need for therapy. "I always say my motto," he wrote, "is 'Art for *my* sake,'" and "One sheds one's sicknesses in books, repeats and presents again one's emotions to be master of them." This is a view not unrelated to André Gide's of the necessary connection between genius and disease, a view later explored by Edmund Wilson in the essays he collected under the title *The Wound and the Bow.* Again, both are specializations of the theory, widely held, of art as compensation, whether for feelings of inferiority or an unhappy childhood or a nagging mother-in-law. It is a view that sometimes approximates the idea of art as revenge. One might mention, too, I. A. Richards's theory of the motive of conflict: a maximum number of appetites in conflict or in imbalance, striving to come into balance or harmony.

Behind most of these ideas lies the theory of Sigmund Freud as he developed it in his paper of 1908, "The Relation of the Poet to Day-Dreaming." The argument here is that creation begins in fantasy or reverie or daydreaming, all of which are simply adult extensions of the play of childhood, in which the child quite frankly creates a make-believe world. "Unsatisfied wishes are the driving power behind phantasies; every separate phantasy contains the fulfilment of a wish, and improves on unsatisfactory reality." Such wishes are generally of two kinds, ambitious wishes and erotic wishes, and these two "are often united." This is a considerably plausible theory, and we must, of course, respect it, yet it is, as I believe, incomplete, partial.

We can agree, perhaps, only on this much as to the beginnings of the creative process, that the will, like rational intellectual process, plays probably no part in it at all. And we would wish to add that a given subject chooses its author at least as much as the author chooses his subject. We need not, to make the point, use the violent language of Nietzsche when he said that the subject of *Alzo sprach Zarathustra* "invaded" him, although that is a powerful word. I am not now thinking of inspiration, but rather of the necessary limitations that are imposed upon every creative being. No more can come out of the subjective life than transfigurations of what has been poured into it. The objective environment necessarily places curbs on the subjective potentialities. Henry Adams felt that his imagination was undernourished because he had been brought up in the United States. "I am too American myself, and lack juices," he said. And, of course, it has long been argued that the American writer in general has found it difficult to fulfill himself because he is nourished on such barren ground. This was the burden of Henry James's eloquent and sad essay on Nathaniel Hawthorne, and the argument has since been applied to many other writers by other critics. Having examined the work of ten well-known twentieth-century American writers, T. K. Whipple, for example, concluded as follows: "Most of their work has a touch of that gauntness or emaciation, a deficiency in variety, body, mass, which springs from underfeeding of the imagination—from having lived, that is, in a world which affords inadequate experience." The world that we create, I am only trying to say, depends in large part on the world that we inhabit. The power of the man, in

Matthew Arnold's phrasing, is not separate from the power of the moment. Even the greatest genius has a collaborator in his environment, and if the collaborator is sluggish, even the greatest genius may fail in the full realization of himself.

Realization is the word toward which I have been laboring. It is the *need* of realization—and it can take many forms—it is the need of realization, I believe, that impels the creative act. Max Eastman, in *The Enjoyment of Poetry*, many years ago employed the word to define "the poetic temper." "Poetic people, and all people when they are in a poetic mood . . . are lovers of the qualities of things. . . . They are possessed by the impulse to realize . . . a wish to experience life and the world. That is the essence of the poetic temper." Realization of experience, and through that, of himself and of his creative potentialities: this is the basis, and without this, I believe, nothing can begin. On this subject, Henry James wrote tellingly. "What kind of experience is intended," he asked, "and where does it begin and end?"

> Experience is never limited, and it is never complete; it is an immense sensibility, a kind of huge spider-web of the finest silken threads suspended in the chamber of consciousness, and catching every air-borne particle in its tissue. It is the very atmosphere of the mind; and when the mind is imaginative—much more when it happens to be that of a man of genius—it takes to itself the faintest hints of life, it converts the very pulses of the air into revelations. . . . Therefore, if I should certainly say to a novice, "Write from experience and from experience only," I should feel that this was rather a tantalizing monition if I were not careful immediately to add, "Try to be one of the people on whom nothing is lost!"

Potentially, at least, the most creative person is the person on whom least is lost.

It is reassuring to find in Dr. Donald McKinnon's summary of the qualities that the creative person shares with other creative persons this quality—"his openness to experience," including his own early experience, "his freedom from crippling restraints and impoverishing inhibitions." The creative process itself may be described as a movement from the un-realized to the realized. It is itself the highest form of realiza-tion. It is a process that begins in the unconscious, yes; but its impulse, beginning there, is to bring that realm into the realm of consciousness, to objectify the subjective, to know and to make known the unknown, to bring the shining new out of the darkness of ancient night.

It is here, I believe, that a distinction made by Carl Gustav Jung—and to use it does not mean that we need follow him back into the darkness of the collective unconscious—is more useful to our subject than the ruminations of Sigmund Freud on daydreams. Daydreams have to do with the fulfillment of our wishes only; but there is also the other part—the contain-ment of our terror and our fears. And, really, if we must weigh one against the other, unfulfilled wishes and uncontained fears, I would say that the latter are much more insistent in their grip upon the creative heart.

I hope that I do not begin to sound like Carl Gustav Jung, who is, of course, so much more "literary" than Sigmund Freud, who, not at all "literary" in that way, is a good writer. Still, Jung can help me now with his distinction between what he calls the *visionary* and the *psychological* literary creation. The second term, at least, is not very exact: for *psychological* I would substitute *social*. Or, better still, if we are really trying to mark out the extremes, we might call the first *apocalyptic*, the second *manneristic*. Whatever we call these two literary modes, the distinction, if we know what we are talking about, is useful.

Jung finds the distinction most clearly exemplified in the two parts of Goethe's *Faust*, and he has other examples of both kinds. One, the "psychological," takes its material from "the vast realm of conscious experience," from "the fore-ground of life." But the other, the "visionary," "derives its existence from the hinterland of man's mind," evokes either a prehuman or a superhuman world, is "foreign and cold . . . demonic and grotesque," plunges us into chaos, into dreams, into "monstrous and meaningless happenings," into "the unfathomed abyss of what has not yet become." And so on. For his own purposes, Jung is eager to demonstrate that these two modes of creative experience are indeed two modes, separate and discrete. I would suggest rather that the distinction is one of degree, that in the material that is concerned with "the foreground of life," the rational analytical intelligence finally plays a large part, and in the material that is concerned with a re-presentation of chaos and the grotesque, the irrational attempts to reveal itself as directly as possible. Helpfully for this argument, Jung himself writes further that "in the day-time he [man] believes in an ordered cosmos, and he tries to maintain this faith against the fear of chaos that besets him by night." The one externalizes chaos, what we fear, and binds it; the other reaches toward moral or social or psychological order, that to which we aspire. I do not think that there is a dichotomy here, but rather that even the extremes, if they are genuine creations, share in one way or another in the qualities of the other. I find some support here in an essay by Jerome S. Bruner, when he writes of "the literalities of experience and the night impulses of life"—"I would urge that we not be too easily tempted into thinking that there is an oppositional contrast between *logos* and *mythos,* the grammar of experience and the grammar of myth. For each complements the other . . ." It is in the complementariness, even the inter-penetration of the one by the other, in my view, that we recognize what is indeed the creative experience.

At the beginning of his lecture, "The Mind as Nature," Loren Eiseley tells how, as a small boy, he lived "in two worlds."

One was dark, hidden and self-examining, though in its own way not without compensations. The other world in which I somehow also managed to exist was external, boisterous, and what I suppose the average parent would call normal or extro-verted. . . . I was living, you see, in a primitive world at the same time that I was inhabiting the modern world as it existed in the second decade of this century. I am not talking now about the tree-house, the cave-building activities of normal boys. I am talking about the minds of the first dawning human consciousness—about a kind of mental Ice Age, and of how a light came in from outside until, as I have indicated, two worlds existed in which a boy, still a single unsplit personality, walked readily from one world to the other by day and by night without anyone observing the invisible boundaries he passed.

Dr. Eiseley seems to think that this is an unusual experience for a child and one that might easily prove psychologically disastrous. My own feeling is that it is the normal condition of childhood and that it is the condition always of the creative man. As T. S. Eliot has written, "The artist, I believe, is more *primitive,* as well as more *civilized,* than his contemporaries, his experience is deeper than civilization, and he only uses the phenomena of civilization in expressing it." The works of Dostoevsky and Henry James, of D. H. Lawrence and Jane Austen—I would argue that ultimately they are not different in kind, only in the degree to which the nighttime and the daytime worlds are given some priority. Even such a writer as Sinclair Lewis, whose work seems to depend on accumulations of social notation alone—even such a writer is moved by an animus of pain and anger, a secret world far back and down into which perhaps he never looked with open eyes, but which, now and then, breaks into the conscious and deliberate structure, and then gives us a glimpse into a nighttime chaos that the sun-parched city blocks of Zenith never knew. Or, to take a slighter but easily illustrative example, the early and the later works of Truman Capote: the nightmare incursions into surrealism that characterize "The Headless Hawk" or *Other Voices, Other Rooms,* and the comic social extravagances of *Breakfast at Tiffany's*—both these arise from the same creative intelligence and both are concerned to objectify the human experience, no matter at what level. From the point of view of creativity, what is important to recognize is the fact that it all begins at the lower level and it ends up in objective externalization, the created fact.

That the line between the created fact and the nighttime world can be very slight I have myself experienced, if you will permit me to use myself, a very minor example indeed.

Once, at least, I dreamed a story, and I believe that it was complete in a way that no direct transcript of waking experience is ever complete. I was living in Boston then, and, having come from the broad flatlands of the Middle West, I had been impressed by a certain kind of narrow, empty Boston street, yet it had never occurred to me to base a story on that impression. The dream took off from such an impression, it was located in such a street, and the dramatic circumstances that the dream unfolded were appropriate to the cruel and binding and yet lonely atmosphere of such a street. This story was slight, to be sure, but as fiction it was, I think, whole. For a dream, if it comes, as I imagine this one did, when one is near to waking, not only contains events and sometimes coherent events, but these events, in a dream, have their own atmosphere and coloration and tone, appropriate to the events. Life, waking life, does not provide these; that is what *style* must create. But in a dream, or at any rate in my dream of the cruelly wounded and wounding boy in the empty lot off a cruel, empty street, even the bleak sentence rhythms seemed to have been given me. And yet I cannot truly think that that dream came to me in language: the emotion that generated the language and colored it when it came, yes, but the language itself was mine and consciously mine. And until the dream was put into language, it existed only as the memory of the dream, not as a story, a created fact.

Yet the need to live largely in the nighttime world has been observed by many writers. "The poet is at the disposal of his night," Jean Cocteau wrote.

Often the public forms an idea of inspiration that is quite false, almost a religious notation. Alas! I do not believe that inspiration falls from heaven. I think it rather the result of a profound indolence and of our incapacity to put to work certain forces in ourselves. These unknown forces work deep within us, with the aid of the elements of daily life, its scenes and passions, and when they burden us and oblige us to conquer the kind of somnolence in which we indulge ourselves like invalids who try to prolong dream, and dread resuming contact with reality, in short when the work that makes itself in us and in spite of us demands to be born, we can believe that this work comes to us from beyond and is offered us by the gods.

Thoreau writes somewhere of the "sleep" out of which his work came, and even such an orderly and rational man as John Dryden wrote of the inception of one of his plays in "a confused mass of thoughts, tumbling over one another in the dark; when the fancy was yet in its first work, moving the sleeping images of things towards the light, there to be distinguished, and then either chosen or rejected by the judgment."

By the judgment! And now we are at my second point—how the creative literary impulse manages to get itself expressed. Marianne Moore has said, "Ecstasy affords the occasion, and expediency determines the form." The seed sprouts in the dark, from the dark, but most generally the plant blooms and is pruned in the daylight. And when the reason takes over, it operates in quite a different way from the indolent somnolence of inception. Now comes a dedication that can be nothing less than fanatical, a furious wilfulness. One thinks of Joseph Conrad, writing *Nostromo*, and, finishing that book, asking his friends to congratulate him "as upon a recovery from a dangerous illness."

All I know is that, for twenty months, neglecting the common joys of life that fall to the lot of the humblest on this earth, I had, like the prophet of old, "wrestled with the Lord" for my creation, for the headlands of the coast. . . . These are, perhaps, strong words, but it is difficult to characterize otherwise the intimacy and the strain of a creative effort in which mind and will and conscience are engaged to the full, hour after hour, day after day, away from the world, and to the exclusion of all that makes life really lovable and gentle—something for which a material parallel can only be found in the everlasting sombre stress of the westward winter passage round Cape Horn . . . a long, long, desperate fray. Long! I suppose I went to bed sometimes, and got up the same number of times. Yes, I suppose I slept, and ate the food put before me, and talked connectedly to my household on suitable occasions. But I had never been aware of the even flow of daily life, made easy and noiseless for me by a silent, watchful, tireless affection. Indeed, it seemed to me that I had been sitting at that table surrounded by the litter of a desperate fray for days and nights on end.

Or one thinks of the agonies of Virginia Woolf, writing *The Years*:

> A good day—a bad day—so it goes on. Few people can be so tortured by writing as I am. Only Flaubert I think. . . . I think I can bring it off, if I only have courage and patience: take each scene quietly: compose: I think it may be a good book. And then —oh when it's finished! . . . I wonder if anyone has ever suffered so much from a book as I have from *The Years*. Once out I will never look at it again. It's like a long childbirth. Think of that summer, every morning a headache, and forcing myself into that room in my nightgown; and lying down after a page: and always with the certainty of failure. Now that certainty is mercifully removed to some extent. But now I feel I don't care what anyone says so long as I'm rid of it. . . . Never write a long book again. Yet I feel I shall write more fiction—scenes will form.

Scenes will form! There is a certain helplessness, first as to inception, then as to the need for execution: or should I say first helplessness, then compulsiveness. Jung wrote,

> The artist's life cannot be otherwise than full of conflicts, for two forces are at war within him—on the one hand the common human longing for happiness, satisfaction and security in life, and on the other a ruthless passion for creation which may go so far as to override every personal desire. The lives of artists are as a rule so highly unsatisfactory—not to say tragic—because of their inferiority on the human and personal side, and not because of a sinister dispensation. There are hardly any exceptions to the rule that a person must pay dearly for the divine gift of the creative fire.

He pays in frenzy and frustration and in possible deprivation of everything else as he submits to his creative drive to realize itself. It can realize itself only through his language, through what in the most general sense we may call technique.

Technique, I know, is a word that has unpleasant mechanical

connotations. I believe that it is a mistake to think of the word with those connotations, and if there were some better word, some word that did not suggest mere mechanical manipulation, I would use it; but I do not know of a better word. By technique I mean simply the means by which a writer gets his initial impulse to create a work out into the open and over to his readers. Technique, in fact, is simply the means by which the writer himself first finds out what he is really trying to say, from all those inarticulate impulses that impel him to say it, and then to say it, that is, to make it a created object.

The example that I would first like to give you is almost ridiculous, after all the exalted language that I have been using. But I would not fall back on my own experiences except for the fact that they seem to me to be simple and therefore relatively clear examples of what I am trying to say, and that I can talk about them with some authority. I hope that no one will feel that I am under any illusion that I am talking about works of art, let alone important works of art, but only that these are examples of something that happens in the mind of a writer.

I was walking home one day thinking of nothing, as far as I knew, when I heard, through an open window of a house I was passing, a little girl practicing her piano lesson. She was diligently working away at one of those extremely simple Bach minuets of thirty-two bars that are commonly assigned to beginners. She had by no means mastered the little piece, but her attempts had a kind of suspense. Would she make it? I wondered, and, leaning up against a tree, I stopped to listen. She kept on for ten or fifteen minutes, adding bar to bar, phrase to phrase, starting over, trying again, and at last, at one successful run, she went through the whole thing without a hitch. She had put the pieces together.

And as I continued along the block or two between her house and mine, I kept wondering, what was that like? The whole effort, so fragile and artificial, and so determined, haunted me. But I do not know why it seemed important at all. By that I mean I do not know what string on the violin of my subjective life she had touched with her bow. But she had touched on something, and as I kept on walking I began to think of a number of marriages I had known—not my own!— that were held together in the most precarious way, often sim- ply by the presence of property, by the furnishings of a house, for example, by all the trappings of what seemed to be solid respectability and even elegance. And then it occurred to me —and this was an entirely rational process by now—it occurred to me that I could write a very short story, probably to be called, as it finally was, "Picking up the Pieces," about a catastrophe in a marriage which, as the man and wife listened to a little girl, across the stretch of a garden, putting together the thirty-two bars of a Bach minuet, was repaired. I got home and sat down at my typewriter and thought up some names for my man and wife who were in the middle of a quarrel, their marriage presumably shattered:

It was early summer and the windows and doors were open, and when Harry Calder raised his voice and shouted, "All right," then, "yes, God damn it, I did!" the little girl next door abruptly stopped her piano practice. And Liza Calder, having forced her husband to this extraordinary admission, did not know what to do, did not even know what to feel. She stood helplessly in the middle of the sudden silence and as her fingers slowly went limp with the rest of her body, the letter she had been holding fluttered to the floor. She looked around the room, and for a moment she could not decide why it seemed so strange. Then she saw that it was as if Harry's shout had blown the familiar and carefully planned room apart. Every object in it stood out separately from every other object in a kind of crazy isolation—the chintz covered chairs, the little lacquered tables, Harry himself, the ashtrays and books, even the prints of birds and flowers indubitably hung in rows on the walls—everything was separated from everything else, without relationship. A trick of her eyes, she thought, and blinked hard; but her second thought was, no, rather, the pieces of her marriage.

The little girl begins to practice again, and while her faltering sounds drift through the open windows, the Calders try to straighten out their troubles, Harry to explain how it had happened that he had been unfaithful, Liza somehow to refix her picture of herself and of her relation to him. The little girl gets better and better and they half listen as they once more move closer together, and presently, at the end of the sixth manuscript page—the story was only about 1,800 words long—just as the marriage is mended, just as the room reassembles itself, the little girl gets it. And the story ends, "Both Liza and Harry smiled for her. You could shut your eyes and almost imagine that the little girl was really good." And so, the implication, I hope, reads: their marriage likewise, as fragile, as shallow, as emotionally empty, yet, patched up as it has been, appearing once more whole and solid.

No one gets *much* credit for that story except as it serves as an illustration for me now; but if anyone gets credit, it is the little girl I heard practicing the piano, and who somehow made me want to write a story, however trivial, about something that had obviously impinged on my subjective life for some time. If it had not been for that external fact of the little girl's practicing her piece, and then beyond that, of my own perfectly conscious attempt to make a hearing of her effort serve to represent something quite different, there would have been no story. But it was only what I am calling technique that made it a story at all. This process I would call not creativity but inventiveness, which is something different from the basic impulse, but something absolutely essential to actual production, and something that should not be dismissed lightly.

May I give another example, if only to suggest that such an impression as the little girl at the piano provided does not usually result in a piece of writing so quickly? It took two years to find the story in this next episode. Here was the inception: on a beach one day, I observed a family near me—father, mother, a small boy of nine or ten. The mother had apparently suffered from some kind of partial paralysis, for not only was the right side of her face a little pulled down, so that she seemed constantly on the verge of leering, but also, she could not extend the fingers of her right hand, but held them in a curious, knotted way. Like many mothers at the beach, she spent a good deal of her time shouting directions at her child, and when she did so, she emphasized her imperatives by throwing out her right arm, with those inflexibly knotted fingers at the end of it. Then, when some little quarrel blew up between the mother and the boy, which I could not hear, the boy abruptly stopped before her, and, exaggerating the paralysis, he imitated her twisted face and, pointing his arm at her, absolutely duplicated the peculiar position of her fingers and shouted "Yak! Yak! Yak!" The mother looked at him in astonishment and then turned over on her face and began to cry, and the father sent the boy down to the tide line and tried to comfort his wife.

This was the actual experience, this was an event, a real thing, and in some ways a rather challenging one for fiction. It was a physical image, and an image which contained a revelation of a relationship. Yet it was in no sense a story. To obtain a story from the experience, a whole different level of events must be made to surround the actual observation. Now I must bring something to it—and what would that be? And again, I don't know why the little episode seemed important to me, but it had, in its small way, "chosen" me to write about it. Finally, remembering it over several years, I decided to make the real story that of an observer; to change the observer from myself to a second woman, also a wife and mother; and to let this second woman discover, through the observed episode and the consequent behavior of her son, that hers was not a paralyzed body, but in some sense a paralyzed soul; and then to see her whole family relationship, and her whole future, in a way that she had never seen them or herself before. The actual incident then was forced into a secondary position, used to illuminate an invented situation, and a different kind, a spiritual dilemma. And the two were meant, of course, to interact, to dramatize one another. This was a distortion of factual truth, quite deliberately and rationally manipulated, for the sake of what seemed to be a larger psychological, perhaps even a moral, "truth." One needs a psychoanalyst, at least, and I think probably someone even more omniscient, to tell one why a given bit of experience such as this observation on the beach strikes that note in one's own inner experience that forces one to force it to become a created work, of whatever value. All I am stressing is that the impulse alone is not enough; it takes conscious thought, planning, manipulation, even mechanics, before that impulse can find any kind of expression.

We must, if I am to say anything on my third point, move on to that now rather abruptly. Journalists and some critics like to talk about the responsibility of the creative writer to society, his function, and to chide writers today for the perversity of their sense of alienation from society. First let us consider the most vulgar example, in order at once to dispose of it quickly. Many readers will remember how, some years ago, the editorialists of *Life* magazine, that unofficial and self-appointed custodian of our culture, published their great polemic called "Wanted: An American Novel." Taking off from Sloan Wilson's remark that "These are, we forget, pretty good times. Yet too many novelists are writing as if we were back in the Depression years," the editorial declared:

> Ours is the most powerful nation in the world. It has had a decade of unparalleled prosperity. It has gone further than any other society in the history of man toward creating a truly classless society. Yet it is still producing a literature which sounds sometimes as if it were written by an unemployed homosexual living in a packing box shanty on the city dump while awaiting admission to the county poorhouse.

We know the writers the editorialists had in mind, and while I have no interest now in trying to judge the value of these writers, I do want to say that the *Life* diatribe shows an extravagant ignorance of the nature of the creative impulse, of the creative writer, of the created work, and, above all, of the creative function and of creative responsibility.

The first responsibility of the creative writer is to his language and to his technique, because only through these can the creative impulse itself find its realization. His second responsibility is to his own freedom to use his language as he must. He must be free to rebel, and in a profoundly basic sense every real writer is a rebel. The rebel, for so many literary genera- tions the hero, has been largely replaced today by "the stran- ger," the outsider, the alienated and disaffected wanderer, the human being who declines to participate in the human enter- prise.

The creative writer, like his heroes, is also the stranger; but there is always this fascinating thing about the artist: he cre- ates what he describes, and in the act of creation, is superior to the object of his observation, which cannot create itself. And therefore the writer, as stranger, is not doomed to that nihilism in which the hero, as stranger, is caught. The artist, always using his freedom, remains a rebel even when he is a stranger; his basic rebellion, in this time or any other, is directed at the universe itself, and the universe cannot be undone by history, it remains, and it provides the stuff which the artist, man of letters or man of paint or stone or the twelve-tone scale, at once rebukes and celebrates. Every truly creative act is an act of rebellion against the universe and a celebration of the universe because it permits this creative rebellion, that is, the freedom of the artist to act.

It is important to society that the artist be free to act for the very reason that the artist is the supreme type of rebel. "Civili- zation may be said indeed to be the creation of its outlaws," said James Joyce, but now, as my vocabulary will have sug- gested, I am thinking not so much of Joyce as of Albert Camus as he writes in *L'homme révolté*. Very boldly, when he comes to talk specifically of the artist, Camus begins with Nietzsche's dogma, "No artist tolerates reality," and, qualify that remark as he does, he recognizes its primary if hyperbolical accuracy.

Camus makes importantly obvious points: the terms "real- ism" (suggesting a duplication of reality) and "formalism" (suggesting a total flight from reality) are meaningless: no art can duplicate reality since all art is selection from, distortion of, and an imposition of order upon reality; no art can totally reject reality since it then would have no materials—"The only real formalism is silence." Yet the very fact of his being an artist means that the man of letters must reject reality as it is in itself. Camus is writing now of the novel, specifically, but his strictures apply to all of the literary arts:

> Here we have an imaginary world . . . which was created from the rectification of the actual world—a world where suffering can, if it wishes, continue until death, where passions are never distracted, where people are prey to obsessions and are always present to each other. Man is finally able to give himself the alleviating form and limits which he pursues in vain in his own life. The novel makes destiny to measure. . . . In this way man competes with creation and, provisionally, conquers death. A detailed analysis of the most famous novels would show, in different perspectives each time, that the essence of the novel lies in this perpetual alteration, always directed towards the same end, that the artist makes in his own experience. Far from being moral or even purely formal, this alteration aims, primarily, at unity and thereby indicates a metaphysical need.

It is the word *metaphysical* that is finally important to our argument. Ezra Pound said, "A work of art need not contain any statement of a political or of a social or of a philosophical conviction, but it nearly always implies one." Camus seems to extend that remark:

> Whatever may be the chosen point of view of an artist, one principle remains common to all creators: stylization, which supposes the simultaneous existence of reality and of the mind which gives reality its form. Through style, the creative effort reconstructs the world. . . .

Now we may add, to language and to the freedom to use it, the third responsibility, which is to the act of rebellion against that which so smugly and chaotically *is*, the universe, society itself. Rebellion, Camus tells us, is the pursuit of values, and that pursuit is the movement from *facts* to *rights*, or shall we say the imposition of rights upon facts. This is, I believe, precisely what Yeats had in mind when he said that the artist must hold "reality and justice in a single thought." Justice takes many forms in the many minds of men; and reality has no form at all. Art, coming out of dark disorder and ascending above the social order, presents the two together.

Lionel Trilling has written that "The function of literature through all the mutations has been to make us aware of the particularity of selves, and the high authority of the self in its quarrel with its society and its culture." The responsibility of the writer then is to maintain the high authority of his free self, which is to say his creative self, which is in turn to say his rebelling self. His responsibility, in short, is to excellence alone. ". . . the oak," said Ezra Pound again, "does not grow for the purpose or with the intention of being built into ships and tables, yet a wise nation will take care to preserve the forests. It is the oak's business to grow good oak."

A wise society will take care to preserve the freedom of its literary culture, of the man of letters, precisely because he has taken upon himself a necessary fight with the world and experience. His task is to force it into shape, into order. And this, the creative act itself, is the only affirmation that he must make: that the artist can and perpetually does create an order that did not exist before he made it. There may be other affirmations, but this is the imperative one, and it is, please observe, an affirmation about man: man creates what the creation does not contain. "The artist," wrote Yeats, "loves above all life at peace with itself." The function of the creative impulse, whether in the man of letters or in any other artist, is not to make peace with the world, but to bring into it, in the creation of his endlessly various forms, those shining examples of peace that are our "monuments of unageing intellect," and that comprise our civilization and our humanity. Only they can put limits on our chaotic nighttime fears and give form to our daytime hopes and dreams. Doing that, they help, with love and work, and for some, still, religion—they help to make reality continually tolerable. And is that not quite enough?